THE VISUAL ARTS

Holt, Rinehart and Winston, Inc., New York

THE

VISUAL ARTS

Wallace S. Baldinger

UNIVERSITY OF OREGON

in collaboration with HARRY B. GREEN

SAN FRANCISCO STATE COLLEGE

Copyright © 1960 by Holt, Rinehart and Winston, Inc.
Library of Congress Catalog Card Number: 59–8691
20788–0110
Printed in the United States of America

Preface

STUDENTS IN ENGLISH literature courses used to commit to memory lines from Tennyson's *Ulysses*:

> I am a part of all that I have met;
> Yet all experience is an arch wherethro'
> Gleams that untravell'd world,
> Whose margin fades for ever and for ever
> When I move.

It is in the spirit of Ulysses that this book has been written. If the book opens new vistas in the visual arts, then it will have accomplished its mission.

The first two chapters deal with elements and principles which apply equally to all the arts. The rest deal with the visual arts in turn. Case studies on a particular art have been included with each chapter. These case studies, analyses of actual works, attempt to determine something of the "why" and the "how" and the "what" of the works in question. These analyses are not mere embellishments of the chapter. They are not to be skimmed over or skipped as though they did not really matter. They are to be absorbed as the chief matter that the chapter offers.

These studies will prepare the reader for the enjoyment of all works in the particular medium. He will make a lifetime's practice of such studies. He will look more and more for himself at corresponding works. He will apply to them with increasing understanding what he has learned about the art. He will come to share more fully the artist's experience in creating such works. He will buy the works which he enjoys the most and will come to live with them.

The summary of each chapter should not be regarded thus as a terminal; it should be treated only as a beginning, a dock from which the voyage of discovery starts. The course of the voyage can be mapped out only as it proceeds, but the notes and recommended readings, referring to the charts of other voyages, ought to be of help.

ACKNOWLEDGMENTS

The scope of this study would have prevented its completion without the assistance extended to the author by many people. To attempt a total listing of benefactors is impossible; the ramifications of the study have been so complex that someone would be overlooked.

Acknowledgments of sources for individual photographs have been made with reproductions, and credit for particular ideas and quotations has been given in the footnotes and the notes at the end of the book. Beyond recognition for such essential services, I owe a special debt of gratitude to certain individuals who have come to my aid in ways which I indicate below:

(1) Harry B. Green, my collaborator and devil's advocate, who always refused to understand an involved passage until I had simplified it and who helped in numerous other ways as well.

(2) Members of the Pacific Coast Committee for the Humanities of the American Coun-

cil of Learned Societies, whose generous grant for aid in research came at a critical moment in the undertaking.

(3) Elizabeth Findly, Frances Newsom, Robert McCollough, and other librarians of the University of Oregon Library, who were always ready to track down some obscure reference or elusive bit of data, or to secure a book on interlibrary loan at the earliest possible moment.

(4) My students, who in more than twenty years of coming and going taught me at least as much about the visual arts as I was able to teach them, and some of whom assembled photographs and information of value to my study.

(5) My colleagues on the staff of the School of Architecture and Allied Arts of the University of Oregon, whose suggestions contributed in a tangible way to the content of the book. Especially extensive was the help of Lynn Alexander for weaving, Victoria Avakian for ceramics, Marion Dean Ross and Wallace S. Hayden for architecture, Mark R. Sponenburgh for sculpture, and Andrew Vincent and David McCosh for painting.

(6) Ulrich Middeldorf, formerly of the University of Chicago, now Director of the Kunsthistorisches Institut in Florence, whose inspiring teaching and careful criticism played a key role in determining the direction of the study, the emphasis made in it, and much of the interpretation and factual presentation.

(7) Gordon Gilkey, print maker of Oregon State College, Bernard L. Freemesser, photographer of the University of Oregon, Howard Dearstyne, photographer of Illinois Institute of Technology, and Ansel Adams, Peter Gowland, André de Dienes, and the late Edward Weston, who read pertinent passages on print making and photography, who offered much helpful advice and encouragement, and who provided indispensable works for illustration.

(8) Carl and Hilda Morris, artists, of Portland, Oregon, whose friendly counsels helped in planning the study and in preparing passages on ceramics, sculpture, and painting.

(9) Marguerite Wildenhain, whose assistance in securing photographs and criticizing the manuscript proved crucial to studies on ceramics.

(10) The late Frank Lloyd Wright, whose personal philosophy and encouragement helped to color the whole approach and whose reading of major portions of the chapter on architecture is partly responsible for that part of the study being what it is.

(11) Herbert Jacobs, who, as discriminating client of Frank Lloyd Wright, read and criticized the passage in which I introduced his first Wright house in Madison, Wisconsin.

(12) Jirō Harada, of the National Museum in Tokyo, whose untiring labor against great odds secured material on Japanese pottery and architecture indispensable to my treatment of Japanese art.

(13) Robert Royston, landscape architect, of San Francisco, who taught me much about garden design and encouraged my studies of relationships of gardens with sculptures and other works of art.

(14) John Rewald, Henry Moore, Anne Kutka McCosh, the late José Clemente Orozco, and the late John Marin, all of whom offered ideas, criticisms, and photographs for the chapters on sculpture and painting.

(15) Albert H. Baldinger, my father, who made many helpful stylistic suggestions.

(16) Perry A. Stamper, James F. Colley, Ellen B. Rice, Jean M. Woods, and other members of my staff in the Museum of Art of the University of Oregon, whose efficient services helped to bring the manuscript to its final form.

(19) Ellen Nichols Baldinger, my wife, who finished typing the first draft of the manuscript ten years ago and the final draft only now, and who stayed with me during the intermediate preparation.

W. S. B.

Eugene, Ore.
March 7, 1960

Contents

Illustrations

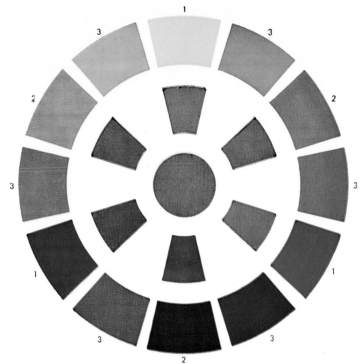

COLOR WHEEL

VALUE SCALE

INTENSITY SCALE

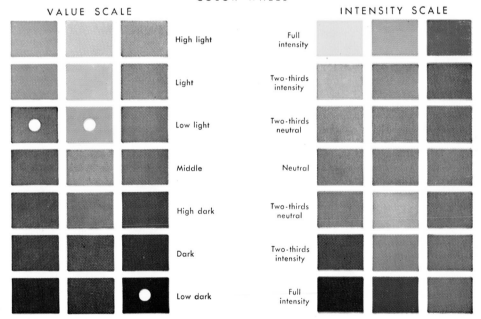

High light

Light

Low light

Middle

High dark

Dark

Low dark

Full intensity

Two-thirds intensity

Two-thirds neutral

Neutral

Two-thirds neutral

Two-thirds intensity

Full intensity

I. The color wheel shows a sequence of hues in the following order, beginning with yellow at the top and proceeding clockwise: yellow, yellow-green, green, blue-green, blue, blue-violet, violet, red-violet, red, red-orange, orange, yellow-orange.

The value scale shows seven values each for three hues: green, orange, and violet. Those containing white disks are at normal value.

The intensity scale shows two different degrees between full intensity and neutral for six hues. (Adapted from *The Art of Enjoying Art* by A. Philip McMahon as adapted from *Commercial Art* by C. E. Wallace; by permission of McGraw-Hill.)

II. *Etruscan Warrior. c.* 500 B.C. Terra cotta, coated with slip as semiglaze; painted in red ocher, black, and white. Height, 8'¼". Courtesy of The Metropolitan Museum of Art, Kennedy Fund, 1921.

III. Sandro Botticelli: *The Birth of Venus,* detail of head. *c.* 1485. Tempera on canvas. 5'3½" x 8'11". Uffizi Gallery, Florence. Courtesy of the Uffizi Gallery.

IV. Rembrandt van Rijn: *Man with a Magnifying Glass*, detail of head. 1665-1669. Oil on canvas. 36 x 29¼". Courtesy of The Metropolitan Museum of Art, Bequest of Benjamin Altman, 1913.

THE VISUAL ARTS

1.1. PLANE, TEXTURE, VOLUME OF MASS, VOLUME OF OPEN SPACE. Kōtarō and Hiko-jirō (gardeners under Tokuhō Zengetsu, Zen Buddhist priest): Garden of Ryoanji, Kyōto, detail of east end. c. 1488. Rocks, moss, and raked sand. 78′ long × 30′ wide. Courtesy Bureau of Tourist Industry, Kyōto Municipal Government.

The Elements of Art

WHEN A MAN GOES to buy an automobile, he listens to motors, tests brakes and steering gears, checks tires, casts an appraising eye at speedometer mileages. He looks for a car that performs well and rides comfortably, but he bases his final choice on an automobile that not only does these things but *appears* as though it would. He asks himself whether the car by its looks promises comfort, visibility, power in getaway, control at high speed, a motor capable of running a few thousand miles before it begins strewing gaskets on the road.

The man who in buying an automobile gives consideration to its looks may know nothing about art but he is exercising his faculties, ineptly or not, in what can only be described as artistic judgment. He will say, perhaps, that the automobile of his choice has good points and lines, weatherproof yet flowing surfaces, upholstery soft but firm to the touch and not too "sticky," coloring pleasant in effect but easily distinguishable on the road. He may remark, perhaps, how low to the road the mass of the body is slung, how spacious are the seats of the car, and how open its sides.

In each such comment the buyer is functioning as a judge of art, but the value of his judgment depends on his understanding of art and the way in which it works. He may not be aware of it, but his evaluation of an automobile is only one of many instances in which he is called upon to make such judgments. Art is all around him. It stands ready to enrich his life and add to his enjoyment exactly insofar as he is able to perceive that art and share in its existence.[1]

[1] See Notes, page 293.

We function repeatedly as both practitioners and appreciators of art. We pick from our wardrobe that dress or suit which we calculate will help us to look and do our best during the day's work. We sit down to a breakfast which we have chosen from the cafeteria line for its looks as well as for its expected tastes. We pull from the library shelf that volume which, other things being equal, seems by its color and proportions to promise the most pleasure in reading. We buy from the corner store that fountain pen, bottle of ink, notebook, or typewriter which attracts our eye both by the case containing it and by the shape which promises efficiency in performance. We select the chair which appears to be most comfortable, and we seek to grace the coffee table beside it with a flower arrangement.

The appreciation of art cannot really be taught. It can only happen inside us. But many things can prepare the way for appreciation, and high among them is an understanding of what the artist is trying to do, what he has to work with, and what should and should not be expected of him. If we are to appreciate the work that he creates, we must know the elements which go to compose it. Whatever the art form to which the work belongs, its elements are held in common with works of every other art form. This is true even of works of the temporal arts, those arts which depend on lapses of time (like music, which appeals to our sense of hearing). For purposes of the present study, however, we restrict ourselves to ways in which these elements operate in the *visual* arts—arts which exist completely in space, which function more in space than they do in time, and which appeal above all to our

3

sense of sight. Authorities differ over the number and the names of the elements; we propose to study a group of seven:

point	texture	mass
line	color	space
plane		

Although for the sake of clarity we shall have to introduce each of these elements separately, in actual practice we shall never find them by themselves but always in combinations. One or another element will dominate, line here, texture there, color or mass or space in a third example, but always in conjunction with at least one other element; and in the long run they will all prove of equal importance. The work of art is a unity and every element it contains needs the help of other elements to bring it into being, even as nerve cells need the help of blood cells and other cells to make the body function.

POINT

The point is the simplest of the elements, for it is nothing but a dot, but through its position in space the dot attracts the eye. It can become a point of focus, whether that focus be a seed pod or one of the seeds scattered by its bursting, whether it be a star or a lighted window at night, a bird perched on a branch, the pupil of one's eye, or simply a period on paper.

On a written page the period indicates a pause or a moment of silence before the flow of words is resumed. On a sheet of written music the point stands either for a rest or for the prolongation of a single note, but in the actual playing of the music the note itself becomes the point. The point must be regarded as the irreducibly basic element, unless space so qualifies because it already exists. Certainly the point is the primary mark in the contact of the artist's tool with his surface. The point is unique among the elements for its essentially static character. Moving nowhere in space, it affords us in our viewing of the work of art the reassurance of a fixed position to rest upon or to return to at will—as concise and brief a visual statement as can possibly be made.

Points in Combination

The ideal shape of the point is a circular one, its ideal size is small, but the artist who varies it in combination with other points has a surprisingly wide range—he may make it square or triangular or irregularly curvilinear, sharp or fuzzy or fractured, larger or smaller than its fellows or uniform in size. If he lets it retain its concentric identity as a point and nothing else, he must be content with the inner tension it maintains simply by being itself. When the artist proceeds to establish a second point somewhere near the first, however, he sets up between the two points tension based on the feeling that each is seeking to retain its position against the pull exerted by the other. If he then introduces a third point nearby, and perhaps a fourth and a fifth, he creates such a complex of tensions and interactions as to approach the richness of form of a simple work of art. Each point remains a world in miniature, but points may assume, through interrelationships as a group, the character of a universe. They may thus afford us, once our eyes have grown sensitive to their invisible pullings and haulings across space, a whole new realm of experience.

When we repeat a point on paper in an orderly or a planned fashion, we create not only tensions but also effects of movement which the point by itself cannot give. We transform the point of focus into a point of departure and induce our eyes to jump along with it in a succussion of repetitions—from one side to another . . ., up and down ⋮, at an angle ∴, and so on. By grouping points in various ways we control effects of action much as though we were controlling our own steps, creating a measured and stately movement ... ..., an accelerating movement . . . ..., a retarding movement .. . . ., and a host of others.

Points in Works of Art

Points figure prominently in works of architecture, especially in those having structural parts which meet at sharp intersections. They give a skyward-rising effect to the roofs of Colonial New England farmhouses and to the towers and spires of Gothic cathedrals. In a Greek temple (4.3b), they punctuate the weight-bearing power of the columns, as exemplified by the shields set above each column; they call attention to the security of the roof, as shown by the rows of terra-cotta ornaments perched along the eaves and at either end of the ridge. Points terminate the upturned eaves and ridges of the roofs in the pagodas, the temples, and the private houses of both China and Japan, recalling the tips of pine tree branches and suggesting that the roof is seeking to merge itself with the space around it. They define the juncture of one brick wall with another about the fireplaces in the Hanna house (4.17a) in Palo Alto, California; they set up a give-and-take with each other inside and outside the house to suggest an active family life.

Points occur in sculpture wherever surfaces or lines come together, and the artist aware of their appeal often uses them effectively for accent. Sculptors have used points to "spot" centers of interest—like those made by the hollow for the heart and the two flanking hair ornaments in the figure of the Toltec Moon Goddess (5.1). An Etruscan sculptor put points to work in the terra-cotta figure of an Etruscan warrior (Pl. II) to exaggerate the belligerence of the subject; points here are ordered into an apparently expanding system of attack —from the crook of the warrior's right arm through the angles at the rear of the helmet to the tips of the crest, the eye, the nose, the beard, and the outthrust fist. An African Negro carver used them in a figure on a burro's back (5.12)—at the angles of the steed's knees, rump, nose, and ears, and of the rider's nose, lips, and beard—to accentuate the jogging movement and the slow but steady advance.

In the use of sharply accentuated points, like the pupil of an eye, the painter is much freer than the sculptor. He does not have to worry about maintaining a general distribution of points of emphasis so as to keep drawing the observer's eyes completely around his work, he works on a flat surface and introduces points as accents to give his picture centers of focus. The ancient Egypto-Roman painter counted thus on the points of eyes, nostrils, and lips in his portrait of a boy (8.3), as did Rembrandt in his portrait of the man with the magnifying glass (Pl. IV).

By the telling use of points a Japanese print maker gave the "feel" of figures, horse, and trees caught in heavy snow (7.7). Using encircled points for eyes, a German print maker re-created the impact of the tragedy of Jesus's betrayal (7.8). The German print exemplifies, in fact, what new sources of expression the contemporary artist has found in the isolated point. Picasso stressed spots of dark and beads of light in his portrayal of a seated woman (8.12). Miró established with points a fantasy suggesting the unknown universe revealed by the microscope, in his *Figures in the Night* (8.13).

LINE

In the painting by Miró just cited for its use of points we find also a pronounced use of lines to connect the points and to play freely around them. In his realization of the interdependence of lines and points, Miró found a positive theme out of which to develop his picture. When points are placed in series and groupings, they tend to go beyond their role as points and to act like the lines which our eyes read into the gaps between them. The point is the simplest element to understand, but the line is the easiest to follow. It is the element which we are continually abstracting ("drawing out") from nature when we note the bare twigs of a

1.2. POINT AND LINE. a. Jed Miller (age 4 years): *Portrait of the Artist's Mother with a Parakeet Alighting on Her Head*. 1956. Pencil. 6 × 5½".* Courtesy of Mrs. Arthur Miller. B. L. Freemesser photograph. b. C. N. Landon (no date available): *Harassed Husband Dashing Homeward*. 1923. Pen and ink. 4½ × 5½". Collection of the author. B. L. Freemesser photograph.

* Height precedes width in all captions.

tree silhouetted against the sky, the blades of grass rising from a hilltop, the cracks zigzagging across the face of a rock, the marks of wind-drift sweeping over a dune, the ripples traced by the breeze on the surface of a lake.

Line as Expression

The point by itself has position; the line has direction as well as position. Whether straight or curved, the line tends to draw our eyes along with it. It suggests an attitude or action which we can associate with it. When paralleling the ocean's or the prairie's horizon, as do our bodies at rest, it becomes the horizontal line, line of repose, stability, breadth ———. When rising at right angles to the earth, as we rise when standing, it becomes the vertical line, line of elevation, dignity, tallness | . When extending obliquely from the earth, like our bodies in movement, it becomes the sloping line, the line of action, transition, unbalance, and above all the line of dramatic and powerful movement ╱ . When curving in a long upward sweep to end in a short downward

turn, like the waves of the ocean, it becomes the line of force that increases to a climax, the line of advance and pull ⌣⌐ . When curving upward to spread and branch, like a growing plant, it becomes the line of unfolding, continuity, exploration) .

In each such apparent direction of movement, line carries with it a sense of mood. But the quality of a line, even more than its direction, can arouse emotional states: tranquillity and assurance when the line runs firmly and smoothly (1.1); emphatic assertion when it becomes alternately thick and thin (1.4b); nervous apprehension and irritability when it splinters and breaks into jagged bits (1.3a); dreamy revery when it doubles and blurs (1.3b); defiance and rage when it jerks about and abruptly changes direction (1.4c and d).

Line for Tactile Expression

We evolve with lines a whole language of expression. We start evolving it as infants when we grasp a crayon and begin scribbling. At first we probably indicate nothing more by our lines than sheer delight in waving our arms, but when eventually we come to translate on to paper what we are learning about our world, we pack new meaning into the lines that we make. We have been investigating everything in reach by touching or squeezing it. When we come to declare what we have discovered primarily through the sense of touch, we resort to line as a way of expressing what we have felt. When Jed Miller portrays his mother with the pet parakeet settling on her head, we sense how aptly through line he can express the experience of running his hands over her face and hair and against the fluttering wings of the bird (1.2a). Our first such drawings resemble the drawings of other children because the procedure of learning by feeling is common to all of us, as is our resort to line to express it.

Line for Ordered Movement

When tactile in appeal, line becomes an abstraction from nature. It stands for what we see as contours, the apparent edges of objects when seen in one position, and it serves in this way to symbolize natural forms. Still more important, line guides our eyes in the direction that the artist wishes them to go. It corresponds to the pointing finger, the speeding arrow, the flying bird. Line indicates apparent movement. It carries the eyes around and through a form, even as the artist meant it to, drawing the spectator into restful pauses, calling on him to proceed, and ultimately bringing him to the place of climax of the entire composition. As in a Mondrian painting (8.14), line can even suggest, without actually representing anything, the structure of the universe —stable as the posts and beams of a building and yet enclosing spaces within which invisible forces seem to be at work.

Our eyes are always seeking lines and reacting to them in one way or another. Since continuous lines, as contrasted with broken or angular lines, convey a sense of order, we tend to line up objects when they stand on a level. We line up pictures on walls so that the tops or

bottoms of their frames give a sense of order. Even our thinking tends toward line in any attempt to organize or make sense out of something. We follow a line of thought, line up prospects, follow a line of inquiry, trace a line of melody. Lines further convey a sense of extension in the direction in which they seem to be moving. An arrow causes our eyes to move beyond the tip of the arrow. A pointing finger impels us to look beyond the finger. Lines thus suggest a distance beyond their actual length and in so doing determine certain effects of proportion.

The artist uses line to underscore an effect. He may resort to this use intuitively but never accidentally and usually with deliberate intent. Take the cartoonist, for example. He knows how expressive line can be and utilizes it to exaggerate our foibles humorously. Consider C. N. Landon's rendering of a man in a hurry (1.2b). The cartoonist knew how to elongate and stretch the man's legs to the limit, but more important than the distortion of anatomy to suggest hurry, he knew just the lines that would make the haste inescapably clear— dipping curves that sweep on into horizontals, but horizontals that give way to inclined lines making angular breaks which point ahead to the right with increasing force.

Line in Works of Art

Architects everywhere and in all ages have used line to work out effects of movement and emotional expression. In an effort to lend serenity to the temples of their gods, whom they conceived as magnified versions of their own order-loving, farseeing selves, the builders of ancient Greece stressed the horizontal lines made by the edges of the forms in the foundations and superstructures and sought to hold these horizontals in check by the verticals which the columns seemed to describe (4.2). For an effect of spiritual aspiration, among a people who looked forward to the attainment of eternal life in heaven, the builders of the Gothic cathedral, on the other hand, developed its parts into a series of vertical lines appear-

1.3. EMOTIONAL EXPRESSIVENESS OF LINE.
a. George Grosz (1893–1959): *The Last Battalion*. c. 1918. Pen and ink. 18½ × 20¼".
Santa Barbara Museum of Art, Santa Barbara, Calif., Gift of Wright Ludington.   b. John Carroll (1892–   ): Head (untitled). n.d. Pencil. 12 × 9". San Francisco Museum of Art, Bender Collection.

ing to soar heavenward one above the other (4.5 and 4.6).

Sculptors have counted on line, which the contours of the masses of their works suggest, to enhance the effects of movement or emotional state prompted by their subjects. Rodin modeled his masses over a system of radiating lines in order to make *The Hand of God* express the opening, unfolding processes of creation (5.10). The quietly enclosing lines suggested by the meetings of the masses give to Maillol's sculptured personification of Thought the desired effect of brooding (5.11a and b).

Painters have made even more obvious use of line for the sake of expression. By repeating the vertical lines in his painting of the village of Gardanne, Cézanne caught the feeling of its hillside location and the climbing required of visitors in exploring it (8.9a). By using a series of whirling lines in his rendering of a landscape after rain, Marin recreated the drama of the retreating storm (8.10). By altering the direction and the character of his lines from one motive to the next, a Japanese artist a hundred and fifty years ago filled the pages of his sketch book with the expressive equivalence to states of action and mood: tripping, lilting lines, for childlike playfulness (1.4a); hard, firmly brushed-in lines with angular break and wall-like rise and bulge, for belligerent defiance (1.4b); short and choppy lines describing inward spiralings, for midcombat madness (1.4c and d).

Line in the Art of Calligraphy

Line came easily to the brush of a Japanese who used that same brush for writing characters which carried even farther expressive abstractions of line. Like the Chinese from whom his ancestors had learned to write in such fashion,[2] he wrote the character for "man" with a one-time representation of the whole figure now condensed into a terse two-stroke summary of the man's legs (1.5a), the character for "tree" with abbreviated strokes standing for the trunk and the outward spreading

2 See Notes, page 293.

1.4. LINE IN ACTION. Page from a Japanese sketchbook. Early 19th century. Pen and ink. $11 \times 7''$. Museum of Art, University of Oregon, Murray Warner Collection of Oriental Art. B. L. Freemesser photograph. a. Childlike playfulness. b. Belligerent alertness and defiance. c, d. Mad midcombat lust to overthrow and kill.

branches (1.5b), the character for "confused and embarrassed" as a tree hedged in so tightly that it cannot move or grow (1.5c). The conventionalization of each rendering released his creative powers of linear expression.

Although we of the Western world do not find in the lines of the letters of our alphabet such expressive directness, we do see much to

1.5. ABSTRACTION OF LINE IN CALLIGRAPHY. a. Chiang Yee (1903–   ): Chinese character for "man." b. Chiang Yee: Chinese character for "tree." c. Chiang Yee: Chinese character for "confused and embarrassed." d. Roman capital letter "N."

admire in the detached movements and the thickenings and thinnings of line in such letters.[3] Take the letter "N," for example (1.5d). We like its serif, that initial little base which supports the first upright. We like the obliquely descending heavy line which follows, and the repeated vertical and serif with which the letter ends.

PLANE

If we combine the letter "N" with other letters to form such a word as "LINE" and follow the beginner's usual practice of spacing the letters equidistant from each other as though each were on a card of the same size as the others (1.6a), we run into difficulty. The letters fail to group together so as to allow us to read the word with ease. The source of our trouble lies in the fact that each letter occupies an area of different size and shape from the areas occupied by the other letters—the area of the "L" open and free, that of the "I" slender and slight, that of the "N" and that of the "E" tending to close. By trial and error we discover that the only way in which to make the letters read easily as one word is to push the "L" and the "I" a little closer together and the "N" and the "E" a little farther apart, thus eliminating awkwardly varying jumps of the eye from one letter to the next and making the spaces between the letters so even and quiet that we are conscious only of the word itself (1.6b).

In the art of lettering, we find ourselves obliged inevitably to shift our attention from stress on line to the equally important employment of the background spaces around the letters. Such spaces are two-dimensional: they have height and width (or length and breadth) but never depth. They compose a plane, a completely flat surface, like the bed of sand in the Japanese garden (1.1). Such a surface may be parallel to the observer. It may be at right angles to the observer. It may be diagonal to the observer. Even as the point has position and the line direction, the plane has extension because it covers area in any direction. This page is a plane; so is the top of a desk or the wall of a room. A level field is a plane; so also, apparently, the ocean in dead calm, an icebound lake, or the flatlands of a river delta.

The Plane in Works of Art

Planes can extend across our field of vision from right to left and from top to bottom, holding us to the flat surface close at hand. They can array themselves in overlapping fashion, conducting us step by step along them or over them into depth. Whichever way they turn,

[3] See Notes, page 293.

LINE

LINE

a

LINE

b

1.6. SPACING OF LETTERS TO FORM A WORD.
a. Letters of word "LINE" spaced equal distances
apart. b. Letters of word "LINE" spaced to read
as a unit.

planes provide the artist an element with
which to simplify and organize and intensify
his effects. The painter is concerned about
planes because he actually does his work on a
plane. Before he can begin to work, he has to
decide the size and shape of the plane on
which he will render his picture. As he proceeds, he has to make up his mind whether to
create the illusion of other planes paralleling
the picture plane or to simulate holes of space
opening out behind it. He may even decide,
as Mondrian did (8.14), to treat the plane for
its own sake, subdividing it into compartments
that depend for their interest on their proportional relationship.

The sculptor faced with a block of stone cut
cubically from the quarry is apt to find its
planes so satisfying that he restrains his carving in order to preserve them as contributions
to the character of his finished work.

Without planes the architect could not work
at all, since it is only with them that he can
create the floors and walls and ceilings and
slopes of roof that form his building. An architect depends on such planes to give a sense
of shelter to his structure. Even where he cuts
holes through or entirely suppresses his wall
planes in favor of doors and windows, he may
seek to remind us of these planes, perhaps by
designing for the panes of glass a framework
which makes a latticelike carry-over of the
planes to either side (4.10).

The Importance of the "Negative" Space

Any area becomes a "positive" space on a plane
when it is defined in some shape and perhaps
filled in by the artist. The areas then left over
around this "positive" space become the "negative" spaces. As surplus intervals, we might
be inclined to ignore the "negative" spaces, but
in reality the artist owes them as much attention as he owes the "positive" spaces, and he
knows that what he does with his "negatives"
can actually make or ruin his work. If the artist
lets a "negative" space get too big, for example, as we did in our first attempt at lettering,
it will outweigh the "positive" spaces set
against it and impair the effectiveness of the
creation. If, on the other hand, the artist
lets a "positive" space get too big, it will en-
croach unduly on the background and confuse
and weary the eye.

Before a "negative" plane that has grown too
large, we experience an effect so chilling that
it numbs our senses to any other element. Before a "negative" space that has been
overlooked by the artist while he determined
his "positive" shapes, we are apt to discover
some accidental and irrelevant shape so fascinating that we forget the artist's message.
Before some "busy" filled-in plane, like that
of a wall covered from floor to ceiling with pictures, we feel so shut in and stuffy that we fail
to pay attention either to the wall or to any
picture on it.

The eye needs "negative" spaces for rest
from overstimulation or as contrast to the
"positive" shapes—even as the ear needs gaps
of silence. Recognizing such need, the actor in
reading his lines pauses for effect, and the
musician in playing a composition stops for
the "rests." The architect reserves broad inter-

vals of plane by which to render more meaningful the intersections of one plane with another or the interpenetrations of a plane with a supporting member (4.8a and b). The sculptor seeks to order the surfaces of his work and give the eye a corresponding series of rests when he flattens bulges sufficiently to make them apparent as planes and leaves them devoid of inner modeling (5.12a and b).

The painter tries to adjust his "positive" spaces to the "negatives" of the plane on which he works, taking care not to let excessive emptiness surround a large but uninteresting shape, and yet sometimes depending on a small and exciting shape to dominate a vast expanse and thus to assume an emotional significance which it would lack if surrounded by other shapes (2.2c).

TEXTURE

Every plane has texture, that element deriving from the physical quality of a work which gives to the plane its own peculiar "feel," smooth, rough, slippery, granular, hard, soft, or whatever. We have illustrated one such texture in the sand bed of a Japanese garden (1.1). The paper of this page has texture, one that avoids glare but is smoother than the texture of newsprint. The top of a desk has texture. So have the plaster of the wall, the rug on the floor, the concrete of the doorstep and the driveway.

Texture appeals to that tactile sense which we begin cultivating the moment we are born. About the first thing that we do as infants is reach out and touch things, learning gradually that an object with a particular "feel" carries with it a particular "look." Owing to the fact that our very safety depended on them, we learned these early lessons well. Even as adults we can still be fooled occasionally, but we are more often right than wrong and the artist realizes this when, counting on our accumulated tactile wisdom for response, he enriches his work with textures.

Texture in Nature and Daily Life

We have become, in fact, intensively texture-conscious. We have developed our sensitivity both to natural textures and to textures which the artist creates to recall them. Consider, in Figure 1.7, for instance, the texture of a piece of rock on the beach and compare it with the texture inspired by that same rock in the coarse-grained wares of a potter. Or observe the textures of leaves as dramatized by the photographer and note how a weaver has developed a corresponding texture in a piece of fabric. We know the natural textures of things and the visual effects peculiar to each texture. We associate certain emotional states with certain textures, and we strive to control and evoke various states from textures by selecting suitable ones for our home surroundings. Assuming that we want a cozy den, do we panel the room in marble or in knotty pine? Assuming that we want an impressive courtroom, do we decorate it with silks and satins or with marble and mahogany? Assuming that we want a dainty boudoir, do we fit it out in burlap and canvas or in diaphanous silk?

We are aware of the textures which work together in combinations. Take that den which we have walled in knotty pine. Would we furnish it with glazed chintz draperies or with something of rough and nubby weave? If we had to choose for it between satin cushions or monk's cloth pillows, which . . . ? If we are going to a dance in a softly lustrous silk evening gown, will we wear rope sandals, knitted wool stockings, a felt hat, a leather jacket? It is interesting to touch the things about us in our room, settle on the roughest texture, the smoothest texture, and the gradations of textures in between; if we then glue pieces of each material to a panel of composition board and make a five-point or a ten-point scale, we may see whether the textures go well together, with neither discord nor monotony of effect.

1.7. TEXTURE. a. Tom Burns, Jr. (1925–   ): *Rock and Foam on Beach*. 1948. Photograph. 10 × 8″. Courtesy of the artist. b. Glen Lukens (1890–   ): *Platter and two small bowls*. c. 1934. Terra cotta; viscous glaze of Death Valley alkalis in decoration of larger bowl. Courtesy of the artist. c. Tom Burns, Jr.: *Leaves of the African Violet*. 1948. Photograph. 10 × 8″. Courtesy of the artist. d. Lynn Alexander (1920–   ): *Woven drapery with surface float*. 1947. Warp: three-ply cotton, yellow and white; weft: nubby cotton, white; floats: nylon rope, white. 12″ wide. Courtesy of the artist. William E. Lotz and Joseph H. Rudd, Jr., photograph.

1.8. TEXTURAL RELATIONSHIPS. a. Bob Stocksdale (1913–   ): Salad bowl and servers, with salt and pepper shakers. 1955. Guatemala mahogany, turned and soaked in mineral oil. Bowl: height, 6″, diameter, 12″. Courtesy of the artist. Gus Pestler photograph. b. Don Doman (1922–   ) and associate designers: Parker "41" fountain pen. 1955. Parker-developed plastic, electropolished chrome-plated brass, beryllium copper, plathenium. 5⅜″ long. Design based on Kenneth Parker: Parker "51" fountain pen, 1931, 1941. Courtesy of Parker Pen Company, B. L. Freemesser photograph. c. Meret Oppenheim (no date available): *Object* (fur-covered cup, plate, and spoon). 1936. The Museum of Modern Art, New York. Soichi Sunami photograph.

Texture in Works of Art

Artists today often exploit texture, sometimes almost to the exclusion of every other element. Frank Lloyd Wright, who worked always, as he put it, "in the nature of materials," developed in his architecture tremendous emotional expressiveness by opposing one texture to another, such as that of wood to that of brick, or that of stone to that of glass. A sculptor explores the entire range of textures, now polishing stone smooth, now letting the marks of the punch show, here polishing bronze, there retaining thumb-marks in the clay. By resorting to technical devices the painter can simulate textures, but beyond their illusions he can add to the emotional impact of his picture by the development of actual textures in the way he applies the paint. Witness, for example, the glossy texture of a painting by Botticelli (8.5), the rough and heavy texture of one by Cézanne (8.9a).

In order to achieve the desired textural effects an artist may treat his material in various ways—polishing, waxing, sandblasting, etching, and so forth. Whatever his treatment of the material, he respects the texture that the material possesses naturally and seeks only to enhance it, never to hide or disguise it. Texture should always be in harmony with the purpose and the form of the surface that possesses it. If something is to be handled, for example, like the objects shown in Figure 1.8, it should be neither extremely rough nor extremely slippery but inviting to the touch. If an article is very small, a coarse surface should be avoided as inappropriate. Probably nothing could be more shocking than to line a teacup and saucer with fur—exactly what an artist once did to vent his spite on art as the symbol of warmaking civilization. Texture needs to be considered again in connection with color, delicate colors requiring a textural treatment quite different from that called for by boldly assertive ones.

COLOR

The element of color conditions not only texture but every other element. Though sometimes missing from a point or a line (when the point or line is black, conceived of either as "the absence of color" in light or as "the presence of all colors" in pigments), it is almost always present in the background of either element. Unless black or white is used for coverage, some color occupies any area. As we shall see later, color ties itself up inextricably with volumes both of mass and of open space. When taken in the broadest sense of the term, it occurs as nearly universally in nature as it does in art. It affects our waking moments, consciously or unconsciously, and also, when we are dreaming, our sleeping moments. It influences—sometimes to a frightening extent—our moods and states of mind, soothing or amusing us, stimulating or revolting us, driving us even to madness.

Color and Its Attribute of Hue

Color comes from sunlight and depends on illumination to make itself apparent. When full daylight is broken up by passage through some transparent medium like rain or the spray of lawn-sprinklers or a glass prism, color reveals its true richness in the form of the rainbow—spreading itself out in all the colors of the spectrum which our eyes can detect, and in others beyond our range of vision. We use "color" as an all-embracing term for any visual sensation deriving from light.

The colors which we perceive in the rainbow we call *hues*. These are immensely diversified in their range. For the sake of convenience in reference, we usually select twelve hues equally spaced from each other in the rainbow:

yellow	violet (or "purple")
yellow-green	red-violet
green	red
blue-green	red-orange
blue	orange
blue-violet	yellow-orange

If we arrange these twelve hues in sequence as a circle with yellow at the top and violet at the bottom (Pl. I), we have made a "color wheel," according to a certain scheme of color known as the Prang system, which is based on hues as pigments, or powdered substances mixed with suitable liquids to form paints or dyes. Each hue tends to blend into the hue next to it and to follow in sequence with the others a circular arrangement. Actually, between each color and the one before or after it in the "color wheel," it should be borne in mind, there are any number of other hues.[4]

Although the hues of the Prang color wheel fall far below the brilliance of the hues of the

[4] See Notes, p. 293.

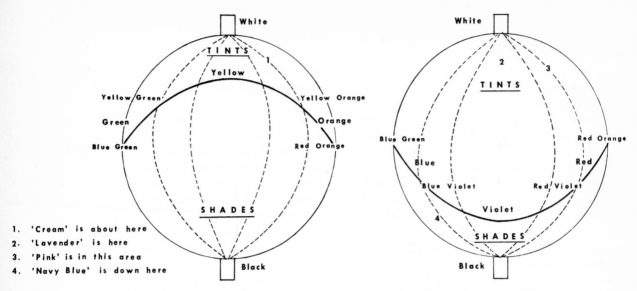

1.9. VALUES. Color Globe—Where tints and shades come from. Diagram by Harry B. Green.

rainbow, each pigmentary hue corresponds on a lower level of brilliance to a given hue in the spectrum as revealed by the rainbow. We can make all but three of the twelve hues artificially by combining one pigment with another. For these three exceptions—red, yellow, and blue—we have to resort to nature, drawing the hue in each case from some vegetable or mineral source. Our medieval ancestors had to depend for blue upon a powder ground from turquoise. Owing to its enormous expense, since it derives from a precious stone, they treasured the color and used it only for specially important or sacred areas such as that of the Virgin's robe in altarpiece paintings or images.

As only nature can give us the three hues mentioned above—red, yellow, and blue—we call them the "primary hues." If we mix any two of these primary hues in equal quantities, we gain the "secondary hues": orange from red and yellow; green from yellow and blue; violet from blue and red. Yellow-orange, red-orange, yellow-green, blue-green, blue-violet, and red-violet are "tertiary hues." We get them by mixing in equal parts a primary and a secondary hue.

Owing to association with certain experiences and objects, we feel that certain hues are "warm" and others "cool." By association with late-afternoon sunshine, fire, or heated iron, on the one hand, and with nightfall, water, ice, snow, on the other, we group yellow, orange, and red together as warm hues and green, blue, and violet together as cool. The artist draws on the ideas which we thus connect with color when he selects and organizes hues, sometimes even making us feel hot or cold by reaction to them. He realizes that hues do not operate in this way by any law of temperature change; he simply depends on our habitual associations to produce the desired effects. It is true that the artist can so modify one color in relation to another as to make red seem cold or blue seem hot, and he may do just this for the sake of novelty and shock. Ordinarily, however, he employs hues for their customary associations.

Color and Its Attribute of Value

We have noted how completely hues depend on light to be seen at all and how through their separation in the rainbow they reveal them-

16 - THE ELEMENTS OF ART

selves as composing light itself. Hues never occur except at some point between the extremes of absolute light and absolute darkness. Each hue has also in its own right, at maximum brilliance, a certain degree of light or dark. Yellow comes the closest to white, violet the closest to black, and each of the other hues ranges itself somewhere between yellow and violet among either the light hues or the dark (Pl. I and 1.9).

This approach of a given color either to light or to darkness constitutes its *value*, the second attribute of color. Value is the relative amount of lightness or darkness as measured against white, the lightest visual effect man experiences, or black, the darkest. We can understand value better if we conceive of color as a sphere, with a north pole and a south pole marking the ends of a line that pierces its center like a hatpin. The "north pole" stands for pure white, and the "south pole" for pure black. Around the outside of the sphere we lay an equatorial band with the color wheel of twelve hues marked out on it. In order to give each hue its proper position of natural value with reference to white and black, we shall have to tip the color wheel in such a manner that yellow comes closest to white on one side of the sphere and violet closest to black on the other side. Each hue has its own place on the sphere, its own value.

We can lighten the value of any one of the twelve hues in the form of pigments by adding white paint to it and causing it to move upward toward white along the outside of the sphere, or darken its value by adding black paint to it and causing it to move downward toward black. Pure yellow has only a few steps to make in climbing toward white, and pure violet has many; the reverse is true when either hue descends toward black. Any hue that has been moved at all in the direction of white is called a *tint*, and any moved in the direction of black is called a *shade*. We see that pink, while a color, is not a hue but a tint of the hue of red. So likewise with khaki, a shade of the hue of yellow, and navy blue, a shade of the

hue of blue. We further see that there can be no such thing as a "pastel shade" but only a pastel tint, because a pastel is a kind of crayon made by adding pigment to chalk, the whiteness of which automatically produces a tint of the pigment.

Although the artist may have only two hues to work with, he can widen his range of colors enormously by resorting to the tints and the shades of each. With the values which tints and shades represent he can really put his colors to work. He can exaggerate the contrast of one hue with another and achieve an effect of great dramatic power. He can reduce the contrast of one hue with another until hues which began by clashing end by working quietly together. He can match the value of one hue with the value of another and introduce them unobtrusively side by side into a background without breaking it up. He can make one area look larger by giving it a light-reflecting tint and another area look smaller by giving it a light-absorbing shade.

Again for convenience, as in the case of the color wheel for hues, the artist adopts an arbitrary scale of values. Those occurring halfway between white and black on such a scale he calls the middle values; those occurring above these he calls the light values and those below, the dark values; the former reach a high light and the latter a low dark at either end of the scale. If the artist keys his colors high, restricting them, that is, to light values, he is apt to get effects of delicacy, lightness, and airiness. If he keys his colors low, he is apt to get effects of forcefulness, heaviness, and gloom. He generally uses values thus to reinforce the mood called for by the character or the subject matter of his creation, whether gay and open or tragic and forbidding, even though he may at times, for dramatic emphasis and shock, actually set the value-scheme at odds with the mood demanded. Whatever the case, the point to remember is that by using values the artist can exploit color to much more telling advantage and with far wider range than he can by relying on hues alone.

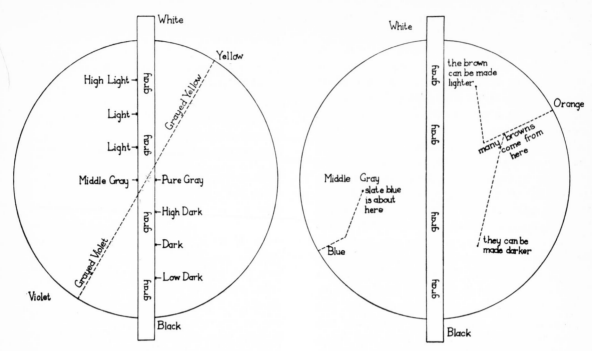

1.10. INTENSITIES. Color Globe—Where neutralities come from. Diagram by Harry B. Green.

Color and Its Attribute of Intensity

The particular value which we have described as natural to a hue can be determined only when that hue is revealed by sunlight in some sort of spectrum. The hue then stands, as we have noted, at the height of its brightness. We have seen how the same hue can then be changed from its natural value, upward to become a tint or downward to become a shade. We have still to observe how it can be reduced from its state of maximum brightness through stages of increasing dullness or grayness until we reach a state so close to total neutrality, or pure gray, that we can scarcely tell the hue from which it originated. The degree of brightness or dullness of a color constitutes the third attribute of color, *intensity*.

In order to grasp the way in which intensity fits into the color system we must slice our sphere in half and see what happens inside it (1.10). We now note that the "north pole" of white and the "south pole" of black mark the ends of a core that runs from white to black in a graduated series of grays, with middle gray exactly halfway between the poles and equal in the amounts of white and black going to form it. On the outer rim of the sphere, far up toward white, lies pure yellow; opposite, on the other side of the rim and close to black, lies pure violet. If we add a little violet to the yellow we get a yellow that is slightly darker and slightly grayer than pure yellow, because the violet has pulled the yellow toward it. A little more violet, and we get a still darker and grayer yellow, the path which our mixture follows moving straight toward pure violet through middle gray at the center of the sphere. If we keep on adding violet, we reach at length a point at which the quantity of violet is equal to that of yellow and at this point achieve, in theory at least, the pure middle gray of the center (impurities of the pigments being used may throw us off in practice). Again in theory if not in practice, continuing to add violet we get a color that grows ever darker and yet brighter and more and more like violet—until at length we reach the original violet on the outer rim, dark but brilliant, like the violet with which we started.

What we did up to the middle point in our process was increasingly to neutralize the hue of yellow by adding violet to it—a process made possible by the fact that yellow and violet operate as a pair of *complementary* colors, colors which serve together to "complete" the color circle. The way in which two colors like yellow and violet are able to do such a thing can best be explained by describing colors as vibrations of light. Light waves of different lengths affect the eye differently. Light waves set to vibrating the rods and cones which form a part of the structure of the eye, and each wavelength has overtones like the overtones of sounds in music. Thus a wavelength that causes vibrations of the rods and cones to register, for example, as the hue of yellow, has overtones which spread out to either side and affect to lesser degrees the rods and cones sensitive to green and orange. When, in other words, we see one color such as yellow, we respond at the same time to hues on either side of it, covering with our eyes one whole half of the color wheel. If we took in simultaneously with our eyes the complement of that color, in this instance violet, and necessarily the overtones to either side of it, we should complete the color wheel and determine a pair of complements. With the color wheel (Pl. I) before us, we can ascertain not only the complements of yellow and violet but of all other hues. Draw a line through the center of the wheel from any given hue to the hue directly opposite. By linking yellow-green and red-violet, green and red, blue-green and red-orange, and so on around the circle, we get the color complements.

Complementary hues are tremendously stimulating to the eye. When seen in equal quantities at maximum intensity, in fact, they become painful, because they set every rod and cone of the eye to vibrating. Unless the inflicting of pain is his express objective, the artist takes some measure, therefore, either to modify the complements or else to avoid them. He may neutralize yellow by mixing vio-

let with it, reserving a hue of high intensity only for occasional accent. Or he may reduce the number of rods and cones stimulated by substituting for one of the complements a hue to either side in the color wheel, blue-violet or red-violet, for example, instead of violet which is the complement of yellow.

Using Color Attributes Together

With twelve jars of colored paint, plus a jar of white and a jar of black, an artist versed in the manipulation of hues, values, and intensities has at his disposal the whole vast sphere of color. If we were to confront this wealth of creative possibilities and have to decide, like him, just what hues, tints, shades, grays, and color accents to use in a given situation, we should feel bewildered. The artist himself relies on his own feelings about color, but his feelings have been refined by years of experience and ours remain relatively uncultivated. About the best that we can do as laymen learning to judge color is to familiarize ourselves with certain patterns which have proved workable through generations of trial and error.

Contrary to the claim often made by those ignorant of the true nature of color, any two colors can be used harmoniously if only proper adjustments are made among their attributes. One such adjustment has to do with quantity of hue. Increase one hue to cover the major area and reduce the other to a tiny fraction of that area, and a harmonious combination will result.

Another adjustment has to do with values, especially when, as we have seen, the artist works with complementaries of the lightest and the darkest hues in the color wheel, yellow and violet. Botticelli adopted complementaries close to these hues when he painted the Goddess of Love being wafted ashore by sea breezes, as the Greek legend described the birth of Venus (Pl. III). In an effort to match in color his concept of the goddess's loveliness, the artist rendered the illuminated portions of her features with a tint of yellow-orange and the reflection of the sky on her forehead with an even lighter tint of blue-violet. Yellow-orange and blue-violet are complements, but Botticelli made them work together harmoniously by drawing them together in value instead of allowing them to oppose each other with their customary strength of contrast.

A third adjustment has to do with intensities. If we let one hue keep its original brilliance but quiet the other hues by neutralizing them, we get such pleasing combinations as that achieved by a girl in a red sweater who wears a skirt of greenish gray rather than of a green as bright as the red of the sweater. The ancient Etruscan artist who fashioned a warrior out of clay and then used color to heighten its effect knew how to mute one color in favor of another (Pl. II). He grayed the colors of the warrior's flesh and armor to make resplendent by contrast the yellow of the ornamental detail.

The Split Complementary and the Triad

The hues used in the Etruscan warrior's figure follow what is called a *split complementary* scheme of color—yellow as the hue of accent just noted and two other hues instead of violet alone as the complement to yellow—the hues lying to either side of the complement in the color-wheel, in this case blue-violet and red-violet. Such a scheme, involving as it does the suggestion through the "split" that dramatic action is in progress, befits a warlike subject. It stimulates the eye and still conveys a sense of purposeful control.

One color scheme somewhat allied to the split complementary uses colors determined by the points of an equilateral triangle inscribed at a given position within the color-wheel (on the twelve-hue color wheel every fourth hue would be chosen). Owing to its employment of *three* hues, we call this scheme the *triadic* and gain with it initial variety of hue beyond that which a two-color scheme can offer. This scheme can be further enriched by variations in value or intensity among the three hues employed.

Analogous and Monochromatic Color Schemes

A scheme akin to both the split complementary and the triadic in its inclusion of at least three hues, but very different from them in its quietness of effect is the *analogous*. In this scheme, the artist employs hues which adjoin each other in the color wheel rather than hues which oppose each other across it. He thinks of these analogous hues as "neighborly" colors, friendly and pleasant in effect but really exciting only when something positive is done with the adjustments in value and intensity. Consider, for example, a brown (neutralized orange) dress that has been relieved by cuffs and collar of cream color (a tint of the analogous hue of yellow-orange) and accentuated by a belt of bright red-orange (the third analogous hue at full intensity). Rembrandt found satisfaction in analogous color schemes, especially those ranging through the red-to-yellow half of the color wheel. A representative instance is the detail of the head in his *Man with a Magnifying Glass* (Pl. IV). Successive varnishings have probably brought the analogous colors closer together than Rembrandt intended, but even before the varnishings he succeeded in catching that magic quality of flesh, illuminated by spotlighting in a dark interior, which only an intimate harmony of yellow, yellow-orange, and orange could yield.

The *monochromatic* color scheme goes beyond all other schemes in assuring harmony, because it embraces no more than a single hue. The artist using it depends on an all-pervading hue not only for its unity of effect but for the mood that it evokes by association; he then goes as far as he sees fit in variations of value and intensity. How cooling in effect a monochromatic scheme of blue can be on a hot summer's day when adopted for dress: navy blue skirt, let us say, with blouse of white (really with a pale bluish tint) and belt of brilliant blue! Or how poetic in appeal in the hands of a master like Hiroshige, the Japanese print maker who recaptured with blue the chill of a winter's evening, when the snow was falling softly and the sounds of passersby were muffled by a frozen blanket already lying thick on the road (7.7)!

The Spatial Effects of Color

The blue of the monochromatic scheme in Hiroshige's print accounts for its coldness of suggestion; it also accounts for the picture's poignant sense of distance. Colors indeed convey effects of spatial depth as well as effects of temperature. Cool colors seem to recede, warm colors to advance; and again it is mental associations which make them seem to do so. The farther away from the eye we move a red or an orange object the more bluish it seems to become. This apparent bluishness is brought about by atmospheric phenomena (dust, smoke haze, smog), and the artist utilizes it to his advantage. He uses colors to create illusions of space, selecting warm hues, widely contrasting values, and high intensities to make things seem close and large, and cool hues, middle values, and lowered intensities to make them seem distant and small. The chubby girl will avoid wearing much red, because it makes her seem heavier, while the girl who is too slight will choose strong colors for a corrective result. The homemaker paints in shades of grayed red or orange the walls of an over-spacious room, because such handling of color in hue, value, and intensity makes the walls seem to advance and thus to reduce the size of the room. Conversely, he paints in tones of grayed blue or green or violet the walls of a room excessively small, because such coloring makes the walls seem to recede and thus to become less confining. The painter can utilize the advancing and retreating properties of color either to create the illusion of great depths of space or else to simulate a solid mass encompassed by luminous space.

MASS

The advancing-and-retreating aspects of color are especially distinctive of painting; in the other arts they play a role subordinate to the *actual* advance and retreat effected in depth by the solid substance of the material. Painting and the graphic arts are only two-dimensional, having height and width, but the other visual arts are three-dimensional, having depth as well. They utilize an element which painting can possess only by illusion: the element of *mass*, which consists in the bulk or quantity of matter.

We think of mass as composing the essence of the earth and the various forms on its surface. We regard our own bodies as masses and read into other masses our experience with ourselves. We recognize the universal pull of gravity which gives us weight, and we take great satisfaction in the physical power with which we resist the pull of gravity and hold ourselves erect. We project this sort of experience into other masses and think of them in a corresponding yielding-resisting relationship to the earth.

Mass in Works of Art

The Japanese find sensuous satisfaction in the masses of natural rock. They go to great lengths to seek out in the mountains those rocks that echo in miniature the shapes of mountain masses and promontories, that manifest in their irregular ruggedness countless ages of battle with the forces of storm and frost. They carry these back, to home or temple, and group their discoveries so as to bring out the qualities of each individual rock. Sometimes, as in the garden illustrated in Figure 1.1, the Japanese so implant the rocks in level gravel beds as to accentuate the solid bulk and upward-rearing power that the rocks possess.

Sculptors respond to the relative degrees of density or compactness of various substances, carving a stone of extreme hardness in simplified bulges that emphasize its massiveness, carving a stone of lighter consistency in dune-like sweeps that suggest the sand from which it originated, carving a block of wood in small-scaled protrusions and withdrawals to accord with the character of the once-growing tree. Architects go out of their way deliberately to emphasize the solidity of supporting masses —by contrasting brick with mortar, for example, to call attention to building blocks, by extending the solid substance of a column into slender shafts and other projecting members, by closing marble walls in solidly, or by making building stones jut out ruggedly (4.13).

The Basic Forms of Mass

Masses can be so fluid as to be subject, like water or soft mud, to easy or continual change by forces from outside. They can hang in suspension above the earth and depend, like clouds, on the temperature and the flow of air to determine their shapes. Or they can rear themselves by their own inner power into forms as varied in expression as those of trees.

Whatever the nature of a mass in a given instance, we can usually find in it some approximation to a standard basic form: the sphere, the cylinder, the cube, the cone, the pyramid. It is recognition of such basic forms that affords one of our most satisfying responses to mass. Man-conceived and man-appealing, these underlying bases of form, or variations and combinations of them, give us our sense of order in nature. However complex its combination of forms, we think we find in nature that order of solid geometry which the artist recognizes as his foundation, freely though he rise above it in the development of his forms.

Architects are apt to use the basic forms of mass nearly unchanged because of the monumental and enduring effects that such forms can give. The builders of ancient Egypt fashioned their tombs into pyramids; the builders of ancient Greece made their temples into cubes or oblongs made of cubes set side by side and punctuated by cylinders (4.2). The builders of medieval France reared their cathedral spires as cones (4.6), and the Byzantine builders climaxed their houses of worship with hemispherical domes.

Sculptors often break their subjects down into corresponding shapes, perhaps working with the cylinder as the essential mass for a bird in flight (5.18a), or with the sphere for the head, the cylinder for the neck and arms and legs of a human figure (5.11a and b). They excite us visually by their use of these forms and their relationships. So likewise we respond to the work of the potters who spare us excrescences of ornament in favor of the pure beauty of the form of their vessels (3.10).

Painters cannot work directly with the basic forms as masses but only with two-dimensional symbols for such forms: the circle for the sphere, the square for the cube, the rectangle for the cylinder, and the triangle for the cone or pyramid. They tell us by their symbols what forms of mass they mean, but only by resorting to various devices can they make us feel the elemental shapes. They realize that shadow is an accidental thing which only exceptionally can reveal the basic form, but they employ light and dark arbitrarily as "modeling" to bring out the essence of a form. Painters can thus reveal to us, even as architects, potters, and sculptors, the universal and enduring qualities of one particular mass, making any departures from a fixed feature all the more timely and significant by contrast with the mass from which they started.

SPACE

For all of the artist's stress on volumes of mass in a given work, we of the Atomic Age know perfectly well how interchangeable mass and energy can be. Let certain conditions occur and the hardest rock can be made to vanish into energy. Let the lens magnify sufficiently and the densest substance can be seen to consist of particles dancing in space. Mass is shot through and through with energy-pregnant space and it is only relative densities which enable us to distinguish mass from space. It is true that we are prone to ignore space as mere surplus room left over after material substance has occupied what it wants. But space in which to live, move about, and breathe is just as important as living matter itself, and open space, potentially occupiable, must be considered another kind of volume important to art as to life. Space goes into the structure of any three-dimensional work of art as integrally, in fact, as a "negative" area entering the structure of a two-dimensional work, and any space not occupied by mass we must regard in like manner as a "negative" space.

The Hindu expresses the significance of "negative" space when he speaks of *prana* as that invisible breath which fills a body-mass with the spirit of God.[5] He builds his sculpture-laden temples accordingly, in balloonlike bulgings of stone (5.2). The Chinese Taoist expresses it, too, when he speaks of *tao*, the Way of Life, as inaudible, invisible, inexhaustible void. Lao-tzu, Taoism's founder, described the key role played by space in life when he declared:

> Is not the space between heaven and earth like unto a bellows? It is empty; yet it collapses not. It moves, and more and more comes forth.

> Assembling thirty spokes by one hub to form a wheel, we find the utility in its void;
> Moulding clay into a vessel, we find the utility in its hollowness;
> Cutting doors and windows for a house, we find the utility in its empty space.*

Prompted by Taoist thought, the Japanese who carved of wood an image of a Buddhist Heavenly Guardian so interfused mass with space as to make them inseparable (5.14).

[5] See Notes, p. 294.
* First paragraph is from Paul Carus. *The Canon of Reason and Virtue: Being Lao-tze's Tao Teh King: Chinese and English* (Chicago: The Open Court Publishing Company, 1931), p. 76; the remainder is a paraphrase derived from two translations, that by Carus, *ibid.*, pp. 79–80, and that by Amos Ih Tao Chang, *The Existence of Intangible Content in Architectonic Form: Based Upon the Practicality of Laotzu's Philosophy* (Princeton: Princeton University Press, 1956), pp. 7, 59.

The Void in Garden, House, and Plot

The Japanese gardener disposes his groupings of rocks about his gravel bed and before his garden wall not alone to stress the masses of the rocks but also to vitalize the open spaces around them and render these volumes as the major element of the whole (1.1). The Japanese may also admit the space of his garden through openings made by rocks and walls, to afford continually inviting glimpses beyond (4.10 and 4.11). He carries this spatial emphasis over into arts like ceramics, making of the hollowness of the tea-bowl, for example, the climax of the pot (3.7).

Contemporary Western artists have set a high value on open space. The contemporary architect treats space as a positive element in its own right, throwing walls and roof around it only when fully satisfied that it will meet every function required and at the same time please the bodily sensations of those moving about in it. The contemporary landscape designer may treat the problem of bringing a backyard garden into relation to the house—with openwork fences of varying heights and extensions, ground planes of lawn and concrete slab, and a massive sculpture of sandstone—ordering spatial volumes into an exciting rhythmic movement comparable to that of the spaces in the house itself. So works any modern artist with a given space to occupy, balancing *something* against the *nothingness* that is there—neither too much of one nor too little of the other, but just the right amount of each to make the work function expressively in terms of his objective and at the same time to stimulate the viewer both visually and emotionally.

Esthetic Distance

One kind of space deserving special attention is that lying between the work of art and the eyes of the beholder. It is the space set off by the orchestra pit at the theater, for example, a space that separates the audience from the stage so as to enable it to view the progress of the play without being drawn too fully into the action. We respond intensively to a play or any other work of art only when able to see it as a creation separate from the affairs of the world, and it is the intervening space called "esthetic distance" which gives us this ability. Esthetic distance figures, for example, in the gap between the gateway of the Acropolis and the Parthenon, built on the highest hump of the rock—a space great enough to make the temple appear especially well proportioned (4.2). The architect always has to reckon with the space around his building if he is to make the structure effectively unified. He learns that the cottage on the side street functions best with little space between it and the sidewalk but that the cathedral demands esthetic distances of far greater magnitude. Lacking ample space around it, the latter suffers like the Cathedral of Granada, hemmed in by dwellings so

that its visual appeal is lost, its main entrance boarded up, and every side entrance forced to accommodate crowds beyond the architect's intent. Blessed by generous openness of surroundings, on the other hand, the Cathedral of Paris gains the effect desired, standing majestically on its island site to dominate the city physically, if no longer spiritually.

The sculptor must similarly take into account the esthetic distance from which his statue is to be viewed. He tries to predetermine such a distance, knowing that once the esthetic distance has been fixed he can proceed in confidence to develop his sculpture at the scale best fitted to the space. For the hilltop or the market place he will carve the piece in the broadest and simplest masses, but for viewing in closer quarters he will fashion the work in more finely scaled detail.

SUMMARY

Space is the one universal element. It is present before any of the other elements come into being and it remains after they are created— to give room for functioning and emphasis by contrast. It plays around the points of a composition like the space around the stars. It stretches in tension between one line and another. It flows along a plane set obliquely to our sight. It sandwiches itself between planes set one behind the other. It huddles between the particles of a substance that lend texture to the surface. It advances or retreats with changes in hue, value, or intensity. It envelops or interpenetrates every volume of mass.

Each element becomes essential at one time or another to the artist's creation. The point

will have to establish a position to which we can anchor. The line will have to indicate a direction for our eyes to move in, or else define and bound a shape within which they can orient themselves. The plane will have to close in or open out a prospect. The texture will have to convey the quality of a substance, and the color will have to contribute to that substance its due degree of emphasis, its "temperature," its "luminosity." Mass will have to awaken our consciousness to the pull of gravity and make us feel the lurch or the fixity of a bulk. But always the element employed refers us back to the space, that void or emptiness which at once contains and controls the whole structure of the work.

RECOMMENDED READINGS

Kuh, Katherine. *Art Has Many Faces*. New York: Harper & Brothers, 1951.

As curator of the Gallery of Art Interpretation in the Art Institute of Chicago, the author developed a series of exhibitions calculated to introduce laymen to the functions, materials, and processes of art. The book, rich in carefully chosen illustrative material from these exhibitions and highly abbreviated in explanatory text, is a useful one with which to cultivate an appreciation of art.

Goldstein, Harriet and Vetta. *Art in Everyday Life*. 4th ed. New York: Macmillan, 1954.

This book succeeds in relating the arts to the workaday world as few other books do. Beyond the scope of the present book, practical studies in interior and dress design in the Goldstein book extend the application of elements and principles of art. Though profusely illustrated, its reproductions are made, unfortunately, at too small a scale to function as they should in a book concerned with the visual arts.

Kandinsky, Wassily (Hilla Rebay, ed.; Howard Dearstyne and Hilla Rebay, trans.). *Point and Line to Plane*. New York: Solomon R. Guggenheim Foundation for the Museum of Nonobjective Painting, 1947. 1st ed. in German (Walter Gropius and L. Moholy-Nagy, ed.), *Punkt und Linie zu Fläche* (Bauhaus Series, Vol. IX), Dessau: Bauhaus, 1926.

Many books concerned with the nature of art and the foundations upon which it is based deal briefly with the elements before passing on to other considerations, even as we do in the present work; scarcely ever does a book devote itself to a study of elements alone. Hence the unique character of this book by a great painter, exhaustive in its inquiry into the character of the point, the line, and the plane, and exceptionally clear in its translation from German into English.

Osborn, Elodie Courter. *Texture and Pattern* ("Teaching Portfolio," No. 2). New York: Museum of Modern Art, n.d.

A box containing forty photographic plates, 10¾ inches by 13½ inches, and a two-page folder describing the sense-appeal of texture and pattern in nature and art. The text makes no attempt to explore the expressive possibilities of texture any more than it does the expressive possibilities of pattern, but the plates exemplify with exciting vividness the employment of texture as a major element in the arts of photography, painting, sculpture, and architecture.

Wolff, Robert Jay (Elodie Courter, Victor E. D'Amico, and Alice Otis, collab.). *Elements of Design*. New York: Museum of Modern Art, 1945.

A box containing 24 cardboard panels, most of them 25 inches by 20 inches, on which are mounted for exhibition purposes a series of carefully planned and executed diagrams, photographs, and reproductions, accompanied by explanatory captions intended to explain the nature and the use of each of the elements in a work of art. A new experiment in visual education.

Wilson, Michael. *What Is Colour? The Goethean Approach to a Fundamental Problem*. Clent, Stourbridge, Worcestershire, England: Goethean Science Foundation, 1949.

This is a small paper-bound volume far more useful to the study of color than its slight format would seem to promise. It is based upon the great German's poet's *Theory of Colors*, first published in 1810, and his principle that the essential nature of color can be understood by visual experience alone, and not by the physicist's concept of lightwaves, which cannot be experienced. The author has made a special effort to avoid technical language and render his presentation easy to grasp.

Bustanoby, J. H. *Principles of Color and Color Mixing*. New York: McGraw-Hill, 1947.

The value of Bustanoby's book lies in its concern for the artist's actual use of data as contributed by the various systems of color. It recognizes the expressive possibilities of color and gives practical directions for the matching and mixing of colors in the form of pigments.

Moholy-Nagy, L. *The New Vision (1928) and Abstract of an Artist (1944)* (Robert Motherwell, ed., "The Documents of Modern Art"). New York: Wittenborn, Schultz, 1947.

Published jointly in a single volume, the earlier of the two essays is based upon the classroom lectures Moholy-Nagy gave when he was a member of the Bauhaus faculty, 1923 to 1928; it is illustrated to a large extent by the work of students in his elementary courses during that time. *The Abstract of an Artist* was written only two years before the artist's death in 1946; in it Moholy-Nagy analyzes his own personal development as a series of "discoveries" of the elements of art.

2.1. BALANCE. a. Symmetrical balance in a furniture group-unit. Lamp stands by Martz, Marshall Studios, Inc.; Carl Morris (1911–   ): *Harbor*, 1953, oil painting on canvas. B. L. Freemesser photograph. b. Asymmetrical balance in a furniture group-unit. B. L. Freemesser photograph.

The Principles of Art

THE MAKINGS OF FORM

IF WE WOULD UNDERSTAND and enjoy a work of art, we must recognize its elements as essential to its structure. We must recognize, at the same time, the ways in which its elements are joined to compose the work's whole. Reconsider the man at the used-car lot buying an automobile. We saw him responding as a discriminating patron to the sensuous appeal of this element or that in the cars examined. Before he could make up his mind which car to buy, he had still to test each prospect for both its operation and its looks. He might become intrigued by flashy fins or bug-eyelike headlights and overlook something else that was seriously objectionable. If he were judging as an enlightened purchaser, on the other hand, he would choose after careful inspection only that automobile which held the road most surely as well as actually appearing as though it would. He would note perhaps about this vehicle how smoothly its contours traced the path of the wind sweeping past, how far to the sides as well as to the front its windshield allowed the driver's unobstructed vision, how well in every other respect it performed and declared that it was performing.

The Three Sources of Form

In deciding on the car to buy, the purchaser was being governed by functional considerations. Every time that he tried to answer a question of function, however, he had to answer some closely related question of form. If the patron stopped to reflect on his experience, he may have been struck by the extent to which the form of the motor car related to its function and yet varied in the nature of this relationship. In one case the form seemed unrelated to the function, chosen only to achieve a novelty of effect. In such a case, when the very life or death of the user might be determined by its performance, the purchaser passed the offending vehicle by. In another case form followed function closely. In a third case form and function joined to make an indissoluble whole. And in a fourth case form actually determined function.[1]

Whatever the case, the patron came to realize that for a utilitarian object like an automobile function was indeed a primary source of form. In the course of his judging, moreover, he discovered two other sources of form which were intimately bound up with function. They were the materials used and the processes, or techniques, employed. Steel, plastic, glass, textile, whatever the material, each had its own peculiar qualities to contribute to the car's behavior and appearance. Only by pressing and stamping and molding and assembling and welding could such materials be controlled and made to participate in rapid machine-production of identical vehicles. No misguided impulse to make the car look like the unique creation of a handicraftsman could be tolerated.

The more sharply the purchaser tried to discriminate between one car and another, the more intensively he imagined himself as sharing in the designer's experience. He tried to follow the refinements of form by which the

[1] See Notes, page 294.

designer sought to express the functions, to bring out the nature of the materials, to make manifest the processes of the production. He found in function, material, and technique the true sources of the form upon which the designer drew in developing his creation.

When the critic turns from automobile design to some other branch of design, whether in industry or in the crafts or in some other art, he finds that works vary in degree of emphasis accorded one source of form or another. Function may dominate at one time to such an extent as to hide the material and the technique, and material and technique at another time to the point where their assertion takes the very place of the functioning of the work. Sometimes even the general effect of the work runs at odds with these three sources of form, masking them under some such dictum as "an art which conceals art." Masking is not always wrong in art. It depends upon the circumstances governing creation. For the sake of cultivating an awareness of the nature of art, however, equal concern for each of the three sources of form will prove central to any study developed in this book.

When the artist designs, he practices no magic hocus-pocus. He simply performs on a more exacting and complicated level an act in which the rest of us engage every day. We design actually when we plan anything. We arrange and order it. We design when we set a table for dinner. Instead of tossing the silverware about haphazardly, we arrange it according to a scheme and we change the scheme every time we change the type of meal to be served. We design when we take notes in class, ordering every page much as the layout artist designs every page of a book to be published. The artist's job is simply more difficult, less conventional, more exploratory, less charted and familiar. In performing it, however, he observes in one way or another certain sure landmarks called principles of design.

The Two Types of Design

Principles of design are not mere shortcuts to creation, rules to be memorized and applied without thinking and feeling. They codify ways of working which, artists have learned through centuries of trial and error, are more apt than other ways to succeed. When we learn to watch for their observance in a work of art, we sharpen our appreciation.

We see principles of design coming into operation in the development of the actual shape of an object. They are then figuring in structural design. When an architect determines the pattern of the brickwork in a wall, he is engaging in structural design. When a potter prompts his clay to rise into the wall of a vessel, or a weaver calculates the interlacings by which to make a textile with his threads, he is practicing structural design. Remove his arrangement and we lose the object itself, because structural design determines the object's existence.

We see principles of design again at work in the embellishment of an object. They are then entering into *decorative* design. When a painter renders a mural on the plaster of a wall, he is practicing decorative design. So likewise a potter when he develops in the clay-coating or the glazing on a vessel's surface some ornamental device, or a textile worker when he stencils or imprints a pattern on his fabric. Remove the artist's decoration—scrape the mural off the wall, chip the clay-coating or glaze from the pot, bleach the print out of the cloth—and the object itself remains. It has lost its decoration but it remains a product of structural design. In either case, structural or decorative, principles of design have governed the creation.

THE PRINCIPLE OF BALANCE

Among the many principles which the artist observes we single out for study four of the most important. Although these principles go by various names, we choose to call them balance, emphasis, rhythm, and proportion.

The principle of balance has to do with stability, whether it be the stability of repose or the stability of equal oppositions. We regard a sense of balance as essential to our physical well-being, and we dread its loss lest some unpleasantness or accident befall. Unless for the thrill of it we entrust ourselves to some contraption that tosses us about and stands us on our heads, we tend to resent any force that throws us off our balance. We carry our resentment over into common speech when we say that a person is "unbalanced," a bank account "fails to balance," or a diet "lacks in balance."

The Force of Empathy

We exercise our sense of equilibrium when we react, unconsciously perhaps but nonetheless physically and intensively, to some object or situation existing outside ourselves. We engage thus in a process called empathy. Through it we project ourselves psychologically into the object or situation. We identify ourselves with it. We feel it operating in ourselves in a positive muscular way.[2]

Why, for example, do we enjoy watching someone dance or ski? The performer is having the fun and we are merely sitting on the sidelines. Aside from appreciating the points marked, the lines described, and the patterns formed by his movements in space (enjoyment also due in part to empathy), we are empathizing. We are dancing or skiing vicariously. We empathize with a quarreling couple when we feel uncomfortable, with a novel when we laugh over the purely fictional episode described, with a performance of music when we say that "we lost ourselves in it." Sometimes, it is true, empathy fails to take place. The motion picture may be so poorly done that the

[2] See Notes, page 294.

misfortunes of the heroine leave us unmoved. The painting may try to "say" so many things at once that each gets in the way of something else in its effort to attract us. Ordinarily, however, empathy is a force determining much of the appeal that works of art exert.

Many of our empathic reactions derive from our need for balance. Have you ever been moved to straighten a picture hanging crooked on the wall? Although it was in no danger of falling, you felt uncomfortable until its balance could be restored. Have you ever been disturbed by a picture of something that was itself out of balance, like the Leaning Tower of Pisa? Once, in the comic strip *Bringing Up Father*, Jiggs and Maggie stopped at Pisa on a trip around the world. They appeared in the first box of the strip looking aghast at the Leaning Tower. That night in bed at the hotel Jiggs tossed about unable to sleep. He got up at last, slipped out of the hotel, found his way to the offending structure, set a prop against it, then returned to bed and promptly went to sleep. The artist knows that effects of disequilibrium in his work will disturb and even repel the observer. He may actually introduce them for the sake of a special effect, but it is one thing to throw a work out of balance because he wants it that way and quite another to have it go off balance because he could not prevent it.

Kinds of Balance

The artist has two common types of balance from which to choose according to the objectives sought—symmetrical (formal) balance and asymmetrical (informal) balance. Symmetrical balance is illustrated by a seesaw with persons of equal weight sitting at equal distances from the fulcrum. An imaginary line drawn vertically through the center of the arrangement will divide it into two equal parts, and each part will appear as the reverse of the other. Symmetrical balance can be secured in a furniture group-unit when a sofa, for example, is set against the middle of a wall and identical end-tables with identical lamps made to flank it (2.1a). Though with variations in the figures to either side, Raphael based his great mural painting, *The School of Athens*, on just such symmetrical balance about the central figures of Plato and Aristotle standing beneath the archway (8.6). In all such compositions the artist gains by formal balance a dignity and aloofness of effect; an effect which is never very exciting, to be sure, but always safe and easily achieved.

Asymmetrical balance, as implied by its name, is lacking in symmetry. It is a "hidden" or "occult" type of balance in which one balancing form assumes some special quality of attraction to make up for its not being a mere reversal of image so placed as to balance another form. Asymmetrical balance may be illustrated by the same seesaw used to illustrate symmetrical balance, except that now one of the two persons on it is heavy and the other light. For one to balance the other, the heavy person has to move in close to the fulcrum and the light person has to move out as far as he can to the other side, placing the fulcrum not in the center of the arrangement but off to that side which bears the greater weight. If we go back to the symmetrically balanced furniture group-unit, move the sofa toward one end of the wall and place beside it, against the shorter area of wall, only one end-table with its lamp, we create an unbalanced arrangement with a large expanse of wall left over. In order to gain the balance required for such an arrangement, we resort to asymmetrical means—hanging a picture, for instance, against the larger of the two flanking areas of wall (2.1b).

The weights of the persons on the seesaw are actual physical weights, to be sure, but the weights of the forms in the furniture arrangement are less physical than psychological—weights of interest rather than weights of physical tonnage. So it is with many works of art: a small plane or mass can outweigh a large one in the attraction of its shape, its texture, or its color, and maintain a balance through superior interest. Asymmetrical balance is informal and intimate in appeal, open to a wide range of expressive possibilities, and exciting to the eye.

The artist seeking to achieve a completely organized whole must resolve not merely one general problem of adjustments but a complex series of delicately determined balances among all the elements employed. If he loses control, he may discover that his shapes are balanced but not his textures, or that both shapes and textures are balanced but not colors. He may find difficulty in tracing the trouble to its source and rooting it out, but his success in making such corrections will depend on his awareness of the principle of balance. If he fails, he will continue to be disturbed by lack of balance and so will those who observe his work, whether or not they detect the reason.

THE PRINCIPLE OF EMPHASIS

The artist may achieve perfect balance in every element of his work and still fail to say anything. He needs to observe the principle of emphasis as well, that principle which calls on certain forms to subordinate themselves to others and to join with them in leading up to, and focusing on, the principal feature of the arrangement. The artist holds us in this way to a matter of chief concern and keeps us from getting sidetracked by incidentals. He resorts to emphasis as a means of imposing order on the world of his creation and through that order clarifying his statement. Without emphasis he merely bewilders us—like the benighted show-window dresser of the variety store who cannot make up his mind what to emphasize and so defeats his purpose, repelling the passerby with the confusion of his display.

When observing the principle of emphasis, the artist is obliged to answer two questions of importance: what does he choose to make dominant, and how can he make it so? Which, of all the potentialities in the subject and the elements ready to be worked with, looms at this moment and in this particular piece of work as of greatest significance? Granted, the artist at another time and in another work may decide differently. Decision in either case is necessary and on that decision depends the structure of the work.

Selective Emphasis in Painting

Three painters on a sketching trip set their easels side by side. They proceed simultaneously to work on the same subject. Cows graze peacefully over the hills before them; a red barn stands in its clump of trees in the middle distance; mountains rear themselves in the distance. The first painter becomes intrigued by the geometric form of the barn against the rolling hills; he is stimulated by the contrast. He seeks to communicate his pleasure. He stresses the barn and the hills; paints them large on his canvas, subordinates the trees and other features, and omits the cows entirely. He calls his painting *Barn* (2.2a).

The second painter happens to like animals. The shapes of the beasts against the rolling pastureland completely absorb his interest. He gives the cattle major emphasis, using the barn and the other shapes simply as an excuse to point up the curving contours of the cattle. He calls his picture *Pastorale* (2.2b).

The third painter looks at the same scene and reviews the same potential elements. He finds nothing of special interest in the barn as barn, the cows as cows, the hills as hills. He responds rather to the visually exciting patterns in space—to the way in which the hori-

2.2. SELECTION FOR EMPHASIS. a. Angelo de Bello (1934–   ): *Barn.* 1957. Oil on canvas. 26 × 34″. Courtesy of the artist. B. L. Freemesser photograph. b. Warren Fairbanks (1934–   ): *Pastorale.* 1957. Oil on canvas. 26 × 34″. Courtesy of the artist. B. L. Freemesser photograph. c. Thomas Wilson (1931–   ): *Space Arrangement IV.* 1957. Oil on canvas. 48 × 54″. Courtesy of the artist. B. L. Freemesser photograph.

zontals and verticals and diagonals interplay with and oppose each other. Seeking to share his emotional response, he develops these patterns. He paints an arrangement of movements in line—vertical trees punctuating the horizontally running fields, patches of terrain repeating the rigid lines of the barn. In order to clarify his patterns, he simplifies the shapes, making the trees little more than strongly vertical dabs of the brush and the fields flat planes of paint. He leaves the cows out because he feels that they would only clutter up his pattern. He calls his composition *Space Arrangement IV* because this is the fourth work that he has rendered in such a manner (2.2c).

Three artists working at the same time from the same subject obtain entirely different results because of the principle of emphasis which each observes, choosing a dominant motive and eliminating everything which would tend to weaken it. Such painters resemble newspaper reporters who describe the same event or the same individual each in accord with his own particular choice—writing accounts which are equally truthful but varied in stress to accord with what each found to be significant, what each liked or disliked, saw or failed to see selectively.

Choice for emphasis has to do with qualities as well as with objects. One group of architectural designers emphasizes the quality of horizontality in a Greek temple, another the quality of verticality in a Gothic cathedral. One sculptor emphasizes mass piled on mass, another the linear movements of a construction. One painter stresses textures, another line and plane.

Emphasis by Placement

The means by which stress is given to a shape or a quality in a work of art, whether building, statue, picture, pot, or other product, are almost infinitely varied, but those most frequently encountered have to do with placement, contrast, ornamentation, and action. In regard to placement, we often find an object made important merely by the position given to it in the whole arrangement. Even as the

lecturer draws attention by standing on a platform in front of his audience instead of sitting in the back row among his listeners, the artist will place his form of principal interest toward the center of the field of vision—usually not at the exact center, because that would be too obvious and therefore less interesting, but either to one side of center or else modified by some device to make it seem off-center. More often than not, he favors a spot a little above and to the right of center, recognizing it as one which we see most readily (just as newspapers recognize by charging extra for an ad placed in that spot).

Emphasis by placement occurs in architecture: the builders of Chartres Cathedral placed a rose window in the entrance wall above the triple doorway (4.6); the designer of a private house placed the shadowed recess of a fireplace between two passageways where it was certain to dominate from any angle of viewing in the living room (4.12b). It occurs in sculpture: one carver hollowed the cavity for the heart in the image of a Toltec Moon Goddess (5.1); another centralized the brooding head of a seated figure symbolizing Thought (5.11). Emphasis by placement figures even more frequently in painting—in the rendering of the left eye of the Egyptian boy portrayed for his mummy case (8.3), for example, or the representation of a church tower in a village scene (8.9a).

Emphasis by Contrast

Emphasis by contrast derives from many devices but that which draws on color seems to be the most common. Furniture becomes conspicuous by the lighter colors of its upholstery as contrasted with dark walls (2.1b), less conspicuous when it tends to match the walls in value or intensity or hue (4.13). Henry Moore counted on shadows of deep penetrations to stress the warm hue and the highlighted protrusions of his *Reclining Figure* in wood (5.15). Edgar Degas employed oppositions of cool highlights to warm shadows in order to bring out the facial features in his portrait (8.8).

2.3. CONTRAST FOR EMPHASIS. a. Chizuko Yoshida (1925–   ) and her pupil, Mrs. Alfred S. Oatman: Rissin-kei style flower arrangement displayed against tokonoma wall. 1957. Iris and rhododendron in white-glazed pottery bowl. Height, 20″. Courtesy of the artists. B. L. Freemesser photograph. b. Chizuko Yoshida and her pupil, Mrs. Alfred S. Oatman: Rissin-kei style flower arrangement displayed against decorated folding screen. 1957. Iris and rhododendron in white-glazed pottery bowl. 20″. Courtesy of the artists. B. L. Freemesser photograph.

Contrasts of line, shape, and size make for dominance of one detail over another. Consider how the vertical lines of a person when standing draw attention by contrast with the horizontal and the broken lines of those who remain seated. The creator of the Etruscan warrior image accentuated the attacking, threatening character of his figure by opposing the angular, broken lines of one arm with the out-thrust, straight lines of the other (Pl. II). Emphasis by contrast of line accounts for the marked sense of order and containment in paintings as far apart in representational intent as Raphael's *School of Athens* (8.6) and Mondrian's *Abstraction* (8.14).

Decoration is certain to attract attention wherever it occurs. Conversely, unexpected lack of ornament, at some spot in an environment otherwise overloaded with it, draws the concentrated gaze; canny old Benjamin Frank-

lin was well aware of this effect when at the French court he called attention to himself and his cause by dressing not in the gorgeous attire of the courtiers, which he could easily have afforded, but in garments startlingly plain. Decoration can, by judicious placing, strengthen qualities of structure in the work of art. It can render dominant a cathedral's entrance wall in the form of sculpture about the portals. It can give accent to some portion of a person's anatomy in the form of jewelry, perhaps, at ears, throat, wrists, as the Hindu sculptor recognized when he fashioned the figure of the dancing god, Siva (5.3).

A plain background by itself can achieve emphasis on something set before it, even as silence provides "background" for effective renderings of music. A flower arrangement (2.3) gains by placement against a "quiet" wall and loses by placement against a "noisy" screen. A pot, escaping notice among others on a gift-shop shelf, dominates in shape and color when set out by itself on a shelf at home. Within the compositional structure of a work itself, emphasis by contrast leads in like manner to a simplification of detail in favor of one dominant note: the entranceway of the Gothic cathedral (4.6); the bowed head of a sculptured figure (5.11a); the brush-drawn figure of the warrior on his charger, against a neutral background (7.4a).

Emphasis by Action

Wild creatures know how dangerously conspicuous they make themselves by browsing or flying. Surprised in their native haunts, they are apt to "freeze" and trust that through their motionlessness they can escape the intruder's notice. Window-dressers seek exactly the opposite result when they introduce moving objects into their displays. Owing to the irresistible attraction of such objects, merchants in a large city once agreed among themselves not to block traffic in the Christmas rush by presenting anything moving in their shop-windows.

Shapes which only seem to move draw attention to a building, statue, picture. Diagonal lines, which always seem to move, when shown in the form of flying buttresses attract the eyes of townsfolk to the Gothic cathedral (4.4b); when shown in the form of inclined axes, to the terra-cotta figure of a warrior (Pl. II); when shown in the form of leaping, advancing flames, to the doomed palace represented as the climax of a Japanese hand-scroll (7.2a). Lines placed so that they "move" one's eye through a painting like Botticelli's masterpiece help to bring the eye to focus on the Goddess of Love (8.5).

Means of emphasis can be multiplied indefinitely, but the artist in actual practice combines them into organizations that vary with his intent. He faces a problem going beyond the mere selection of something for accent and abandonment of the rest to take care of itself. He recognizes that everything in the arrangement, from point to line, plane, texture, color, mass, space, must be given its due. Something will have to register as of chief importance, something else as of a little less importance, and so on in sequence throughout the structure of the work. Even a composition that seems simple may in reality represent the juggling of many factors to bring them all into close relationship with each other.

THE PRINCIPLE OF RHYTHM

Rhythm has been called the common denominator of the arts. Obvious in music, poetry, and dance, but less readily perceptible in the visual arts, it remains essential to the structure of any work of art. One definition calls rhythm a succession of expectations and their satisfactions. When a drum is beaten in a succession of light and heavy beats, the hearer learns to anticipate the pattern and to feel at ease only when the pattern is fulfilled and repeated. The rhythmic arrangement of openings in a building depends for its effectiveness upon the emotional satisfaction experienced by us when we find the pattern measuring up to what the architect teaches us to anticipate, but when the rhythm of the openings departs from the pattern in size or height or some other obvious quality we are apt to feel unsatisfied and disturbed or even repelled.

Other definitions call rhythm "a measured succession of accents and intervals," "a series of lingerings and leapings," "a relation of part to part and of parts to whole in a recognizable pattern of arrangement." In all such definitions rhythm is taken out of the realm of the accidental or casual and placed in that of the planned, the ordered, the systematized. It is not just any old relationship which sets up a rhythm; it is a relationship of organized movements, whether actual or apparent.

Rhythm in the work of art is important to us because rhythm plays such an important part in our physical lives. Our bodies conform to many physiological rhythms of which the beating of the heart is only one. We live in a world that conforms to rhythms, from the rhythm of the succession of day by night to the rhythm of the sequence of the seasons. We learn to expect the recurrent rise and fall of the frogs' chorus in the marsh at night, the regular flap of the wings of birds in flight, the steady hoof-beats of the galloping horse.

Rhythm helps us to find order in the world about us. Some pattern that we can count on, some kind of predictable order, becomes to us a profound psychological necessity.[3] This is especially true today, when the uncertainty of our times, the very elusiveness of such a pattern, makes us frightened and neurotic. Turning from our Age of Insecurity, we seek in art that sense of order denied by our environment.

The artist projects into his creation the order that we crave. He underlines and clarifies it beyond any kind of order casually encountered in nature and he departs in that process from any attempt at nature's imitation. He senses beyond ordinary mortals "the life movement of the spirit through the rhythm of things.[*] He abstracts and heightens it, incorporating it into the structure of his work to afford himself and us the satisfaction of an expectation fulfilled. Hence the rhythmic arrangement of the stripes in a weaver's fabric, the windows and planes of wall in an architect's design for a dwelling, the limbs about the torso of a carver's figure, the points and lines and color-passages of a painter's landscape.

The rhythm may prove obvious and tiring because too easily grasped, as in singsong poetry. It may prove subtle and exciting, rewarding our study every time we turn to it, as in epic poetry with an oceanlike roll. In either case the rhythm remains essential, be-

[3] See Notes, page 294.
[*] Poetic English rendering by the Japanese writer, Kakuzō Okakura: *The Ideals of the East* (London: John Murray, 1905), p. 52. More literally translated as "rhythmic vitality," the principle serves as the first of the Six Canons of Hsieh Ho, a Chinese painter writing about his art in the middle of the fifth century A.D.

2.4. RHYTHM. B. L. Freemesser (1926–   ): *Bucking Bronco.* 1954. Photograph, made with 4 × 5″ Graphic camera, shutter speed 1/500 sec., under daylight; XXX film. Negative: 5 × 4″; enlarged detail, 9½ × 7¾″. Courtesy of the artist.

cause its absence from the work results in chaos, and chaos destroys us, if only emotionally.

Rhythm by Repetition, Progression, and Continuity

The artist can achieve rhythm in a number of different ways, most commonly by repetition, progression, and continuity. He can repeat something like a column in a building, a slat or a post in a garden fence, a ball of flame in the nimbus surrounding a figure cast in brass, or the climbing feet in a photograph. On the stage the Rockettes of Radio City Music Hall achieved their fame by resorting to this very type of rhythm, forming a line of thirty girls of the same height and all trained to dance in unison.

2.5. RHYTHM. André de Dienes (1913–   ): *Nude on Dunes.* 1956. Photograph, made with 2½ × 2½″ Rolleiflex camera, shutter speed 1/100 sec., under daylight with overcast sky; Panatomic X film. Original print: 11⅛ × 10⅝″. Courtesy of the artist.

When the artist resorts to progression to establish a rhythm, he follows a plan that sets up expectations of each succeeding step— making shapes from the base to the top of a building either smaller and smaller, for example, or bigger and bigger. In developing such progressions he follows a pattern of rhythm often found in nature—in the plant, for example, which grows leaves in diminishing succession toward the end of its branch, or in the chambered nautilus, which grows convolutions in increasing amplitude from the center outward.*

When achieving rhythm through progression, however, the artist does not always utilize in numerical order the continuous sequence of changes in size or in other attribute which he has established. He alternates these changes in some way in order to make them less obvious and often more interesting. Look at the Greek temple or the Gothic cathedral (4.3b or 4.6),

* A profound study of rhythmic progressions in nature is that of D'Arcy Wentworth Thompson, *On Growth and Form* (Cambridge, England: University Press, 1917).

and note how varied, for instance, are the heights of succeeding parts from foundations to roof. Rhythm gained by progression in this way becomes more active, seemingly, and more forceful in expression than rhythm gained by repetition alone.

A third way to achieve rhythm is by the provision of an easily connected and continuous flow from one form into another. Dancers and actors resort to this device in moving their arms and legs and shifting their positions on the stage, because they know how important rhythmic movement is to the effectiveness of their roles. They never move by chance or whim, but rehearse hour after hour just to guarantee the proper continuity. Architects exert corresponding care to provide transitional features between the major forms of their structures—no architect more than Frank Lloyd Wright, for example, in the details of his design for a private residence, carrying the lines of the horizontal boards and battens of the wall over into corresponding window openings, then shifting to the mortar-marked courses of brick in a pier, and continuing into a horizontal succession of vertically proportioned window-doors (4.12). Sculptors, photographers, and painters do likewise. Witness a sculptured figure by Maillol (5.11a), with its pulsating follow-through from one contour, one surface, one mass, into another. Witness a photograph by Dienes (2.5), with its coordinated rise and fall of contour in dune and figure. Witness a painting by Botticelli (8.5), with its irresistible continuity of lines and forms from one figure to the next.

Complexities of Rhythmic Structure

Ordinarily artists use all kinds of rhythm in the same composition. They develop a combination of rhythms in any building, statue, painting, or product of the crafts, planning skillfully and subtly to make them all contribute to the total effect desired. They may choose at one time and in one piece of work to give prominence to one kind of rhythm and at another time and place a totally different kind.

One sculptor may create out of marble a swirling mass of forms in the process of emergence into being, increasing or decreasing depths of modeling and repeating in various sizes the predominant spiral. Another sculptor may choose to emphasize the drooping form of a sorrowing mother, and focus for contrast on another rhythmic system of straight lines and angles composing the rigid figure of her son, held dead across her lap. Or a mosaicist may glorify the walls of a church with repetition after repetition of flat figures held rigidly erect, but within these larger forms vary the rhythm through progression and continuity from one fold of drapery to the next. The artist thus draws heavily on the principle of rhythm to bring order and expressive power into his use of basic elements.

THE PRINCIPLE OF PROPORTION

Proportion is a matter of relationships—relationships of height, width, depth, and surrounding space. Any one dimension is by itself neither right nor wrong. When dimensions are placed together, however, relationships are established, and it is these relationships which we judge when we say that a table is too narrow for its length, a lampshade out of proportion with its base, and so on.

The Question of Scale

The amount of open space around an object creates a factor called scale. Scale, too, is a matter of relationship. Look at a chair, for example (3.16). Is it too large? You can only ask in return, "Too large for whom or for what?" The chair is too large for a three-year-old, too small for the fat lady of the circus, but just right for yourself. The chair is too large for a hallway at home, too small for the foyer of an auditorium, but just right for your living room. The chair is right or wrong in scale only as it is related to the nature of its user and the nature of the room in which it is used.

Note how frequently the principle of proportion figures in daily life. We go downtown to buy a lamp for an end-table in the living room. In the high-ceilinged showroom we find one which pleases us, and we buy it. We carry it home and set it up in our small living room, only to discover that it now looks very large and clumsy. We have not changed the lamp a bit but we have changed its relationship to its surroundings and thrown it out of scale.

Alterations of scale do at times heighten the artist's expression. Consider Michelangelo's marble carving in St. Peter's at Rome (5.9). The sculptor wanted to glorify the idea of divine motherhood and to intensify the pathos of the sacrifice of Jesus. He did it by enlarging the figure of the Madonna and reducing the size of the body of her full-grown Son lying dead across her lap. Expecting the normal human scale in the two figures, we are shocked by the distortion into a heightened realization of the meaning of the subject. Note again how the figures of Adam and Eve in Rodin's *Hand of God* become by diminution mere lumps of clay, dependent for support upon the Creator's giant palm (5.10).

Static Proportion and Its Compositional Role

Certain generalities still hold regarding effectiveness of proportions. When height and width or height and width and depth are all the same, the relationship is obvious and for that reason less interesting than dimensions which offer the surprise of the unexpected or the fascination of the subtle. Yet even the square is useful in places where the artist wants to quiet a motive or subject it to a unifying discipline. An interior designer will call upon a floor to be tiled in squares in order to subordinate it to the furniture or the pictures of a room. An illustrator will equalize the rhythmic sequence of images evoked in a poem by disposing around an invisible square the succession of miniature incidents (7.5).

When an area is divided in half, whether by an actual or by a psychic line, its parts bear to each other an obvious, static relationship, less interesting than some unequal subdivision. In a wall painting that needs to maintain a feeling of stability already achieved in the architecture, the artist may deliberately seek a formal proportioning. Raphael did so in his famous mural, *The School of Athens* (8.6), and gained by his arrangement an imposing effect of order. As always when an artist starts out with such a daringly static layout, however, Raphael found it necessary as he proceeded to overcome the resulting lack of interest by personalizing and diversifying his rendering of the figures on the steps to either side of the central figures of Plato and Aristole (including even a portrayal of himself in the distinguished assemblage to the right).

Correcting Proportional Defects

It becomes necessary sometimes in art as in life to work with a disagreeable proportion which cannot be avoided. Orozco faced such a necessity in a mural that he was commissioned to paint toward the end of his life (8.16). Sentiment demanded that a squat and florid old doorway be retained—set obtrusively into the multistoried wall upon which he had to work. He used spiraling forms to one side of it and rectilinear forms to the other, to carry the doorway so integrally into the picture that he made the handicap seem an asset intended from the start. Line can be employed in clothing to disguise undesirable proportions, with vertical stripes for the attire of an overly bulky person and horizontal stripes for the attire of a

person overly tall and slender. Sarah Bernhardt had excessively bony arms that would have interfered with her career on the stage; to correct the deficiency, she invented the "cartridge sleeve," a sleeve of great length which folded into a multitude of lateral shadows when caught back by the cuff at her wrist and which made her arm in this way seem plump. We have noted in our discussion of color how the manipulation of values and intensities can make objects seem larger or smaller. Knowing how to achieve such effects, the artist can off-set unfortunate proportions.

The same applies of course to scale. Puppets at a marionette performance are of miniature size but the audience does not realize how small they are, thanks to the careful control of scale in costumes, properties, and stage sets, until the manipulator appears beside them. A kindergarten teacher will sit on a very low chair when talking with the children of her class, bringing herself into scale with them for the sake of the emotional harmony created, but she rises to tower above them when order needs to be restored. Someone entering St. Peter's in Rome, largest church of Christendom, may fail to realize at first how colossal it really is, because even the sculptures within it match the scale of the structure, and only upon noting another visitor standing antlike beside the huge base to a pier is the vastness of the building recognized. A photograph of some object by itself is apt to puzzle anyone looking at it over the question of its size, but a photograph of the same object with a human figure standing beside it gives the viewer assurance of the scale. More often than not, the artist makes the human figure the norm, because the average height of a person is known or assumed and that height gives the viewer something definite to go by in grasping the scale of the rest.

INTERRELATION OF PRINCIPLES: SUMMARY

The principle of proportion goes hand in hand with the principles of balance, emphasis, rhythm, hand in hand, in fact, with any principle. Although for the sake of convenience in studying them we have talked about principles of design one by one, in practice we appreciate how closely interwoven they are, supporting each other toward an integration of the whole. The creation of any work of art represents a complex task of juggling factors and fitting them together, so that each will contribute properly toward making the finished work do everything that the artist wanted. The fact that the artist performs this complex task intuitively, feeling the problem through rather than working it out logically or mathematically, does not lessen the magnitude of the task nor reduce the respect due him for succeeding as well as he does—even though we may not happen at the moment to like what he has done.

RECOMMENDED READINGS

Goldstein, Harriet and Vetta. *Art in Everyday Life.*
  Already listed for reading in connection with the study of the elements of art (Chapter 1), the Goldsteins' textbook is even more helpful as a supplement to the study of the principles of art.

Teague, Walter Dorwin. *Design This Day: the Technique of Order in the Machine Age.* New York: Harcourt, Brace, 1949.
  The personal philosophy of life and art which animates the work of an industrial designer. Since the book offers a sound and thorough treatment of principles as generally applicable to art, it can be read with profit in connection with studies based on the present chapter.

Scott, Robert Gillam. *Design Fundamentals.* New York: McGraw-Hill, 1951.
  This book, based upon many earlier studies of the principles of art, supersedes them. It is clearly and simply written, and illustrated by lucid diagrams and photographic reproductions all of which are closely related to the text. A concluding chapter presents a step-by-step analysis of the process by which the design of the book itself was evolved—a case study of principles in action.

Small, Harold A., ed. *Form and Function: Remarks on Art by Horatio Greenough.* Berkeley, Calif.: University of California Press, 1947.
  Horatio Greenough (1805–1852) was a sculptor from Boston, Massachusetts, who practiced his art most of his life in Florence, Italy. He was the first American writer to formulate the peculiarly American philosophy of functionalism. In *The Travels, Observations, and Experience of a Yankee Stonecutter* (New York: G. P. Putnam, 1852), published under his pseudonym of Horace Bender, and in *A Memorial of Horatio Greenough* (New York: G. P. Putnam, 1853), edited by Henry T. Tuckerman to include additional written fragments and articles by Greenough, the sculptor-critic makes "form expressive of function" the criterion for evaluating both the art of his own day and the art of the past.

Weyl, Hermann. *Symmetry.* Princeton, N.J.: Princeton University Press, 1952.
  Originating in a series of lectures delivered by the author-mathematician at Princeton University in 1951, the book offers a comprehensive study of the principle of balance as it holds in both nature and art. Instead of classifying types of balance as we have done in this book (symmetrical and asymmetrical), Weyl treats symmetrical balance as bilateral symmetry and distinguishes four other kinds of symmetry: translatory, rotational, related, and ornamental. He develops an essentially heavy subject with occasional light touches.

Lee, Vernon (pseudonym for Violet Paget). *The Beautiful: An Introduction to Psychological Aesthetics.* New York: G. P. Putnam's Sons, 1913.
  A volume disproportionately small considering the extent of its influence on the English-speaking art world. The author invented the term "empathy" to correspond to the German word *einfühlung* as formulated by Robert Fischer (see Note 2).

Ivins, William M., Jr. *Art and Geometry: A Study in Space Intuitions.* Cambridge, Mass.: Harvard University Press, 1946.
  A book requiring considerable background in art and mathematics to follow in detail, but entertaining reading for those who look for the author's conclusions: that ancient Greek art and geometry were based on purely tactile-muscular intuitions of the simplest and the most inhibiting sort, and that Renaissance art and geometry, creating the perspective of central projection and section, liberated the Occident from the Greek tradition and opened up a whole new vision of the world.

3.1. Raymond Loewy (1893–   ). The first organically designed American automobile, the 1948 Studebaker Commander. 1947. Courtesy of Studebaker Corporation of America. Kaufmann and Fabry photograph.

Industrial Design and the Crafts

THE PROBLEM OF FINDING a motor car worth purchasing led us to think of it as a work of art. It obliged us to study both the elements composing the automobile as an art-object and the principles governing their employment. We learned the importance which elements and principles shared in all creations of the artist. We must also, however, evaluate a third set of features—those making the automobile uniquely a creation of industrial design.

Industrial design, newest comer to the realm of the arts, belongs to the oldest class among them, the arts of utility. Originating in everyday living needs, the arts of utility produce objects having usages apart from their looks. Men can fashion objects for use without any artistry at all, to be sure, and still manage to make such objects work. They can even manage to lend to their nonartistic abortions a charm of quaintness, of wonderment that products so "rattle-trappy" in appearance do actually run. Experience with objects of use is beginning finally to convince both manufacturer and patron, however, that the thing which feels best to the hand and looks best to the eye is apt also to be the thing which works best in practice.

Relationship of Industrial Design to the Crafts

The man who shapes utilitarian objects with his own hands has an advantage over the manufacturer who depends on employees to make the same objects in quantity with machines. If the craftsman takes pride in his work, he is almost certain to be inspired by the feel and the look of the object taking shape under his hands to form it expressively in terms of functions, materials, and processes.

Arts practiced by craftsmen are generally referred to as crafts. They are the oldest arts known to man, even as some of their descendants, absorbed by industrial design, are the newest. Crafts stand apart from industrial design by no hard and fast line of demarcation; they tend to approach it or to merge with it in a hundred different ways. No one can tell, for example, how many assistants a craftsman may require before he has to convert his studio-workshop into an industrial plant. No one can tell at what point a simple tool becomes complex enough or big enough to transform the handicraftsman into a factory worker in one direction or into an industrial designer in the other. About all that we can say is that certain utilitarian objects like pots or brooms were once the individual products of the craftsman, and still are to some extent, while other objects like radios or refrigerators have been industrial products from the very beginning, with the forms of some determined expressively by industrial designers.

Industrial design has not replaced any of the crafts but it has come to occupy an important field allied to each of them. It has given rise to esthetic standards which have been extended to cover not only the mass-produced article, which is its particular concern, but even the craftsman's creation. These standards are founded upon the concept of the clear, clean forms of use, smooth-surfaced, precision-cut, uniform of type, and interchangeable in part. The grace possessed by the living creature has become the criterion—a grace of form shared with a bird, a cat, a fish, but always a form

41

uniquely itself because its function is unique; its need is to look that function, inviting use.

A century ago industrial design, then nameless, busied itself with fashioning machine-made decorations to fasten on to manufactured articles as disguises of their factory origins and their everyday uses. Too frequently today it still does. When functioning as we now think it ought, however, industrial design can tolerate no decoration which pretends to an individuality that the product lacks; it can accept only the hard core of the work itself.

If ornament is to figure at all, then that ornament can never be more than an accent here or there to suggest the object's readiness to perform as intended. No straining to look like something else, but contentment to be itself— if a craftsman's creation, then warmly personable, sturdily upright in the strength of the manual process by which it was brought into being; but if an industrial product, then coolly impersonal, with exactitude of contour and "seamlessness" of joining to serve as constant reminders of the factory process behind it.[1]

INDUSTRIAL DESIGN: PROCEDURES AND PRODUCTS

Far from leaving machine-made objects to evolve their forms automatically, which they never will, industrial design now begins to play a positive form-determining role. It exacts of its practitioner the most painstaking research, requiring months or even years to attend to properly. Only after such preliminary investigation can the artist of industry settle down to his drafting board. He makes hundreds of sketches to develop the ideas which occurred to him during his studies. He makes working drawings for the most likely forms developed in this way, checking them repeatedly against data showing the proportions and measurements and characteristic attitudes and actions of the human figure, not only the average male figure, the average female figure, the average child figure at different ages, but the known extremes of each, the tallest, the shortest, the heaviest, the lightest.[2]

The designer translates such forms into miniature models of wax or clay, continuing to alter them freely in process as ideas for possible improvement occur to him. He converts the most likely form into a full-scale dummy or mock-up, constructing it of wood or cardboard or other temporary material. He presents this dummy to his clients and goes over it with them critically. If it fails to satisfy completely, he makes another dummy and still

another until one does finally satisfy. He has the full-scale prototype then built out of the actual materials of the factory, and the machinery tooled around it for mass manufacture.

Throughout such procedure the designer serves continuously as the critic of his own work in progress, responding to defects noted by altering the forms to correct them. When we as prospective consumers view the final product, we imagine ourselves in the artist's place, responding to it as he did in an active "give and take."[3]

Is the product to be a vehicle? Then its form must meet, and must declare that it is meeting, the product's intent: transportation that is safe and comfortable, rapid, and economically feasible. Is the vehicle to be a motor car? Then its form must make evident to touch and sight the properties of the metals, alloys and plastics, glass, rubber, and upholstery that are used in its making. Is the motor car to be duplicated in quantity? Then its form must be made to tell the story of its assembly-line production, with features appropriate to the industrial operations involved: die-casting, stamping, punching, welding, and the like.

[1] See Notes, page 295.
[2] See Notes, page 295.
[3] See Notes, page 295.

Style in Industrial Design

When we learn to appreciate the form of an automobile, as of any work of art, we respond to its style—that character of the form which results from a distinct manner of expression. If we find the character common to works of the same artist, we call it an individual style. If we find it common to works of the same society, we call it a cultural style. If we find it common to works of the same time, we call it a period style.

In the case of automobiles we fail to detect any clearly definable individual style. We can tell the differences between a Ford and a Chevrolet or a Buick and a Studebaker easily enough, but we are at loss to say whether such differences reflect individual styles peculiar to a Harley Earl or a Raymond Loewy, or whether they stand for the supposed preferences of consumers at a certain income level. We suspect the latter, because we know how anonymously industry operates and how fittingly collective the form of a factory product should be. Even when we learn that the Buick has been designed by Harley Earl and the Studebaker by Raymond Loewy, we still have to recognize that the former artist is merely the man in charge of a design department of General Motors Corporation and the latter the head of a whole organization of designers. Such an artist does not say, "I designed it"; he says, "We designed it," and by "we" he means perhaps scores of other artists working with him. He means perhaps any number of other collaborators as well: engineers, company executives, presampling consumers willing to serve as "guinea pigs." Few other arts operate as anonymously as industrial design, but its practitioners find ample compensation for lack of self-expression in the satisfaction of watching their creations go into mass production and fulfill their purpose at the hands of a thousand or a million users.

The cultural style of an automobile reveals itself when we compare an American Chrysler with a German Volkswagen or an Italian Cisitalia. Even though one car may at times influence the design of another in another country, even though for the sake of some particular advantage it finds a market abroad, the automobile still offers in such comparisons a direct approach to the character of the culture in which it is manufactured—the culture of the individuality-loving Italian aristocrat, the culture of the economy-minded German, the culture of the conspicuously consuming, speed-and-comfort-minded American.

The period style of a motor car is identifiable in a comparison of the historical models displayed in a museum of science and industry or in some corporation's pavilion like the Ford Rotunda at Dearborn, or in automobile ads in old periodicals. We see thus in context, for example, that the emergent automobile merely imitated the familiar forms of the buggy, winning for itself the name of "horseless carriage." We follow the vehicle through its primitive stage, when every part was bolted on separately to compose a contraption as "jumpy" and "noisy" to operate as it appeared. We follow it through its classic period, when every part, though still sharply defined, was made to conform to an over-all effect of streamlining and easy harmony of proportion, regardless of consequences in added weight of body and decreased vision of driver.

We come at length to the revolutionary model of the late nineteen-forties and early nineteen-fifties, when, pioneered by the Studebaker of 1947 (3.1), the automobile entered an "organic" era. Out of renewed endeavors to gain efficiency in production and performance, out of exhaustive "aerodynamic" studies like those already devoted to the airplane, emerged a form unlike any that preceded it. We note that this Studebaker is distinguished by lightness in appearance as in fact. We observe how its running board and fenders come to merge with its body and how that body tends to assume contours suggestive of ease and speed in movement, like the body of a greyhound or a panther.

The better of the new forms of the automobile, as of other industrial products, have come to be called "organic." They are called by such a name not so much in the biological sense as in the philosophical: "having a complex but necessary interrelationship of parts, similar to that in living things." * They are called "organic" not because by any intent they represent or imitate the forms of living creatures. They are called "organic" because they are evolved like a living organism out of its environment, evolved at the hands of the designer out of an environment conditioned by functional need and factory-production with factory-made materials, and made to express these conditioning factors in the same way as the living organism was shaped by evolution to express its adaptation to environment. Insofar as earlier forms met the formative forces of their own day squarely they could also be called "organic." But the newer forms are especially well qualified to own the name because they reflect a definite attempt to lay *equal* stress on functions, on materials, and on processes as their determining sources.

Each stage in the history of the automobile was marked by a period style to which automobiles generally conformed and from which minor variations were made, sometimes annually.[4] Deterrents to change were the enormous costs of retooling machinery for production and the assumed conservative "taste" or "tastelessness" of the buying public. So impressive was the increase in sales following the "organic" transformations of the automobile after 1947, however, that manufacturers were encouraged to adopt a policy of basic redesign every two or three years with minor alterations of trim in between.

The new policy did not mean, unfortunately, that every biennial or triennial design was a good one nor that every innovation of trim during the interim actually enhanced the form. The policy was supported by popular demand because of high-pressure advertising and snob appeal, but it served only to demoralize the average designer and to relegate car design to the same tyranny of changes in fashion that

* *Webster's New World Dictionary of the American Language* (New York: P. F. Collier and Son, 1953), Vol. II, p. 1032.
[4] See Notes, page 295.

ladies' dress and ladies' millinery have suffered for generations. So much does fashion reign in the automobile industry, in fact, that we dare not illustrate the latest model of any make lest it seem outmoded and therefore somehow insignificant before the ink on this page has dried.

Superficial dressing-up of a product is known as "styling." A perversion of the art rather than true designing, styling substitutes novelty for creation and standardizes fads. In the automobile industry it is responsible for the annual rash of chromium strips, cowcatcherlike grilles, multicolored bodies, airplanelike fins, and kindred excrescences which veil the forms of the automobile itself. Fads and fashions are popularly called "styles," but they are only passing ripples on the surface, tricks of the drafting board aimed at stimulating sales. True styles are just the opposite: unconscious manifestations of integrity of design, putting first things first, starting with the roots of the problem in the nature of functions and performance, of materials and manufacturing processes, and working gradually upward and outward without prejudice to the final form.

The Telephone as a New Industrial Product

Manufactured goods have multiplied until they extend their services into every corner of our lives. They support us when we sleep, buzz us into waking, douse us with water, shave us, dress us, cook our meals, percolate our coffee, preserve our food, wash and dry our dishes and our laundry, carry us to work, give us something to sit on and to work over, take our dictation, type our letters, file our papers, connect us in conversation with persons at a distance, entertain us over the air, provide us with a smoke and a book and a light by which to read, do for us practically anything else that we can think of. More factory products minister to us than ever before, and scarcely one of them now goes through the factory and ultimately reaches our hand without having had some artist scratch his head over its form-to-be.

3.2. THE BELL TELEPHONE. a. Bell Telephone Laboratories: No. 20-AL desk stand telephone. 1914. Granular carbon transmitter. Height, 11½″. Courtesy Bell Telephone Laboratories. b. Bell Telephone Laboratories: Handset telephone. 1927. Phenolic plastic. Height, 5¾″. Courtesy of Bell Telephone Laboratories. c. Henry Dreyfuss (1904–): Combined No. 300-type telephone set. 1937. Phenolic plastic. 5½ × 5⅛″; mounted as handset, height, 8¾″. Courtesy of Bell Telephone Laboratories. d. Henry Dreyfuss: Combined No. 500-type telephone set. 1950. Cellulose acetate butyrate. 5 × 5½″; mounted as handset, height, 8½″. Courtesy of Bell Telephone Laboratories.

Many such objects were unknown a century ago. They claim no ancestors whatever. But they have entered so much into the fabric of our lives that we now take them for granted and treat them as necessities. There is nothing fixed nor final about them. With the advent of atomic power, in fact, they open a prospect the horizon of which fades before us as we move. Unless atomic power destroys us before we learn to employ it exclusively for our benefit, they will keep on evolving, in forms the nature of which we can now scarcely guess but which are certain to grace man's existence as long as the designer treats the human body and its needs as his frame of reference.

The unprecedented type of industrial product is well exemplified by the telephone, that popular symbol of progress. The telephone may be bound down by the never-relaxing demands of engineering but it affects our lives probably more intimately than any other product. When it rings we answer, not knowing till we do whether the call is a wrong number, an insurance salesman's request for an appointment, or a bid for a date. We escape only to a cabin in the woods and then not for long, because our own work, like that of most people, is geared to the telephone.

Unlike most products, the telephone cannot be shopped for and bought. It remains the company's property, waiting to be installed in our home when we subscribe to the company's services. Freed thus of sales-pressuring and fashion-styling, it allows unprejudiced critical inspection as a work of art created by industry.

Engineers used to be employed by the Bell Telephone Company to develop forms of the telephone out of purely technical and functional provisions.* They probably never even thought of "beauty" in connection with their product. If the idea ever did occur to them, they probably banished it from their minds at once as something entirely alien to their work and apt to interfere with their product's efficiency of operation. Art meant to them what it meant to most engineers of their generation —a mere wrapping to conceal and prettify the "works."

Take the old stand-up Bell model of 1914, for example (3.2a). Form never followed function more faithfully—and, if the functionalists of design are right, the telephone of 1914 ought now to be sitting with the immortals of art. It lasted a long while, to be sure (officially until 1927 and in out-of-the-way places long after that). It bespoke its usage honestly. Probably no one ever started talking into its earpiece by mistake, and that is more than can be said for some of its successors. With its ringing apparatus hung separately on the wall, however, and its angular combination of iron foot, post, mouthpiece, hook, and earpiece reflecting the piecemeal procedure of its engineers, the telephone of 1914 remained throughout its active career the artless little brother of the flivver and the biplane.

In 1927 Bell engineers came forth with a combination stand-up and handset model (3.2b). For it, in the interests of economy in manufacture and comfort in use, they approached the problem of design mathematically. They kept the bell-box on the wall, but broadened the base, shortened the post, and developed a joint mouthpiece-earpiece unit that would reach from the average user's mouth to his ear. It looked better than the old model, and it worked better as well.

In developing the Bell telephone of 1927 the engineers made a radical change in material. They abandoned iron, that nature-extracted metal which had to be shaped by machinery and joined together piece by piece as a carpenter joins pieces of wood to build a house. They turned to the new phenolic resin, a plastic unknown until 1909, when a chemist, Leo Baekeland, had managed to fuse under heat and pressure the powdered chemicals phenol and formaldehyde. When cast hollow, as it had to be to house the phone's mechanism, phenolic became its own supporting structure, a shell, a stressed-skin construction. It occasioned thus

* *Industrial Design*, Vol. III, No. 2 (April, 1956), pp. 42–45; Henry Dreyfuss, *Designing for People* (New York: Simon and Schuster, 1955), pp. 100–109; and Don Wallance, *Shaping America's Products* (New York: Reinhold, 1956), pp. 30–40.

at the hands of Bell engineers a significant change-over from tectonic (piecemeal) assembly in iron to a new, potentially integral-designing procedure implied by the word "plastic." * This word, open to a large variety of uses, has been appropriated by industry to cover a variety of newly invented synthetic materials. It derives from the Greek word *plastikos,* meaning "fit for molding," in contradistinction to the Greek word *tekton,* meaning "carpenter."

Molded phenolic pieces still had to be combined to complete the instrument. Suddenly, however, the Bell researchers found themselves facing a question never faced before: if phenolic assumed its final shape at the moment of its creation, why not reduce the total number of pieces and design something more unified at the very outset? A form determined by measurements alone no longer seemed to satisfy.

For the first time in its history the Bell Telephone Company felt the need of an artist. But it was still thinking of engineering as one thing and of art as another. With the telephone apparatus predetermined, the company commissioned a number of artists to work out alternative proposals for a molded phenolic "package" which might at once contain the telephone and look attractive to users. The company failed in this endeavor, as of course it had to. Artistic creation simply fails to function when conceived as nothing but "face-lifting."

In casting about for "a little art to wrap the telephone in," however, the Bell Telephone Company unearthed a young artist just starting out in the new profession of industrial design. The designer needed a job but he refused to sacrifice his principles to get it. He would have nothing to do with the Bell project until the company authorized him to start at the bottom and work up, collaborating with the engineers themselves to evolve an organic form rooted in performance and func-

* J. Gordon Lippincott, *Design for Business* (Chicago: Paul Theobald, 1947), p. 110–115.

tion and the peculiarities of the molded plastic composing it.

The recalcitrant artist who so impressed the telephone company that it finally agreed to his terms was Henry Dreyfuss. Starting in 1930, in 1957 the designer was still working for Bell. He had collaborated with a host of other designers, technicians, executives, and factory workers to bring forth two artistically distinguished models, the combined handsets of 1937 and of 1950.

The earlier model was a handset (3.2c) that combined the ringing apparatus with a cradle for the earpiece-mouthpiece receiver. It represented a decided advance over anything that preceded it, in compactness, convenience, and expressiveness of form. Twenty years after its first appearance it was still in active use in many parts of the United States. But it was beginning to look heavy and clumsy as the general trand of industry toward lightness of form gathered momentum. And the phone behaved imperfectly. Sometimes it "howled" because of faulty transmission. When the baby was sleeping, its bell rang too loudly. When a user was careless in replacing the receiver, it failed to lower the two plungers in the cradle so as to open the circuit for another call, necessitating a serviceman's trip to correct the difficulty. Reflections from the smooth black phenolic surface tired the eye. The number plate under the dial kept getting dirtier and more defaced with pencil marks, with no provision for easy cleaning, and the flicker of the dial over the number plate made the numbers hard to see, causing errors in dialing. The dial was too small for easy operation by the average finger.

The later model got rid of these defects (3.2d). A new plastic lightened the instrument, insulated against "howling," yielded a stronger stressed-skin support. A volume-control wheel under the base plate allowed turning of the bell to the subdued note desired. The handle connecting the earpiece with the mouthpiece fitted the hand better and offered a lighter unit to hold; its flattened back reduced the tendency of the old receiver to slip out of position when

3.3. THE ERICOFON. a. L. M. Ericsson Telephone Company, Stockholm: Ericofon, as set on desk and as held for dialing. 1955. Styrene copolymer housing, molded in three parts and cemented together. Height, 9¼″. Courtesy of North Electric Company, Galion, O. b. L. M. Ericsson Telephone Company: Ericofon, as held while telephoning. Acrylonitrile dial, nylon switch button. Base, 4½ × 3⅞″. Courtesy of North Electric Company, Galion, O.

grasped. The housing shell was reduced in height to a point where light-reflections no longer struck the eye. A larger dial and a number plate projecting the ring of numbers beyond the rim of the dial, with simply a white dot in the center of each hole to facilitate lining up with the proper number, made dialing an easy and accurate operation. Best of all from the serviceman's point of view, the cradle prongs were lowered to the point where the receiver would slip into position over the plungers almost automatically, opening the line for another call.

The 1950 combined handset behaved well. It also looked its part—clean-cut, quietly functional, impersonal, unobtrusive. Coming in black or in a choice of colors, it was ready to fit into the color scheme as well as into the furniture arrangement of the average American household for another score of years.

With the Bell model of 1950, Dreyfuss succeeded in alleviating the troubles arising from the "receiver-off-the-hook" situation (known to servicemen as ROH). He was unable, however, to make the instrument completely foolproof. The ROH problem remained to be met and solved by L. M. Ericsson, head of a telephone company in Sweden. Ericsson and his designers developed the Ericofon as a one-piece telephone with a stand-switch on the underside of the base (3.3a and b).* When the instrument was picked up, the switch-button shot out to close the circuit for a call. When it was set down again, the switch-button was pushed back in, opening the circuit for another call.

The user found the Ericofon bottom-heavy enough to guarantee its always being set down in an upright position. He had to pick the entire instrument up to make a call, but it was so light, thanks to the light plastics molded to form both its mechanism and its housing, that it weighed in its totality no more than the receiver alone in the Bell model of 1950.

Sensitive to the qualities of the newer plastics employed, the designers of the Ericofon created a form equally attractive when in use and when at rest. They developed a phone with a stable spread of base and a tuliplike rise of handle to mouthpiece—as inspired a creation of industrial design in its field as had yet appeared.

THE CRAFT AND INDUSTRY OF FABRIC MAKING

It is easy to distinguish the form of the buggy from that of the motor car. The buggy was the work of the lone craftsman who never let two carriages go out of his shop alike. The motor car was the joint work of any number of men—designers, engineers, and factory employees—who always turned out motor cars alike. In the first case the work bore marks of individual shaping and refining. In the other any object differing from the one before it or the one after it on the assembly line was sure to have suffered some accident along the course, betraying a defect which needed to be tracked down and corrected. When allowed to be itself, the industrial product affirmed its factory origins by the nature of its forms, always precise and smoothly functional, always impersonal.

Forms of some other products are certain to keep us guessing. However hard we try, we cannot tell whether their origin is the studio or the factory. The forms of most fabrics (kinds of cloth) are like that. As with baskets, which change little when their making is transferred from hearth to factory, so with fabrics. Almost any textile produced by the artist-craftsman can be multiplied in identical form by the factory. The product remains the same because the art of fabric making is one in which handwork and machine-work tend to coincide.†

The Materials and Processes of Fabric Making

Fabric making is the art of making cloth out of pliable fibers. The fibers employed in the

---

* For further description and illustration of the Ericofon, see the "Redesign" section of *Industrial Design*, Vol. IV, No. 1 (January, 1957), pp. 80–81, and *Modern Plastics*, Vol. XXXIV, No. 8 (April, 1957), pp. 117 and 236.

† Alastair Morton, British weaver, has written on the relationship of the craftsman to the textile manufacturer in a book the introduction to which was written by Herbert Read, *The Practice of Design* (London: Lund Humphries, 1946), pp. 25–38.

process can be animal or vegetable or mineral. If animal, they can come from the sheep, as wool, from the Himalayan goat, as cashmere, from the cocoon of a moth, as silk, and so on. If vegetable, the fibers can come from flax, as linen, from the cotton plant, as cotton, from the cellulose (woody part) of many other plants. If mineral, the fibers can be manufactured from a silicate of calcium and magnesium, as asbestos, from a regenerated cellulose, as rayon, from various synthesized chemicals, as nylon, Dacron, Orlon, and a host of others. Each such fiber has its own peculiar properties; it is porous or dense, sheer or opaque, absorbent or repellent, or whatever—properties which carry over into the fabric itself to determine much of its functional, tactile, and visual character.

Fabrics can be made in one of three ways: by rolling or pounding, by lacing, or by intertwining. When wool or fur fibers are rolled together under heat and pressure, they become interlocked to form a compact and even sheet called felt. When inside layers of mulberry bark are pounded together (by the Polynesians), the bark becomes tapa cloth.

Lacing involves the fastening of yarn to itself in a regular pattern. It makes use of nothing but a single thread element and depends for its effect upon the way in which the securing is done, whether by knotting or knitting, crocheting or tatting, hooking or looping. At the hands of primitive man, lacing produced snares and nets; at the hands of modern man, it produces a great variety of meshlike fabrics much prized for their ornamental charm.

Intertwining involves interlocking threads, one set with another. It embraces a number of techniques—braiding, bobbin-lacing (for tapestries), and so on—but it flourishes most generally in the form of weaving. In weaving the intertwining is always done at right angles, to produce fabrics called textiles. One set of yarns, called the warp, runs vertically; another, called the weft or the filling, runs horizontally. It would be possible to make a fabric by threading each weft yarn, called a pick, into a large needle, and passing it by hand alternately over

and under each warp yarn, called an end. This is exactly what is done in darning. But the procedure would soon prove intolerably tedious and clumsy for fabrics of any size.

Weaving on the loom is the only practical alternative, whether it be done on the weaver-craftsman's handloom or on the industrial weaver's power-loom. On the handloom, much as on the power-loom, ends of warp are stretched parallel to each other between the warp beam and the breast, or cloth, beam (3.4a). They are threaded in two or more sets, each end of one set through the eye of a wire in a series of wires framed as a harness, and each end of the other set through an eye in the second harness, and so on, depending on the number of harnesses of the loom in use and the degree of intricacy of the pattern to be woven.

Each harness is connected with a pedal called a treadle. When the weaver presses one treadle down, he pulls its harness down. Since one harness is connected with another across the top of the loom, the weaver makes the second harness come up in the same operation. The first harness in this way draws its set of ends down and the second harness its set of ends up, forming a triangular opening called a shed. Through the shed from one side to the other he throws the shuttle (3.4b), a wooden receptacle trailing behind it the yarn of the weft from a spool running freely inside the shuttle—to form the first pick of weft.

If in the process of threading ends of warp through their respective harnesses the weaver has threaded them also through a grill work in the hinged batten (the beater), he can now swing the batten against the pick, driving it against the breast beam to make the first pick of the textile to be woven. Pressing on the other treadle, he now reverses the shed, throws the shuttle through in the other direction, and leaves behind it in the shed the second pick, ready in turn to be driven against the first pick. He continues the process, pressing first on one treadle and then the other, changing the color or the texture of the yarn in the shuttle as often as required by the pattern

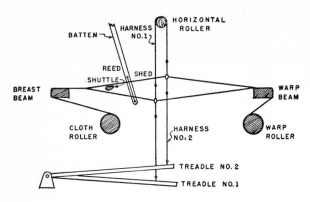

3.4. THE HANDLOOM. a. Diagram of section of handloom. b. The handloom in operation. Courtesy of Lynn Alexander. William E. Lotz and Joseph H. Rudd, Jr., photograph.

and rolling the textile up on the breast beam as it is completed.

Form and Ornament in Weaving

Any art has natural limits which the material, the technique, and the intended functions of the creation all impose upon its practitioners. Rather than regarding these limits as strait jackets which cramp their style, artists who recognize the nature of their art welcome its bounds as disciplining and form-determining forces.

Weaving is no exception to this rule. Its craftsmen lend distinction to their products by working within its limits to express their response to the material of the yarn, to its behavior on the loom, and to the nature of the usage to which the fabric is put. Weavers relish the warmth of wool, the coolness of linen, the delicacy of silk, the tensile strength of horsehair, and so on, bringing such qualities out in the textile which they weave. They accept the basic rectangularity of the intertwining of warp and weft and find in it their justification for the complex of stripes and plaids developed.

Weavers design from the outset with a definite function in mind and proceed to weave accordingly: for canvas, denim, and uphol-

stery, for example, beating the picks tightly together to make a dense, heavy and durable fabric; for scarves, veils, and curtains, beating the picks loosely together to form a semi-transparent or translucent fabric. For drapery, as they could not for clothing, weavers may develop a float in either their warp or their weft (1.7d)—a motive consisting of ends or picks which skip across a passage of the cloth before being caught in again (and one that can be very attractive, in fact, in a household free of cats).

Weavers face questions having to do with the wear and the strain to which the fabric will be subjected. Must the cloth be washed or must it be dry-cleaned, and how often? Must it convey a rich and luxurious effect, one light and delicate, or tight and resistant, or loose and flowing, or whatever? Their answers to such questions help determine in turn their yarns and their methods of weaving.

The over-and-under intersection of threads of warp and weft creates the textures of the fabric, especially when the yarns employed have distinctive textures of their own. If the

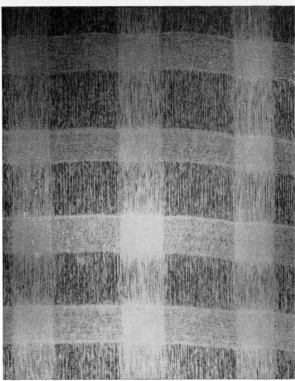

3.5. A WOVEN CURTAIN. a. Lynn Alexander (1920–): Woven curtain with open weft, draped before window. 1947. Warp: lemon yellow bouclé and chenille; weft: blue violet two-ply cotton. Width of whole curtain, 42″. Courtesy of the artist. William E. Lotz and Joseph H. Rudd, Jr., photograph. b. Lynn Alexander: Woven curtain with open weft, detail stretched flat as on loom, lighting from in front. Courtesy of the artist. William E. Lotz and Joseph H. Rudd, Jr., photograph. c. Lynn Alexander: Woven curtain with open weft, detail stretched flat as on loom, lighting from behind. Courtesy of the artist. William E. Lotz and Joseph H. Rudd, Jr., photograph.

textile is sheer, then the play of light through the interstices becomes an additional factor in the fabric's appeal. When the ends and the picks are grouped into units large enough to be noticed by themselves, and especially when the yarns are dyed in different colors, then the textile assumes a pattern as well as a texture. Its ornament is integral with its structure.

Fabrics can be woven in such a fine and even texture that their forms scarcely call any attention at all to the manner of their making. They are textiles which become mere supports for a decoration to be applied to them after they are finished, usually by a print-making process which the designer shares in common with the artist who creates pictures for duplication. In applying decoration to textiles there is much confusion as to its purpose, textile printers sometimes attempting elaborate pictures with insistent illusions of depth. Considering the utilitarian nature of the art, this practice is wrong. Only flat and highly abstracted or completely nonrepresentational motives fit a textile that is flat in itself but depended on for use as tablecloth, window curtain, or clothing. When the textile itself extends into deep space, any spatial illusion in the ornament tends to contradict that extension.

The printing of textiles is a branch of the art of fabric making to which standards of critical judgment must apply as rigorously as to any other art. But the central core of fabric making is weaving itself, and our case-study of the artist at work must be the weaver at the handloom. Lynn Alexander was accustomed to creating draperies of various sorts for specific uses by interior designers and architects, and in this particular instance he was commissioned to prepare window curtains for a newly finished residence. The building in question was foursquare in its simplicity, with abundant window area opening to the south and an adjoining fireplace of comparable rectilinearity. It called for curtains accentuating the structural clarity of the interior but softening at the same time the linear hardness of the edges (3.5a).

In following the weaver's step-by-step procedure we note how consistently he dealt with the elements and the principles of all art as his visual language, along with considerations which applied exclusively to the craft of his specialty. Alexander was prompted by the architectural simplifications to adopt the tabby weave, that plainest of all techniques in which weft threads are carried alternately over and under successive threads of warp, much as in darning socks. In order to achieve the degree of translucency necessary for a curtain, he planned for both a loose weave and a series of bands of alternating closed and open (or omitted) weft.

Again in keeping with the severity of the architecture, the weaver decided to restrict himself to a single material. He chose cotton because of the range of its qualities, from its high tensile strength and nonelasticity to its affinity for dyes and varied techniques of spinning (3.5b). For the more open of the two bands of warp decided on, Alexander chose bouclé, a thread spun in "buckles" or ringlets to bring out the lightness and fluffiness of the cotton. For the alternating opaque bands of warp, he chose chenille, a tufted and velvety caterpillarlike thread, which he stretched in double thickness on the loom so as to enhance the luxurious softness of the cotton.

In order to determine the type of yarn and weave for the single band of closed weft the artist wove a sampler, a length of cloth in the making of which he could actually try out for himself his possible selections. From this sampler Alexander finally chose a tightly spun, two-ply cotton yarn accentuating by its contrast in hardness the softness of the two yarns of the warp and bringing out still another quality of cotton, its long-fibered tensile strength.

The weaver was seeking a richly textural effect. He realized that he could not achieve it without a strict subordination of color to texture. He was careful, therefore, to mute the colors of the dyes by graying them. But within the range of grays which he allowed himself, Alexander still gained considerable expressiveness. He dyed both the bouclé and the chenille in lemon yellow, a hue suggesting sunniness, and the two-ply yarn in violet, the complement setting the yellow off by contrast. Since, as we noted in the first two chapters, complements equal in value and intensity weaken each other by competition, Alexander developed a violet dye of lower intensity and higher value than the yellow dye (principle of proportion).

3.6. A Woven Drapery. a. Margery Livingston (1918–   ): Woven drapery with tabby weave, detail stretched flat as on loom, lighting from in front. 1956. Warp: rayon chenille and rayon nubby; weft: tow rayon and cotton-and-rayon bouclé. Courtesy of the artist. Ira Latour photograph. b. Margery Livingston: Woven drapery with tabby weave, detail, as hung on wall. Courtesy of the artist. Ira Latour photograph.

Ends of warp and picks of weft, spun and dyed and woven as we have described, put the two-harness handloom into the kind of operation at which it is happiest. As if by magic under the light above the loom, the tabby weave brought forth rectangles of fabric now dense, now open; now hard, now soft; now oblong, now square—in a strong rhythmic succession (3.5b). When it was taken off the loom and hung at a window with daylight behind it, the curtain underwent, moreover, a spirited change of effect (3.5c). The bands of closed weft reversed their value-sequence from halftone-white-halftone to halftone-black-halftone and the bands of open weft became a series of lush textural passages in alternate succession (principle of rhythm). When pushed to the side of the window the curtain gathered into folds which enhanced the simple pattern instead of confusing it, while continu-

ing to function in its double capacity as a window-softening and a window-frame-repeating textile (3.5a).

In weaving his curtain with open weft, Lynn Alexander explored the range of expression possible to cotton alone when spun according to different techniques. Another weaver, Margery Livingston, worked with corresponding directness to explore the qualities of cotton when spun in combination with rayon. She threaded her warp in an alternating sequence of one end of rayon nubby and three ends of cotton spun with rayon as chenille, and wove her weft in a tabby weave of corresponding picks, one of rayon tow and three of cotton spun with rayon as bouclé (3.6). She brought out in this way the characteristic gleam and crinkliness of these combination materials and managed to lend to the basically formal pattern a sense of casual informality.

THE CRAFT OF POTTERY

Among the utilitarian arts taken over more or less completely by industrial design, none has maintained its identity as a craft alongside the industry more vigorously than the art of ceramics. Deriving its name from the Greek word for potter's clay, *keramikos*, ceramics is the art of making vessels out of clay, fashioning them hollow, baking them in a kiln until the clay is hard, and sometimes finally glazing them for both watertightness and appearance.

Potter's clay appeals to us as few other substances can. Known to us as mud, it is capable of exerting over us, when we do not have to walk or drive through it, that same magic spell which it casts over children making mud pies. Behind it as behind the stone of the carver lie its origins in "rock-ribbed mother earth." From "mother rock of clay," as the potter puts it, the forces of wind, rain, frost, and sun extract the clay's ingredients—its silicate of alumina, its alkalis, its sand, iron, and various "impurities." Down the mountain torrent the ingredients have to be carried, to some stagnant backwater on the plain where they settle into beds and weather for ages, until at length they can be called good clay and dug out for the pottery.

The commonness of clay may deceive the novice into thinking it of little consequence, but it is not just any old mud that the potter uses to make his pots. Out of a single deposit of twenty or more layers, each a different clay, he may find only one layer satisfactory for his purposes. Even then, most likely, he will not find the clay of this particular layer quite right. He may find it too "short," as the potter says when it is too sandy or brittle, in which case he must add proper amounts of ball clay, a secondary clay with a strong attraction for water. He may find the original clay too "fat," too rich and sticky, in which case he must add proper amounts of a graded sand or a pulverized brick called "grog."

From the start the potter has to have his mind made up about the nature of the pot he is going to make. He has to prepare his clay with his end product in mind, making sure that it will have just the right composition to respond efficiently to the particular techniques of shaping and of firing involved. There is a wide range of possibilities for this end product. In general, however, the possibilities lie within one or another of three main classes based upon the nature of the clay: earthenware, stoneware, and porcelain.

If the ceramist's pot is to be of earthenware, it will be composed of a coarse clay, porous when not glazed (covered with a glassy coating), fusible at a low temperature of firing (from red heat at about 750° C to intermediate orange heat at about 1000° C), and soft enough after firing to scratch with a knife. It will have an opaque and thick but brittle wall. If the vessel is to be of stoneware, on the other hand, it will be composed of a finely textured clay, vitreous (nonporous even when unglazed), fusible only at a white heat around 1300° C, and hard enough to withstand any attempt to scratch it with a knife. It will have an opaque wall, like that of earthenware, but the wall will look firm enough and strong enough, even though very thin, not to break under considerable rough usage. If the work is to be of porcelain, it will be composed of clay as fine and vitreous as that of stoneware, fusible at the same white heat, and fully as hard. Porcelainware differs from stoneware in its employment of an ingredient made from decomposed granite and called kaolin, which renders the clay dazzling white when fired and often also translucent. When struck, moreover, porcelainware will ring like a bell.

Even when the potter has composed his clay satisfactorily for one of these three wares, he is still not ready to shape it into vessels. He must soak the clay in water, weather it in the open, age it in warm, damp storage bins. He must dry it on "bats," slabs of cast plaster which soak the water out of the clay until it no longer sticks to his fingers. He must force all air-pockets out of the clay by a process of vigorous cutting and beating called "wedging." He must

3.7. HAND-BUILT POTTERY. Ninnami Dōhachi (*fl.* 1804–1842): Raku tea bowl. Early 19th century. Hand-modeled earthenware, black glaze; exterior ornament, white crane; interior ornament, white tortoise. Height, *c.* 3″. National Museum, Tokyo. Courtesy of Jirō Harada.

give the clay an even consistency by kneading it as a baker kneads dough. Only after all this preparation can he be satisfied that the clay is ready for use.

Handbuilding a Pot by Pinching

Clay readied for pottery production has a plasticity inviting emphasis. It leads at the same time to different effects depending on differences in techniques. A potter as responsive to processes as he is to materials will, for example, develop out of hand-building irregularities of form appropriate to it, even as he will develop out of wheel-throwing (shaping on a whirling wheel) contrastingly regular and symmetrical forms.

As an outstanding instance of the irregularities expressive of hand-building, take a Japanese raku-ware tea bowl (3.7).[5] The potter

[5] See Notes, page 295.

making it felt his clay to be a naturally friendly substance. In a society secure in its isolation from the rest of the world and long at peace under a strong government, Ninnami Dōhachi at the beginning of the nineteenth century feared his material no more than he feared anything else about him. He cherished his clay, in fact, treated it with a reverence that amounted to a religion. He worked in the service of the tea ceremony, a ritual inspired as much by art as by religion, a kind of super-art that demanded as much from the potter as it demanded from a score of other craftsmen. In accord with the ideals of the tea ceremony, calling for quiet and age-mellowed harmonies of effect, he resorted as most appropriate, he thought, to pinch-potting, simplest of all hand-building pottery techniques.

That Dōhachi knew what he was about is clearly apparent in the tea bowl illustrated. Its foot makes a secure stand; it also records the lump of clay which the potter held at the start in the hollow of his hand. It marks in spread from foot to base of belly the second step in the process—a widening and raising of the wall by squeezing the clay between the fingers until it reached about three inches in both height and width. It reflects the potter's upward pinching in the irregular curvature of its lip. Thick and heavy walls, asymmetrical bulgings of surface, and uneven modulations—it declares in such features not only the clay out of which it was formed and the way in which it was made, but also the purpose for which it was produced. The bowl was made to hold in the hands without burning them, to contain a brew of tea the color and texture of the leaves of which it suggests in its own color and texture, and through such suggestion to arouse in its user a mood of quiet thoughtfulness.

Most remarkable of all facts about this tea bowl is that none of its qualities came automatically as by-products of the process. Once Dōhachi had reached the desired general shape and size of his bowl, he let it dry to what the potter calls a "leather hard" condition. He then subjected it to a *turning* operation, scraping the bowl with a turning-tool until it assumed a smoothsided cylindrical shape ready to receive, by cutting and gouging, irregularities deliberately introduced by him to express his experiences with the pinch-potting process. In such designing he followed by positive intent the way that every artist follows, determining by his own expressive will even features which seem to the outsider nothing but happy accidents.

Since the tea bowl was made to serve hot tea in, Dōhachi had to render it watertight. He made his vessel so by giving it a glassy coating called a glaze. Mixing water with chemicals which would turn white when fused by the heat of the firing, he painted inside the bowl the form of a tortoise and outside it the form of a crane, symbols of long life which the guest would understand for good-luck wishes when the bowl was offered. Elsewhere over the bowl's surface the potter painted a black-yielding glaze, taking care only to stop it short of the foot in an irregularly curving edge. By so doing he was able to accentuate its original state as a liquid, the manner of its application, and the nature of the clay underneath. He proceeded to fire his bowl in a wood-burning kiln, by a single exposure to heat converting his clay to "biscuit," as it is called in its hardened state, and at the same time fusing his glazes. The tea bowl emerging from this process was calculated especially to appeal to the Japanese using it, because they had the background to appreciate the subleties of its irregularized form. The rest of us at least sense the bowl's vitality, because we see how honestly it declares its purpose and its medium.

Throwing Pottery on the Kick Wheel

Much faster than building a pot by hand is the process of throwing it on a wheel. For wheel-thrown ware the potter cuts a lump of clay just large enough for the predetermined size of the vessel to be thrown. He slaps it down and centers it on a whirling wheel-head. He coats his hands with water, braces himself securely, and, while the wheel continues to rotate, shapes the pot by balancing one hand against

3.8. THE KICK WHEEL. Cutting wire being drawn under a pitcher which has just been thrown on the wheel-head. Courtesy of Marguerite Wildenhain. Otto Hagel photograph.

the other in a series of forcible but delicately controlled operations: hollowing the whirling lump of clay to the exact diameter of the inside of the foot, bringing the walls out and up and in almost as though the clay were raising itself, then choking in the neck and rounding out the lip.

Potter's wheels are legion. Some are designed to be twirled by hand, some to be kicked or pedaled with the foot, some to be driven by motor. Each wheel has its advantages and its disadvantages. Each claims its devotees. Tra-

3.9. Marguerite Wildenhain (1896–   ): Coffee set, Pond Farm Ware, Guerneville, Calif. 1946. Wheel-thrown stoneware with speckled glaze. Courtesy of the artist. Otto Hagel photograph.

ditionally preferred, the old-fashioned kick-wheel is a contrivance consisting of the wheel-head set at one end of a vertical shaft, a much larger and heavier fly-wheel set at the other end, this coupling installed inside of a wooden scaffolding and bench, and the point at the lower end of the shaft made to turn in a bearing (3.8). Successful operation of the wheel requires a sense of timing and rhythm like the dancer's; as the potter sits at his bench, alternately kicking the wheel and working the clay, his every action must flow imperceptibly into the next, and every part of his body must function in unison with every other part.

The smoothly coordinated stages of the process have made themselves felt in the water pitcher which the California potter, Marguerite Wildenhain, is shown as about to cut from the head of her wheel with a cutting wire, preparatory to setting it aside to dry. The potter has just modeled a spout by stroking outwardly the freshly shaped lip; once the vessel has dried into its "leather hard" state, she will add a handle, stroking a roll of clay into the desired shape and luting (gluing) each end with slip (liqueous clay) to the body proper. Oherwise she has given the pitcher that perfectly symmetrical shape around a vertical axis which constitutes one of the chief distinctions in the form of a thrown pot.

The techniques of throwing this pitcher have made themselves felt in the contours of its body, for they rise more rapidly than do the contours of a hand-built pot; if a widely extending curve natural to a coil-built vessel had been attempted here, the centrifugal force of the whirling wheel would have caused the vessel to collapse. The techniques have made themselves felt, again, in the subtly varied grooves made by the knuckles against the wall of the piece, grooves retained as ornament, perhaps, but an ornament as effectively integrated with the form as it was intended to enliven the surface.

As exemplified in the coffee set next presented (3.9), Marguerite Wildenhain's art resides in the clear, clean forms of use and of clay well thrown. The pieces in her set have a dynamic quality which attests eloquently to the process by which they were made. They bespeak the texture and hardness of stoneware clay, strikingly unlike the clay going to make the earthenware tea bowl.

High-fired stoneware, in fact, drawing from Marguerite Wildenhain some of her most inspired creative efforts, is here shown at its best. It betrays, for one thing, a peculiarly bold functional directness. It looks its serviceableness for daily life—coffee pot well-balanced for handling and pouring, and generous in capacity; cream pitcher matching the pot's utility on a miniature scale; cups sitting securely in their saucer wells, strong-handled, opening hospitably to the lips; and so on. The coffee set assumes the quiet coloring characteristic of stoneware, with a speckled but transparent overlay of glaze which accentuates the "shortness" and the orange-skinlike texture of the clay employed. It continues to make to its users the same appeal to touch and sight which it made to the potter herself, a standard of quality which she describes as exacting of herself:

3.10. Arthur E. Baggs (1886–1947): Cooky jar. c. 1938. Salt-glazed stoneware. Height, 13½". Everson Museum of Art, Syracuse, N. Y.

The test for the quality of a pot is the simplicity of the result. If it looks as if it had simply grown out of the earth like a stone, then it will be a good pot. If it can stand next to ancient pots, Chinese or Greek or Italian, without losing its distinct personality and the character of its period, then it will be a good pot. And if it has a good shape and a material appropriate to its use, it won't even need a glaze, and it will still be a good pot. A glaze should, like a well-tailored dress enhancing the bodily beauty of a well-built person, increase the beauty of a well-shaped pot, but not cover a formal monster with the glamour of its shine and luster. . . . The most artistic glaze is nothing without a pot to put it on, while a pot can be a masterpiece without any glaze on it at all. A pot is thrown in a few minutes. It is nearly as natural a reaction of the potter, as, say, walking is.*

Like Marguerite Wildenhain's coffee set, the stoneware cooky jar thrown by Arthur E. Baggs (3.10) suggests a certain assurance and power

* Quoted by courtesy of the potter from the manuscript for a lecture; later incorporated in the text for her book, *Pottery: Form and Expression* (New York: American Craftsmen's Council, 1959).

in reserve. The jar makes its very usefulness as a storage receptacle depend on its shape, which is basically spherical. Against the regularity of this nucleus it asserts its power of movement by its extensions of foot, handles, and lid.

In the handles of the shoulder and lid, the jar utilizes a certain form commonly encountered in the midst of throwing but scarcely ever preserved. When a pot in process falls short of its objectives, as it often does even in the studio of a master, the artist lifts it from the wheel-head, crushes it together and returns it as salvaged clay to the storage bin. The walls of the piece as they are pressed together sometimes assume curves which are startlingly dynamic, curves which potters have often admired but rarely thought to exploit as Arthur Baggs has done. He has put such partially collapsed forms deliberately to work as handles. Grooving them deeply as accents to the run of knuckle grooves across the body, he has made these handles express not only the plastic nature of the potter's clay and the activated nature of the process; he has even crooked them to accommodate the lifter's fingers.

Industrial Ceramic Processes

Every pot examined thus far, whether by a Dōhachi, a Wildenhain, or a Baggs, was created by a handicraft technique rendering it unique. It appeared to have been worked on only the moment before we saw it. Coming directly from the potter's hands, it declared its origins.

When, from the middle of the eighteenth century on, industrial processes came more and more to replace the handicraft techniques, confusion resulted. The quality of pottery production declined. The ideal remained the craftsman's but the methods of making were wholesale. Factory-produced wares became imitations of the handmade, and poor imitations, too, because the industrialized production line was ill suited to meet the old ideal.

Pottery emerging from the factory was either slipcast or pressed or jiggered-and-jolleyed. If slipcast, the pot was made in a two-piece plaster mold by filling the mold with slip (clay mixed with water until creamy in consistency), letting the slip stand in the mold until the plaster had soaked up enough water to form a deposit of clay wall of the desired thickness inside the mold, then pouring out the remainder of the slip, letting the clay wall dry and shrink inward from the cast, and finally opening the mold to remove the cast pot. If pressed, the pot was made by rolling short clay out as though it were dough for a piecrust, pressing the resulting slab into a mold to make it assume the desired shape, and removing it when dried. If jiggered-and-jolleyed, the pot was made with the use of a motor-driven wheel. A plaster mold was attached to the wheel-head and a chunk of clay was pressed down around it, if the mold was solid, or into it, if the mold was hollow. The wheel was set to revolving and a metal template, cut to follow either the outer or the inner contour of the piece to be produced, was brought down on a hinged arm, to trim away in a flash all of the surplus clay and determine the shape of the pot.

None of the three industrial techniques lent itself to the surface modulations natural to handicraft production, and any attempt to make it record such modulations ended in a blurred and slovenly impression. In order to conceal imperfections, therefore, factory producers resorted to ornamentation, either painted on or else stamped in a mold and luted on as relief. In this attempted concealment, they usually succeeded in turning out nothing but cheap travesties of the handmade wares.

By a curious reversal of influence, an occasional potter-craftsman like Glen Lukens of southern California tried to create unique pots out of such a technique as pressing in a mold (1.7b). It is true that Lukens found his sources of form in clay peculiarly suited for pressing and in the action of the pressing itself. He prepared a coarse grog, clay mixed with particles of crushed biscuit. He rolled this grog into a thick layer and pressed it loosely into the mold, often leaving folds of clay to show on the surface as reminders of the process. He then turned the pressed ware on a wheel, using a sponge to smooth out areas for contrast with the original texture. As a further contrast, he even trailed a thick glaze of intense color over the biscuit or into grooves cut into the green ware to receive it. Giving exaggerated emphasis thus to the elements of mass, texture, and color, Lukens cared little for functions and their expression in his ware but much for poetic allusions to the nearby desert, whence came his clays and glazes and the motives for his forms, like cracked earth, and rock and sand in combination.

Pressed ware by Lukens is about as far away as one can get from industrial dinnerware, whether chinaware or chinaware's post-World War II cousin, plastic ware. Especially does it differ from the latter. Substitute chrome-plated metal molds for plaster molds, join the casting and the firing of the plastic, melamine, in a single operation, and the plate, cup, saucer, or bowl which emerges from the mold is bound to be identical with every piece preceding or following it. This contrasts with industrial porcelain, even the best of which sometimes shrinks or warps in the firing, rendering it unfit for sale save as a second.

Plastic dinnerware is by nature clearly and cleanly functional about its forms. It is strong, light, smooth, unvaryingly precise about the fitting of every cup to saucer, of every lid to bowl. It comes, when cast in melamine, with a translucent, lightly mottled body that shows up well in tints of blue or yellow and shades of red or blue-black. Plastic dinnerware has at the same time many obstacles to surmount before it can gain general acceptance at the hostess's dinner table, where its very strengths are apt to count as weaknesses. People are conventional about their expectations at a meal. They want dishes that are fragile and look fragile, dishes that weigh enough not to slide too easily, dishes that have a little touch of embellishment about them, dishes which the habitual use of wheel-thrown wares in the past has demanded to be rounded if not circular and symmetrical in shape. When made to meet the conventions of ceramic wares, plastic dishes are stretched beyond the quality of their material, betraying their uneasiness in their forms.

The problem of designing a plastic dinnerware that can be itself and still win general acceptance has to be solved before melamine dishes can prove their survival value as products of industrial design. Perhaps an adaptation of the shapes traditional to Japanese lacquerware, or else the development of absolutely free forms in which the sole associations are those with the forms of an organically designed and furnished kitchen, will demonstrate itself to be the best solution. In the meantime, and perhaps always as a valid alternative to plastic tableware, industrially designed and manufactured porcelainware will continue to challenge the creative powers of the artist.

About the time when melamine was first beginning to be cast as dishes for picnics and tray-lunches, Eliot Noyes, staff-member of New York's Museum of Modern Art, projected a tableware in the range of pure porcelain that could be produced impersonally on the factory assembly line and yet merit place in the museum alongside masterpieces of the individual potter-thrower. Noyes persuaded Louis E. Hellmann, head of the Castleton China potteries in New Castle, Pennsylvania, to invest the firm's resources in production of the line. Together they commissioned Mrs. Eva Striker Zeisel, potter as well as industrial designer, to develop the forms of the ware.*

Mrs. Zeisel met her challenge with a rare vitality of imagination. She cleared her mind of preconceptions of what tableware might be. She reexamined the nature of the kaolin-rich clay required for porcelain manufacture and evolved out of it shapes able to meet the hardest and the most exacting of usages. As apparent in the plate, the butter plate, and the cup and saucer forming part of the place-setting illustrated (3.11), Mrs. Zeisel utilized the hardness of the high-fired material to draw the edges out to translucent thinness and allow a

* _Arts and Architecture_, Vol. XIII (June, 1946), pp. 28–29, etc.; and _Interiors_, Vol. CXI (November, 1951), p. 124, and Vol. CXI (February, 1952), p. 114.

3.11. WORKS OF ART IN A TABLE SETTING. Eva Zeisel (1906–   ): Dinner plate, butter plate, cup, and saucer. Designed 1942 for Castleton China Company, New Castle, Pa. Porcelain. K. P. C. de Bazel (1869–1923): Goblets. Designed for Koninklijki Nederlandsche Glasfabriek Leerdam, Leerdam, The Netherlands. Leerdam crystal. John Van Koert (1912–   ): Contour flatware. Designed 1950 for Towle Silversmiths, Newburyport, Mass. Silver. Setting from exhibition at Walker Art Center, Minneapolis, January–December, 1951. Will Hoagberg photograph.

concentration of weight for stability's sake toward the center and the foot. By way of counterpoise to such massing she lightened the effect of the frequently lifted cup by raising the saucer into a small well around it (exactly fitting its foot) and curving the walls of the cup into upward-moving contours. She treated all handles like those of the cup—straplike lengths of clay luted securely to shoulder and belly and looped to fit the thumb and fingers. Although to enhance the popular appeal of Castleton tableware she designed some sets with gold bands around the rims and a few painted abstractions applied with great restraint, she counted in her basic set on the ivory tone of the porcelain, its reflections and translucencies, and the food served in it, for the only embellishment.

WORKING GLASS BY HAND AND BY MACHINE

Mrs. Zeisel intended Castleton china to be viewed not in isolated display but in use at the table in conjunction with other serving things (3.11). Recognizing that, in mid-twentieth-century art, relationships count for more than entities, she calculated that her porcelainware would glow most appealingly against the transparent sparkling glass and the opaque but polished silver to be set beside it. For a super-art of table setting that embraces tributary arts, she counted on her chinaware's holding its own with any crystalware or flatware of comparable integrity.

The Dutch artist K.P.C. de Bazel evolved for manufacture by a glass factory of Leerdam, Netherlands, the goblets shown in our setting. For them de Bazel had to resort to the craft of glass-blowing to make the original models, but in so doing he was practicing an art far closer to its industrial equivalent than was the case in ceramics. A blast furnace melts the silicates of various bases under action exerted on them by potash or soda; it also keeps the slag molten in the crucible while the artist works. Into this slag the artist dips his blowing-iron (or hollow metal rod), collecting on its pipe-nose a pearshaped gathering of the glass-to-be, and then on a metal table rolls it into conical shape. Through the blowing-iron he blows the gathering into a bubble (3.12); with pincers he removes the bubble and with scissors and shaping-tool he trims and fashions it into the form desired. He reheats the gathering periodically to keep it workable, and attaches to it in its semimolten state whatever hollow or solid pieces may be required. He anneals the heated work by putting it slowly through a long oven of gradually diminishing temperatures so as to strengthen it without causing breaks or flaws. If the glassworker can then go on to make molds from original pieces and attach the molds to machinery that will gather, blow, and join for him all by itself, he can convert an already industrialized craft into assembly-line production. And if he is in tune with both processes, as this designer was, he can develop forms for goblets distinctively expressive of the glass so worked. The Leerdam Crystal goblets possess such forms—sparkling in their clear transparency, lightly bubblelike of belly, broad of foot, solid of stem—proclaiming at once the ductility of the slag and the ordered regularity of the wheels of industry. The goblets hold liquids hospitably, sit

3.12. Craftsman blowing glass, Corning Glass Works, Corning, N. Y. Courtesy of Steuben Glass, New York.

on the tablecloth firmly, conform securely to the grasp, curve efficiently to meet the lips.

Although glassworking is an art of practical utility in which the craft tends to merge with the industry, it sometimes becomes an art of "free" creation in which function is ignored and material and technique are dealt with only decoratively. Sidney Waugh approached the easel painter and the studio sculptor when he created decorative glassware like his *Gazelle Bowl* (3.13). Waugh shaped a bowl to recall by its thick-walled spherical belly and chunkily cut legs the original heaviness of the slag. Against the extraordinarily massive forms resulting from such treatment he opposed a frieze of lightly scampering animals the lilt of whose movement and the threadlike attenuations of whose forms startle us by their contrast to the forms that they grace, even as the ductility of the molten glass surprises us by its contrast to the weight. The forms of the gazelles assume at the same time a voluminosity

3.13 (*left*). Sidney Waugh (1904–   ): *Gazelle Bowl. c.* 1934. Engraved Steuben glass. Height, 7¼″; diameter, 6½″. Metropolitan Museum of Art, New York.

3.14 (*right*). George Thompson (1913–   ): Flaring bowl on open base. 1940. Steuben glass. Height, 4½″. George Lazarnick photograph.

corresponding to the bowl's—an effect made possible by the technique of the engraving process which Sidney Waugh employed, pressing the glass wall in turn against a series of rotating copper wheels of varying diameters and thicknesses, grinding into it an intaglio (a design cut below the surface) which affords the firmest of edges, the smoothest of curves, the most convincing illusions of relief and airy depth.

Although craftsmen employed by the Steuben Glass works made replicas of the *Gazelle Bowl* so faithful to Waugh's design as to find their way into museum collections, the original bowl retained a certain elusive sense of vitality which the replicas were bound to lose, a sense of uniqueness which the bowl as a "show piece" properly conveyed but which the replicas missed. Probably more than anything else, it is the ornamental frieze which distinguishes Waugh's bowl as a studio creation. Had the

frieze been less in evidence and the bowl fashioned for some particular use apart from itself, the process of reproducing it would have seemed more fitting, even as it does for the Flaring Glass Bowl on Open Base designed by George Thompson for Steuben Glass production (3.14). In Thompson's bowl, unlike Waugh's, the basic industrial processes were invited to make their appeal in the forms that they created, all subordinate to the idea of the possible use of the bowl as a flower container. The elementary bubble form determined the belly, the contrastingly heavy, viscous slag determined the lumpiness of the foot and the robust spread of the legs, the ductile molten mass the extension of the rim, and the crystalline transparency of the glass in play of light and shadow its only "ornament." No representational ornament was added to draw the observer's attention away from such qualities as evolved organically.

THE CRAFT OF METALWORK

While the knives, forks, and spoons displayed in our placesetting (3.11) harmonize in simplicity with the porcelainware and glassware employed, they preserve their own identity through the solid material composing them. The material might have been clay or wood, used from time to time for tableware. In this case, and usually by preference, it is metal, because metal resists breakage better, retains a cutting edge or a point, and facilitates control by adjustment of weights to the hand for leverage and momentum. The metal might have been a natural material like iron or platinum. It might have been an alloy like pewter or steel. In this case, and again by preference, it is sterling silver (an alloy of 92.5 parts of pure silver and 7.5 parts of copper). Although silver tarnishes in air and reacts to salt in storage, for ordinary table contacts sterling needs no protective plating to keep it from eroding or from staining foods or altering their taste. Sterling warms to the hand or the lip. It has about it a softly glowing effect. It responds readily to a refinement of form or a subtlety of finish.

The very workability of silver has operated to its disadvantage. Especially in the making of flatware it has often succumbed to an overloading of ornament for the sake of ornament, a sentiment which ignores the functional utility of the tools when it does not actually impair their efficiency. Feeling the need to break with this tradition of meaningless ornamentation, D. S. Defenbacher, then Director of the Walker Art Center in Minneapolis, came to play the same role for flatware as Eliot Noyes had played for porcelain. In 1950 he proposed to the firm of Towle Silversmiths in Newburyport, Massachusetts, that the lay members of his museum organization act as "guinea pigs" for models of knives, forks, and spoons to be projected for the open market by Towle's designer, John Van Koert. Climaxing the joint efforts of artist, consumer, and producer, Towle Silversmiths went into wholesale manufacture and the Walker Art Center featured by exhibition the "Contour Flatware" thus evolved.*

Van Koert modeled the utensils not only to fit the grasp like sculptured "handies" but to continue and actually to complement the movements of the hand in eating. The artist might have developed his forms blindly, so pleasurably shaped and balanced are they to the grasp, but he did not evolve them automatically. He trained the contours of each piece, rather, to "glide" in easy directness from its upturned end over the elongated, concave handle to the culminating accent at its "business end." The designer recognized how much softer food has become today, and developed forms accordingly—a spreading, short-bladed knife; a scoop-shaped, closely tined fork; a lip-fitting, round-bowled spoon. He fashioned his pieces, finally, for easy "raising" into shape by the mechanical equivalent to pounding with hammer by hand—stamping a punch into a die with a massive press.

As long as the eating habits of a society continue to require knife, fork, and spoon in preference to chopsticks or some equally more refined tool, the art of forming flatware of silver will remain an industrial offshoot of the metalworking crafts. On the other hand, since silver platters and tankards meet a luxury demand, the making of hollow-ware with the metal will always remain more of a studio craft.† Although a designer of hollow-ware like Margret Craver may maintain connections with such industrial-silver concerns as Handy and Harmon of New York, such connections are primarily for purposes of marketing, and the artist remains above all a handicraftsman.

---

* The catalogue prepared for this exhibition stands as an authoritative reference in its field: D. S. Defenbacher, *Knife: Fork: Spoon* (Minneapolis: Walker Art Center, 1951); it includes an exhaustive bibliography.
† Perhaps the standard reference for silver hollow-ware in the United States, treated historically, is that by John Marshall Phillips, *American Silver* (New York: Chanticleer Press, 1949). The technique of making hollow-ware is clearly presented in the 16 mm. film, *Handwrought Silver* (Handy and Harmon, New York).

3.15. Metal for Use and Adornment. a. Margret Craver (1907–   ): Handwrought bowl. 1946. Sterling silver. $3 \times 5''$. Newark Museum, Newark, N. J. Courtesy of the artist and the Craft Service Department, Handy and Harman.   b. Irena Brynner (1917–   ): Ring. 1955. Half-round platinum wire, black pearl, and diamonds. Courtesy of the artist. Ruth Bernhardt photograph.

Like other craftsmen, Margret Craver had to sharpen her conception of the form for such a vessel as the sterling bowl illustrated (3.15a), first working it out on paper. Once fully under way with its execution, however, she responded to the impulse of the metal under her hands, departing increasingly from her preliminary study until the drawing was completely forgotten and something unique created.

Even as the silversmith prepared her sheet of metal for working (softening it by heating, and cleansing it by "pickling" in sulphuric acid solution), she found the growing whiteness of the silver a quality worth preserving. Cutting from the sheet a disc of silver of the required diameter, she proceeded to "stretch" it over the concave end of a wooden block, hammering it into the hollow and gradually deepening its curvature with a ball-peen hammer. The artist sensed the increasing animation of effect induced by the "stretching," but with imaginative restraint stopped her hammering short of the maximum effect. Lest the dents of the hammering remain to interrupt the surface "flow," she transferred the piece to a round-ended iron stake upon which to pound it smooth with a planishing hammer. After polishing with emery cloth, she brought the contours of her bowl to spirited termination by thickening the rim with a rawhide mallet. In the making of a foot upon which the bowl could stand, finally, Miss Craver sought to recall by

each of its parts the shapes her sheet of silver had assumed in the earlier stages: by the circular base, the disc which she had cut, and by the short, scalloped pier above the base, the curving surfaces resulting from the "stretching." Once soldered to the belly, these elements not only called attention to the technical procedure followed; they provided an effective "springboard" for the rising contours of the bowl itself.

Making Jewelry

Among the metal-working arts jewelry design remains even more of a studio craft than the hammering of hollow-ware. If we recall what we observed in the preceding chapter about the purpose of jewelry, we can understand the reason. Jewelry is created by the artist not to clothe the body but to embellish it. It is intended to lend distinction to the physical person. Imagine every woman one came across wearing an identical necklace. Other features might vary, but the common necklace would tend to blunt other charms and reduce all women to an average. A woman chooses a piece of jewelry for its uniqueness and its power to enhance some personal trait, not because it matches an ornament that she has seen other women wearing.

It is true that jewelry has been perverted into decorating not the figure but the dress, making it into "costume jewelry," often on the level of junk. It is true that jewelry has also been perverted into advertising wealth and rank, making it into "conspicuous-consumption jewelry" on the level of tinsel.* When designed by an artist-craftsman for its proper functioning, on the other hand, jewelry can be made to grace the human body much as incised or painted decoration can be made to grace the body of a pot—to give accent to an especially comely foot, belly, shoulder, neck, or lip. Consider the Hindu dancer. Note how effectively she makes her jewels emphasize every part of her form in movement—from the bells on her toes or ankles to her anklets, her girdle and girdle-pendant, her brooch and pectorals, her bracelets and finger rings, her necklaces and earrings, her nose rings and headbands. Her dance, eloquent of a life in which art and religion are one, would by itself qualify creatively. But let her be divested of her jewelry and her dance would suffer.

Superb jewelry has been made out of the commonest and cheapest of materials, from the animal claws and teeth strung together by cavemen to the tortoise shells and seashells carved by South Sea islanders, to the powdered glass melted into enamel inlays by Byzantine artisans and the iron collar-rings fashioned by craftsmen of certain Burmese and African tribes for stretching the necks of their fairest females to astonishing lengths. Most jewelry has depended for at least a part of its effectiveness, however, on the rarity of its materials, much as some pottery depends for its value on its obvious fragility. Hence the preference in jewelry-making for gold, platinum, and silver, for jade, rock crystal, and pearls, and for the precious and semiprecious stones which are together called gems. Other things being equal, in fact, it might be said that the rarer the materials used in jewelry, the more exclusive-seeming the quality of the ornament. Gems can appear so precious, to be sure, that the vulgar jewel-setter and his clientele are car-

ried away by their costliness, letting "the tail wag the dog" at the expense of the design. But the artist who understands precious stones and cherishes them, who goes to great effort to find a rare gem, and who recognizes the type of female beauty with which that gem can be worn to best advantage, is the craftsman qualified to design and fashion the highest quality of jewelry.

Such an artist-craftsman is Irena Brynner.† Heir through one parent to the most exacting traditions of Swiss workmanship, she is heir through the other to the age-old flair for exotic jewelry common to the Mongol. From Manchuria to San Francisco and thence to New York, Miss Brynner brought a refined old-world sensitivity to precious metals and gems. Turning to the art of jewelry design, she cultivated that delicate touch and infinite capacity for taking pains without which the small-scale operations of the jeweler's art would have been impossible. She developed the power to grasp essentials and in their favor to design with simplicity and directness.

Such a seemingly effortless creation as the finger-ring illustrated (3.15b) bears witness to these qualities of artistry. Miss Brynner found her motivation for the work in an exceptionally large and perfectly formed black pearl, rare product of the oysters in the Gulf of California. She felt that the soft luster of the orb called for abandonment of glittering gold, usually employed by her for gem settings, in favor of the more gently gleaming platinum—even as the pearl's rarity seemed to demand the special security of setting which the immensely harder metal would afford.

The craftsman heated the platinum until it was malleable. She shaped it into a narrow band with tapering ends. She twisted it into a double loop just large enough to fit the average size of a lady's middle finger. She drew its ends securely down around the pearl as though they

* These evaluative terms are used by Fred Farr, himself a jewelry designer, in an article on jewelry in *Collier's Encyclopedia* (New York: P. F. Collier & Son, 1954), Vol. XI, p. 402.

† Further works, accompanied by a brief biographical account of Irena Brynner, are reproduced in *Craft Horizons*, Vol. XVI, No. 5 (September–October, 1956), p. 27. For jewelry design see also Marianne Ostier, *Jewels and the Woman: the Romance, Magic and Art of Feminine Adornment* (New York: Horizon Press, 1958).

were well-manicured fingers holding the pearl to view. As a final note of emphasis, she set into the platinum bands to either side of the pearl two diamonds the sparkling whiteness of which called attention to the pearl's resonant darkness.

WORKING WITH LEATHER AND WOOD

Natural forces make jeweler's gems and precious metals out of the chemicals of the earth, break "mother rock" down into potter's clay and glass. Oysters make jeweler's pearls out of grains of foreign matter. Plants grow fibers and animals grow hair for the yarns of weavers. These time-honored contributions of nature to the crafts now tend to be superseded for industry at least by man-made synthetics. But there are two materials which nature gives the artist to work with, materials which plastics may never quite succeed in replacing even for industry: the skins of animals and the trunks of trees.

Leather comes into use by everyone, whether as shoes, pocketbooks, gloves, and suitcases in an industrial society, or as shields, quivers, jackets, and sails in a primitive society. Wood comes into similar use, if not in the construction of the house, then at least in the composition of its furnishings, its utensils and tools. Any use of either material calls for a certain source and a certain manner of preparation—from the patent leather made of cowhide for the traveling bag to the chrome-tanned, emery-buffed, and glass-polished leather made of pigskin or kidskin for dress gloves; from the paper-thin cedar of the boat-racing shell to the hand-fitting, moisture-absorbing walnut handle of the meat-cleaver.

An artist working with leather has its natural texture to exploit, a texture akin to partially dried clay (clay which we have already noted the potter calling "leather-hard"), one which he can actually heighten by running the leather through cork-covered rollers. The leatherworker finds that leather cuts easily and accurately with a sharp knife, that it sews together readily with leather thongs and makes for expressive effects of joining. He learns that beyond such qualities leather when wet can

assume the permanent impress of blunted modeling tools, lending itself to ornamental patterns. So receptive is leather, especially calfskin, to this modeling treatment that the craftsman may be tempted to overdo the ornamentation and even to create tricky pictorial effects in it. But recognition of the utilitarian nature of the craft and of the properly subordinate nature of any embellishment keeps the leather-tooler's work within the bounds of enhancement of the object's form and purpose. In the leather binding of a book, for example, the craftsman under such discipline may impress with modeling tools nothing but the title and the name of the author in plain lettering and some highly simplified abstract motive symbolizing the nature of the contents.

The woodworker has a material of wide diversity to work with, because wood is an organic material and an organic material varies as life varies, even from cell to cell. Wood is composed of tubelike cells of cellulose bound together by lignin, cells that differ in their organization not only from one kind of tree to another, but from one tree to the next of the same kind and even from one block of wood to another cut from the same trunk. The block varies in itself, moreover, owing to its affinity for water and its continual shrinking or expanding in accordance with the humidity of the atmosphere. The cellular structure accounts for the grain of the wood and the grain in turn for its strength, its texture, and its pattern. Wood is very responsive when worked along the grain, but less so when worked across the grain or in shear against it. Patterns and their accompanying textures vary with the kind of wood and the manner of cutting it, ranging from knotty pine and bird's-eye maple to peanut-figured Japanese ash, flake-figured lacewood, and stripe-figured zebrawood.

Wood can be whittled with a pocket-knife, cut with a saw, drilled with a brace and bit, smoothed with a plane. It can be turned—fashioned with a chisel while rotating on a lathe. It can be joined—one piece cut in a certain way to hook snugly in with another when the two are pushed together and fastened. It can be finished—sanded, its pores filled and stained, and its surface waxed, oiled, shellacked, or varnished, either to accentuate the grain or to conceal it.

What the artist does with wood to be turned, for example, depends on his understanding of the nature of the particular wood and his ability to alter its form creatively in process as hidden qualities come to light. He chooses the wood to begin with because he knows that it will work well for the utilitarian object which he has in mind. But he knows that the turning of the block of wood while it rotates on the machine-driven lathe is always a new adventure, calling for alertness to unsuspected deviations, unflagging sensitivity to expressive values, just as throwing clay on the kick-wheel demands of the potter.

Take Bob Stocksdale, San Francisco woodturner, for example, and the set of salad bowl, serving paddles, and salt and pepper shakers which he turned for use as tableware (1.8a). Salad served with the set would seem to the user more or less palatable by association of sight of the bowl and its accessories with the sight and taste of the food, and Stocksdale knew that for such a stimulus no ordinary oak or walnut would do. Much, therefore, as Irena Brynner chose a rare pearl around which to fashion her finger-ring, the woodturner hunted down a block of Guatemala mahogany exceptionally beautiful in color and grain.

On his workshop bandsaw Stocksdale sawed from this block of mahogany a smaller block, or blank, for each object in the set: the bowl, the serving paddle for each hand, the salt cellar, the pepper shaker. For the bowl and each of the shakers the craftsman mounted the blank on his lathe, screwing one side of the face-plate to the top of the blank and the other side to the lathe. While rotating the blank on the lathe, he shaved the outside gradually away with his chisel, subtracting surplus material until the shape of the mass approached completion. After turning the bottom flat to guarantee secure stance on the dinner table, the artist removed the blank from the lathe and drilled a hole carefully down through it to the exact point of the inside surface of the foot, to guarantee that he would not make the foot too thin.

Stocksdale then screwed the foot of the blank to the faceplate, attached it to the lathe, and proceeded to rough out by turning with a large chisel the hollow interior of the piece. Checking the thickness carefully with calipers and removing any unevenness detected, the craftsman then completed the turning both inside and out with increasingly fine abrasives. He took the vessel off the lathe, plugged the screw holes in its foot, and set the piece in an overnight bath of mineral oil to finish and reduce the absorptive power of the wood. He carved the paddles by hand and subjected them to the same treatment with oil. Only then was he ready to polish each of the five pieces and send them out into the world, confident that they would meet every functional and esthetic demand made on them.

The woodturner exercised the self-restraint of the master craftsman in subordinating his own work, the form in its symmetry and smoothness, to the qualities of the wood itself, its deep-toned color and its dipping, swirling run of grain. He calculated that these qualities would further operate in a supplementary way, to emphasize by contrast of color and texture the salad to be served. He designed thus in anticipation of actual function, to permit display of food on the table at its tempting best.[6]

Designing and Making Furniture

Making vessels by the turning of wood is a craft closely akin to metalworking, glassworking, and ceramics. In spite of its dependence on the motor-driven lathe, it remains more than any of its relatives, perhaps, a traditional

[6] See Notes, page 295.

handicraft. Making furniture by the working of wood, on the other hand, exploits not only turning but every other technique as well, from whittling to joining and finishing. It exploits above all the art of joinery, a structural technique bringing the art of furniture design closer to that of architecture than to any other craft.

The craft of furniture-making has tended to survive to a considerable extent even in the factory. Machinery can saw up the posts and planks and process them for storage in quantity. All that it needs is a workman to feed it the proper wood. But only skilled craftsmen can join and fasten and finish the furniture units, even though these craftsmen are not the original designers. It is fitting, therefore, to start one's acquaintance with good furniture by a look into the craft.

As with works of any craft, the form of a piece of furniture is appreciated by actually trying it out and noting how the designer has called into play the elements of art and put to work the principles of art, to meet every functional and technical requirement. Of the three general classes of furniture—chest, table, chair—consider the chair as a case in point. A chair is made to sit in, but it must be designed beyond that for a particular kind of sitting. Some chairs are made for dining at a table, some for writing at a desk, some for lounging in a corner. The chair shown beside the fireplace in the rustic interior illustrated (4.1a) was made for dining. Since in dining one leans forward toward the plate at the table and supports oneself partly against the table's edge, one might require a mere bench or stool like that illustrated in the same room. Although backless seats are sometimes used for dining, as at picnics, they deny relaxation desirable for the process. When seated in an erect position for eating, one's back should be supported, one's arms and head left free, one's thighs supported comfortably from underneath, and one's feet planted securely on the floor. A person of average height has certain proportions and certain habitual attitudes which he shares with his fellows. Ascertain what they are,

apply them to the design of the chair as related to the design of the table, and you have fixed the height of the seat above the floor, its other dimensions, and the angle by which its back should be inclined. Trial would show, in fact, that this particular piece, called the Windsor chair, reached its shape by just some such procedure.*

As a work of art, at the same time, this chair evolved no more automatically out of its program of requirements than did a pot, a woven fabric, or a wooden salad bowl. It needed shaping by the artist. Only expressive ordering, no mechanical matching of a shape with a demand, can account for the stable splaying (spreading) and bracing of the legs, the saddle-like carving of the seat to fit the contours of the body in a sitting position, the hospitable rise and curve of the back to accommodate the shoulders. The chair not only lends itself to easy grasping and moving; it affirms its qualities.

Observe how expression of function merges with expression of materials used and processes employed. Wood for legs, seat, and back is thick where support is required, tapering where mortise-and-tenon joints must come, and skeletonlike in its combined openness and strength. The wood is warm to the touch, lightly animated to the eye. It is also frankly revealed for what it is: hickory, tough and resilient, to form the legs and back; pine, light and easily carved with the grain, to constitute the seat.

So also with the way the wood was worked. The chair was made two hundred years ago for such early New England interiors as that shown by a local wheelwright who could turn on his hand-driven lathe the legs, the stretchers, and the spindles of the chair as easily as he could the spokes of a wheel. The anonymous craftsman creating this Windsor type of chair was a true artist-craftsman with pride in his materials and his ability to carve and join them functionally.

* J. Gordon Roe, *Windsor Chairs* (London: Phoenix House, 1953).

3.16. Charles Eames (1907–   ): Dining chair. Designed 1948. Molded plywood. Manufactured by Evans Products Company, Detroit, Mich.; distributed by Herman Miller Furniture Company, Zeeland, Mich.

The eighteenth-century wheelwright also designed his chair, as any artist will, for his own time, its life and methods of production. A saddle seat, a spindle back, and splayed legs are elements which belong to an earlier day, and the chair into which they fit is properly today nothing but a museum piece. For all of the functional efficiency of these features in Colonial New England, they become in the accelerated tempo of the mid-twentieth-century household only awkward relics. In the hurry of modern life, one trips over the spreading legs, cracks the seat, springs the joints, dislodges the spindles. Industrial manufacture,

moreover, even though with assembly by skilled workmen, cannot replace the craftsman who chose his wood with care, shaped the pieces individually, and joined them delicately.

The Windsor chair belonged to the life of the early-eighteenth-century villager of New England for whom it was fashioned, but the principles governing its creation are as valid today as they ever were.* Contemporary counterpart in adherence to such principles of design is the dining chair created by Charles Eames during the nineteen-forties (3.16). For

* George Nelson, ed., *Chairs* ("Interiors Library," 2; New York: Whitney Publications, 1953).

this chair, it is significant to note, an industrial process had to be adapted and developed along totally different lines from the techniques of the furniture craftsman: a process of plywood manufacturing and molding. The designer sought to evolve a seating surface of utmost comfort, a structure of lightness, strength and grace, and an accessory as intimately a part of contemporary life as the airplane and the motor car. The resulting form proved daringly novel, but not because the artist proceeded self-consciously to make something "original." He simply followed a step-by-step procedure that the "give-and-take" of creating the prototype determined. The outcome was a chair belonging as inseparably to the world of modern life as the Windsor chair belonged to the world of Colonial New England.

Plywood composes the Eames chair—a material the development and application of which we owe to machine manufacture. When a log is steamed, it can be sawed not only into the usual cross-section boards, with the diameter of the tree delimiting the width of the pieces, but also into continuous sheets unrolling around the log as the shaving proceeds. Thin sheets so produced have no strength to support a weight parallel with the grain of the wood, but surprising resistance in the opposite direction. Glue one sheet of such laminated wood against another with the grain of each running at right angles, add further sheets, or plies, in similarly alternating layers, and you have fashioned a structural material as flexible as it is strong, and, when well bonded, proof against warping.

When plywood is manufactured in this way, it can be treated again with steam and molded to bend in only one direction, as at the juncture of chair-back with seat. The resulting chair can be sat in but not with comfort, because the flat planes fail to conform to and support the contours of the body. Eames attacked this problem, confident that a solution could be found, but it took many years to find it, with discouragements along the way which would have induced the average designer to give up the project.

Since plywood refuses to stretch in forming, unlike metal, the artist had to resort to a painfully laborious process to achieve the compound-curving shapes required, a process involving the actual fabrication of the plywood by hand. Over the mold he laid thin and individually precut strips of wood veneer this way and that to adjust to the curves, and gradually built the plywood up to the needed thickness. He found that he could make a comfortable plywood chair in this way, but the process by which he did it was slower and more laborious than the building of a conventional chair by established techniques of woodworking. It was totally unfit for industrial production.

Prolonged trial and error brought into collaboration not only the craftsman's artist-wife but numerous other designers and technicians. With their assistance he tried cutting slots here and there to give some slack in bending. This device eliminated the need for laminating piece by piece. But the unitary seat-and-back which he was trying to achieve by molding had finally to be abandoned, because molds could not be made deep enough to cast seat and back in one process. He developed instead of it a "petal" type model—one in which seat and back, as well as legs, were each molded separately and then joined to each other by sponge-rubber shock mounts borrowed from airplane manufacture. Once the plywood was treated with a resin to integrate finish with material, Eames's molded plywood chair was at last ready for industrial production—as smoothly functioning, flexible, and self-protecting a form as the body of the human being using it. Only the problem of costs in production still eluded the designer. Molding plywood remained the most expensive of all the molding processes. For low-cost, large-scale chair-production Charles Eames ultimately turned to plastics—losing the vitality of effect of the natural color and grain of plywood in favor of efficient and economical production of molded Fiberglas chairs with wire-cage bases attached.[7]

[7] See Notes, page 295.

SUMMARY

The field occupied by the crafts and their industrial descendants is enormously vast and complicated, and it keeps changing all the time. Some of the crafts are the oldest arts on earth, while some branches of industrial design constitute the newest. Some crafts, like weaving and jewelry design, manage to hold their own against any attempt of industry to take over. Others, like pottery, glassworking, metalworking, and woodworking, manage to keep going along lines of their own, parallel to design for mass production under their descendants in industry. Some arts of industry, like automobile design, acknowledge ancestors among the crafts, though with little real credit. Other arts of industry having likewise to do with the molding of plastics, like telephone design, own no ancestors whatever but forge out by themselves into fresh territory.

Whatever the case, all crafts share in common with the arts of industry their designing for use apart from the forms of their products. They share in a design for use out of which the artist derives much motivation for the forms themselves. They share also in a concern for the nature of materials, whether natural or synthetic, and for the processes involved, whether individual or collective, as corresponding sources of forms.

Expanding industry surrounds us closer and closer with its products, forces us willy-nilly to judge them as works of art. Recognizing the elements universally composing works of art —point, line, plane, texture, color, mass, space —and the principles governing their composition—balance, emphasis, rhythm, proportion, and the like—we sharpen our faculties continually as we select and put to work objects of daily use which it is the job of both the craftsman and the industrial designer to refine and fashion.

RECOMMENDED READINGS

Read, Herbert. *Art and Industry: the Principles of Industrial Design*. New York: Horizon Press, 1954. 1st ed., London: Faber & Faber, 1934.
> Published in England, this was the first definitive book on industrial design of the twentieth century. Short but penetrating and lucid in criticism, the study is abundantly illustrated. Herbert Read here lays foundations for an esthetics of industrial design.

Van Doren, Harold. *Industrial Design: a Practical Guide*. New York: McGraw-Hill, 1940. 2d ed., 1954.
> Harold Van Doren was one of the first industrial designers to practice in the United States, and his book has performed something of the same role in the New World as Read's book did in England. Van Doren addresses himself to the student considering industrial design as a spe-

cialty. He offers helpful pointers on composition and technique, even though his illustrations seem as time passes to be more and more "dated."

Lippincott, J. Gordon. *Design For Business*. Chicago: Paul Theobald, 1947.

Although as an industrial designer Lippincott addresses his book primarily to the industrialist, he offers anybody a challenging piece of reading. He sees the field with a fresh perspective and argues for current concepts of industry which are condemned by most writers on art, including the present author. Declaring that the sole reason for the existence of industrial design is "to keep merchandise moving," he defends any practice effective in doing so: "styling" for new annual models, designing for speedy obsolescence, using women's fashions of dress as the determinant for all stylistic changes, calculating through intensive advertising to foster popular demand for the newest product.

Ritchie, Andrew C., *et al. Good Design Is Your Business*. Buffalo, N. Y.: The Buffalo Fine Arts Academy, Albright Art Gallery, 1947.

The catalogue of an exhibition prompting preparation of an Index of Industrial Design from which were chosen for display only objects at once low in price and high in quality. Introductory articles were written by Walter Dorwin Teague, representing designers; Richard Marsh Bennett, representing educators; Edward S. Evans, Jr., representing manufacturers; and Charles P. Parkhurst, Jr., then the Albright Gallery's assistant curator in charge of the exhibition, representing consumers. Rapid changes in style render the products illustrated increasingly out of date, but critical analyses make the catalogue still a useful reference.

Kaufmann, Edgar, Jr. *What Is Modern Design?* "Introductory Series to the Modern Arts," 3. New York: The Museum of Modern Art, 1950.

Restricted in text and illustrations to home furnishings, this brief cataloguelike publication prepared by a staff member of the Museum of Modern Art lays down a set of precepts for evaluating industrial products as works of art. It goes on to compare in well-chosen illustrations and explanatory captions, often too cursory to be informative, objects grouped together under categories of use.

Gump, Richard. *Good Taste Costs No More*. Garden City, N. Y.: Doubleday, 1951.

A book addressed by a prominent art dealer of San Francisco to the average American consumer. Witty in style, it goes perhaps too far in its use of epithets and sarcasm to convert the typical antique collector to buying objects for their intrinsic artistic worth rather than for their rarity and novelty. A series of illustrations comparing objects similar in function and style, one superior in design to the other, and captions explaining the bases for judgment, make a feature nonetheless worth study.

Dreyfuss, Henry. *Designing for People*. New York: Simon & Schuster, 1955.

This highly personal, autobiographical account by an industrial designer covers more of the history of industrial design than any of its predecessors. Its attractive layout, with marginal notations and sketches reproduced in sepia, groupings of illustrations showing a great diversity of products in process of being designed and in actual use, and a text with easily readable type, makes the book itself a worthy example of industrial design.

Gallinger, Osma Couch. *The Joy of Hand Weaving: the Complete Step-by-Step Book of Weaving*. New York: D. Van Nostrand, 1952. Originally published, 1950, by Laurel Publishers, Scranton, Pa.

The art of weaving has many manuals on techniques to guide beginners as well as professionals. It has a few historical studies on textiles. But no one has written a book dealing with weaving from the appreciational point of view. Perhaps the author of this book comes nearest to qualifying, although she has written her text primarily for students following courses in weaving in the public schools. In extremely simple and clear English she coaches the beginner through initial projects carried out on an elementary cardboard frame to more advanced projects on increasingly complex looms.

Digby, George Wingfield. *The Work of the Modern Potter in England*. London: John Murray, 1952.

Pottery suffers almost as much as weaving from how-to-do-it books that neglect to establish a frame of reference for determining quality. Digby's study is a welcome exception. Owing much to Dora M. Billington, potter-author of the best previously published study, *The Art of the Potter* (London and New York: Oxford University Press, 1937), and to Bernard Leach, one of whose books is alluded to in a footnote for the present chapter, Digby ties his theory to the criticism of actual wares. He makes frequent quotations from, and references to, contemporary potters of England and Japan.

Plaut, James S. *Steuben Glass*. New York: H. Bittner, 1948.

Although the monograph deals with the products of a single firm, the emphasis upon glassware as art and upon the basis for judging it esthetically makes this publication superior to any other book on the subject. Affiliated with the Corning Glass Works of the same city, Corning, New York, Steuben specializes in glassware as art and enlists the services of such designers as Sidney Waugh, one of whose works has been dealt with in the present text. Waugh has himself written about his art, *The Making of Fine Glass* (New York: Dodd, Mead, 1947).

CHAPTER 4

4.1. THE FAIRBANKS HOUSE. a. Jonathan Fairbanks (*c.* 1595–1668): Fairbanks house, Dedham, Mass., interior of original unit. Begun 1636. To right of fireplace, Windsor chair, of type originating *c.* 1725. Courtesy of the Fairbanks Family in America, Inc. b. Jonathan Fairbanks and descendants: Fairbanks house, exterior from southeast. East (nearest) section added 1648 for oldest son and his bride; west (farthest) section added 1654 for hired help. Courtesy of the Fairbanks Family in America, Inc.

Architecture

THE NATURE OF A BUILDING

THE CRAFTS and their industrial-art descendants meet on common ground when they enter into the art of interior design. Indeed, without the contributions made by each craft or branch of industrial design to the others, the art of interior design could not function at all. The practice of designing interiors once consisted (and still does in some quarters) of treating an existing room as though it were a stage. This practice amounts to the arrangement of odds and ends of furnishings for their decorative effect alone. Called interior decoration, such practice operates as a branch of decorative design but a branch that suffers impoverishment because of its divorce from construction.

Interior design is different. It exists to complete and emphasize the structural composition of a room or, preferably, of the whole interior of a building. It cannot be dismissed as a matter of wrappings and trimmings, for it functions as structural as well as decorative design. Interior design is, in fact, an inseparable part of the mother art of architecture.

Architecture Defined

Architecture is the art of organizing space for shelter. Space for shelter implies a roof. A roof requires support—posts, piers, columns, arches, walls. If the space has to be enclosed, as most often it does, then shelter demands walls. A floor is added—above the damp or dusty ground—and the ingredients essential to a building are all present.

A building which is no more than a shelter cannot automatically qualify as a work of art.

Structure becomes architecture only when created by those sensitive to its possibilities of visual appeal. It becomes art only when created by those responsive to the proportioning of a wall, the relating of one wall to another, the interaction of one mass or space with another, the coordination of parts within a whole.

We found the crafts exacting enough, but architecture is immensely more so. The craftsman weaving a curtain, throwing a pot, or blowing a bottle can make a mistake, and the chances are that he will cause no serious damage. But let the architect make a mistake and anything can happen. He and his client and the general contractor may all go into bankruptcy. They may have to answer for manslaughter if the building collapses while people are in it. They may be sued for recovery of damages, from rain-water due to leaky construction or from fire due to faulty wiring.

Like the industrial designer, the architect works on a characteristically big scale. He participates in enterprises involving heavy investments. He faces responsibilities to large numbers of people and sometimes even to a whole society. He tries to keep the multitudes of participants in his creation working smoothly together—from the associated architects and landscapers and draftsmen at his office to the members of the building committee, the municipal authorities and lending agencies, the contractors and subcontractors, the unionized technicians and construction workers, and even the consultants on regional and urban planning boards.

The art of building is at the same time closely akin to the crafts. Since its productions have uses apart from actual appearances, it operates like the crafts as a utilitarian art. Since its productions are exceptionally durable, it may play a historical role, portraying the life of people. Like pottery especially, it deals with walls and the volumes of open space embraced by walls. In our first chapter we noted an ancient Chinese philosopher pointing out that walls exist for the sake of the space contained by them. Empty space, or interval, does indeed give a building its reason for existence, just as empty space gives a pot its reason for existence. The architect exploits volumes of open space. He employs wall areas, pier masses, and other solids about the structure simply to advance both the utility and the visual effectiveness of the intervals inside. He transforms these intervals into dramatizations of space as excitingly a fulfillment of Taoism's "doctrine of the void" as man has ever achieved. From the narrowly compressed chambers of Egyptian tomb or Hindu temple to the expansive openings-out of Persian palace or Gothic cathedral, the existence of intervals within walls makes a construction a building and gives it character. Interval-events are the stuff out of which true architecture is made.[1]

Conditions of Architecture as Sources of Design

Whatever spatial composition may be required by a building, the architect designing it must always consider certain conditions. He will have to face and find ways of dealing with five basic limitations: site, function, climate, materials, and methods of construction. Rather than enduring these restrictions as strait jackets to design, however, he will actually work with them as opportunities in disguise, a fertile soil out of which to make his forms grow and mature.

The architect should, and sometimes does, have a hand in selecting the site.[2] He considers the type of building called for and seeks a site best fitted for it, whether sloping or level, whether forested or cleared, whether adjacent to river, railroad, or highway or sequestered, whether favored or hindered by neighboring structures. For the site selected he determines areas, contours, and surroundings. He ascertains what natural growth exists on the site and decides what can be utilized and what needs to be destroyed. He digs a test-pit to find out what the subsoil is like and how deep he needs to sink his foundations. He tracks down the locally accessible utilities and figures how best to connect his building with them.

Every location will make a difference in the forms of building, in the materials used, and in the methods of construction. The site has ordinarily required special designing if the building is to take on architectural character. Copybook plans and patterns, offered on the assumption that any old site will do, have usually brought a builder to grief, for some local feature or other always seems ready then to work against the accommodation of the structure to the ground on which it is built.

The architect must match knowledge of the site with knowledge of those for whom he is designing. He draws up a program of requirements and incorporates in his subsequent design every possible adaptation to the clients, the potential users of his building. He draws up this program only after repeated consultations with everyone concerned, seeking continually to educate the clients to recognize and define their tastes and prejudices, their habitual movements and characteristic states of mind.

Limitations of function seem obvious. Only too often, however, they have been ignored in favor of some imposing or novel effect. A good building is not designed from preconceived ideas of its exterior appearance. It is not started with a choice of style thought "nice," then tailored to fit that style. It is started with a program of requirements which causes the plan to grow meaningfully, and the walls to rise from that plan with a surefooted grace of service.

[1] See Notes, page 295.
[2] See Notes, page 296.

Out of functionally motivated planning comes the particular quality or flavor of a building. The Greek temple [4.2], for instance, is small, for only priests were meant to enter it, while the populace stood outside. The Gothic cathedral [4.6], by contrast, had to be large enough for the congregation to witness the rites at the altar as the main feature of their worship. A good building does indeed look its part, declare its reason for existence.

Along with ascertaining the nature of the site and completing the program of requirements, the architect must take into account the climate. At what latitude does the site for the building lie, and consequently at what angle will the sun's rays fall in the course of each season and through the hours of each day? In what direction, then, should the windows of each room face in order to benefit from sunlight in winter and from shade in summer; in other words, where should each room be for proper heliotropic orientation (the position in relation to the sun's rays)? [3] What is the path of prevailing winds for each month of the year and what is their velocity? How can breezes be welcomed in summer and gales excluded in winter? What modifications will orientation for wind impose on orientation for sun?

What is the average precipitation for every month of the year; how many inches of rain and how many inches of snow? How many hours out of a possible total does the sun shine each year? What is the average temperature in the shade for each month of the year, and what humidity accompanies such temperature? How can heating and ventilation and drainage be best designed to assure maximum comfort under natural conditions? To what extent is the region subject to earthquakes, tornadoes, or hurricanes, and how can the structure be strengthened to withstand such onslaughts and ensure the safety of its occupants?

Where rainfall or snowfall is heavy, a sloping roof is needed. Where rainfall is slight, a flat roof is cheaper, and cooler, too, for no peak traps the heat of the sun. Window-arrangement, known as fenestration, is governed by climate. So also are thickness of walls and the materials out of which they are made. Where climate is mild and change in weather slight, as in portions of California, thin wooden partitions can be employed, interior space opened up, and rooms made to face on garden patios. Where climate is severe and changeable, as in New England, thick stone or concrete walls or walls containing heavy insulating material have to be provided, and interior spaces closed in more tightly.

Climate influences much about the shape and the materials of a building.* So does the culture nurtured by that climate. Any ancient city in Europe or Asia has an architecture which distinguishes it. The buildings of Heidelberg, for example, differ from the buildings of Venice or Barcelona, and the buildings of Kyoto differ from those of the northern Japanese city of Sapporo. Each community builds with the materials and according to the manner which time has shown to be right for its climate and its way of life. Each has developed out of reactions to its climate a definite architectural unity.

The architect must choose the materials of his building early in his preliminary investigations, because much of its character will depend on this choice.[4] He can do things with wood that he cannot do with stone, things with stone that he cannot do with brick or concrete. Since the perfection of the Bessemer openhearth process in the nineteenth century, the architect has also been able to work with steel; and with steel and its indispensable companion invention, the elevator, he has been able to send his building high into the air. He has been able to do with steel things undreamed of with other materials, to break with tradition in unprecedented fashion.

Learning to design with steel, the architect has become receptive to other new materials—glass, glass brick, reinforced concrete, concrete block, plywood, metal alloys, plastics. Dis-

---

* Jeffrey Ellis Aronin, *Climate and Architecture* (New York: Reinhold, 1953).
[4] See Notes, page 296.

[3] See Notes, p. 296.

covering new possibilities in their employment, he has been encouraged to take a fresh look at old materials and the ways in which local traditions of building have put them to work: various kinds of lumber in forested regions, for example, or of stone in rocky regions or of adobe and brick in desert regions. He has reconsidered the properties of such materials and put them to unexpected uses. He has found, by way of contrast to the impersonal synthetics of industrial production, a warming personality and a sense of belonging in materials which are natural to a region. By using them expressively, he has been able to relate a building to its site. With the regional effects thus defined, he has been able in turn to bring even the new synthetic materials into harmonious site-relationships.

The architect in reviewing possible materials very soon finds himself reflecting on how they can be used. He realizes the predilection of a particular material for a certain type of construction and the impetus of both material and construction toward certain expressive forms.

Let us consider the igloo of the Eskimo.[5] The Alaskan native constructs his igloo out of the material most abundantly at hand—the packed snow underfoot waiting to be sliced out and used in the form of cubical blocks. The Eskimo stands within a circular area destined to become his floor. While members of his family cut blocks of snow outside and hand the blocks across to him, he raises the wall around him spiralwise, each convolution smaller than the one before it until at length there remains overhead a single hole just large enough to juggle the last block of snow into, to serve as his "keystone," completing the dome. The Eskimo is then imprisoned in his own house until he cuts a small door through it at the base and crawls out. The igloo is not very strong at first, but alternate thawing under sunshine and freezing at night convert the dome of snow into a homogeneous ice-coated shell capable of withstanding the strongest gale and conserving every bit of heat from the whale-oil lamp which the Eskimo lights inside.

[5] See Notes, p. 296.

Types of Structural Support

The Eskimo's igloo, a hemispherical, self-supporting, stressed-skinlike structure, is a creation of the plastic technique which we noted in the preceding chapter as promising to revolutionize industrial design. In architecture before the twentieth century it was virtually unknown and it is still, even after mid-century, quite rare (4.18a and b). A "monolithic," monococcic, or shell type of construction, as it is variously called, this plastic process is based on the principle of the eggshell. We have only recently learned to apply this thermoplastic technique to materials other than snow, and even the Eskimo must abandon his igloo when heat from the summer sun finally melts it, forcing him to resort to the old familiar tectonic construction to build his summer hut, a skeletal-framed and sealskin-covered dwelling.

We could now design most buildings to employ this technique if only the construction industry were willing to change over to mass production of prefabricated structures and the public were willing to accept the product. We could utilize that integral molding process which we found the industrial designer perfecting for production of the Ericofon (3.3a and b); we need only allow flexibility in assemblage of standardized units to meet changes from one site to another, in orientation, insulation, view, and regional expression.

Inherent conservatism, however, exhibited by builders no less than by laymen, together with the unionized craftsman's fear of automation, stands in the way of new techniques of construction, and especially in the way of plastic techniques which might tend to supplant the tectonic. Such obstacles often oblige the architect to proceed as though he, too, were a handicraftsman. He concentrates on each individual structure by itself, even as the thrower concentrates on each pot and the jeweler on each article of adornment. He continues to design an edifice for erection as the craftsman did the Windsor chair— fashioning parts piece by piece and joining them by hand. And the consequence is that in an industrialized society with a growing population the production of buildings lags behind the need. The process is too slow for the modern tempo.

Even among the tectonic techniques, however, though they have been used for thousands of years, there is much to challenge the architect's creative powers. Using them, he has at his disposal two alternative methods of developing supports.

The two methods of developing architectural supports are akin to those in organic life which the biologist calls respectively the invertebrate and the vertebrate. Just as invertebrates are creatures with their skeletons on the outside (oysters, snails, crabs, and the like), so invertebrate buildings are structures with exterior skeletal supports. They may be plastically created, like an igloo, or tectonically built up brick by brick or stone by stone with load-carrying, roof-supporting walls. Again, just as vertebrates are creatures with their skeletons on the inside (human beings, birds, snakes, and the like), so vertebrate buildings are tectonically assembled with a skeletal support and an outside skin hung from the skeleton to protect both it and the interior through which it rises. The Gothic cathedral is a vertebrate structure of great apparent lightness. Its stone skeleton was developed with such engineering skill that the weightiness of the stone serves only to stress the openness by contrast.

Just as buildings may be classified according to type of support, so may they be classified according to method of spanning space. Open spaces are spanned tectonically either by the post-and-lintel method or by the arcuated method. The post-and-lintel method is still the most common. It consists simply in erecting uprights, or posts, and in laying beams, or lintels, across them. For this type of construction, wood serves better than stone; it imposes problems of downward pressure and static support so simple of solution that the architect's energies are largely freed for concentration on refinements of detail in the interests of balance, emphasis, rhythm, and proportion. The architect cannot provide a large interior space without interrupting it by additional walls or posts to keep the beams from breaking under the load that they must carry, or even, with stone lintels, under their own weight. He can span with a system of wooden brackets, called the truss, spaces larger than he can with unsupported wooden beams. But within the traditional post-and-lintel system he can span very broad spaces only with steel beams cast in such a way that one plane reinforces another and intersects with it to make a shape in section like that of the letter T, U, or I.

Another kind of post-and-lintel construction, however, offers the architect greater possibilities of openness. This is cantilever construction—the projection of a beam or other structural member from a wall or column, strong enough in itself and securely enough balanced or embedded to carry its own weight over open space and sometimes to bear a large additional load as well. Stone does not permit projection to any great extent, but wood has been used, in China and Japan, through systems of bracketing from walls, for extreme overhangs of roof [4.10]. And modern structural materials are even better adapted to cantilever construction. Thanks to the perfection of steel and ferroconcrete (concrete reinforced with steel beams and steel mesh), we no longer need to sit behind posts supporting balconies in a theater or a church, for huge balconies can now be cantilevered into auditoriums far out over the main-floor seats. An architect can now extend a ferroconcrete roof slab so far beyond the supporting posts or walls that it actually seems to float in mid-air (4.8a and b, 4.9).

The second class of construction for spanning space gives stone a chance to rival or surpass even the most daring of cantilevers, whether the cantilevers are made of wood in Oriental building or of ferroconcrete in contemporary. Based upon the arch and therefore called arcuated construction, it consists in placing a series of wedge-shaped blocks of stone (or a series of bricks) in such fashion that they lean from either side of an opening until they meet each other at the center in a keystone. The keystone serves to equalize the two opposite thrusts so that, if the supporting walls are thick enough or additional masonry is piled up as buttressing outside the arch, the stones forming the arch are held securely in position. By making the series of wedge-shaped stones describe a curve, the pull of gravity exerted on each stone and transferred to its neighbor, because of its wedge shape, to constitute a lateral or sideways thrust, can be carried in the same curving direction down into the supporting construction and through it to the ground. The fact that stone does not yield under pressure, but merely transmits pressure, makes it an ideal material for arcuated construction.

The round arch, sometimes called the Roman arch because the ancient Romans used it so extensively for their public buildings, amphitheaters, aqueducts, and bridges, is capable of supporting a heavy load especially when strengthened on top by concrete, a type of which the Romans knew how to mix and pour. But the builders of the Gothic cathedrals, innovators who fused engineering with architectural design, discovered that a pointed arch, one coming to a point at the keystone instead of rounding out through a circular curve, had greater resistance to downward pressure and hence greater power to bear loads. They used this pointed arch, therefore, to support walls of extreme height and to contribute so effectively to the apparent vertically upthrusting space that the arch of their invention became known as the Gothic arch (4.4a and b, 4.5).

Building from Within Outward

The process by which the form of a building evolves, out of the experience of erecting it or even of living in it while it is being erected, best evidences itself when architect, builder, and client are combined in one person. Such a combination was traditional in New England back in the early days of settlement, when Jonathan Fairbanks and his family came to make their home in the infant settlement of Dedham. A farmer-craftsman like his fellow migrants and the heir to a build-your-own-home tradition among the rural folk of England, Fairbanks at his arrival lost no time in erecting his house. He knew that he could not tarry, for winter came early in New England and his family's survival depended on the shelter that he could rear.

In the new and hostile environment, Fairbanks realized, the hearth would literally have to become the heart of family life. To its construction, therefore, he gave top priority, laying the brick masonry for it in the center of the area selected for the site and making the fireplace open to either side of the chimney so as to gain maximum heat for the two ground-floor rooms intended (4.1). Around this central nucleus he built the walls of the house, using heavy, square-cut timbers for the posts, beams, and braces of the post-and-lintel framework, and filling in between them sticks encased in rushes and mud (wattle and daub, or stud and mud, construction). To shed the heavy snows of winter, he built a steeply sloping roof above his two-room dwelling and counted on the garret space thus created to serve as additional sleeping quarters for his growing family.

If Jonathan Fairbanks had used straw (thatch) to cover his roof and then called his structure complete, he would have had a conventional English open-timber house—a frame house, that is, with the heavy skeletal framework showing on the outside. The severe climate and the lack of adequate straw, however, demanded modifications. Instead of thatch for roofing he was obliged to use shakes, large and heavy shingles split by hand from sections of a log, and over his open-timber wall to apply a newly invented type of veneer (coating) of boards overlapping featherwise, called clapboarding (4.1b).

Like the utensils fashioned by hand and hung in their appointed places about the fireplace, every brick, timber, shingle, nail had to be made individually and given its designated spot. Each minor unit, as precious to the builder as though it were endowed with a personality of its own, had to be joined to its neighbor with the utmost care and kept reassuringly visible as one moved about the house. Visible, tangible things made the settler feel secure. They formed his refuge against uncertainties outside, like the depths of the forest, the storms of winter, the wild beasts and wilder savages. The more closely and tightly he could press the things around himself and his family, the safer he felt, and was. Hence the compactness of the forms of his house, its small and infrequent openings, its firmly defined walls and sharpened angles of intersection.

As the family expanded in size, even the attic failed to accommodate the overflow. The older sons married, brought their brides to live under the same roof, and proceeded to rear families of their own. Lest the enclosing walls burst outward, additions had to be made. A lean-to was built against one of the sides. New units were erected to adjoin either end of the original structure, and their attics converted into full-fledged second stories through roofing with a newly invented roof of four slopes, called the gambrel. Growing piece by piece, each tight little part made to look as separate as it was, the house took on at the start and continued to embody a vital primitive quality.

The house which Jonathan Fairbanks constructed for his family used the post-and-lintel form to which the wooden frame is naturally adapted. Such was the restraining effect of New England Colonial life, however, that not for a hundred years or so after the completion of the original nucleus of the Fairbanks House did house-builders get around to ornamenting more than an occasional beam-end. As long as the house could be augmented in any direction by a simple process of addition, little time was spent in worrying about the proportions of a wall or the ornamental accent of a window, a door, or the peak of the roof.

When the prosperity of New England life in the eighteenth century led to a growing demand for the enrichment of the forms of the dwelling, builders found the source for their motives in a post-and-lintel architecture of sophisticated embellishment whose ultimate origins could be traced from its adoption by English aristocrats to the temple-builders of ancient Greece. Under this influence New England builders sought to treat their wood as though it were stone, because the Greek models were themselves of stone. The anomaly of the situation lay in the fact that the Greek originals —in stone—had in turn been developed from wooden-frame prototypes.

BUILDING FOR RELIGION

Abode for a Patron Goddess: Ancient Greece

The religion of the ancient Greeks was responsible for this translation from one material into another. On supposed visits to a town in ancient Greece, the patron deity of the community was thought to need lodging. A mansion was required for this god, appropriately bigger and better than even the local ruler's dwelling, and to it as to the king's palace people were expected to come to pay their respects, to make offerings, or to plea for favors. They were not, however, expected to partake of any ceremony in the house of the deity. While they waited for the priests to open the door, they needed shelter from the sun. It was natural to extend the roof beyond the walls, supporting it on posts to form a porch at either end of the building and eventually all around it (4.2, 4.3b).

The temple was still not quite what it ought to be. Man was mortal; his house could well be a temporary affair of mud. But a god lived forever, and his house needed to be permanent. Hence the shift early in the history of Greek temple-building from wooden to stone construction (a shift which the exhaustion of the forests also prompted); hence also, thanks to religious conservatism, the fashioning of the stone in forms natural to the old construction in wood. The Greeks lived much in the open air; their climate encouraged outdoor life; and the exterior appearance of their temple came inevitably to mean more to them than the inte-

4.2. THE GREEK TEMPLE. Phidias (500?–432 B.C.), designer; Ictinus and Callicrates, architects: Parthenon, Acropolis, Athens, as seen from the Propylaea (entrance portico for the Acropolis). c. 447–432 B.C. Pentelic marble. G. E. Kidder Smith photograph.

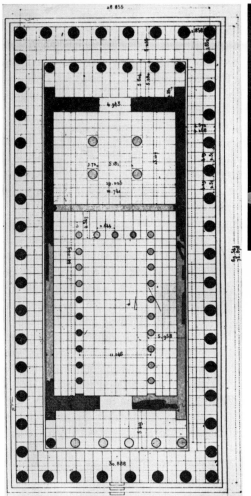

4.3. THE GREEK TEMPLE. a. Plan of the Parthenon. From Pierre Chabat, *Fragments d'Architecture* (Paris: A. Morel, 1868), pl. IV. b. Model of the Parthenon, restored, as seen from the northeast, looking toward main entrance. Courtesy of Metropolitan Museum of Art, New York. c. The Greek orders. 1. Doric order (Parthenon); 2. Ionic order (Erechtheum); 3. Corinthian order (Choragic monument of Lysicrates). From B. Heathcote Statham (Hugh Braun, rev.), *A History of Architecture* (New York: B. T. Batsford, 1950; 1st ed., 1912), fig. 56, p. 48.

rior. The further they refined the proportions and the details of this exterior, the more they thought to honor their god. Owing to the fact that stone lent itself to such refinement, especially a fine-textured marble quarried on Mt. Pentelicus and thus called Pentelic marble, the Greeks of Athens preferred this material above all for their temple-building. Thanks to the responsiveness of Pentelic marble to subtleties of finish, the Athenians were able to bring to its ultimate refinement of mass and detail the temple which is now about to be examined.

The Parthenon was, to a peculiar degree, the work of the community. Pericles, ruler of Athens, sponsored its building, begun in 447 B.C., as his favorite project. Phidias, leading sculptor of Athens, acted as master designer and supervisor of construction. Ictinus and Callicrates, leading architects of Athens, collaborated in designing its architectural details. And large numbers of marble workers worked for fifteen years to bring it to completion.

Rising on its sacred rock, the Acropolis, high above the city which the goddess Athena Parthenos protected, the Parthenon became the manifestation of civic pride and imperial ambition, expression of a common objective and a common tradition of building. Since absolute formal clarity of form was demanded of it in keeping with the classic ideal, the temple had to be built according to a single predetermined design, individual artists had to control the entire progress of the work, and the work had to be finished within a single generation. So much did the unity of the whole depend upon adherence to the master design that styles of later times could not be incorporated without impairing the classic effect.

The procedure followed in building was the direct opposite of that which we have traced in the construction of the Fairbanks House. Instead of building outward piece by piece from the central chimney, adding a unit whenever a later need prompted, the Parthenon was formed so that greatest emphasis could be placed upon the exterior, with its effect of noble repose derived from the ordered relating of one solid element to another as the work proceeded. Since, as we have noted, only priests entered the temple while the townsfolk stood outside, the main thing was the exterior effect. Unified and self-contained, the temple was built to dominate the rock at its highest eminence, withdrawn from the natural landscape and the workaday world below it. Little did it matter that the entrance be hidden by a row of columns, and refinements restricted to the exterior. Such peculiarities were the outcome of selecting certain things to emphasize at the expense of others.

This pagan temple of Athens may have been the abstraction of a wooden prototype, but the response to the marble used in it led to a building unlike anything man has created out of wood alone. The structure seems literally to pulsate with the thousands of nuances possible only to stone.* So sensitively were the visible elements adjusted to delight the eye that no straight line was allowed to show, lest it seem to sag and lack vitality. Nor was any obviously bulging curve permitted to occur anywhere in the building, lest it seem to break the Greek rule of "nothing in excess." Maximum richness is thus packed into the simplest of structural forms.

Since the exterior is a singularly unified mass, with each side subordinate to the ends and the east end dominant over the west, and since its component elements build up to a climax at the gable (that triangular piece of wall under the sides of the ridged roof), a brief description of the east end will serve to indicate how parts were everywhere put together (4.2, 4.3b and c1). The initial statement is one of bold contrast—columns upthrust from a multitiered foundation. Grooves called flutings ac-

* The lengths to which the builders of the Parthenon went in elaborating subtle refinements of proportion and curvature are followed minutely by William Henry Goodyear, *Greek Refinements* (New Haven: Yale University Press, 1912). For scholarly treatment of the whole of ancient Greek building, see A. W. Lawrence, *Greek Architecture* (Baltimore: Penguin, 1957). An earlier account written in the light of Greek culture in general is that by Rhys Carpenter, *The Esthetic Basis of Greek Art of the Fifth and Fourth Centuries*, B.C. (New York: Longmans, Green, 1921).

centuate the vertical supports and make them look less bulky, but the capitals on the tops of the columns make a transition to the repeated horizontals of the marble cross-pieces above. These cross-pieces consist of three layers of stone: the architrave, the frieze, and, topmost, the cornice. The frieze is divided up into two alternating units: fluted slabs, triglyphs, above each column, to recall the ends of beams in the old wooden construction; and slabs called metopes, designed to plug the gaps between the fluted slabs, and sometimes, as here, carved in relief. The cornice overhangs the other cross-pieces protectively and provides the base of a triangle completed by the slopes of the roof. The area within this triangle is called the pediment, a space here filled with sculpture. Terracotta ornaments on the roof give final echo to the more broken forms below and a relaxing touch to the severely compact self-containment of the composition.

Suggestive of the nature of the classic ideal is the name "orders" by which the styles of Greek architecture are known. Three such orders are to be distinguished: Doric, Ionic, and Corinthian; and they are distinguished by reference particularly to the columns of a given building. In the Parthenon, which exemplifies the Doric order at its best (4.2 and 4.3a, b and c1), the columns are sturdy, simply tectonic and structurally articulate. Each column sits directly on the topmost layer of the stone foundation; it has no base. Its flutings, originally cut drum by drum (block by block, that is) on the ground, so skilfully that when the drums were assembled they matched up perfectly, were made to meet each other in a sharp, vertically running edge. The fact that these flutings seem so uniform in the shadows that they cast, in spite of the tapering of the columns toward the top, is due to the extremely gradual reduction in the depth of the groove as the carver proceeded upward from one drum to the next.

In the Doric order the column culminates in a capital designed, as any capital was, to serve a dual function: structurally, to provide a wider bearing on which to lay the lintel without

having to sacrifice floor area by having a bulk of column that would otherwise have been necessary; and visually, to help the eye make a graceful transition from the vertical movement of the column to the horizontal movement of the lintel. The Doric capital rises above a horizontal groove at the top of the column to form two simple, clearly defined parts: a cushionlike block curving outward from the column, and a flat bearing-slab on top. The Doric frieze above the lintel, another distinguishing feature of the order, we have already described as consisting of alternate fluted blocks and filling slabs.

The Doric order was named after the Dorians, a branch of the Greek peoples originally settling on the mainland of Greece. It composed a vigorously masculine style showing clearly its translation into stone from the earlier wooden construction prevailing when forests abounded. It was the manner of expression of a ruggedly vigorous civilization far removed as yet from any over-ripe and overly sophisticated stage.

The Ionic order was named after the Ionians, a branch of the Greek peoples originally settling on the islands of the Aegean Sea and the coasts of Asia Minor. It composed a gracefully slenderized, feminine style reflecting clearly the architecture of the Ionians' neighbors, the space-loving, ornament-affecting Persians. Its columns (4.3c2) had ornate bases and flutings that met each other not in sharp edges but in flat vertical strips. Its capitals had volutes (spiral motives) which balanced each other around a curving cushion block (possibly originating in the rams' horns once hung at the ends of columns as trophies of the chase). Its frieze had no alternating members like the Doric frieze but either a plain marble surface or one sculptured in continuous relief.

The Corinthian order was named after its supposed originators, the people of the seaport of Corinth on the Greek mainland. It was a more florid version of the Ionic order, reflecting the taste of a cosmopolitan and luxury-loving trade center. Its columns (4.3c3) had even more ornate bases than the Ionic but the same kind of flutings. Its capitals had smaller volutes than the Ionic, dwarfed in scale by a series of outward-curving leaves carved more or less imitatively from the acanthus, an indigenous plant growing abundantly in the area.

Whatever the order in ancient Greek architecture, it was applied mostly to temples and public buildings and considered too expensive or vainglorious for mere dwellings. The Romans had no compunctions in this regard. They used the Greek orders freely; they magnified and elaborated on these orders and employed them indiscriminately for palaces and mansions as well as for temples and public buildings. Peoples of Europe and the Near East continued through the Middle Ages and the Renaissance to use the Greek classic orders more decoratively than structurally, and from the Renaissance almost until today to use them as decorative symbols.

Later modifications and perversions fail, however, to dim the glory of achievement of the builders of the Parthenon. In employing the Doric, simplest of the three orders, they recognized the legitimate sources of form in site, function, climate, material, and structural procedure. They did so in spite of the fact that they were following a post-and-lintel construction translated from wood into marble; in spite of the fact, again, that they were concentrating on the exterior to the neglect of the interior, and leaving the interior a mere shadowy recess for the gods and priests.

A House of God for Communal Worship: Medieval Europe

A goddess's abode perpetuated in marble can function as long as her worship in the temple needs to be offered only by priests in private. A gabled post-and-lintel structure affords all of the interior space needed. A house for deity that requires an assembly hall for congregational worship, as does the Christian church, is a different matter, and the prolonged struggles to solve the problems of erecting and maintaining it make an instructive chapter in the history of architecture.

Solution to these problems was finally reached at the end of the Middle Ages in the French Gothic cathedral (4.5, 4.6). As the seat of a bishopric (its name comes from *cathedra*, Latin for "bishop's seat"), the cathedral had to be big enough to accommodate at Mass even greater numbers of worshipers and officiating clergy than attended an ordinary church. When fire destroyed it, as often happened in medieval Europe, the loss was severe. How could one design at once a commodious house of worship and a fire-resistant structure? Stone masonry construction like that employed in building the Parthenon would solve the second problem. But stone masonry construction calls for walls thick enough to bear the weight of the building, and windows small enough not to weaken the supporting power of the walls. If the ceiling and roof are of wood, the building is subject to the hazards of fire, but a ceiling composed of stone beams must, as we have noted, have a very limited span if the stone is not to break under its own weight. An interior spanned by stone lintels, therefore, would have to be dark and cramped, defeating the very purpose of the Christian Mass as a sacrament performed by the priest in full view of his assembled parishioners.

Arches were used in Christian church-building from the very beginning, but only in minor capacities, the larger spaces being spanned in wood by the post-and-lintel method inherited from the Greeks. In France, however, losses from fires induced the medieval cathedral builders to abandon the post-and-lintel method in favor of the arcuated. The use of the arch and its extension as a tunnel, or barrel, vault was a better choice than the combination of techniques, since through it broader interiors were possible. But the tunnel vault still fell short of a satisfactory solution because it required even thicker walls and fewer and smaller windows than ordinary construction demanded. The source of the difficulty lay in what the Hindus had remarked concerning the Moslems' use of arcuated construction, that "the arch never sleeps." The very existence of an arch depends, as we have seen, on its con-

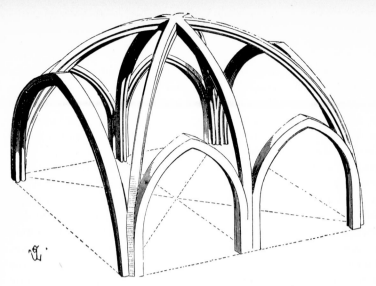

4.4. THE GOTHIC CATHEDRAL. a. Perspective drawing of a Gothic sexpartite vault, with nave spanned by single arches, coupled arches opening into side aisles. Reproduced in E. E. Viollet-le-Duc, *Dictionnaire Raisonné de l'Architecture Française du XIᵉ au XVIᵉ Siècle* (Paris: B. Bance, n. d.), vol. IV, p. 34, fig. 21. b. Cross section of the nave of a Gothic cathedral (Notre Dame, Chartres). c. Ground-floor plan of a Gothic cathedral (Notre Dame, Chartres). d. Plan of a Gothic quadripartite rib vault (Notre Dame, Chartres). b, c, and d all reproduced in A. de Baudot and A. Perrault-Dabot, *Les Cathédrales de France* (Paris: Henri Laurens, n. d.).

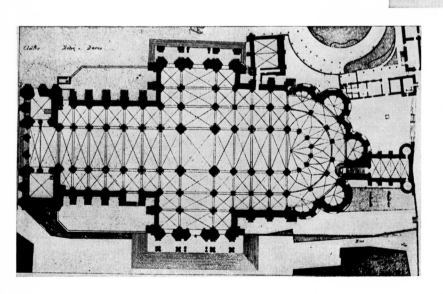

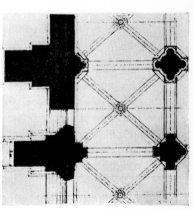

4.5. CATHEDRAL OF NOTRE DAME, Chartres, interior, looking toward choir and apse. 1135–1280; 1507. Levy and Neurdein photograph.

through it at the piers as points of support instead of along a continuous wall, they found themselves able with the rib vault to transform the previously thick-walled masonry into a skeletal system of construction (4.4a). When covered with rib vaulting, the cathedral was divided by arches running across it into separate units called bays. Diagonally across each bay were built two additional arches called ribs, to intersect in a common keystone and support a masonry-filling between the ribs in the form of four correspondingly arcuated webs (4.4c and d). The thrust of one web was thus made to counterbalance the thrust of that adjoining, and the thrust of each bay of vaulting to concentrate in the haunches of each rib. Stone piers were made to serve as isolated supports for arches and ribs, and stone buttresses as external projections to meet the thrusts of the ribs (4.4b). In order to take their weight off the vaulting of the lower side aisles, as well as to economize on materials, the buttresses supporting the vaulting of the nave, or lofty middle portion of the cathedral, were carried obliquely across to the base of the outside walls of the side aisles by inclined half arches and piers which together came to be called flying buttresses. The exterior construction was thus induced to proclaim the vaulting within.

With the development of the pointed arch, which not only reduced the thrust of the arches and ribs, but also supported a greater weight than the round arch and made all vaulted bays of uniform height, the finishing touch was added to this masonry frame. The walls of the structure became merely screens, replaceable at will by seemingly endless expanses of glass, which needed for support only a system of stone piers and arches, called tracery, to flood the interior with daylight.

Out of the solution to this structural problem, then, came the opportunity to enlarge and elaborate the traditional type of plan for the Christian church. The apse (4.4c), where the altar stands and the clergy officiate in the sacrament of the Mass, remained the cathedral's focal center. In the fully developed structure a corridor came to encircle the apse, often

tinuous counterbalance. The arch and its projection as the tunnel vault exert a continuous outward thrust causing the structure to collapse unless the walls are thickened and piled up over the haunch of the thrust (the place of maximum thrust).

The medieval builders finally invented the rib vault, a device which solved the problem perfectly. Surprisingly, moreover, because the weight and thrust could be concentrated with chapels radiating from it. In the front of the apse the choir continued to accommodate in flanking stalls the choir boys at the sacrament. In front of the choir a space called the crossing continued to represent the intersection of the nave with two arms called transepts. But the new climax of the composition became the tremendous horizontal expansiveness of apse, choir, and nave, to take in undreamed-of numbers of worshipers, and a corresponding vertical expansiveness, to create the effect of a heavenward surge.

The divisions in elevation came to correspond to the major divisions in plan (4.4b). A decorative arcade was designed above the side aisles to mask the space taken up on the wall of nave by the lean-to roof over the vaulting of the side aisle. An area called the clerestory was allowed to rise above it to the vaults for the main expanse of windows.

Although movement upward became the dominating motive, the use of isolated supports gave opportunity for limitless spatial expansion, and the builders made the most of it. Through partial concealment of vistas by the piers, they suggested unending progressions of space (4.5). By projection of chapels at various points they enhanced this spatial effect. Outside as in, by means of piers and flying buttresses, of chapel walls and windows, they maintained a continuous ebb-and-flow of rhythmic form, a movement picked up and accentuated by countlessly varied features—some purely structural, like spires, to weight down the piers of the flying buttresses; and some ornamental, like wall arcades or capitals of piers, to emphasize construction.

In marked contrast to the Greek temple, the Gothic cathedral became a dynamic thing, the activation so strikingly evidenced being the consequence of an organic approach to problems different from those of the Greeks. Quite in keeping with the nature of these new problems, the form of the cathedral changed, not to meet some predetermined idea of what the whole should be like, but to accord with changing states of mind held by successive generations.

4.6. CATHEDRAL OF NOTRE DAME, Chartres, western façade and flanking towers. Façade and south tower finished c. 1145; north tower and spire finished 1507. Clarence Ward photograph.

No Gothic cathedral was built in a year or even in a decade or two. The cathedral of Chartres (4.6), here selected to illustrate the type, took more than a century to complete (1135–1280),* and its North Tower, destroyed by fire before the end of the twelfth century,

---

* A sympathetic and largely accurate account of the building of Chartres Cathedral was written by Henry Adams, *Mont-Saint-Michel and Chartres* (Boston: Houghton, Mifflin, 1913; 1st pub., 1904). For a more scholarly treatment refer to Otto von Simson, *The Gothic Cathedral* ("Bollingen Series," XLVIII; New York: Pantheon Books, 1956).

was not rebuilt until 1507. Such, however, was the uninhibited strength of the culture producing the building, and so nearly universal its expression through art, that the builders of any successive generation seem never to have felt that the new addition they were erecting should follow the style of some preceding part.

Witness to this is the austerity of the South Tower (that to our right in looking at the front of the building), built in the Romanesque manner of the early twelfth century, and the contrasting exuberance of the North Tower, a Flamboyant Gothic composition. Such diversity of expression might have resulted in nothing but a combination of unrelated fragments.

It is to the credit of the later builders that, while following the manner of designing of their own day, they also sought to restore the western façade to its original symmetry. Since they were making the North Tower light and open in form, they found it necessary to increase its height so as to match in the total of its mass that of the more solid South Tower. It was the nature of the Greek classic spirit that the Parthenon, to exist as an entity, had to be completed in a single generation. It was the nature of the French Gothic spirit, on the other hand, that a building like Chartres Cathedral could go on from one generation to another receiving contributions to its structure without losing its unity.*

BUILDING FOR MODERN TRADE

While French Gothic builders at Chartres carried the arcuated techniques of construction to extremes of daring height, airy openness, and luminosity, it remained for Western architects of the twentieth century to carry a cantilevering form of post-and-lintel construction to corresponding extremes of horizontal extension and spaciousness. They were able to do this through a new technique of skeletal steel construction which we have already described as belonging to the vertebrate class, a technique at first called "Chicago Construction" because it originated in this American metropolis of the Middle West during the city's rebuilding after the fire of 1871.

Chicago architects learned to bolt, rivet, or weld steel beams together to form the skeleton of a building extending almost any number of stories in height. Steel beams buckled, to be sure, under the heat of fire. They offered little resistance to pressure. But the fire-resistance of these structural members could be improved with terra-cotta casings. The high tensile strength of these steel beams could be combined with the compression strength of concrete to form a new material called ferroconcrete. With a ferroconcrete skeleton for framework, architects working in Chicago at the end of the last and the beginning of the present century revolutionized the processes of building. Among other unprecedented types of building, they created out of this ferroconcrete skeleton the epoch-making skyscraper.

It is unfortunate that few of the architects engaged in such a remarkable technical advance appreciated its possibilities for design. They found that they could hang almost any kind of wall on their ferroconcrete skeletons, and almost any kind they did hang on these skeletons before they were through. A look at downtown Chicago confirms how easily skyscraper-builders succumbed to temptation, for there in the city's heart a forest of tall buildings still rises, nightmarish in vagaries of fancy that remain oblivious to the realities of the construction underneath.

One early building in downtown Chicago does stand out, however, as a noteworthy exception. This is the Carson-Pirie-Scott (originally the Schlesinger-Mayer) Department Store (4.7), designed by Louis Sullivan in 1899.

---

* The concept of Greek architecture as an art of "being" and of Gothic architecture as an art of "becoming" is elaborated by Wilhelm Worringer in *Form Problems of the Gothic,* translated from the German by John Shapley (New York: G. E. Stechert, 1918).

In it form-and-structure and form-and-function achieve a significant synthesis. The building not only meets the program of requirements for a department store but, neutrally balanced and open and cagelike in form, is made to say that it is meeting that program. Its exterior has retained its effectiveness, although the interior is now somewhat dated. In an article Sullivan published shortly before he received the department-store commission, we can trace the clear-seeing analysis which brought him a generation ahead of his contemporaries to the threshold of a new type of organic design. One passage of the article reads, in fact, like a prophecy of the sort of thing Sullivan was soon to create:

Beginning with the first story, we give this a main entrance that attracts the eye to its location, and the remainder of the story we treat in a more or less liberal, expansive, sumptuous way—a way based exactly on the practical necessities, but expressed with a sentiment of largeness and freedom. The second story we treat in a similar way, but usually with milder pretension. Above this, throughout the indefinite number of typical office-tiers, we take our cue from the individual cell, which requires a window with its separating pier, its sill and lintel, and we, without more ado, make them *look* all alike because they are all alike. This brings us to the attic, which, having no division into office-cells and no special requirements for lighting, gives us the power to show . . . that the series of office-tiers has come definitely to an end.*

From the time of the Carson-Pirie-Scott building a whole quarter of a century had to elapse before architects could rid themselves of the idea that an edifice had above all else to symbolize something. Among the first to free themselves from the notion was Ludwig Miës van der Rohe, German architect later to identify himself with America's architectural develop-

4.7. Louis Sullivan (1856–1924): Schlesinger-Mayer Building (Carson-Pirie-Scott Department Store), Chicago. 1899–1904. The farther section, designed by Daniel Hudson Burnham in 1904 and built in 1906, follows closely Sullivan's original design. Chicago Architectural Photographic Company photograph.

ment.† Miës van der Rohe came to base his effects on the definition of the differing usages to which each part of his building would be put, on the frankest revelation of the neutral skeleton, the severest flatness of white stucco veneer, the starkest contrasts of openings. He made every feature and relationship clearly perceptible, sharpening edges and proportioning bands of windows to areas of white stucco with an exactitude rivaling that of Henry Dreyfuss in the designing of the telephone (3.2d).

Perhaps the most important single creation of the first half of the century was, ironically enough, a temporary structure designed by this

* From Louis Sullivan's article, "The Tall Office Building Artistically Considered," *Lippincott's Monthly Magazine*, Vol. LXVII (March, 1896), pp. 404–405.

† Philip C. Johnson, *Miës van der Rohe* (New York: Museum of Modern Art, 1947).

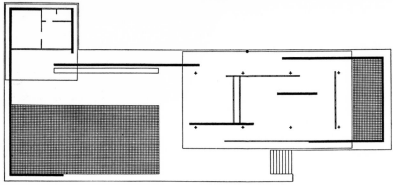

4.8. a. Ludwig Miës van der Rohe (1886–   ): German Pavilion, International Exposition, Barcelona, exterior, looking toward entrance terrace. 1929. Foundations and lighter-colored walls: Roman travertine; free-standing partition in hall: onyx; pool lined with black glass. Courtesy of the architect. Hedrich-Blessing photograph. b. Ludwig Miës van der Rohe: German Pavilion, International Exposition, floor plan. Courtesy of the architect.

architect: the German Pavilion at the Barcelona Exposition of 1929 (4.8a and b). Proceeding with relentless self-discipline to follow a principle formulated by and for himself, that "less is more," Miës van der Rohe eliminated from his pavilion everything superfluous, focusing upon the few remaining elements the utmost concentration. He allowed himself nothing but walls, a floor slab, two pools, a few chairs, a potted plant or two, and a dominant

accent gained by a single piece of sculpture (4.9). With the same painstaking care the architect-builders of the Parthenon devoted to refining a simple form, Miës van der Rohe worked and reworked his materials into a corresponding epitome of organic form. He drew a plan which was in itself a model of refinement (4.8b). He made every piece of material stand intensively by itself. Concrete, marble, onyx, glass—the architect made each at one and

4.9. Ludwig Miës van der Rohe: German Pavilion, International Exposition, sculpture pool. Walls surrounding pool: bottle-green transparent glass. Sculpture by Georg Kolbe (1877–1947): *Standing Woman*. Bronze. Courtesy of the architect.

the same time a part of the structure and a product exhibited by it.

Foremost of all the features in the Barcelona Pavilion, Miës van der Rohe planned to make the open spaces of his building interlock with the solids, and in so doing succeeded more than ever before in liberating the units of architectural construction. Disciplined by points of support marked by slender piers and originally established as basic units of measurement, the architect was able to disassociate each unit from the other in such a way as to yield its own maximum expressive flavor and still gain by relationship to the ensemble. He provided a continuous plane of floor to be seen through the glass partitions from one area to the next. He developed slender piers with chromium-plated steel skins, completely free-standing walls, and a hovering roof slab of widely cantilevered extensions. Through the alternate opening and closing of space he expressed in a new twentieth-century idiom the rhythms of actual life. However direct his expression of the functions of the building as a reception hall for the exposition, however frank his emphasis upon the materials and their respective roles in its construction, he managed in the Barcelona Pavilion even more boldly to assert the new spirit of the age in which he lived—one in which the boundaries of space and time dissolve and a new "fourth dimensionality" emerges.

BUILDING FOR DAILY LIFE

Housebuilding in Japan

Some features of this twentieth-century Western architecture trace back to Japanese influence—flatness of surface, sharpness of line, proportioning of intervals, and asymmetrical balance. They occur in Miës van der Rohe's architecture, however, divorced from the necessities of a climate which had originally in Japan made dwellings what they were.[6]

The Japanese house (4.10) is a weatherworthy structure, as adaptable to changing uses as it is to changing states of weather, and as boldly assertive of materials and processes of formation as is a living organism. It proclaims by its wide overhang of roof, solid walls to north and west, and removable screens to south and east, that it is built to shelter its occupants from the hot sun and heavy rains of late spring and summer, to open its heart to the autumn foliage and the blossoms of every season, and even to the winter snow and sunshine. The cantilevering of eaves is extensive and functionally justified; orientation for sun, wind, rain, sound, and view is efficiently adjusted; and the relating of house to site is intimate and personal.

When the translucent paper screens are in place on the south and east sides of the Japanese house, their panel-like effect provides a true structural motivation. From within the house one realizes how foliage out-of-doors casts on the surfaces of such screens ever-changing patterns. When the screens are pushed back into a cupboard built for them in the thickness of a wall, the house becomes more open in character than would be possible through broad expanses of immovable plate glass. The three-foot-wide veranda (beyond the range of screens in the Japanese house) is an extremely utilizable sheltered space. Functional woven reed screens hang from the eaves above this veranda: partly unrolled, such screens shield the interior from the glare and

[6] See Notes, page 296.

the heat of the sun; fully unrolled, they protect the interior from driving summer rains while continuing to admit the ventilation.

Upon entering such a house one finds quarters as freshly ordered and livable as the outside promises (4.11). Straw mats called tatami cover the board sub floor in simple geometric patterns; spotless, fragrant, inviting to the touch, they furnish a surface not only to walk and kneel on in one's bare or stockinged feet, but also to work and eat on, and even to sleep on. Manufactured in standard sizes, they contain the horizontal module (basic unit of measurement) on which the whole building is designed—as a four-and-a-half-mat, a six-mat, an eight-mat house, and so forth. Since the heights of the structure are correspondingly standardized, the structure embodies an underlying discipline making every variation in the smaller forms a meaningful departure.

Particularly noteworthy is the simple range of furnishings and accessories: no furnace, merely a charcoal-burning hearth in a pit in the floor; no chairs, only cushions; no tables, only short-legged stands; no bedsteads, only bedding. And every movable article may be stowed away behind the sliding doors of cupboards built into the walls.

A pair of alcoves is similarly incorporated with the architecture at one end of the room, the smaller one fitted out with shelving to take the place of bookcases and a desk, the larger one, the tokonoma, to accommodate a carefully arranged display of a flower arrangement, a piece of pottery or sculpture, and a kakemono (scroll painting suitable for hanging). The works of art thus shown can be changed to accord with such changing circumstances as the weather, the seasons of the year, the annual festivals, or the personalities of invited guests. In our illustration, for example, the room was prepared for an autumn festival. A kakemono featuring a mountain landscape in autumn hangs on the tokonoma wall. An arrangement of autumn-blossoming zinnias stands below it in a metal vessel. To the other side, on a low

4.10. Attributed to Kobori Enshu (1580–1649): Tanaka house and garden, Kyoto, seen from the garden, looking northwest. Mid-17th century. Photograph courtesy of Hirojirō Onishi.

4.11. Seibei Kimura (1869–1955): Jirō Harada residence, Tokyo, living room, seen from entrance of room. 1937. Photograph courtesy of Jirō Harada.

cupboard used to store scroll paintings, the terra-cotta effigy of a Buddhist abbot sits, while a temple bell hangs above it, suggesting a monastic contemplation appropriate to the season of mists and mellow fruitfulness being featured.

The Japanese hold special reverence for natural materials. No paint was allowed to mask the materials. No piece of wood was cut mechanically; it was sawed and planed so as to accentuate its grain, and matched in run of grain to accord with the other pieces cut from the same log. Again, as in the room illustrated, woods are used expressively. Against the pale green tone of tatami straw the warm reds and yellows of cryptomeria, cypress, bamboo, and other woods, stand forth vigorously, and against the natural textures of both straw and wood the varied granular surfaces of the mud plaster gain in their appeal to touch. As a note of major stress in the ensemble, the all-important post of honor that separates the alcoves was chosen from a special wood, here a log of cryptomeria with its bark preserved to remind one of the forest yielding the material out of which the house was made.

The spatial volumes are vigorously composed in such Japanese dwellings as that here presented. The paper screens have much to do with the open spatial quality—screens not only removable but, in our example, constructed in sections with a backing of glass, so that in cold weather when the lower half is raised to afford an outside view, the screens may protect the interior while emphasizing its spaciousness by contrast of translucent with transparent surfaces. Important to the spatial effect is an ornamental window inserted between the two alcoves and a piece of wooden partition hanging part way from the ceiling; in the latter case, when interior screens of paper are set into place between the partition and the tatami, the openings through the partition maintain not only the ventilation but a sense of spatial flow.

This flexibility enters into every part of the structure of the Japanese house. The skeletal frame, on which everything else depends, rests simply on a row of stones set beneath the posts. The occasional stretches of fixed plaster wall are subordinated to the broad expanses of removable screens and, together with the latter, the floor mats leave the house so light in weight that a wind would blow it away were it not for the anchorage affected by the heavy roof of tile laid in mud. All parts are prefabricated before the house is raised. Cut and fitted together in sections on the ground and numbered piece by piece, they are pulled apart and piled in careful order. When every section is ready, the building itself is put together in little more than a day. A structure so readily assembled is as speedily demounted. In the path of a sweeping conflagration, the greater part can be speedily dismantled and hauled to safety, leaving little even of the framework to be consumed by the flames.

It has been contended that the Japanese art of building, uniquely the expression of Japanese beliefs and way of life, could never be exported to the Occident. But the principles so strikingly evidenced by it are universally valid; and from the observance of such principles architects in sympathy with the Japanese attitude have found their way into an organic design deeply rooted in the site and the function, in the materials and the method of construction.

Housebuilding in Contemporary America

Among those who discovered the Japanese house was Louis Sullivan's one-time apprentice, Frank Lloyd Wright, an architect destined to pioneer in an organic approach to architecture fully a third of a century before Miës van der Rohe at Barcelona. Already at the turn of the century launched on one of the most revolutionary careers in the history of art, Wright responded to Japanese example as an encouragement to follow organic procedure in domestic design.[7] If you develop the form of a house as though it were growing upward from the ground like a tree, Wright reasoned, then your

[7] See Notes, page 296.

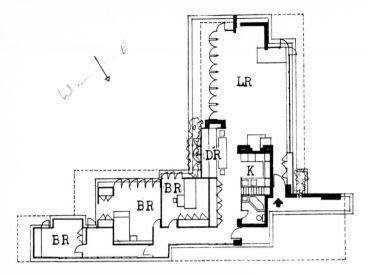

4.12. A PRAIRIE HOUSE. a. Frank Lloyd Wright (1869–1959): Herbert Jacobs residence I, Madison, Wis., plan. 1937. Courtesy of The Museum of Modern Art, New York. b. Frank Lloyd Wright: Herbert Jacobs residence I, house as seen from street, looking east. Courtesy of Herbert Jacobs. P. E. Guerrero photograph.

house will be unique even as the site and the conditions of life for which it is planned must always be unique. That each such structure had to assume an individual character because of the architect's response to the site and the character of his clients is demonstrated by tracing the development of the forms of one particular example: the residence which Frank Lloyd Wright designed in 1937 for the Jacobs family in Madison, Wisconsin.

As in any sound architectural procedure, Herbert Jacobs and his wife had to participate actively as clients in the creation of their dwelling. This they did by fixing severely restricted limitations to the cost of the house and drawing up for it with the architect an extensive program of requirements. They located a site near the outskirts of the city, one which Herbert Jacobs made acceptable to the architect by combining two ordinary lots into a plot of land,

120 feet square, a plot which sloped gently away from both its northern corner and the street on its western edge.

If we would retrace step by step how the house came into being, we must start, as did the architect and his clients, with the plan (4.12a).* Considerations of good drainage, good view, and maximum unbroken space for garden all called for placing the house on the knoll towards the northern corner of the lot. Since only a heating unit needs to be accommodated below the ground-floor level, excavation was limited to a single small pit. Since snowfall is heavy during a Wisconsin winter, labor of shoveling was minimized by making the driveway and footway as short as consistent with allowing the driver of the family automobile a view in either direction before backing on to the street. The garage and porte-cochère were combined to form a "carport" and provide a welcoming overhang at the entrance to the house. Privacy was guaranteed by turning the main entranceway at right angles to the street and running a screen wall outward from it part way toward the street.

The favorable lay of the street permits the house to parallel it, like the other houses in the block, and profit at the same time by favorable orientation. Madison, with a latitude of 43.5°, lies well to northward in the United States, at a point where the declination of the earth on its axis (that phenomenon which accounts for seasonal changes) causes the sun to "ride" low in the southern sky during the winter and high overhead during the summer. The city suffers from extremes of heat in summer and of cold in winter, extremes tempered solely by an occasional south breeze in summer or a sunny day in winter. With the back of the house to the street, a continuous screening wall protects against the noises of the street and also, in this case at least, against the winter's storms and the summer's sunshine.

* The client's account of the building of this house is contained in the book by Herbert Jacobs, *We Chose the Country* (New York: Harper and Brothers, 1948), while the architect's account is published in the first Frank Lloyd Wright Feature Issue of *The Architectural Forum*, Vol. LXVIII, No. 1 (January, 1938), pp. 78–83.

With a continuous expanse of glass doors, the front of the house is open to the winter's sun and the summer's breezes and affords a view of the lot and access to the terrace.

When the architect turns to the development of the plan itself, he proceeds to work from the inside outward. The utilities are the vital organs of the house, relegated to a central location and grouped as closely as possible to gain economies of unitary plumbing. The walls surrounding this central core are put to good use—to enclose the areas for bathing, cooking and basement-access, to encompass a fireplace and flues for it and the kitchen stove, to bound an entrance hallway, and to make their mass the major weight-bearing element for the entire dwelling. The service core is flanked by two entrances to the street, facilitating answer to the doorbell, delivery of groceries from carport to "kitchen," and private access from outside to bathroom and bedroom. Other pierlike supports are distributed at such points as might perform similarly extra duties: one to frame the shelves at the end of the dining table and screen the table from the living room; a second to flank the service doorway; and a third to make a secluded alcove for lounging and reading at the far end of the living room. This multiple-purpose type of planning must eventuate, if it is thorough, in a compactly efficient design.

So effective is the orientation described that even in sub-zero temperatures the sun is sufficient, when the sky is clear, to heat the whole house. At other times the roller screens across the doors reduce heat loss by conduction through the glass, and an ancient Roman device, here used for the first time in America, approximates the effect of solar heat. Two-inch piping is laid in a gravel fill beneath the concrete floor-slab; through it circulates hot water from the boiler; thus the floor of the house itself becomes the heating element, a radiant heating device which warms the ankles but leaves the air about the head healthfully cool.

By reducing the kitchen area to a cooking alcove and the eating area to a dining alcove, by placing them close together for almost effort-

less serving, and by incorporating them with the living room in a partially sequestered fashion, there is eliminated the drudgery of housework in a servantless household. Since the living room is intended for the family's social life, it is large and open, using the space gained by abolishing the conventional dining room and kitchen and transforming the conventional library into a reading nook with a built-in table and a wall of bookshelves. Since bedrooms are for quiet retirement, they are ranged in a private wing of the house, stepped back one behind the other for the sake of privacy when opened to the terrace. In order to shade the walls of both the social wing and the bedroom wing from the summer sun, the roof is cantilevered into widely overhanging eaves, indicated on the plan by means of dotted lines.

Such considerations, though essential to the process, do not carry the plan for the house beyond a nebulous state. In order to crystallize it into something workable, we need to determine, even as the architect does in consultation with his clients, exactly what activities are to go on in each area, how much of the area is to be occupied by the equipment for such activities, and how much clear space is needed to perform them. The architect himself knows by past experience how to define such areas directly, but we can approximate his work at this stage only by following an elementary exercise.

We lay out on a sheet of paper a network of lines forming squares to correspond at reduced scale to the module to be employed—a square two feet on a side. To the same scale we cut rectangles of colored paper representing floor areas to be occupied by various articles of furniture and equipment. We move these pieces about on the network, trying different groupings for each activity called for. We try the spaces out full scale for ourselves, finding that a major traffic lane like that from the main entrance to the wardrobe demands a width of at least three feet four inches, a secondary lane like that into the bathroom calls for a width of at least two feet, a clearance between an armchair and a coffee table requires a width of one foot, and so on. Anything less in a given instance would feel cramped, anything more would throw the interval out of scale. Once we have disposed our furniture group units and the intervals between them, we lay the walls in around the ensembles, map out storage units, retain openings for doorways and windows, relate rooms to each other, and bring the plan methodically thus to completion.

A house so planned can be efficiently practical. As far as our description has gone, it might be no more. On the plan for the Jacobs house, however, a sensitive artist was at work, one who made its features express their respective purposes and the whole house its welcoming and sheltering role. Though advanced no farther than the plan, the Herbert Jacobs residence was already promising to become a true work of art. We may observe in the plan how protectingly, for example, the main pier-masses seem to cluster about the entrance but to awaken responses in the smaller piers. We see how buoyantly sociable the extensions of the living room seem by contrast with the masses of the piers, how quietly apart the bedrooms seem to lie in a wing to themselves. We realize how much like tree-growth the social wing and the sleeping wing seem to branch from the trunklike core, how much, again like a tree, intervals of light and air interpenetrate the branches.

Although the detailed study we have been making has by no means exhausted the subject, it should demonstrate how formidable is the task of evolving a plan. Inescapably interdependent with it, moreover, are questions about the elevations of the house, its materials and construction, its ultimately tangible form. In the interest of simplicity we have tried to omit them from our analysis of the plan, but time and again they have intruded. That is as it should be—when a real house is the objective, and not merely a two-dimensional drawing.

The architect insisted that the Jacobs house have a carport for the sake of its welcoming effect at the entrance, and he depended on

4.13. A PRAIRIE HOUSE. Frank Lloyd Wright: Herbert Jacobs residence I, living room, looking toward library and lounging alcove. Courtesy of Herbert Jacobs. P. E. Guerrero photograph.

cantilevering to roof it (4.12b). The cooking alcove would have become impossibly dark and smelly were it not for a low monitor tower permitting windows to light and ventilate it; this tower became the expression on the outside of the house of the central core within, while pushing the red-brick masonry of the chimney still higher to register the weight-supporting masses of the central pier.

Screen walls, thin but solid, were finished identically inside and out. Boards of white pine, dovetailed with strips of redwood for battens, were screwed together on each side of a core of other boards insulated from the outer layers with nothing but building paper (4.12b, 4.13).

Since it is common knowledge that wood supports considerable weight against the grain but buckles easily under weight set parallel to it, boards laid on their sides to complete the walls of the house were revealed frankly as nothing but screening. So also the treatment at the head of the walls, where a continuous band of windows was installed, was revealing—making visible from inside how directly the composition-board ceiling served as roof and protective overhang of eaves.

The fireplace as the focal center of the house came to sum up the composition of the whole —the use of a solid, to support the structure, and the use of asymmetrical balance, canti-

4.14. A PRAIRIE HOUSE. a. Frank Lloyd Wright: Herbert Jacobs residence I, as seen from the garden, looking north. Courtesy of Herbert Jacobs. P. E. Guerrero photograph. b. Frank Lloyd Wright: Herbert Jacobs residence I, living room, looking north toward fireplace, main entrance, and dining alcove. Herbert Jacobs photograph.

levering, and interplay of vertical with horizontal units to quicken the flow of space. Such themes were repeated with rhythmic variations throughout the rest of the structure. Observe how forms were made to succeed each other, for example, in the horizontal extension of the redwood battens along the wall, the change of pace and texture in the masonry pier, the lighter run of horizontals in the framing units of the vertical strip of windows, the brief interruption of another pier, the renewal of the window motive with the horizontal framing units, and the climactic succession of vertical oblongs in the window-doors opening on the terrace. No matter where we go, into a bedroom, onto the terrace, back to the entrance walk, we experience the same rhythm, for the house seems inexhaustible in this play of forms.

Regional Building

When Frank Lloyd Wright designed the Jacobs house in 1937 he had been following for half a century a line of procedure directly opposite to that followed at Barcelona by Ludwig Miës

4.15. A BAY REGION HOUSE. Frank Lloyd Wright: Paul R. Hanna residence, Palo Alto, Calif., living room, looking west toward play room. 1937. Roger Sturtevant photograph.

van der Rohe. Instead of trying to fashion architectural forms which might be valid on any site, Wright from the outset had been striving to evolve forms which might in their variety affirm the uniqueness of the locale. From the clod of earth at one's doorstep to the mountain ridge of one's horizon, the American architect was looking for qualities of the locale out of which to motivate his art.

Wright saw in the site for the Herbert Jacobs house something more than a neutral hillock upon which to build. He saw it as the minute fraction of a landscape rolling oceanlike from the Alleghenies two thousand miles to the Rockies, a vast Middle Western prairie in which, so to speak, he sought to "plant" a structure as native to it as the hawthorn or the cottonwood. "I loved the prairie by instinct as a

great simplicity—the trees, flowers, sky itself, thrilling by contrast," the architect declared.*

I saw that a little height on the prairie was enough to look like much more—every detail as to height becoming intensely significant, breadths all falling short . . . The climate being what it was, violent in extremes of heat and cold, damp and dry, dark and bright, I gave broad protecting roof-shelter to the whole . . . I like the *sense of shelter* in the look of the building. I still like it. The house began to associate with the ground and become natural to its prairie site.

* Frank Lloyd Wright, *An Autobiography* (New York: Duell, Sloan and Pearce, 1943; 1st ed., New York: Longmans, Green, 1932), pp. 139–147.

Such was the Jacobs house, such any prairie house created by Wright's hand in the Middle West, because the architect felt the character of the region in which he was working. To say that his houses belong to a "Prairie Style," however, is to contradict the architect's intent. The sources for their design, deeply rooted as they were in the locale, make for kinship, but they differ as much from each other as Madison differs from Aurora, Illinois, or Wichita, Kansas.

Wright's houses differ from each other in accord with their locations, even as every subregion differs from another within the Middle West, and more still as every major region differs from another within the North American continent. Consider, for example, a house designed by Frank Lloyd Wright for the San Francisco Bay region (4.15, 4.17a) and, by way of contrast, another designed by him for that desert region of Arizona known as Paradise Valley (4.16, 4.17b).

The landscape of the Bay region is one of undulating hills enlivened by constantly changing effects of fog, wind, and sunshine. The unbroken, curving contour predominates in the forms of both the land and the clumps of oak and madrone distributed over its face. Responding perhaps to this environmental stimulus, people have grown characteristically energetic, easily informal and friendly. When Wright came to design a house for Professor Paul R. Hanna of Stanford University, therefore, this constant "to and fro" of both nature and man suggested to him for his planning module a shape borrowed from the beehive: the hexagon or "honeycomb unit." With it as his basis in both plan and elevation, he proceeded to evolve a gracefully animated form, as light and free and welcoming in effect as the landscape and the life it fosters.

The setting of Paradise Valley is, on the other hand, extremely rugged and dramatic. Mountain mass and dense volcanic rock are baked in almost constant sun, but their coloring is compensatingly gorgeous and intense. The dotted line—the interrupted contour— prevails, making staccato sequences of form.

4.16. AN ARIZONA HOUSE. Frank Lloyd Wright: Rose Pauson residence, Phoenix, Ariz., living room as seen from entrance to dining room. 1940. P. E. Guerrero photograph.

Everything exists on a scale of superhuman grandeur, dwarfing man and regulating his existence. Alone in the vastness of space, he hides from the heat of noonday but does his work toward evening in concentrated mobility. The house that Wright designed for the Pauson sisters became correspondingly big-scaled and colorful. A solid concrete platform from which the multihued local boulders twinkled intermittently was made a foundation for the superstructure of redwood. Battered walls (walls with obliquely inclined planes) were built to play outward and inward like the rocks of the nearby Camelback Mountains—massive, shadowed retreats from the heat of the desert. A two-story living room was designed to open south, its elongated spatial volumes emphasizing by dramatic contrast the bulky volumes of the terrace and the mountains beyond.

In creating forms to catch the flavor of a landscape, Wright used the prevailing natural materials—its woods, stones, and clays. He managed thus to develop such regionally expressive buildings as prairie houses, Bay region houses, and desert houses. Whatever the natural materials used, however, the architect always finds certain contradictions in the forms fashioned from them. Trees, rocks, and beds of clay take on forms quite different from the shapes of boards, blocks, and bricks used in construction. In their natural state, trees, rocks, and clay beds are irregular in contour, double-curved, continuous, while the building materials derived from them are regular in contour, rectilinear, intermittent, and the structures employing such materials are correspondingly square of plane, cubical in volume, and disassociated from the site. Wright always had to break these basically formal shapes into small-scaled units extending in zigzag fashion into the landscape in order to make them fit the site.

With such compounds, synthetics, or plastics as we found industry adopting for its products, the architect can avoid these contradictions. Compounds are, to be sure, uniform and impersonal in nature; they get their final shapes at the moment of their birth in molds; and they are cast with little or no thought for any specific site. In shell construction with reinforced concrete, on the other hand, a compound offers the best chance of all to achieve forms organically expressive of a region. There are laws of physics which cannot be violated. There are human preferences, for walking on flat and level floors in multi-story buildings, which cannot be ignored. Nevertheless, for one-story structures with uninterrupted interiors, like civic auditoriums, shell construction can take on forms as organically related to the locale as are the forms of a shell fish or a crab. The Eskimo's igloo fits perfectly into Arctic wastes covered with the same natural material as that entering into its erection. The icy crust carries over from one to the other. The igloo's days are numbered, of course, when the sun of summer shines, but the shell of which it is composed could be easily rendered permanent if made of reinforced concrete.

When used by itself, concrete is probably the oldest compound used in building; it goes back at least to ancient Rome. It is made by mixing water with a binding element (gypsum in earlier times, for example, and Portland cement today), and two aggregates—a coarse aggregate such as gravel and a fine aggregate such as sand. If this fluid mixture is poured into a mold and there allowed to harden and set before removal of the mold, the resulting concrete will prove remarkably resistant to compression and fire. It will at the same time prove hopelessly weak in tensile strength; it will bend under pressure and crack up and break.

Steel makes a perfect complement to concrete. Though weak in resisting compression or fire, steel compensates for its weaknesses with an extraordinary tensile strength. It has, moreover, almost the same expansion-coefficient as that of concrete under increase in temperature. In combining steel with concrete, as nineteenth-century builders discovered, one ingredient's weaknesses are offset by the other's strengths. The resultant ferroconcrete, or reinforced concrete, is remarkably efficient for today's construction needs.

Until recently, however, architects have been so habituated to post-and-lintel that they have overlooked the properties natural to ferroconcrete and forced it into structural service ill-suited for it. They have entailed in consequence much waste of labor and material and much excessive weight. After experiments with ferroconcrete for shell construction, however, architects have come to employ the material for single-storied types of structures with unobstructed interiors.

True shell construction consists in building a structure the covering of which serves simultaneously as its support, its walls, and its roof. Such is its nature that a stress exerted at any point on its surface is transmitted with equal force throughout its mass. As in industrial production, only compound plastic types of materials lend themselves to the necessary

4.17. a. Frank Lloyd Wright: Paul R. Hanna residence, view from entrance court, looking southwest. Roger Sturtevant photograph. b. Frank Lloyd Wright: Rose Pauson residence, view of living-room end of house and its terrace, looking northwest. P. E. Guerrero photograph.

4.18. Felix Candela (1910–   ), structural designer; Joaquin Alvarez Ordoñez, architect: Los Manantiales Restaurant, Floating Gardens, Xochimilco, Mexico, view over water to landing. 1958. Hyperbolic paraboloid: half-inch shell of ferroconcrete, interior painted white; vertical panes: glass, frames painted black with red accents; floor, gray granite; roof waterproofed with black-tar paint sprinkled with white gravel chips; mural screen at entrance, *History of Xochimilco*. Spread, approx. 150′; maximum height, approx. 34′. Erwin Lang photograph.

shaping. Natural materials, even when converted into plywood or hollow tiles, refuse to conform easily to curvilinear shapes, whereas ferroconcrete automatically assumes such shapes.*

Ferroconcrete shell construction has made particular headway in Italy, Spain, and Mexico, where architects are accustomed to doing their own contracting and determining their own methods of construction. In each of these countries, moreover, whether or not they intended, architects of shell construction have evolved forms expressive of the locale.

Felix Candela, the Spanish exile residing in Mexico, was not thinking of regional forms when he worked out at first by intuition and later by mathematics, that only one type of curvilinear shape rendered a structure self-supporting without either ribs or buttresses to strengthen it. This is the hyperbolic paraboloid,† familiarly exemplified by the shape of the Western saddle. Thanks to its doubly curved extensions, even when thinned to a shell of less than half an inch in thickness, it withstands almost any tensile stress.

When Candela was commissioned to design a restaurant (4.18) for Xochimilco, the float-

* So does ferro-cemento, a variation of ferroconcrete consisting of steel-mesh reinforcement and a mixture of Portland cement, sand, and water, without any gravel. For both, see Pier Luigi Nervi (Giuseppina and Mario Salvadori, trans.), *Structures* (New York: F. W. Dodge, 1956; 1st ed. in Italian, 1955).

† Felix Candela, "Understanding the Hyperbolic Paraboloid," *Architectural Record*, Vol. CXXIV, No. 7 (July, 1958), pp. 205–207 and 215.

ing garden near Mexico City, he designed for a site of tropical luxuriance. Between one-time floating islands on which flowers are still cultivated for the market, Aztec boatmen pole their punts, either gathering flowers or guiding visitors. The garden does indeed make a colorful setting for a restaurant and the architect in this case made the most of it. He created a structure which was itself like a flower—with eight ribless vaults merging at the center in a gracefully flowing transition. He looped each vault upward from its stemlike pedestals, letting the interior open outward from it through glass on to the garden landscape. Permitting the shell to sport no ornament, he made the shell itself an ornament to the garden. Rearing nothing but a wire mesh over a wooden formwork, he had concrete troweled over it by hand before removing the forms and leaving the marks of the troweling as the texture of the shell.

Candela understood the effect which this unprecedented structure would make on the restaurant's patrons. Its extraordinary openness and lack of conventional walls and ceiling would at once stimulate and disquiet them, much as would an unsheltered and unfamiliar spot in the out-of-doors. The Spanish-Mexican designer insisted, therefore, that the shell follow a form uncompromisingly logical both inside and out, appealing visually to a popular confidence in mathematical equations. He insisted that it relate to every means by which to convey a sense of human scale: from the tables and chairs of obviously normal size, to the low terrace supporting the building, with its small-scaled rockwork for facing, its boxes for flowering plants, and its stairways with standard dimensions for risers and treads. That the stimulus actually outweighed the threat felt inside the shell came to be obvious by the patrons' enjoyment and appetite.

LANDSCAPE DESIGN

Shell construction can thus be made to meet the client's requirements, the site's geography, and the architect's expressive will. In the process of evolving its forms, however, we saw the architect obliged to stop short of his goal. He was unable with the structure alone to relate the restaurant to familiar and effective human uses. He had to resort to something which the structure alone was powerless to do: that marriage to site and human usage which only a landscape designer is able to perform.

Needs of site, beyond placement, orientation, and designing of house, carry us over into the realm of landscape design, and it is these needs that we shall now consider. Landscape design does have much in common with architectural design. It exploits space as its major element and disposes masses, planes, textures, colors, points, much as architecture does. It finds its sources of form in the same five factors which inspire architectural design: site, function, climate, material, and technical procedure. It, too, creates a "floor" and a number of containing "walls."

Landscape design differs from architectural design, on the other hand, in certain respects which make it the exclusive concern of an artist-specialist. Landscape design creates no ceiling nor roof to cap its "walls," unless it be the open sky. It treats the site not so much as something in which to establish firm foundations, but as a soil in which to set the roots of plants. It extends the usage of the living areas of the house at such times as the weather permits; at other times it creates a satisfying view from the windows of the house. Landscape design also provides for utilities and activities at least partially conditioned by the season and the weather: laundry-drying, vegetable-raising, sources of materials for indoor flower-arrangements, disposal units for garbage and waste, a pool for swimming, facilities for late-afternoon entertaining, and screening for privacy.

Landscape design is much more dependent on climatic conditions than is architecture, because one of its principal classes of materials is growing plants, and plants are inescapably concerned with such natural conditions as composition of soil, amount of sunlight and shade, direction of sunlight throughout the year, velocity and direction of wind, amount of rainfall, frost, and snow. It utilizes structural materials to crystallize the form of the garden and provide its skeletal support, but it finds such materials definitely less crucial than does architecture. Much more than architecture, on the other hand, it can never rest content with the supposed completion of any one of its creations. Nothing about such a creation can be made to stay put. Everything is in a process of change, if not in itself (a terrace, for example), then certainly in its relationship to the plant materials and the lighting—from year to year, season to season, day to day, and even minute to minute. Architecture is an art of "being." But landscape design is an art of "becoming": its product changes with changes in climate; and it rapidly reverts, when neglected, to weeds and nonexistence.

The needs which a dwelling requires of its lot often go neglected by the architect. He may attempt to meet them in some fashion, but more often only the occupant tries to meet them after he moves in. In desultory layman's manner he strings a clothesline, plants a row of onions, sows a patch of grass seed.

The direct opposite would be true of Japanese homes. However poor a household in Japan, the owner almost always tries by some bit of gardening to fit the house to the site. Japanese, in fact, insist that no house is complete without a garden, and no household normal without its daily accompaniment of works which abstract and rearrange forms derived from nature.[8] They thus patronize and practice certain arts which have scarcely existed in the Occident, making compositions out of sand and weathered rock (1.1), fashioning miniature landscapes on trays, pruning roots and training branches to control and compose the growth of miniature trees, arranging cut greens and flowers and driftwood in works of pottery (2.3). Japanese have demanded of such arts that simple directness of statement in terms of function, material, and technique to which we called attention in the Japanese teabowl (3.7). They have worked through such arts toward that unity in which house and garden are treated together as a single creation.

It took close collaboration of builder and gardener to complete the old Tanaka house and garden in Kyoto (4.10), and the result of their joint efforts is a structure that seems to grow from the ground as naturally as the pines, wax tree, and maple which rise protectively nearby.[9] It took, moreover, the unremitting care of successive owners who followed the first owner-maker, a hydraulic engineer of seventeenth-century Japan, and his presumed designer, Kobori Enshu. Each such artist-owner needed to understand the way in which the forms of garden and house contributed to each other as he continually renewed the planting and the structure to keep them both intact. He had to prune and train each tree and shrub as it grew, to replace it when it died, to maintain its proper relationships to the garden and the house—in scale, in echo of shape and inclination of roof, in repetition, through interstices of foliage, of the openings of the house, in play of lights and shadows cast upon the walls.

Thanks to the labors of the original owner and gardener and of their descendants, we can explore the garden today with the same pleasure that visitors have felt for three succeeding centuries. We can discover how its makers utilized the elements of art in accord with such principles of design as we have studied, to complete a complex whole. Starting, for example, with the stone bridge and the uptilted rock beside it, we proceed to the contrastingly open forms around. We pause for the dramatic light-and-shadow shapes of the ferns enfolding the rock. We pass to the crisp hatchings of the

[8] See Notes, page 296.

[9] See Notes, page 297.

Acorus on the left, relishing their opposition to the softened blur of fatsia beyond. We glance across a level stretch of water framed by plant masses, rest our eyes on a far bank of shrubbery, then turn to the stretch of miniature meadow for which the inlet of the pond has prepared us.

Much of the garden's effectiveness depends on contrast of curvings of plant growth to rectilinearities of house. When we focus our attention on the house, we realize the important role which the garden plays in reverse. We sense the dwelling's stability, but enjoy by analogy its treelike branching of posts and beams and outward-spreading roof, its foliage-like intervals and mergence of inner with outer space.

We discover that the materials and the construction of the house are as frankly revealed for what they are as the plants in the garden, and view with even greater satisfaction than before the features designed to bring the outdoors in (4.11): the tree trunk composing the *tokobashira*, the ink-painting hung in the tokonoma as poetic allusion to the mountain scenery of autumn, the metal container on its polished wooden stand, bearing a composition of seasonal cut flowers as subtly disposed to suggest the workings of natural forces as the clumps of shrubbery outside. Whichever way the designing started, whether with the house or with the garden, the proper functioning of the forms of one depends on the forms of the other. If the garden is designed to enhance the house, then the house must bear extensions of its forms. If the house is designed to open on the garden, then the garden must be developed to justify the view.

Frank Lloyd Wright early learned this lesson of Japanese house-and-garden design. In the Jacobs house-and-garden (4.12 to 4.14), for example, he committed himself and his clients to the development of a garden as an integral part of the whole complex. The lot had to be landscaped in order to complete the view from both the living room and the bedrooms. Thanks to the wood and the brick employed, the walls of the house had to be rectilinear and firm. By frequent changes in their direction and interruptions in their course, however, they were made to accommodate growing plants as well as light and air. Built-in furniture and built-in planting boxes integrated more than the furniture with the architecture; they fused the garden with the house.

The gap in the wall beside the entrance walk not only receives a climbing vine; it affords a glimpse of flowers behind it. Outside the windows of the dining alcove a box of luxuriantly growing plants punctuates the juncture of one wing of the house with the other, and, along with vines growing from the concealed-lighting trough, provides a pleasant setting for summer meals. By means of terraces, formalized banks of ground cover, and rectangular beds of flowers, grass, and vegetables, the architecture extends in turn into the recesses of the garden. Gradually slackening in the severity of its geometry as it withdraws from the house, the architectural motives tend to merge imperceptibly with the landscape beyond.

The arts of architecture and landscape design are rarely practiced by a single person, and rarer still is the chance to complete a house and garden in a single operation. Owing to the fragmentary way in which most of us do our thinking, the landscape architect is usually obliged to accept only remedial jobs—concealing behind screens of planting the more glaring of the architect's mistakes, tricking a revivalistic façade into looking as though it fitted its site, making living space out of a yard which the architect in his original design for the house had ignored.

The landscape designer, Robert Royston, once came to the author's rescue in the third of these respects. The writer was living with his family in a two-story-and-attic structure on filled land overlooking a piece of an old cherry orchard. Seven of the cherry trees remained to shade the rear of the house from the late afternoon sun of summer, but nothing had ever been done to make the lot other than a fragment of a rundown orchard. Fifty feet wide and a hundred and twenty feet deep, the lot lay largely to the rear of the house (4.19a), a

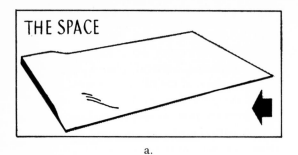

THE SPACE

a.

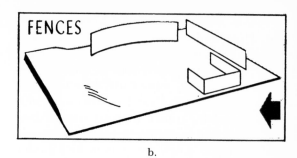

FENCES

b.

TEXTURE

c.

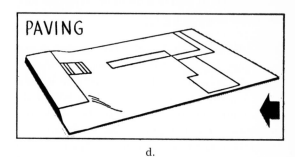

PAVING

d.

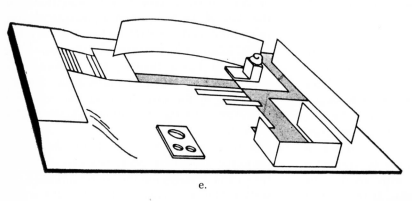

e.

f.

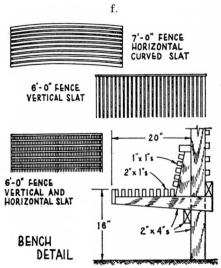

7'-0" FENCE HORIZONTAL CURVED SLAT

6'-0" FENCE VERTICAL SLAT

6'-0" FENCE VERTICAL AND HORIZONTAL SLAT

20"

1" x 1's
2" x 1's

18"

2" x 4's

BENCH DETAIL

4.19. Robert Royston (1904–   ): Wallace S. Baldinger garden, Eugene, Ore., procedure by which the plan was developed. Diagrams from illustrations in *Sunset*, November, 1953, pp. 50–51. Courtesy of the editors of *Sunset*.

shapeless weed patch painful to look on as to cut. Then, under winter rains, filled land supporting the back porch began to slide downhill, carrying the porch with it. Under stress of the emergency, more earth-fill was hauled in, retaining walls of random stonework were built around the trunks of cherry trees nearest the house, and a reinforced concrete slab was laid to support a new porch, to make a garden terrace, and to lead to a flight of steps reaching the lower slope of the hill.

Since a garden terrace without a garden made the weed patch still more painful, it was necessary to convert it. A gravel walk leading from the steps toward the rear of the lot was laid; a sculpture on a pedestal to bound the view from the terrace down the walk was proposed; and in front of the sculpture-to-be the walk was turned at right angles to lead to some projected garden nook along the north edge of the lot. But all this seemed too stiff and narrowing for a lot already cramped.

Then, the landscape architect called in, Robert Royston, noted at once the source of the trouble—the thinking in terms of lines and axes rather than of areas, and so he began with the ground area itself (4.19a).[10] Letting trees serve as fixed determinants, he designed three free-standing fences, each of a different height (4.19b). With one fence he created a three-sided "garden room," with another he screened off the vegetable plot at the end of the lot, and with the third he divided the main portion of the garden from the laundry area and the children's play area. He made this third fence the dominant one in height and interest, determining its variations in height solely by eye so as to prevent its seeming either to slide downhill or to take off into the air. He curved it so as to introduce a sense of extension from side to side, and placed it at such heights as to allow branches of two cherry trees to hang over it as though it had always been there. He had the fences painted with colored creosote stains, not only to preserve the wood but to form a background of color for the plant mate-

[10] See Notes, page 297.

rials: the curving fence a quiet "battleship" gray like that of the house, the rear fence black, and the "garden room" fence eucalyptus green.

By disposing vertical planes against the flattened slope of the hill in this way, the landscape designer was working structurally. By designing the fences composing these planes in varied patterns of "one-by-ones" and "one-by-twos," he was working texturally (4.19). He now laid out a series of concrete blocks carrying the structural motive of the terrace itself out into the garden (4.19c)—in a landing for the steps, an emplacement and a pedestal for the sculpture, two plant containers opening into the ground below (one for a single plant specimen and the other for three), and two rectangular stepping "stones." By having the concrete of the landing and the emplacement scored with parallel lines while it was still wet, he introduced a "repeat" with variations for the slats of the fences and a pleasing change in textural quality for the material. As an additional contrast to the concrete he called for rolled gravel as a "flooring" for the walks, the "garden room," and the laundry area (4.19d).

It was in the disposition of concrete and gravel areas (4.19e) that Royston broke clearly with the original idea of axes and lines. He eliminated the intersection of the two walks, projected an oblong plant bed over the area thus gained, staggered the continuation of the walk to the rear fence, and pushed the sculptural pedestal and emplacement far enough to the side to put the sculpture out of the direct line of vision from the terrace (4.21).

Everything up to this point involved the "architecture" of landscape architecture. It established the structure of the garden, its supporting skeleton. It fell short, however, of giving the garden a head and humanizing center. Every line, plane, and texture converged with powerful impact upon the pedestal, and with nothing on the pedestal the garden framework remained incomplete and impersonal. At the very outset arrangement had been made with the sculptor Mark Sponenburgh to collaborate with the landscape architect in furnishing a suitable piece of sculpture wherever

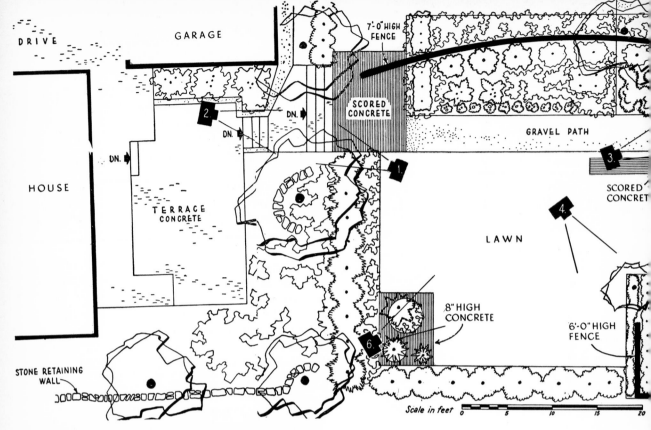

DRIVE

GARAGE

7'-0" HIGH
FENCE

SCORED
CONCRETE

2

DN.

DN.

DN.

GRAVEL PATH

3

1

HOUSE

SCORED
CONCRET

TERRACE
CONCRETE

4

LAWN

.8" HIGH
CONCRETE

6

6'-0" HIGH
FENCE

STONE RETAINING
WALL

Scale in feet 0   5   10   15   20

4.20 (*above*). Robert Royston: Wallace S. Baldinger garden, the developed plan. Adapted from *Sunset,* November, 1953, pp. 50–51. Courtesy of the editors of *Sunset.*

4.21 (*left*). Robert Royston: Wallace S. Baldinger garden, view from concrete terrace behind house, looking west. 1951. Tom Burns, Jr., photograph.

needed. When the sculptor saw the plan (4.20) and realized the key role that his carving would play—big in scale, powerful in sweep of contour and massive in effect, drawing the converging movements of the garden into its bulk only there to resolve them, he was ready to withdraw. The garden sculpture had seemed to him in prospect a minor work to be placed more or less casually. But Robert Royston had loaded on his shoulders a responsibility that only he as sculptor could discharge. Much trial and error ensued, much searching of studio and storeroom. It ended in the sculptor's decision to establish, on a pedestal to be cast especially for it, one of his major creations in

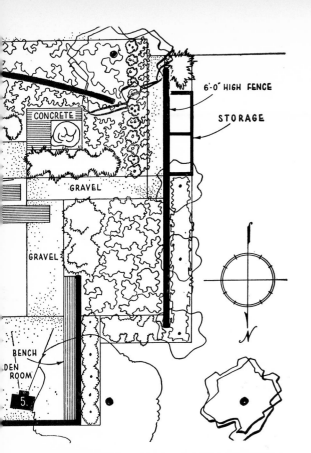

6'-0" HIGH FENCE

STORAGE

CONCRETE

GRAVEL

GRAVEL

N

BENCH

DEN ROOM

5.

stone: a highly simplified mother-and-child abstraction appropriately called *Earth*.

Once the sculpture was in place in all its massiveness (4.22), every structural member of the garden seemed to come to life and, in reverse, every plant to take on structural meaning—from the planes of fence, lawn, and ajuga-bed to the sculpture-echoing but looser masses of cryptomeria, dogwood, and pine, the gesturing lines of cherry branch, japonica, and rhododendron, and the rhythmically contracting and expanding spatial volumes. The carving, a work of the primary art of mass, set the key. It evoked the mood, contemplative and domestic. It invited enjoyment for its own sake as a representational sculpture. It provided a hub, finally, around which the garden's forms could move in rhythmic coordination.

4.22 (*below*). Robert Royston: Wallace S. Baldinger garden, view from concrete plant container, looking southwest. Sculpture by Mark Sponenburgh: (1917–): *Earth*. 1948. Brownstone. Height, 20½". Tom Burns, Jr., photograph.

SUMMARY

Architecture is, like any craft or branch of industrial design, a utilitarian art. It has to do with the provision of human shelter. It operates like some super-craft conditioned by necessities—necessities of site, function, climate, building materials, construction techniques. More than a craft or branch of industrial design, however, it has to begin with paperwork: data concerning site and surroundings, sketches, plans, elevations, sections, construction details, perspective renderings, specifications to guide the builders. Only after all such paperwork has been attended to can it proceed with the actual construction. But as the structure rises, working upward and outward like a tree, it may seem to require changes in the form originally envisioned, again like a tree in response to the actual environment.

Concerned with qualities of space which it governs by masses and planes, accentuates by points, and enriches by colors and textures, architecture owes its very reason for existence to its voids. It controls these voids through techniques of construction, whether post-and-lintel or arcuated, whether skeletal or shell techniques which can be made to contribute as expressively to the form of the building as the materials employed by them, as the functions prompting its construction. Hence originates the vitality of such masterpieces as the Parthenon, a post-and-lintel structure in marble, the cathedral of Chartres, an arcuated structure in stone, the Carson-Pirie-Scott Department Store, a skeletal structure of ferroconcrete, and the Xochimilco Restaurant, a shell structure of ferroconcrete.

In order to heighten the expression of the function of such works, to make them belong to the site and the region, to extend their usefulness beyond their walls, architecture is often obliged to call on other arts for assistance. Assistance may take the form of architectural ornament, although this ornament is scarcely recognized as such when integrated with the structure. It may comprise the furniture and furnishings created by the various crafts and branches of industrial design. It may consist in a process of interior design intimately interrelated with the architecture itself. It may involve the development of the site as a process of landscape design. It may embrace sculpture or painting, either incorporated with the building or shown separately. Even among such arts as become collaborators, one art may have to call on another to help it meet its own collaborative program: witness the garden just studied, demanding the masses of a sculpture for climax to its composition.

RECOMMENDED READINGS

Zevi, Bruno. (Milton Gendel, trans.; Joseph A. Barry, ed.). *Architecture as Space: How to Look at Architecture*. New York: Horizon Press, 1957.

> This is one of the best books ever written on the nature of architecture as distinguished from the other arts. In an excellent translation from the original Italian, it maintains an objective point of view, treating architecture of the past with the same penetrating insight as architecture of the present. Volumes of open space in architectural composition take on new significance at the hands of Zevi as he relates them to a "fourth" dimension of time.

Scott, Geoffrey. *The Architecture of Humanism*. New York: Doubleday Anchor Books, 1954. Charles Scribner's Sons, 1924.

> Geoffrey Scott makes an able defense of Renaissance architecture on the grounds of its ability to afford esthetic pleasure independent of any structural or functional expression. His use of the word "taste" as synonymous with "sound critical judgment" is no longer valid, because "taste" may now connote the snobbishness of "fashion" and the arbitrariness of "styling." His book continues, nevertheless, to hold a place of fundamental importance in the criticism of architecture.

Giedion, Sigfried. *Space, Time and Architecture.* Cambridge, Mass.: Harvard University Press, 1954. 1st ed., 1941.

Written with appreciation of the great architectural styles of the past and a clear grasp of what makes the architecture of the twentieth century unique, this book continues to exert sound influence. Analogies with other arts are superficially drawn, but the treatment of "space-time" as a new element in recent architectural creation, pp. 425–608, and the treatment of innovations of construction and design originating in Chicago, pp. 345–424, make outstanding contributions.

Pevsner, Nikolaus. *Pioneers of Modern Design from William Morris to Walter Gropius.* New York: Museum of Modern Art, 1949. Revised ed. of *Pioneers of the Modern Movement from William Morris to Walter Gropius.* New York: Frederick A. Stokes, 1937.

Nikolaus Pevsner brings to the writing of this book firsthand contact with contemporary art and severely disciplined scholarship in the historical origins of contemporary architecture.

Mumford, Lewis. *Roots of Contemporary American Architecture.* New York: Reinhold, 1952.

Both Giedion and Pevsner recognize the historical importance of certain developments in American architecture. Mumford tracks down the formative ideas from which these developments emerged. He traces them to their literary sources, reprints significant passages, and prefaces them with an excellent introduction.

Gutheim, Frederick. *Frank Lloyd Wright on Architecture: 1894–1940.* New York: Duell, Sloan and Pearce, 1941.

Rarely if ever before in history has an architect as prolific and creative as Frank Lloyd Wright written so voluminously about his own life and work and critical evaluations. In contrast with his personal letters, models of brevity, Wright's books suffer from verbosity and redundancy. Hence the value of such an anthology as this, edited with discriminating intelligence. It completes a Frank Lloyd Wright trilogy published by Duell, Sloan and Pearce, the other two of which have been cited in the footnotes for the present chapter: Wright, *An Autobiography* (1943; 1st pub., 1932); and Hitchcock, *In the Nature of Materials* (1942).

Hamlin, Talbot, ed. *Forms and Functions of Twentieth-Century Architecture.* 4 vols. New York: Columbia University Press, 1952.

This ambitious work in four heavy volumes does more than simply review in pictorial and statistical form outstanding examples of building during the first half of the twentieth century. It provides an introduction to the whole art of architecture and its allied arts, in the light of contemporary building. The first volume is devoted to elements, the second to principles, and the third and fourth to building types. In spite of enormous detail, the text is simply and clearly written.

Hudnut, Joseph. *Architecture and the Spirit of Man.* Cambridge, Mass.: Harvard University Press, 1949.

Written in smaller compass, this is a more readable book than the monumental four-volume work for which Hamlin served as editor. The second half of the book is devoted to city planning from the architect's point of view. Hudnut is particularly penetrating in his critical comments on the garden and the element of space which the interior of the building shares with the garden, pp. 133–142.

Nelson, George, ed. *Living Spaces.* "Interiors Library," 1. New York: Whitney Publications, 1952.

Since the early nineteen-twenties many picture-books of contemporary interiors have been published. Often printed from plates already used by some magazine, they are valuable chiefly as documentary material and of limited use to a reader seeking bases for critical judgment in interior design. George Nelson's book is a welcome exception. It is introduced by an intimate and stimulating essay by the designer himself and followed by a wide range of interiors both in time and in character of effect, each well-analyzed.

Eckbo, Garrett. *The Art of Home Landscaping.* New York: F. W. Dodge, 1956.

Many books on garden design have been published. None of them approaches the present book for down-to-earth practicality from the home-owner's point of view. The author relates the practice of garden design closely to that of domestic architecture. He starts with a "groundwork" of climatic and soil conditions and demonstrates correct subsequent procedure. The book suffers, however, from the smallness of the illustrations.

Church, Thomas D. *Gardens Are for People.* New York: Reinhold, 1955.

Thomas Church's book gains a distinct advantage over Eckbo's by its use of color plates as well as black-and-white illustrations, all of generous size. Church writes with a lightly humorous touch as he conducts the reader on a tour of his own California gardens. His book is worth consulting, even though limited in application to a small portion of the United States.

5.1. *Goddess of the Moon* (*Chalchihuitlicue*). Before A.D. 770; found in 1889, half-buried, southwest of plaza in front of the Pyramid of the Moon, Teotihuacán. Andesite; hole in breast originally inlaid with precious stone. Height, 10′6″. Museo Nacional, Mexico City. Hugo Brehme photograph.

Sculpture

THE LANDSCAPE ARCHITECT who employed sculpture to complete the author's garden (4.22) knew enough to let a carving be itself. He recognized that sculpture was an art of independent studio creation, not a utilitarian art like his own nor one competing with industrial design. He observed the principle of emphasis, allowing the single sculpture called for to assert its qualities.

Sculpture is an art of expression in volumes of solid mass: volumes whose rise against gravity and attendant sense of power can alone give the work its theme; solids whose balanced oppositions across space express the nature of their element; masses which can, and often do, assume shapes representing things apart from the work itself—here, for example, a mother bending over her baby, with an enfolding cloak so suggestive of cloud-wrapped Mother Earth as to prompt the title.

BASIC FORMATS OF SCULPTURE

Sculpture in the Round

Sponenburgh's *Earth* is a statue in the round; space surrounds it on all sides. The appeal of the work depends on the way in which the space goes around it, even though the spectator may not be able actually to go behind it and must view it from a few vantage points to the front and sides.

Sculptures in the round have almost always been created as thickly opaque and solid-looking as they can be made. They affirm by their density that element of mass which is the art's chief stock in trade. They continue to be produced, as solid as they ever were. In our advanced industrial society, however, a society in which speed of travel and communication has revolutionized experience with space and time, the conventional massiveness of sculpture is apt to seem inappropriate. Modern sculptors have turned more and more to effects of reflection, translucency, transparency, even openness and hollowness. They have replaced mass with point, line, and plane to define the spaces occupied by their works (5.16, 5.19 to 5.21a and b).

Sculpture in Relief

Sculpture in the round constitutes one of two main classes of sculpture based on degree of projection into space and relation to background. The other class is sculpture in relief. Whereas sculpture in the round projects full volumes in a spatial envelope that has no background of its own, sculpture in relief projects less than the normal projection of an object represented and requires that a background be a part of it. If forms project almost as much as would the object represented or up to about half as much, the work is classified as high relief, sometimes by using the French term "haut" (pronounced "oh") for "high" (5.2, 5.8). If the forms project about half as much as the normal relief of the object represented down to the slightest bulging of the surface, the work is classified as low relief, sometimes using the French term "bas" (pronounced "bah") for "low" (the front of 5.1).

The simplest of all forms of relief, so close to drawing as often to be treated with that branch of the art of painting instead of being treated with sculpture, is incision. The artist

119

simply grooves a contour into a surface, letting the shadows cast inside the incision register on the eye as lines. If, as the ancient Egyptians sometimes did, the forms are hollowed out instead of being raised from the background, we have intaglio, the opposite of relief (though usually classed with it).[1]

Since in all forms of relief the figures are incorporated with the background, no view save one, that from directly in front, is effective. The movement of such figures is mainly from side to side or up and down and only to a minor extent, if at all, forward and back in space. This differs sharply from the movement of sculpture in the round, which is fully as much forward and back as it is up and down and side to side.

Whether devoted to relief or to the round, sculpture as an art of mass appeals above all to our sense of touch, our tactile response. Ideally, we ought to be able to run our hands over a statue before we do any looking at it, even as the sculptor did while the work was in progress. We ought to be able to touch it, fondle it, caress it, even hug and, if possible, lift it. Only in that way can we grasp its full expressive meaning—in terms of textures, shapes of volumes, bulk, the tactile space that it occupies. The sculptor Brancusi was so conscious of the need for the primary tactile appeal of his art that he labeled one of his creations simply *Sculpture for the Blind.* Inspired by the same idea, sculpture students are sometimes asked to make "handies," small pieces intended to be handled rather than seen. Sculptures on public view ought ideally to be so strong, so secure on their pedestals, so resistant to soiling that spectators can handle them freely.

PROCEDURES AND MATERIALS

Subtractive Procedure vs. Additive

The artist who fashions a work of sculpture follows one of two standard methods of procedure: the subtractive, or the additive. The subtractive is the glyptic method (from the Greek *glyptikos*, meaning "carved"). The artist in following it cuts material away until the creation stands forth "revealed," so to speak, as though it had been in the material all along, simply awaiting the moment of emergence. He feels impelled by the material's resistance to his attack to eliminate multitudinous detail. He recognizes its stubborn refusal to brook mistakes. Hence the nature of his carving, simple of surface, round of contour, big-scaled in its counterpoisings of one mass to another. Mark Sponenburgh followed the subtractive, the glyptic, technique when he carved *Earth* out of sandstone (4.22). Other sculptors have carved figures with correspondingly expressive features: the Toltec image-maker, for example (5.1), the Hindu craftsman (5.2), the Egyptian portraitist (5.4).

The additive is the plastic method ("plastic" deriving, as noted, from the Greek *plastikos*, meaning "fit for molding"). The artist in following it adds some material, usually clay, to itself until the work is finished (Pl. II, 5.5). He makes changes easily as he proceeds. If dissatisfied with the way in which the work is going, he may slice the material back to the beginning and start all over again. The method thus allows great flexibility and freedom, directly the opposite of the subtractive method. It responds to every slightest expressive impulse—pinching, pulling, punching, smoothing—to record the action faithfully. It lends itself to spontaneity of effect, leaving to the artist himself exertion of any required restraint.

Sculpture cast in metal is produced by the additive method; the metal merely records a shape originally fashioned in an additive material (5.3, 5.6, and 5.7). For such casting, clay is ordinarily the preliminary material, and for a shape designed to exploit the self-supporting power of the metal, the clay must be built up

[1] See Notes, page 297.

around an armature—a skeletal framework made of wood, iron pipe, twisted wire, or the like, to support the figure temporarily during the course of the modeling.

Clay, Metal, Stone, and Wood

The sculptor has to have the same understanding of basic elements and principles of design as other artists have, and he is no more able than they to apply elements and principles without understanding the materials with which he works. Observers need in turn to know something of these materials and their ways of behaving in order to appreciate what the sculptor is trying to do. Clay and metal, for instance, permit greater freedom than other materials. They invite an active pose, an open composition, with limbs flung out, head tossed back, body thrown off center, drapery flying.

Clay lends itself to spontaneous and spirited effects when, as in pottery, it is fired in a kiln and converted into the self-supporting ultimate material. It can, by craftsmanship that involves phenomenal speed in modeling and absolute certainty in constructing interior walls of support, be rendered into a statue of colossal size (Pl. II). Ordinarily, however, lest the fragility of the fired clay lead to breakage, it prompts the creation of works on the miniature scale of the statuette (5.5). On a limited scale it prompts a lively, playful rendering of detail and an anecdotal, poetic, or even pretty development of theme. When colors, made possible by glazing, are added to grace the work, a terra-cotta or ceramic sculpture can be said to have reached its ultimate possibilities (Pl. II).

The strength of brass or bronze permits a sculptural figure to be supported on even a single toe (5.3). Such a metal allows the figure to be contorted into practically any position. It encourages opening the forms out into space, sometimes even to the exclusion of mass entirely (5.19, 5.20, and 5.21). It offers a wide range of colors, dependent on chemical reactions either within the metal itself or in reaction with the atmosphere; it further receives and holds the brilliant colors of enameling.

While clay and metal invite open forms and broken contours, stone and wood demand more closed and compact forms (5.1, 5.9, 5.11, 5.12, 5.13, 5.15). Stone forbids by its relative brittleness, in fact, any sharply outflung limb or narrow support of foot. It militates by its hardness against elaboration of detail, and it encourages powerful massing. Michelangelo, supreme carver of the Italian Renaissance, realized the limitations of stone and rose to meet its challenge. He conceived of the ideal stone statue as having so little projection anywhere that it would roll downhill without breaking.

More than either stone or metal, wood has warmth and personality that varies from one piece of material to the next. It allows greater freedom of handling than stone but less than cast metal or modeled clay. It requires special handling to bring out the run of its grain (5.15). It has little strength to support a thin projection out across the grain, but it lends itself well to joinery when a sharply protruding form is carved separately and inserted into the mass (5.12, 5.13). By its relative darkness and active effect of grain, wood prompts sharp angularities of cutting and deeply shadowed penetrations for accent. Again, because of the run of its grain, wood predetermines the direction of its cutting—with the grain or across it, but never against it, lest the wood be split and ruined.

New Materials and New Combinations

Sculptors are always experimenting with new materials. Today they are investigating the possibilities of stainless steel, welded iron and steel, aluminum, blown or molded glass, any one of a score or more of the newly invented plastics (5.16, 5.19 to 5.21). They are continually finding in this way ideas for new motives and new ways of heightening old themes.

Sculptors are learning to combine these new materials and broaden their expression. The materials which they use may be new, but the idea of combining them is old. Twenty-four hundred years ago, in the shrine cities of ancient Greece, gigantic statues of the gods were being fashioned of precious materials laid over a core of cheaper substance. The image of Athena housed in the Parthenon, for instance, was not merely of marble; it was constructed out of gold and ivory, materials which gave the name *chryselephantine* to this type of statue, because it meant in Greek "made of gold and ivory." [2]

SUBJECT MATTER OF SCULPTURE

Sculptural materials have great power to evoke moods, because they usually enjoy a close alliance with subject matter. Sculptors aware of this power may choose a particular material to enhance the appeal of their chosen subject. Whatever their reason for choice of a particular material, however, one thing is sure: they never choose it for the sake of literal imitation of something else. Sculptors realize that the purpose of their art, as of any art, is always other than deception. They may be tempted merely to reproduce natural forms because the masses native to their art correspond to the masses found in actual objects. If they succumb to the temptation, however, they trick us into confusing the sculpture with the thing represented and deny us any chance to regard the sculpture as a work of art.

Sculptors realize that their office is not to imitate nature, but to abstract from her and re-create. They look to her as their source of subject matter, and especially to her animate creatures, the masses of which assume relationships in movement. They find in animals, for example, forms full of meaning, masses shaped to facilitate movement, bodies ordered to suggest emotions. Sculptors find in the forms of animals a graceful, clean efficiency which they marvel at and long to emulate. They abstract from such forms. They modify the motives selected, exaggerating and distorting them, investing them with an empathic appeal so that we as observers can come to share in the animal's existence (5.16 and 5.18).

However strong our empathic response to a piece of animal sculpture, we remain human beings, and any response we may make to a sculptured animal can be multiplied a hundredfold when we turn from it to the sculptured human figure. Sculptors see possibilities of mass-relationships not only in the pose of the professional model but in the attitudes assumed unconsciously as any person moves about: leaning against something, lounging in a chair, walking along a street, performing a thousand and one workaday occupations. They study these relationships as they would those of an animal's form. They draw from them, re-create them, and in the process open our eyes to a world of unsuspected experiences (5.5, 5.6, and 5.11).

Often a sculptor develops drapery about the figure which he is creating, because with it he can emphasize some feature much as the potter does with painted ornament about the body of his vessel (3.7). With the representation of drapery the sculptor can intensify the massiveness of a figure (5.1), increase the firmness of its stance (5.6), accelerate the effect of its action (5.9). He needs simply to know the "anatomy" of drapery, how it falls in line-creating and potentially expressive folds, how it conceals the body here and reveals it there in terms of the creative needs which he feels his work to have.

The question of drapery in sculpture again brings up the question of clothing. We have already noted in our chapter on industrial design and the crafts how fickle are the fashions of dress. Prompted by need to keep the wheels of industry turning, women's fashions change every season. Under such circumstances a dress that really enhances the beauty of the body is extremely difficult to design. If the reader doubts such a statement, let him go to the files of some ladies' magazine and look for even one illustration of a "well-dressed" woman twenty years ago. The chances are that he will fail in his search, so ridiculous will

[2] See Notes, page 297.

even the most fashionable appear. If he dips farther back into history, beyond the Industrial Age, he will find that fashions changed more slowly and sometimes reached a high peak of expressive design.* Seldom even then will he find a dress that really seems to have more than a narrowly "dated" quality about it.

The consequence of fickleness is disqualification of most contemporary attire for representation in sculpture.[3] Sculpture ordinarily admits only the most generalized kind of drapery, universally appealing because of its lasting materials and epiclike massings of form.

Owing to changing styles of dress and their frequent contradictions to the changelessness of both the human body and the typical sculptural material, sculptors find the unclothed figure preferable for subject (5.9, 5.10, 5.11). Laymen recognize this preference but they often misinterpret its motives. They are apt to judge sculptors "immodest" or "indelicate."

Most sculptors prefer the human body without its clothing, but that does not mean that they conceive of it as "naked." They insist on going beyond the dictionary, which treats the words "naked" and "nude" as synonymous.† They hold that "naked" implies accidental exposure of the body to the public, connoting shame and secret sin. They hold that "nude," on the other hand, implies pride and glory in a well-formed figure, not the conventionally "perfect" athlete or triumphant "beauty queen," but an idealized re-creation of the human body as the noblest thing in nature.‡

The sculptured nude, even at the hands of professed realists among artists, is very different from actual physical specimens in a nudist camp. It is not even a "composite" of the best points drawn from the bodies of, say, five handsome athletes or five charming maidens, nor even of a hundred. No ideally beautiful sculptured figure was ever created by combining parts chosen from different living figures. It always emerged as the unique creation of an artist, not as the super-generalized "average" figure which a measurer would put together.[4] It became the creation of a sculptor who worked as a true artist, disposing the elements for their apparent movement and balance in deep space, stressing physical features regarded by him and his society as desirable, developing rhythmic movement throughout to complete an "organism" which seems to live in its own right as a statue.

Except in societies like those of medieval Europe or Japan, in which social bathing seems to have offered a satisfactory substitute, the appeal of the sculptured nude has always run deep. The ancient Greeks expressed this appeal in two legends still illuminating to us, their cultural descendants. One legend tells of the beautiful youth called Narcissus. Although many nymphs pursued him, he spurned them all. One day, however, leaning over a clear pool, he fell hopelessly in love with the image he saw in its depths—his own reflection. Unable to embrace the image and unwilling to leave it, Narcissus pined away, finally turning into the flower which bears his name.

None of us is quite so self-absorbed as Narcissus but we all have more or less self-love. We have an insatiable curiosity about our personal appearance. We gaze into mirrors as well as fountains, but no matter which way we turn we can never quite manage to glimpse the whole of ourselves. Frustrated, we turn to the sculptured figure as a projection of ourselves. Solid and strong in both tactile and empathic appeal, it fascinates us as an object of self-realization.

The other Greek legend deals with Pygmalion, king of Cyprus and accomplished sculptor. Pygmalion, disillusioned with the wickedness he saw in women, carved his ideal female nude out of ivory. Truly a labor of love, the statue was so comely that he fell in love with it and prayed to Venus that she grant him a

* Bernard Rudofsky, *Are Clothes Modern?* (Chicago: Paul Theobald, 1947).

[3] See Notes, page 297.

† *Webster's New World Dictionary*, op. cit., 1953 ed., Vol. I, pp. 974 and 1007; *New Century Dictionary* (New York: D. Appleton-Century, 1946), Vol. I, pp. 1120 and 1157.

‡ Kenneth Clark, *The Nude: a Study in Ideal Form* ("Bollingen Series," XXV, 2; New York: Pantheon Books, 1956), Ch. I, "The Naked and the Nude," pp. 1–29.

[4] See Notes, page 297.

wife as fair. Touched, the Goddess of Love answered his prayer in unexpected fashion. When Pygmalion returned to his beloved statue, he was amazed to find the flush of life coursing through his work and the lovelight coming to its eyes. Overcome with joy, Pygmalion married his gift from Venus.

The legend points up an interest which most of us have in good measure. It is an interest which extends from our own bodies to the bodies of others and especially to those of the opposite sex. Like Pygmalion, we carry our interest over from real life into the art of sculpture. We do not expect our nude statues to be transformed into mates, but we continue to contemplate them, to some extent, at least, for their sex appeal.

The remarkable thing about the nude in sculpture, however, is not the sexual stimulation exerted by it. The marvel is the way in which the sculptured nude catches us up into its ennobling operations as a work of art. Sculpture takes our object of desire and removes it from the immediate time and place. It sublimates and depersonalizes our sexual desire, to deepen and enrich our experience beyond the mere moment.

The appeal of the nude in sculpture does not end in ministry to our narcissistic or erotic impulses. Thanks to its tactile and empathic appeal, its reference to a lifetime of experience with our own bodies, the sculptured nude becomes in a sense the source of all art. It becomes the source for our sense of scale, our systems of proportioning, our repertories of artistic form. It becomes, as it were, the instrument with which the artist plays symphonies, on such themes as emergence into life, bearing of burdens, triumph of achievement, pathos of death.

The sculptor knows the feel of form emerging out of mass, because the very process recurs at his hands; he lifts the solids of his material into the swellings of the body's emergence (5.2). He knows literally what it means to put one's weight behind an effort; he adjusts the masses of his sculptured figure to intensify the sense of purposeful struggle (5.3). He knows the empathic response of the organism to deep emotion, how every muscle from toe to ear seems to undulate overwhelmingly upward and forward (5.13). He knows the lassitude of the body at the point of death, when every part sags into the hollows of the bed and sets the mold for the *rigor mortis* to follow; he carries this empathic experience across into re-creation of a body from which the life has gone (5.9).

POTENTIALITIES OF SCULPTURE

Experience with the preferred subject matter of sculpture helps the sculptor to dispose the masses of his work. He shares the human figure as subject with photographers, printmakers, painters, but he alone among his fellows can endow the forms by which he represents it with tangible substance in deep space.

Limitations

If the sculptor would make the statue express his message, he must abide by certain conditions affecting his creation. If he fails to do so, they can defeat and break him. Sometimes we call these conditions limitations, as though they hedged the artist in like prison walls. We should, rather, call them opportunities. Weak artists fret over limitations, but true sculptors glory in them as challenges. Sculptors respond to three such conditions: illumination, placement, and relationship to other arts.

The sculptor has to consider not only the way in which his image feels to hand and body. He must watch constantly for play of light and shadow about the work in progress. He may not know exactly what kind of light is destined in the end to fall on his creation, but he tries to guess what it will be and to shape his masses in the hope of meeting it. He tries to make reasonably sure that the masses will meet without accidental form-distortion any combination of lights, shadows, and reflected lights.*

When lighted indifferently, sculpture shows up badly. Sculpture badly lighted indoors is distorted enough, but sculpture exposed to the shifting light of the outdoors is the major victim. Sculpture usually undergoes exposure to sunshine with "light-sickness." At one particular moment of one particular day it may appear in utter perfection, exactly the way its maker intended. Earlier that morning the play of lights and shadows may have rendered it completely invisible. Toward sunset on the same day the lighting may convert it into a monstrosity. And this is to say nothing about its appearance on any other sunny day of the year, or under a cloudy sky, or veiled in fog, rain, or snow. Uncontrolled lighting is indeed the enemy of sculpture. It flattens forms. It eats away at contours. It digs holes where highlights fall and tears masses to pieces.

What can a sculptor do about the accidents of lighting? Ideally, of course, he can require that the ultimate site of the relief or the statue in the round be fixed in advance—chosen, say, for a minimum of changes in outdoor lighting throughout the course of either a day or a succession of seasons, close, for example, to the north side of a wall (4.22), or likely to be viewed only at a time when the lighting is kind (5.11b). The sculptor can study the conditions of lighting peculiar to the site selected and design his sculpture specifically to meet them (5.14). He can secure assurance that his work will never be shown except indoors under lighting specially prepared for it (5.9).

The sculptor can make his masses assert themselves so powerfully that they more than offset the encroachments of a blazing sun (5.2). He can make his masses project so boldly that the shadows cast by them upon their background serve only to define and emphasize their bulk (5.13). He can choose a material

with a mat surface so light-absorbent that it can declare its mass consistently through a normal range of lighting (5.15). He can make the light itself do his form-creating work for him, cutting and joining pieces of material to catch the highlights and cast the shadows (5.16). He can even dispense with mass entirely—and with all the plaguing problems of illumination—by merely delineating the space otherwise occupied by mass with the slender forms possible to metal (5.19 to 5.21b).

The placement of a piece of sculpture has as much influence as its lighting on its effectiveness. A statue set up in the open with only distant points from which to be seen needs a bold silhouette and a grand simplicity of plane (5.1). If provided with much detail within the silhouette, it would lose its sense of power and irritate the observer by presenting forms incapable of comprehension at a distance and yet visible enough to be confusing. By way of contrast, a sculpture established indoors, with limited space in front of it and around it must be designed for intimate viewing. It might have an interesting silhouette but it would need above all a rich play of inner rhythms of form, much delicacy of detail and surface modulation (5.3). Rhythms of contour and rhythms of inner form are both essential to sculpture, but they reverse themselves in relative importance when placement changes from the far site to the near.

Miniature sculptures, statuettes, form a class by themselves (5.5), especially those made to be carried about and handled as much as seen. Such works are free of any limitations of site, but they require because of this portability a highly developed tactile appeal and completely felt-through composition on all sides, even on the bottom where the larger work might be merely squared and flattened to fit its pedestal. Their lack of fixed placement gives the artist a chance to provide distinct surprises of detail on the underside—as is usual in the ivory, bone, jade, and marble miniatures of Japan known as *netsukes*.[5]

* Read, *The Art of Sculpture, op. cit.*, pp. 105–123. See also the instructive 16-mm. film directed by Alexander Shaw, *Looking at Sculpture* (distributed by British Information Service, New York; black and white; English sound track; 10 mins.).

[5] See Notes, page 297.

Sculptors sometimes incorporate the pedestal with the work itself, but when they do they find it necessary to differentiate from the statue either the material forming this integral support (5.9) or else its composition, from a more organic to a more geometric character (5.18). Whether or not they work the pedestal into the composition of the sculpture, sculptors insist upon some device like a pedestal or a niche or a bracket to set the work apart from the actual world around it. Especially if the image has some representational significance, they recognize the need to make it obviously a work of stone, wood, bronze, or whatever its material, and not of fur or feathers or human flesh and blood (5.2). As pointed out already in the present discussion, our enjoyment of such a work of art depends on our recognizing this difference. The moment we begin mistaking a statue for an actual human figure, that moment we cease to respond to it as a work of art.

A pedestal harmonizes in its mass with the masses of the sculpture, but its regular shape takes on the more impersonal character of a building and gains some accord with whatever architecture may adjoin it (5.8). Its impersonal and intermediate character guarantees, moreover, that esthetic distance from the observer about which we have already written in an earlier connection (pp. 23–24).

Sculpture is definitely a nonutilitarian art. Its reason for existence lies in expression of personal experience with volumes of mass and re-evocation of that experience in the observer. It has a realm in which to operate wide enough to occupy it independently as long as there are artists to practice it.

Sculpture's specialty in masses, above all the abstracted but still recognizable masses of the human body, qualifies it nonetheless for out of doors: in a garden (4.22, 5.11b), on or around a building's exterior (5.2, 5.8), within the structure of a city and the region surrounding it (5.1, 5.2). Such employment is always esthetic, never utilitarian. Far from enslaving the sculptor to some overlord in architectural, landscape, or urban design, it can and should embrace him as collaborator on a level of equality and mutual respect. Only under such conditions can he do his best work.

Often, as in the Baldinger garden (4.22), a sculptor creates his work in advance of a possible purchase for specific use. He gives it forms free of outside suggestion or command. The designer, needing a statue or a relief of such and such a character, prospects in museums, dealers' showrooms, and sculptors' studios. He may find the very piece he needs, buy it forthwith, and install it at the point he had in mind. Or he may find only that the works of a given artist follow the right direction. He then enlists the sculptor's aid, not only to find the right work but to install it with proper adaptation to its newly determined use —designing a pedestal, installing adequate lighting, or disposing adjacent forms for mutual enhancement.

If the sculptor accepts a commission from a designer in another art, he assumes a role of subservience to the artist employing him, a role fraught with dangers of disagreement and misunderstanding and even of perversion of his art beyond its normal province. The sculptor anxious to preserve his integrity as a free creator can indeed point to cases in which collaboration has debased his work. He can point to excesses of advertising zeal—those roadside stands which masquerade as big oranges, beer kegs, and the like. He can point to the caryatids of ancient Greek shrines, columns carved as market women carrying baskets on their heads for capitals (truly sculpture gone wrong when it arouses an empathic response of backache). He can point to the gargoyles of the Gothic cathedral—rainspouts carved into heads of beasts and monsters, all waiting open-mouthed for the next shower, when they vomit elements down on shelter-seekers.

Sculpture perverted to serve either as architecture or as digression from it is unworthy of acceptance as great art. But sculpture about a building has usages which are more difficult to dismiss. There are cases of employment for particular effects within the architectural composition itself: lightening effects accomplished by a rippling light and shadow, interest-lending effects of niched statuary on an otherwise monotonously plain wall, softening effects at corners which might otherwise seem abrupt.*

It would be incorrect to say that the better the use made of sculpture by architecture, the poorer the sculpture. Sculpture which seems decorative or pictorial from a distance may reveal itself, when examined closely, to be rich in representational significance. It may perform a function of which it is uniquely capable —representing masses of figures in motives common to humanity, themes that help to personalize the building and underscore its functions.

It would also be incorrect to say that sculpture made for incorporation with an edifice becomes a mangled fragment when detached from the structure and exhibited in a museum. Good sculpture maintains its inner cohesions, its tensions between opposing masses, any of which are sufficient to preserve its unity when the work is removed from the architecture of which it was once a part and shown by itself. Such is one distinction unique to the art of mass.

Sculpture as a Religious Adjunct: Stone

For sheer density of mass, that major element in sculpture, it would be hard to find a more impressive figure than the ten-foot stone image of a moon-goddess which stands today in a gallery of Mexico's National Museum (5.1). Confronting it as we enter the gallery, we marvel at the powerful way in which it seems to rise from the floor, as it once rose from the earth, to compress itself. Approaching it empathically, we experience something of that sense of immovable steadfastness which the carver must have sought to evoke from the stone. We are reminded of the ancient Greek personification of such power in the earth giant, Antaeus, who grew stronger every time Hercules threw him to the ground.

The statue was made to represent Chalchihuitlicue, moon-goddess whom the Toltec tribesmen of Mexico worshiped fifteen hundred years ago as source of physical prowess. In keeping with their idea of matchless strength, it was carved out of a block of stone as big as could be quarried while remaining portable to its sacred site. Although assuming somewhat the human form which the Toltecs imagined the moon-goddess to have, the image had to retain the original squareness and density of the block as evidence of a harnessing of power to the needs of man.

For his material the Toltec sculptor chose andesite, one of the hardest stones of Mexico. Instead of treating his job as a grievous one, he actually welcomed the stone's resistance. He made the figure hug in massive austerity the four flat planes with which he started. In order to maintain these planes, he reduced to low relief all forms of the human body which would normally project. He worked for the sharpest possible silhouette at the front of each of the four major planes, and he treated each plane as a field for equally sharp detailing. Committed to the rectangular face of the block, he seems to have relished its confinement, bounding most of the inner forms with a similarly closed and rectilinear frame. By subdividing areas according to a consistently geometric pattern, the Toltec sculptor finally completed an image as aggressively stonelike as could be imagined and almost painfully severe.

In its tight plane-boundedness and sharp angularity the Toltec moon-goddess is similar to the Fairbanks house of Dedham (4.1). In both, physical environment played a formative role. As in a mountain-hemmed valley of New England, so on the arid plateau of central Mexico where the Toltecs lived, human life persisted in a state of ceaseless war with nature.† Insecurity lurked everywhere. Fear of the unknown haunted the mind. Control of the environment, denied in real life, had to be sym-

---

* In the perspective of mid-nineteenth-century romanticism, John Ruskin wrote a penetrating study of architectural sculpture. See *The Stones of Venice* (New York: John Wiley and Sons, 1885; 1st English ed., 1851), Vol. I, pp. 211–357.

† For study of Toltec culture, see George C. Vaillant, *Aztecs of Mexico* (Garden City, N. Y.: Doubleday, Doran, 1944), pp. 50–70.

bolized in the image of the deity. It had to be projected into stone in those obviously man-made patterns which we have learned to recognize as primitive.

To call the Toltec statue "primitive" is not to argue, as people used to do, for its creator's incompetence. Such carving would stretch the capabilities of a modern sculptor with even the best of tools. And the Toltec carver had no finely tempered chisels with which to attack the andesite. He had only chips of still harder stone, tools with which he could scratch the stone away bit by bit. He performed a remarkable feat of skill, therefore, in grinding the stone down until the goddess stood revealed in knifelike precision.

The block of carved andesite was set beside a sacred way that cut through the heart of a temple-city the Toltecs had built to curry favor from their gods. By the sheer weight of her image, the Toltecs hoped to pull the goddess from her perch in the moon to receive their sacrifices and answer their prayers for rain and fertility. In actual practice, though, they found the magic of their image working fitfully. Some years would go well and the harvest abound. Other years the goddess would turn her back.

If an image of colossal size and dense material sometimes failed to bring the moon-goddess to their midst, then, perhaps the Toltecs reasoned, they could climb after her. High mountains soared not far away and probably at one time or another the Toltec priests did climb the loftiest to make their sacrifices. Mountains still had their drawbacks for such a purpose. They were products of nature's handiwork, not man's. Wild beasts haunted their slopes and natural forces played around their peaks.

The only solution seemed to be an artificial mountain which the Toltecs could erect in their holy city itself, a mountain the construction of which would outdraw ten thousand times over the sweat drawn from the sculptor by his carving—and by this increased labor strengthen the magic. The Toltecs built a pyramid to represent a mountain, therefore, and

dedicated the colossal pile to the Goddess of the Moon. They were careful to avoid irregularities in its slopes, because these might lead the moon-goddess to confuse it with a real mountain and fail to recognize man's labors in her honor. They built their mountain as massive as a natural one—using clay blocks and waste materials for filling and stone blocks for covering—but they made it rise pyramidally true as a die to the platform reserved on top for an altar around which their priests could make their offerings.

Even the Pyramid of the Moon, larger and larger though the Toltecs made it by successive additions, eventually failed its builders. The rains stopped, vegetation wilted, famines took their toll. The survivors fled, never to be heard of again, but leaving behind them gigantic works of art to attest to their onetime power.

Man-made mountains, inspired by a riper culture, have been allowed at times to relax from their original severity of pyramidal shape and assume forms more representational. Such, for example, are the temple-mountains which have been erected in India for at least two thousand years.

Like the Toltecs of Mexico, the Hindus have always taken emotional satisfaction in the density of stone and its suppression of space. In order to increase the sense of enclosing mass, they have hollowed cave-temples out of live rock. Again like the Toltecs, piling mass on mass to get closer to their goddess of the moon, the Hindus have made their temple-mountains into shortcuts, over the ledges of which to climb toward the supposed Infinite.

Unlike the Toltecs, on the other hand, the Hindus did not seek security in the stone's inertness. They made the stone seem, rather, to swell and pulsate with vitality. They were impelled in this by their faith, which anticipated, as a matter of fact, discoveries of modern science.

Hindus long ago conceived of our universe as composed of matter and energy in continual interchange. They conceived of mass and spirit as coming to focus in the human body to make of it the noblest of creations. Since matter

5.2. Mallikarjuna Temple, Pattadakal, view looking northeast. *c.* A.D. 745. Sandstone. Height, *c.* 60′. Courtesy of Stella Kramrisch and the Phaidon Press.

manifests itself in the body's flesh and energy in the body's breath, by controlling the breath man controls his flesh; by controlling the energy within, he can hope eventually to control the energy of the universe. Intensification of the power of energy can narrow to a lifetime or even half a year that gap of millions of eons of time which the soul otherwise needs for transmigrations from atom to Supreme Being.

The way to do this, according to the Hindu faith, is to practice yoga, an art of religion which unites prayer with ritual and every other form of worship.* Great seers need no help in the practice of yoga but ordinary mortals require outside aids. They need a temple (5.2) that can be regarded as embodying the Supreme Being who is himself practicing yoga. The Hindu architect thus began with a solid

* See Swami Vivekananda, *Raja-yoga: or Conquering the Internal Nature* (New York: Ramakrishna-Vivekananda Center, 1946).

stone foundation, at once the altar of dedication and the seat supporting the temple.

Since the tower, the temple proper, was regarded as an equivalent both to the human body and to the world conceived as one gigantic mountain, it had to be made as massive as possible. Save for a tiny cubicle which served as sanctuary and a narrow passageway around it for the priest to use, therefore, the architect rendered the superstructure completely solid in appearance and reality. He piled one block above the other in diminishing sizes but identical shapes—to accentuate by the open passageway left around each terrace the essential massiveness of the building. Such matter had to seem to breathe. The architect developed in the mass of each story alternating protrusions and recessions to correspond to breathing.

The builder of the Hindu temple not only worked sculpturally but also depended on sculptors to complete the structure. For the sanctuary he required sculptors to fashion the cult statue. For the hall of approach he required them to carve columns into reliefs elaborating the god's attributes and exploits. For layer upon layer of the "World Mountain's" exterior he required them to people the stone with the life of the world and the activities of the gods, and above all with the operations of that Supreme Being who through his incarnations turns the wheel of life: Brahma to create the wheel, Vishnu to sustain it, and Siva to destroy it.

Provided at last with sculptures essential to the structure's functioning, the temple was ready to offer welcome to the aspiring pilgrim. When the pilgrim on his "mountain"-climbing expedition reached a relief representing Siva, he could indeed rejoice, because Siva as destroyer-god marked a cycle's end. The pilgrim could rejoice especially when he came upon a relief of Siva dancing the dance of life, for by identifying himself with the dancing god he could hope to speed the turning of his own cycle of existence. Dance is a common form of praise in most religions, but in Hinduism the art of bodily movement plays a role far more important than in any other faith. It enjoys divine sanction because Siva is himself the Lord of the Dance. He dances to re-create like Brahma, to sustain like Vishnu, to embody himself in, end, and bring release from every new cycle of existence. To praise Lord Siva is to engage in Siva's special art, whether as a dancer oneself or as a patron supporting sacred dancers in the parish temple.*

The way in which the moving body of the dancer draws into play a volume of open space, like a universe speeding in its orbit through space, makes the dance a satisfying means by which to accelerate the present cycle of existence. It is satisfying as long as the dance continues or the memory of it lingers in the mind. The trouble with the dance, however, is its fleeting character. A dancer cannot keep on performing forever, nor can his place be taken continuously. Memory fades, letting the wheel of life slow down.

At this point, Indian sculpture comes to the rescue. It fills the temples outside and in with reliefs representing Siva and his hosts in every conceivable movement of the temple dances. From the devotee's point of view, however, such sculpture still falls short. It has to remain fixed in place, an inseparable part of the temple for which it was carved. The temple of pilgrimage is apt to lie at a distance, too far to visit often, if at all. And practice of yoga by the average mortal needs concrete objects on which to focus his faculties.

Sculpture as a Religious Adjunct: Metal

Solution to the problem lay in the creation of statues of the Lord of the Dance which would conform to an orthodox size of three to four feet and yet prove light enough to be carried in processions or taken home for use on the household altar. Stone was too heavy and brittle for the purpose. Cast metal could, on the other hand, meet the demand, because it is, as we have seen, strong in self-support. It lends itself, moreover, to slender, wirelike forms that are easily carried. It can stick out in all directions to approximate a dancer's movements, and it can underline such movements by its contour-following strips of highlight and shadow. Such considerations led to creation of the metal image of Siva, Lord of the Dance, chosen for illustration (5.3).

Cast in brass, this sculpture of the dancing Siva attests to its maker's mastery of the *cire-perdue,* or "lost wax," method. Before casting the work the sculptor had put to the most, expressive use each step of his procedure. He had given the metal armature a spirited skeletal rendering of one of the most difficult attitudes in the dance represented. Using wax rather than clay, he modeled over

---

* Ananda K. Coomaraswamy, *The Dance of Siva* (New York: The Sunwise Turn, 1924), pp. 56–66. Two instructional 16-mm. films document the Hindu dance as inspired by the cult of Siva: *Bharatnatyam* (produced 1944; black and white, sound; 10 mins.); *Lord Siva Danced* (features Ram Gopal and troupe; produced 1953; black and white, sound; 24 mins.). Both films are circulated by the Government of India Information Services, Washington, D. C.

5.3. *Siva, Lord of the Dance.* Early 14th century. Brass. Height, 36¾". Denver Art Museum, Denver, Dora Porter Mason Fund.

this armature a figure that anticipated by its graceful flow of contour and delicate refinement of detail qualities which the metal would naturally assume when poured. He built up a mold of clay around the wax figure and allowed it to dry thoroughly before subjecting the whole combination to slow heating in a kiln— heating at a rate which would harden the mold without warping it and at the same time melt away the wax.

Into the hollow left by the wax the artist poured his molten metal—in this case brass.[6] With so large an image, 3 feet in height, the work of a less competent craftsman might have been ruined by the cracking of the metal as the solid mass cooled. This would have resulted from unequal rates of contraction at its heart

[6] See Notes, page 297.

and on its surface. The fact that the brass did not crack as the statue cooled was a final test of its creator's mastery, for the artist knew just how thin he would have to make each part to accommodate it to the cooling process, and just what parts were so much thinner than the others that they would have to be cast separately and welded into place (marks of welding do actually appear on the back of the image). So successful did the final casting prove to be that the sculptor was stimulated to perfect the surface of the image—polishing it, chasing it (incising around its details and engraving their surfaces), and probably even gilding it, although the gold has disappeared. Taking shape over a skeletal armature by a process of addition with modeled wax, and planned to meet and express the later necessities of the metal casting, the image came freely to extend itself into space and ultimately, when the thinnest pieces were attached, to embrace as much open space in definitely designed shapes as it did masses.

It is as outsiders that we of the Occident view this sculpture of a Hindu god. We bring to our study what we know about the use of the human figure for a sculptural subject, the techniques of carving and casting, the elements and the principles of art as they operate in sculpture. But we still fall short of grasping all that is set before us because we lack the background in the Hindu faith of those for whom the sculpture was made.

In order to appreciate fully a work of art we must put ourselves in the place of those for whom it was originally intended. If we manage to see such works even dimly through the eyes of Hindu believers, we can add considerably to our appreciation. Let us look again at the brass image of the dancing Siva as we would if we were devotees at prayer. Like heat hidden in firewood, Siva carries within him the source of all energy. He dances at the center of the universe and all nature in a ring around him dances in tune, bursting out everywhere as it dances into the flame of the energizing spirit. Hence the repetition of the circular face of Siva in the ring of fire and the crackle of energy carried out from Siva's whirling locks to the tongues of flame.

Siva dances in the human heart as well as in the heart of the universe. Since Hindus speak poetically of "the Lotus of the Heart," we note how fittingly the sculptor has conceived of the god as dancing on a double-lotus pedestal. Since the universe is a transitory creation, caught in the snare of illusion and deformed by ignorance, and since our hearts as part of such a creation are similarly afflicted, we relish the artist's reminder of this in the form of a dwarf upon which Siva dances with his right foot—destroying our ignorance.

Siva also brings release. He raises his left foot high into the air in token of salvation and points downward to those on earth, both with the toes of this foot and with the fingers of one

hand above it. Siva reassures us that he will save. He points upward with the fingers of another hand and extends its palm in blessing.

Siva orders creation. He raises another hand above the upward-pointing one but with its back turned toward us. With this hand Siva grasps the drum on which he begins the pulse-beat of new life. Siva guarantees preservation. From every finger tip and strand of hair he broadcasts energy. With the breath of life he quickens even negative spaces, repeating rhythmically in them the shapes of the positive forms.

Siva brings destruction. In the fourth hand, extended in asymmetrical balance against the other three hands in a group, he holds the ball of fire by which creation must be consumed before a new era can start. Cobras wrapped about the god's head and around one arm co-operate with their venom in destroying, as with their coils in evolving and with their periodically shed skins in reincarnating. As a sculpture at once inspired by intensive religious belief and intended to inspire a like fervency of belief in the observer, this image came thus at the hands of a true artist to assume the expressive power of all great art.

Portraiture in Stone

Like Toltecs and Hindus, Egyptians had a passion for sculpture. They craved the tangible and definite, and thought, felt, saw, and fashioned things in terms of the unyielding surfaces of solids. Like Toltecs but unlike Hindus, they adhered to a primitive (archaic) convention and maintained it as absolute law for thousands of years.

We noted an arid plateau keeping the Toltecs primitive-minded for the duration of their existence. In ancient Egypt a combination of river valley and desert operated in the same way to keep the archaic ideal in force. To early inhabitants of the Nile Valley, survival meant avoidance of the Sahara Desert pressing in on one side and of the Arabian Desert pressing in on the other. It meant sticking close to the bountiful river. Considering the proximity of boundless wastes, we can understand how the Egyptian should have developed an aversion to open spaces.* We can understand how he came to enclose his fields solidly with mud fences, to wall his gardens tightly, to mass the mud-plaster of his dwelling against wind, sand, and sun. Endeavoring to continue the present existence as long as possible and to assure endless existence in the hereafter, he demanded that house and tomb be snug and tight, and made to look that way.

The architect could do much to meet his fellow Egyptian's needs. He could thicken walls, omit windows, reduce open spaces. He could still not quite achieve the effect of total enclosure which his clients wanted. In an effort to do so, he called in the sculptor. The sculptor carved columns as palm trees and bundles of papyrus stalks or lotus plants—symbols of ever-renewing life. He represented the very dwellings themselves in relief in the faces of cliffs and in the caves hollowed from them—to make hidden abodes for the dead.

Beyond this collaboration with the architect, the sculptor performed independently an even more vital service. He provided the tombs with portrait statues of his patrons, individuals who regarded preparation for their passing to the other world as the most important business of their life on earth.

Egyptians thought of themselves as possessing several souls, one of which composed their shadow or "double." Their *ka* they called it—a guardian spirit which accompanied them in their daily work but went off at night on trips of its own. This *ka* would accompany them in the life after death providing that the body, which always cast the shadow when the sun shone, could be kept intact to serve as its home. Undertakers perfected an art of mummification to preserve the body for this purpose—and sometimes they succeeded so well that the face of the mummified corpse has survived unimpaired to the present. They were not uni-

5.4. Thutmose: *Portrait Bust of Queen Nefertiti*. *c.* 1370–1360 B.C. Limestone, gessoed and painted. Slightly less than life size. Egyptian Museum, Berlin, Amarna Gallery.

formly successful, however, and some corpses decayed. Too, enemies might break into a tomb and destroy the mummy.

In order to forestall such calamities, Egyptians hit upon the idea of having sculptors create portrait statues as substitute homes for their *ka*—images which could be hidden away in the tomb, where at least one image might escape destruction in case the tomb was sacked.

In accord with that same primitive ideal which we noted in Toltec society, the Egyptian sculptor carved his portrait statue in unmistakably man-made shapes. He kept the essential shape and feel of the cubical block of stone as it issued from the quarry. He carved the block primarily for its front view, only secondarily for its right profile, and never for any other. He held to a rigid law of frontality, carving the figure, whether erect or seated, with such symmetrical balance that a plumb line dropped from the center of the head would bisect it. So completely was the body of his statue subject to rule that the Egyptian sculptor

* Environmental interpretation of Egyptian art is based on Wilhelm Worringer (Bernard Rackham, trans.), *Egyptian Art* (London: G. P. Putnam's Sons, 1928; 1st ed. in German, 1927).

could finish most of it in advance of any commission, making it identical with any other statue and leaving only the head for portrayal from the sitter. Sometimes he achieved considerable lifelikeness in the carving of a client's features. Usually, however, counting on the *ka's* reading ability to decipher the name inscribed underneath, the portraitist idealized the features of his sitter almost as much as he had the prefabricated body.

It is phenomenal, therefore, that out of this convention-ridden land and its sculpture there should eventually have come such a bust as that shown here (5.4). Explanation lies in transformations of Egyptian society during the two centuries preceding its creation about 1370 to 1360 B.C. Such changes broke the restrictions of a hemmed-in river culture and flooded Egypt with new ideas, new motives, and new styles in art. Egypt could no longer restrict itself to an isolated local outlook conditioned by the Nile, for it had now become the center of a great empire embracing not only the lands to the south, at the headwaters of the Nile, but the whole of Asia Minor as far as the Euphrates River. Powerful monarchs had by conquest and trade brought unheard-of prosperity to the land of the Nile and launched a building boom under which all of the arts flourished.

At this time the pharaoh Akhnaton and his queen, Nefertiti, took particular interest in religion and art. Akhnaton was resolved to found a new religion based on worship of one god, Aton, the Sun, after whom he had named himself "He who is beneficial to Aton." Nefertiti, whose slender proportions and delicate features set the style of female figure and dress in Egypt for a generation, became such an enthusiast for her husband's new religion that she outdid him in advancing it.

Under Akhnaton and Nefertiti worked a master sculptor, Thutmose, one of a handful whose names have come down to us. Probably Thutmose's genius had as much to do with setting the fashions in figure, dress, and art as did the persons and the personal tastes of the king and queen. At any rate, we have gained insight into the Egypt of that era through Thutmose's portraits of the royal pair and their children, and above all, perhaps, by the bust of Nefertiti found in the ruins of the sculptor's own home at Tell el 'Amarna—a bust which the artist seems to have made from the life and kept in his studio as a model from which to carve other works.

Thutmose was fired by Akhnaton's creed of devotion to "Truth" to undertake in his portrayal of Queen Nefertiti an innovation as daring in sculpture as her husband's was in religion. He substituted for the old tradition of idealized representation a new individualism designed to match the delicately proportioned, sharp-featured aspects of the lady's head. For creating her nearly life-size bust Thutmose apparently realized that only the fine-textured responsiveness of limestone could measure up to the queen's fragile type of beauty, for this stone is what he chose.

The sculptor had no intention, it would seem, of breaking with the traditional Egyptian law of frontality; to his mind it probably had to be accepted as enduring, like the Nile itself.[7] But Thutmose could reject his predecessors' plane-boundedness in carving. He could round the planes of his bust into depth, modulate them in minute swellings and hollows. He could repeat in smaller forms about the head the long sweep of curve of the queen's neck— elongated and tilted gracefully for animation of effect.

Thutmose's last refinement was the introduction of color. He glued linen to the limestone surface, covered it with gesso, and on this ground applied color in simple but gently varied passages. If we saw the original, we should note how judiciously the master handled his coloring of Nefertiti's features and crown. Suffice it to say, beyond calling attention to the remarkable comeliness and "stylishness" of the portrayal, that the sharpening of detail effected by painting brought the archaic tradition in this bust to the very point at which decorative daintiness was about to take over. Only the self-disciplining power of the master

[7] See Notes, page 298.

himself, perhaps, kept him from sacrificing individuality of interpretation to the pleasantly decorative.

Human Substitutes in Ceramic

Some eight centuries after Thutmose's time in Egypt, a society along the west side of the Italian Peninsula reached a brief moment of power and prosperity. Though comparable to that of the Egyptian Empire in luxury of life, it differed markedly in character. This was a confederation of city states known as Etruria, a union which invaders of Italy had organized five hundred years before. Building walled cities on hilltops for defense, the Etruscans had first secured to themselves the surrounding valleys and then had turned to foreign adventure. They had amassed a huge treasure by falling suddenly on other peoples' settlements and ships, and bearing home the spoils.

Since the Etruscan way of life depended on wealth acquired by violence, it was necessarily precarious. Robbers live by the sword but they stand at any time to die by it, too. Indignant victims have a way of forming alliances and staging surprise attacks which can overwhelm a stronghold unless sentries are kept posted to give warning of their approach. Buccaneers taking refuge behind the battlements of an Etruscan hill town were haunted by fear of attack, obsessed by need to secure the fortifications in every possible way. After working to provide utmost protection in the walls, they looked beyond that limit into magic, commissioning the best sculptor of the community to create a colossal image of a warrior (perhaps the God of War himself) to stand perpetual guard over the city's approaches.

The guardian or god of war here represented was so conceived (Pl. II), but the modeler did more than merely represent a man advancing into battle. He managed to convey by his expressive ordering of the figure's points, lines, planes, masses, and colors a sense of the Etruscan will to dominate.

Though with archaic stiffness of rendering, the Etruscan master caught something which

no mere pose of an actual soldier could: the very sense of combat. Perhaps we should say "because of" rather than "though," for in this very stiffness the artist found a source of expressive strength. He joined part to part in sharp, angular breaks that gave to the contours those motives of action in conflict to which we have already referred in our discussion of line (pp. 9, 33). Again, as we have noted in our discussion of color (p. 20), he used color contrasts to enhance this same effect of separateness and aggressive advance: blue-black for the flesh, reddish brown for the tough oxhide leather of breastplate, arm-rest for shield, and sheathing for legs, and so on.

With such intensity of accent in line and color, the figure was well calculated to carry its effect to a distance—impressing the worshiper as he approached the temple or alarming the enemy as he crept up the hill for a surprise attack. In either case, as the spectator drew near, he suddenly discovered how mighty the image was, how it towered over ordinary mortals in its 8 feet of height. He was overawed, if not terrified, by the dominating eyes. Its maker had muted every detail in favor of the exaggerated size and color of these eyes, making them the centers for a series of spiral-like forms unleashing themselves, as it were, around the crest of the helmet and over the arms and legs, to end in the outthrust fist.

The *Etruscan Warrior* is remarkable for its sharpness of joint, linear edginess of detail and flowing effect of contour—qualities which we have learned to identify with metal casting. It is astonishing to discover then that the Etruscan sculpture is not made of metal. It is made of clay.

Why, we ask, should a work of such size be rendered in terra cotta? It had to be modeled with lightning speed and complete assurance, lest the increasing weight of the clay cause the piece to sag out of shape and crack in drying. We cannot answer this question. All we know is that the craftsmen of Veii, the Etruscan city from which the image may have come, were famous for their colossal terra cottas. And from the same site may have come another colossal head of the Etruscan war-god, more than three times life-size, displayed today beside the striding figure in the Metropolitan Museum of Art in New York City. Similarities of style indicate that it must have been done by the same artist, and the fact that it came without accompanying fragments of a body suggests that this artist overreached himself in attempting a terra-cotta figure too big for even his skill in modeling and firing.*

The sculptor achieved in the surviving 8-foot figure a triumph rare in the history of ceramic sculpture. Except for the missing weapon and shield, which appear to have been made separately out of metal and then attached, he modeled and fired the gigantic ensemble as a single piece. Building the clay up around a core of straw which was destroyed in the firing, he left only a single small hole in the top of the head for the escape of steam and smoke. The artist no doubt knew the techniques of bronze casting as well as he knew those of clay modeling, for he carried over into the form of his terra cotta qualities for which he would have planned had the work been cast in bronze.

The epic scale on which the *Etruscan Warrior* was modeled accounts for some of its effectiveness as a work of art. The psychological functioning of the subject represented depends in this case at least on the magnitude of the figure. But terra cottas do not have to be big in order to be great. They do not always need to amaze us with the feats of craftsmanship involved in their making. They can be of miniature size, as they usually are, and still rank with the best in all ceramic sculpture.

Terra-cotta statuettes played a role in man's transformation from savagery to civilization by allowing him to abandon a religious custom of the greatest cruelty. There was a time in the ancestry of all of us when our forefathers practiced human sacrifice. Sometimes it was thought that their gods had to be appeased with human flesh. We recall, for example, the Bible story of Abraham, how he came within an inch of sacrificing his son, Isaac, because he believed that Jehovah demanded it, or our study of the Toltec Moon Goddess in the present chapter—the sacrifices made to her were of human victims. Sometimes it was thought that the departed family head or clan chieftain needed the continued services of his household in the after-life. Then, at his funeral were killed all those nearest him, from his favorite wife to his last servant. Prehistoric graves in Egypt have been found so filled with skeletons of the funerary victims that the slaughter must have been wholesale. The same is true of ancient China.

Apparently, however, neither Egyptians nor Chinese felt at ease about burying the living with the dead. If the victims' wailing did not touch their hearts, then the waste involved touched their pocketbooks. Lest they depopulate their own society, they looked for substitutes. Prisoners of war, yes, but better still, because prisoners could be made into slaves, sculptured effigies of those who would otherwise be slain. By having the spirits of the would-be victims instilled by magic into their sculptured representations and interring these images, both peoples thought at once to meet the needs of the dead and to spare the living.†

The artist specializing in tomb statuettes had every incentive to make his figures lively. He had no august dignity to offend as he would have had in representing the deceased overlord. He regarded the servants and even the women of the chieftain's household as common folk like himself, and so could model them as uninhibitedly as he could the barnyard animals. He could indulge in the current comedy of manners, multiplying details and exaggerating personal traits as he pleased.

The livelier the image for the grave, the better it was supposed to do its job. And the

---

* See Gisela M. A. Richter, *Etruscan Terra-cotta Warriors in the Metropolitan Museum of Art* ("Papers," No. 6; New York: Metropolitan Museum of Art, 1937). Published in the same number is a report on the structure and technique of this sculpture and other Etruscan terra cottas presumably found with it. It was written by the English potter, Charles F. Binns, who taught Arthur E. Baggs (see 3.10).

† For Egyptian tomb statuettes, see James Henry Breasted, Jr., *Egyptian Servant Statues* ("Bollingen Series," XIII; New York: Pantheon Books, 1948). For Chinese tomb statuettes, see C. Hentze, *Chinese Tomb Figures: a Study in the Beliefs and Folklore of Ancient China* (London: Edward Goldston, 1928).

more of these vital images about the dead man, the better he would be looked after. Hence the vast depository of statuettes which the graves of either country constitute—surest source of knowledge of the way in which people of their times felt, looked, and worked. No doubt thousands of these miniature sculptures await the excavator's shovel, but we have enough of them already at hand to know that the art of making them flourished in Egypt for three thousand years and in China for two thousand. The vast majority are of clay because the demands made of them could best be met by the flexible terra-cotta medium. The art flourished as the idea took hold and spread. It came to an end in Egypt only when Roman conquerors imposed different ideas about the soul's needs after death. It came to an end in China only when excesses of extravagant use impoverished working families and prompted imperial decrees forbidding burial of tomb statuettes in favor of burning paper effigies at funerals.

Probably the best artists ever to make funerary figurines in China were the Tartar tribesmen known as the T'o-pa. This people migrated from the steppes around Lake Baikal to invade China in the fourth century A.D. and establish in the Yellow River valley a vigorous state called Wei. Within a century or two after their conquest, their conversion to Buddhism, with its teachings against the taking of life in any form, led them to do away with sacrifices at funerals, even the formerly popular sacrifices of horses. Horses came thus to be modeled in terra cotta, and along with the steeds their grooms—men of either Tartar or Indo-European origin whose nomadic life on the steppes had qualified them as ideal keepers of stables for the Chinese. For this kind of modeling T'o-pa artists had been ideally prepared by a centuries-old art of bronze-casting for harness and tent trappings and personal ornaments.

Just such a groom, his hand raised to lead by the bridle the horse now lost, made the subject of the present figure (5.5). Turk or Hun perhaps, this groom was modeled by the Tartar sculptor with the freedom natural to clay and yet with the artistic reserve governed by the

5.5. *Turkish Groom*, Ming Ch'i (tomb statuette), from Wei River valley, Shensi, China. 4th-6th century A.D. Clay, individually modeled and fired in kiln, originally polychromed. Height, 14″. Museum of Art, University of Oregon, Murray Warner Collection of Oriental Art.

5.6. *Charioteer*, from a monument at Delphi, Greece. 475 B.C. Bronze, with enamel and silver inlay. Height, 5'11". Museum, Delphi. Alinari photograph.

principle of emphasis through elimination. The sculptor employed the additive technique expressively, to be sure. He brought out, with the heightened relief of clay pellets loosely applied to the mass, the distinctive features of the stable-keeper's face—bulging eyes, protuberant nose, and pointed mustache and beard. But he shaped these features with a rhythmic repetition of bulges and lines which gives the face an animated, even a twinklingly humorous, effect.

The modeler kept the detail of the figure strictly subordinated to that of the head, rendering split leather apron, riding breeches, and undershirt in simple slabs and rolls of clay. He followed no formula, but he kept his rendering always within bounds of his design as he varied details. He no doubt ended by coloring the form as simply and yet vividly as he had modeled it, though only bluish and yellowish traces remain. When the sculptor brought his figure to the firing stage, he was confident that it would withstand the heat without cracking because he had planned it from the outset for that ultimate test. His patron must have been as delighted as we are when we come upon the image amid a group of typical grave figurines. Barely 14 inches high, it can stand as a masterpiece beside the 8-foot image of the Etruscan warrior.

Idealization in Bronze and Marble

Like the Etruscans, who raided the settlements of the Greeks to the south of them and were in turn overwhelmed, the Greeks supported for centuries mainly sculptors in bronze. Even after abandoning wood for marble in temple construction and embellishment, the Greeks continued to do sculpture in metal or in a combination of metal with other materials.

Fifty years before Athenian builders completed the Parthenon (4.2), a Greek master cast the bronze portrait of an athlete (5.6). The artist found his subject in the winner of a chariot race held at Delphi in honor of Apollo in 475 B.C. We know all this through a lucky accident. A landslide buried the figure before barbarians could destroy it, keeping it hidden until a modern shovel turned it up. Pieces of the reins found with the figure suggest that originally it formed a part of a larger work consisting of the chariot and the horses as well, but that the landslide failed to cover these other parts, leaving them ready victims for the armorer's crucible.

It is a tribute to the power of a classic ideal already achieved at the end of the first quarter of the fifth century B.C. that this bronze figure, fragment though it is, should now form a complete work of art in itself. For that is the way in which a classic artist works—perfecting the internal organization of each part within the ruling harmony of the whole. Although he must have intended the figure to be an individual portrait, moreover, this artist so modified the rendering as to idealize the athlete's form in terms of classically ordered composition.

The youth was conceived as standing firmly erect, pride of mastery over his steeds shown by his face and carriage. Unlike the primitive dispersal of interest over the entire field which the Toltec image displays (5.1), concentrated emphasis has here resulted in the bringing of the parts of a human figure to climax in the face, in the eyes, even in one eye, which is larger and more sharply defined than the other. Though symmetrically disposed about the vertical axis, the Greek athlete's figure is subtly varied from one side to another in such manner as to make the entire rendering instinct with life. No two folds of drapery are alike, no two locks of hair nor modulations of surface. Yet over all, thanks to the repeated verticals of the drapery folds and the tall proportions of the silhouette, a sense of dignified calm prevails.

The bronze *Charioteer of Delphi* meets requirements of human-figure representation in a classic manner. With the same forms it meets expressively the challenge of its medium. Cast in bronze, it could be nothing else. When a plaster cast is made of it, the grotesque travesty resulting becomes readily apparent if we compare its head with the head of the original. Details are either lost or blurred in the plaster, but details of the bronze come forth as a marvel of

5.7. *Charioteer*, detail of head and shoulders. Museum, Delphi. Alinari photograph.

craftsmanship (5.7). What the plaster misses is the subtle refinement which chasing of the actual metal surface effects—to give texture to the hair, protuberance to the eyelashes, sharpened contours to the lips. Inlaid for final accent, the sunken silver fret of the headband and the black enamel pupils of the eyes once accounted for an even greater air of vitality than still pervades the work. Nevertheless, for all of its final delicacy of detailing, the original simplicity of form remains—perfectly adapted to the flow of metal in casting and eloquent of that classic ideal which the Greeks posed in the adage, "Nothing in excess."

Prevalent though bronze-casting remained as late as the fifth century in ancient Greece, and masterly though such a work as the bronze *Charioteer of Delphi* is in conception and technique, the growing desire of the Greeks for classic clarity and permanence of form turned them more and more to carving in marble.

They felt the challenging resistance of the marble to their attack and the ultimate yielding of the stone to a treatment calculated to bring out both its own qualities and the qualities of classic art.*

The Greek sculptor learned to attack his marble with a single tool: the bronze point called the punch, grain-respecting and mass-accentuating in its action. He spared no pains to perfect with it such form as might favor the stone and the cutting, holding the punch always at right angles to the surface and bruising the marble crystals gradually away until the form stood revealed. He ended with a restrained smoothing of surface with pumice or emery which often left punch marks showing here and there and always preserved the underlying solids. The result was a carving which looked like stone, with a velvety, opaque bloom of surface in which every grain of marble seemed to come to life.

Under stimulus of marble for material, especially that Pentelic marble the virtues of which we have noted in the preceding chapter, the Greeks developed an enthusiasm for sculpture comparable to that of the Toltecs, the Egyptians, and the Hindus. Unlike other peoples, however, they exploited the art of marble carving in pursuit of a classic ideal conceived in terms of the well-proportioned human body. They glorified man as the noblest of organisms, transformed him into a type after which to pattern his gods, and looked to him as the basic unit of all measure.

We have seen how Athenians of Phidias's day honored the city's goddess by erecting to her a temple humanized with bodylike refinements of structure. We have seen how, not satisfied even then, they commissioned the greatest sculptor of their time not only to supervise the architects on the job but actually to invest the building with monumental sculp-

*The best general reference is that by Gisela M. A. Richter, *The Sculpture and Sculptors of the Greeks.* For techniques of carving, however, see the authoritative studies by Stanley Casson, *The Technique of Early Greek Sculpture* (Oxford: Clarendon Press, 1933), and Carl Bluemel (Lydia Hollands, trans.), *Greek Sculptors at Work* (London: Phaidon Press, 1955; 1st German ed., 1927).

ture. To stand enshrined within the temple, towering to the roof, Phidias carved out of the same Pentelic marble as made the structure (plus additions of bronze, gold, ivory, and other materials) a colossal image of Athena herself. He assembled every Greek sculptor worthy of the name and set him to carving—to crown the head of the temple wall with a continuous frieze celebrating the procession held annually in Athena's honor, to enrich the metopes of the frieze above the colonnade with representations of Greeks battling centaurs and triumphing thus symbolically over the barbarism of nature, to fill the pediments, finally, with statues telling the stories of Athena's birth and victory in the contest for favor of the townspeople as their patron deity (4.3b).

With their sculptural enrichment of the Parthenon the Athenians accomplished more than a visual determination of the temple's function. They created an architectural composition which their architects and stonemasons, for all their subtleties in proportioning and curvature, were powerless to complete. Looking again at the Parthenon in its present ruins (4.2), we can imagine it restored, its roof intact, but without even the terra-cotta ornaments on top. Would the blank superstructure not combine above the alternating columns and voids to make the composition top-heavy, marring in this way the classic repose demanded of the whole? The Athenians must have felt it so, because the model of the Parthenon (4.3b) offers a satisfying general appearance that the surviving original does not, its sculptures for the most part having been taken by Lord Elgin at the beginning of the nineteenth century and presented to the British Museum.

That the Elgin Marbles were intended specifically for their designated places on the Parthenon is only too apparent in a critical examination of the sculptures as they are shown at the British Museum. The Parthenon frieze was intended to be seen from a distance below, and only at a sharply oblique angle of viewing. In such a position it was illuminated solely by reflection of sunlight from the pavement beneath. The sculptors calculated their respective

5.8. *Kings and Queens of the Old Testament,* west portals, Notre Dame, Chartres. Second half 12th century A.D. Limestone. Life size and over. Vizzavona photograph.

panels to meet exactly such conditions, rendering the upper parts in higher relief than the lower parts, correcting for the abrupt foreshortening occasioned by the angle of viewing, and modulating surfaces to look best only when "footlighted."

As the floor-level display and overhead lighting of the sculptures in the British Museum demonstrates in reverse, the architectural sculptor is as dependent on the architect as the architect is on him. Lest his contributions become misshapen masses and fail to perform the jobs asked of them in the structure, the

sculptor must adjust his forms to the forms of the building and the lighting controlled by it.

Cathedral Sculpture

Like the Greeks, the Early Christians conceived of the building in which to conduct devotions as a House of God, Whose divine presence could be sensed in every smallest part. Owing to differences in form of worship, however, it was necessary to develop a different kind of structure—one designed, not for solitary prayer in the presence of priest alone, but for congregational worship before a priest performing the sacrament of Mass.

When a thousand worshipers had to be accommodated at once, a church had to open up inside and become a primary exploitation of architecture as an art of space. The evolution of the Christian church for the performance of Mass brought forth the Gothic cathedral, that achievement of stone cage construction which we examined in the preceding chapter (4.4 to 4.6).

We saw how effectively the Gothic system of isolated supports, rib vaults, and flying buttresses eliminated the convention of weight-bearing walls in favor of an unprecedented openness of space. We saw how frankly this system declared itself the stone skeleton that it was and how naturally it determined the dynamic effect of the building. We saw how effectively it received enrichment through the use of minor features like wall arcades and pier capitals.

We must now recognize that the Gothic cathedral was meant to be more than mere construction to shelter a God and a multitude of worshipers. It was meant to be an expression of the believer's yearning for heaven—a heaven located, to be sure, somewhere above the earth, yet at the same time on earth and in the devotee's heart. Hence the verticality of emphasis in proportioning the building and disposing its parts. Hence likewise the thousand and one allusions to God's creation, conceived as mirroring His goodness.

Allusions to a Heaven on earth could be made by the architect-builders of the cathedral —through a harmony of form like that which the universe is supposed to compose, gained professedly by the magic of numbers and proportions; through a symbolism that treated such elements as piers and rib vaults as trees; through a stress on stonemasonry in the form of piers as solid as rock-ribbed earth itself. But architects found their allusions falling short of the original intent, for only the representational arts of the sculptor and the painter could make direct reference to the outside world. Sculptors, as well as painters, were asked to complete the building. They carved reliefs from the same stone, to grace doorways, arcades, piers, and pier capitals.

Along with painters, sculptors did much for the cathedral with these reliefs. They told Bible stories and stories of the lives of the saints, catalogued the labors of the months, and reviewed the virtues and the vices of man. They represented, in short, all of the manifold details of the workaday world itself. By such enrichment of the structure, carvers made of the cathedral so instructive a study, even for those who could not read, that they won for it the name "Bible of the Poor." They were content to remain masters in their own art, striving in no way to rival the builders but in every way to help them achieve the desired effect.

For example, sculptors elongated into strongly vertical elements those figures of Old Testament royalty which gave to the western entrance of Chartres Cathedral (5.8) the name of "Royal Portal." * They rendered these figures stiffly upright, like the colonnettes and piers between and below which they stood, and undercut them deeply, as though they were about to stand forth like the free-standing piers inside. The artists also made the figures in their austerity a psychological reassurance to the worshiper as he passed through the doorway, because statues at this point seemed to steady the active-looking building and keep it from collapsing.

The sculptors worked with maximum condensation and dramatic intensity, but they never forgot as they developed their images that they were striving to complete the building, not to disguise it. They required every sculptural detail to affirm the apparent structural role of the block out of which it was carved—a pillar statue as a vertical support, a capital as an extension of the bearing surface, a carved arch-stone as a unit dependent for support on its neighbors, a decorated lintel to span an opening, and a sculptured panel above it to fill the head of an arch.

* The sculptures of this three-arched entranceway are studied in detail and illustrated, Whitney S. Stoddard, *The West Portals of Saint-Denis and Chartres* (Cambridge, Mass.: Harvard University Press, 1952).

Carvers at Chartres used the same local sandstone as was used in the masonry. Aside from its convenience and economy, they probably found it satisfyingly regional and natural, close to the earth which they conceived as a "mirror of God." Romans and their Italian descendants used their native Carrara marble with like expressiveness. With this snow-white, translucent stone they developed forms quite different from those of the medieval French. They carved their marble with an elaboration which the Greeks never dreamed of imposing on the Pentelic variety. Barely beginning their carving with the punch, restricting the use of the tool to roughing out, they went on to layer after layer of increasing refinement, striking the stone obliquely with claw chisels and flat chisels until a smooth-surfaced form was reached, ready for polishing till it shone.

Michelangelo, sixteenth-century Italian master, shared the Greeks' respect for material and tools, and when he came to execute a commission for a Roman cardinal the needs of his own time and people led him to choose this different medium and to treat it in the Italian manner.* He was asked to sculpture, not a Toltec moon-goddess to whom sacrifices were to be made, but a *Pietà*, a Mother of God mourning her Son, Himself a sacrifice of atonement for the sins of Man (5.9). The subject had been rendered many times before, usually with exaggerated emphasis on the grief portrayed. Current efforts of the Papacy to extend beyond earlier control the temporal power of the Church were certain to affect the forms. The new state of mind called for grandeur of treatment with figures heroic and impersonal.

Michelangelo exploited the qualities of his block of Carrara marble to modify the original planes in favor of gradual transitions and broadly rendered surfaces, all of which he trained within the pyramidal structure to lead to the Virgin's head. In the dazzling whiteness and translucency of this marble and its response to polishing, he found the opportunity

* For a full account of this commission, see Charles de Tolnay, *The Youth of Michelangelo* (Princeton, N. J.: Princeton University Press, 1947).

5.9. Michelangelo (1475–1564): *Pietà,* Chapel of the Pietà, St. Peter's, Rome. 1498–1502. Carrara marble. Height, 6′3″. Alinari photograph.

to play with highlights and half tones until the block seemed to emit a light of its own.

The Italian carver marshaled such features to the treatment of his theme. He rendered the Christ like a Greek Apollo, marred to the least possible extent by the Crucifixion. He represented the Virgin like a Greek Demeter, goddess of earth, sorrowing, to be sure, but with dignified restraint. He sought in such analogies an echo of antiquity that might redound to the glory of the Christian church. Encouraged by qualities of the marble to idealize the forms of the Virgin and the dead Christ, Michelangelo went on to development of a still more startling concept. At the time of the Crucifixion Mary was a woman in the later years of her life; and so she had been portrayed in earlier *Pietàs,* her ebbing strength barely sufficient to support the weight of her Son. Michelangelo shifted the scale of his figures. He reduced the size of the Christ and made the figure of the Mother gigantic by contrast. He portrayed Mary unwasted by her suffering, eternally young and comely.

Such breadth of form and grace of movement as we see in this sculptured *Pietà* have become the norm for a type of beauty which we are accustomed to calling classic. They are the traits which evolve naturally, as we have seen, out of search for the utmost clarity of form. In order to achieve such clarity the sculptor is obliged to create an ensemble which seems, as it does here, and as it did in the *Charioteer of Delphi*, to be completely self-contained—disassociated, that is, from the surrounding space. In Michelangelo's case there was probably no conscious choice of classic as the best type of composition in which to make his revolution in subject. The state of mind which he shared with the churchmen of his day brought forth both the form and the content of his sculpture, and his choice of material as well.

The Romantic Ideal and the Search for Form

The forms of Michelangelo's *Pietà* can still be regarded as symbols, because they suggest something about religious beliefs that can be put into words better than they can be stated visually. As in all classic art, symbols play subordinate roles to the organization of the actual visual forms. Sculptures of the romantic nineteenth century, however, make symbols uppermost. They represent an art which was never content with the form immediately at hand but always intent upon converting it into something else, something fanciful and remote. They represent an art of emotive fragments, an art in which pieces of representational form are treated more for their associational appeal than for themselves.

Romantic sculptors are apt to find the carver's materials too resistant and inhibiting for this art of remote suggestion. For the veiled half-statements of romanticism they find only clay completely satisfactory: not the clay composing the final form, as in the *Etruscan Warrior* or the Chinese tomb statuette, but the clay of temporary convenience, modeled fluently,

cast in plaster, then torn down and returned to the storage bin.

At the hands of romantic sculptors, clay responds to the vaguest of formulations. It can be made to appear to blow itself apart, to hover indecisively in space, to vibrate in an atmospheric play of half tone and shadow, conforming to any kind of sketchiness. Auguste Rodin, foremost modeler to use clay for romantic effects, became marvelously adept at seizing the fleeting gesture of an arm or the flickering expression of a face. This French master of the late nineteenth century gloried in the sketch. He made his plastic medium into a kind of poetry in which pellets became words and flourishes with his thumb phrases of the fancy by which to suggest ideas.[8]

From Rodin's point of view, it was unfortunate that clay did not behave properly after being modeled, requiring translation into another material. Rodin thought of plaster-casting and translation into bronze or marble as nuisances too bothersome to waste time over himself. He hired artisans who made no pretense of being artists themselves—to make the plaster cast from his clay original and from it in turn to cast the bronze or make the marble copy. He counted on a craftsman's doing an expert job of reproducing the original, to be sure, but he remained indifferent to the material in which it would ultimately appear.

The art of emotive fragments reaches its climax in such of Rodin's creations as *The Hand of God* (5.10). This piece was copied by commercial craftsmen into marble through the use of a pointing machine, which makes holes in a block to depths measured off on the cast from a common starting point, controlling by depths of the holes the amount of marble to be removed. Some of the workmen's points, drilled too deeply with the pointing machine, had to be left in the finished surface. But from the romantic point of view such blemishes were not serious. Rodin made a fetish of the unfinished. He broadened the range of his expression by making highly polished fragments seem to emerge from shapeless masses. And

[8] See Notes, page 298.

minor mistakes made at the factory were in keeping with the effect.

The marks of clay-modeling here copied into marble contribute to the poetry of the subject, for it was out of clay, according to the Book of Genesis, that God fashioned the first man. Pushing upward from what seems to be a lump of raw clay in which folds still persist, the hand of God holds another lump upon which is being brought to completion the figures of Adam and Eve. By way of contrast with the roughness of unmodeled clay, the hand and the two miniature figures were carved as though slicked to the utmost with clay slip (see p. 60), and the impress of the thumb strokes sweeping around them was reproduced as though all were still in progress. Marble treated as clay and clay as poetry—this is the essence of the romantic procedure as Rodin followed it.

Scarcely a sculptor reached maturity during the early years of the twentieth century without coming in one way or another under the influence of Rodin. Aristide Maillol was an apprentice who learned from the older man how to develop sculptural effects independently of any one particular medium. Maillol revolted at the same time against the exaggerated sentimentality and tortured symbolism of his master's sculptures.

The purifying tendency inherent in Maillol's reactions is well represented by an early work of his career, one entitled *The Mediterranean*, or *Thought* (5.11a and b). Maillol's alternative titles suggest a source of inspiration in that Mediterranean coast of southern France where the classic tradition lingered and where the sculptor himself preferred to live and work.[9] We can read into the seated nude figure certain connotations of a brooding sea and the mysteries of thought. Actually, the work needs no such title. Sometimes known simply as *Woman Leaning on Her Elbow* (a title preferred by the owner of the original stone version), the sculpture is able by its forms alone to hold the observer's attention. It is a work of pure and independent sculpture.

[9] See Notes, page 298.

5.10. Auguste Rodin (1849–1917): *The Hand of God*. 1902. Marble. Height, 29″. Metropolitan Museum of Art, New York.

When the young French master came to work on this sculpture, he was deeply moved by his growing awareness of the female body—its sculptural massiveness, its big-scaled earthiness and hint of mellow fruitfulness. He created under this inspiration a figure which goes far beyond any literal transcription of a model who may have posed for him. Impelled by an artist's sensibilities, Maillol did what any artist must in order to create. He abstracted and exaggerated; he even distorted the human figure in order to re-create it as a work of art.

Perhaps our eyes are so accustomed to the kind of sculptural treatment presented by *The Mediterranean* that we have come unthinkingly to accept it as though it were a norm for female beauty. Habits of seeing lead to ready acceptance. Nevertheless, if we were to compare the sculptured figure with the form of a living model posed in the same position, we should be surprised at the liberties taken by the artist. If the sculpture were an actual woman, she would prove so heavy that her movements would be

5.11. The Classic Ideal in Twentieth-century Sculpture.   a. Aristide Maillol (1861–1944): *The Mediterranean,* or *Thought,* three-quarters front view of original in modeled plaster. *c.* 1901. Stone and other materials. More than life size. Courtesy of John Rewald. Vizzavona photograph.   b. Aristide Maillol: *The Mediterranean,* or *Thought,* three-quarters rear view of stone replica in garden of Dr. Oskar Reinhardt, Winterthur am Römerholz, Switzerland. Photograph courtesy of the owner.

impaired. Her biceps and thighs would be clumsy, her wrists and ankles enormous.

Why should exaggeratedly heavy proportions seem right in the statue? Our discussion of sculpture as a representational art yields the answer. Because a deeply felt response motivated the work and determined its design, Maillol had to magnify the woman's bulk. He had to broaden her joints and spread her haunches over the base. He had to re-create the form that inspired him, making it parallel the living figure in its apparent vitality and yet remain distinct.

When we see the figure in three-quarters front view, as here illustrated (5.11a), the forms impress us with the majesty of their movement. Their major planes face broadly towards the front. But subordinate planes recede from us, and before long we are drawn by them to shift our position. From a new vantage point we discover a whole new series of formal interactions. Compositions in depth succeed each other as we encircle the statue in a series of pauses to observe it, and a rear view, though subservient to that from the front, is still filled with meaning (5.11b). Freestanding and self-contained in its mass, the figure can be grasped only after contemplation from all sides. It is fully in the round.

In reaction to Rodin, Maillol approached his work more as a stone-carver than as a modeler. He continued Rodin's practices of modeling, but he found preferable to clay for modeling a partially-set modeling plaster applied and built out with a spatula. He continued to call on craftsmen to cast replicas in bronze or carve copies in stone, but he planned his original study in plaster for such forms as might look especially well in stone, and it is in stone that *The Mediterranean* appears at its best.

SCULPTURE IN THE NATURE OF MATERIALS

The generation succeeding Maillol carried still farther its revolt against romanticism. Sculptural mass became of prime importance. Material began again to make its contributions to form, and they could never now be the same contributions from wood as from stone, or from bronze as from clay. The eyes of the younger generation began to be opened to the potentialities of the new approach by discovery of works produced in widely different times and places. Whether prehistoric, African, or East Asian, these works were as vigorously organic, in our sense of the term, as any ever created.

One such work, vitalized by marriage of material with subject, comes from Dahomey, on the African Guinea coast (5.12). Ostensibly the portrait of a man riding a burro, the piece interprets its subject with utter freedom of expression. The artist was a woodcarving specialist who lived toward the end of the nineteenth century or the beginning of the twentieth, in the eastern part of Dahomey where the neighboring culture of Yoruba predominated. The man who commissioned the image was

5.12. *Equestrian Figure*, or *Schango, God of Thunder*. Perhaps 19th century. Polychromed wood. Height, 15¾". Collection of Louis Carré, Paris. Courtesy of the owner and The Museum of Modern Art, New York.

5.13. Unkei (d. A.D. 1223), Kaikei, and others: *Heavenly Guardian,* one of two guardian warriors, main south gate, Tōdaiji, Nara. A.D. 1203. Polychromed wood, carved in multiple separate blocks and assembled hollow. Height, 27'2⅖". Asuka-en photograph.

probably the chief of an important local clan claiming descent from one of the four Great Gods of Dahomean religion, the thunder god Schango. Since Schango was a public god who nourished and protected his people when they did their duty by him, it was important that his favor be courted. To win his proper care he had to be represented in objective form and his image enshrined in a typically thatch-roofed shelter. There the priest could perform the daily ritual of rubbing the image with a gradually accumulating crust of palm oil, blood, corn meal, and other such offerings, a crust fortunately removed from the present sculpture.

Since a woodcarver was an individualist in Dahomean society and had to be accorded respect and careful handling, we can imagine the patron waiting long, if not patiently, for the moment of the artist's inspiration to arrive. When it did arrive, we can be sure that the sculptor was at last completely in tune with the block of hard wood and the sharp gouges. Allowed considerable freedom of representation and style for the statuette of even a god, the carver developed a concept of the thunder god that was novel in the extreme. He conceived Schango as driving his burro across the sky, the hoofs of the galloping steed kicking up the thunder.

Specialist in a single material, the artist never forgot that it was wood with which he was working. He managed with true artist's ingenuity to direct the features prompted by the wood into enhancement of the subject. The carver followed the run of the grain faithfully through the core of the work, but cut subordinate parts out of the other pieces of wood, to be inserted into the core with a uniform insistence on their separateness. He repeated with like angularities of juncture a whole series of vertical and oblique forms, and with these he set up a rhythm so powerful that the observer may feel in himself the jog of the rider's body and think he hears, as well as sees, the clatter of the burro's hoofs.

The Dahomey sculptor held to the initial block for all major masses, helping thus to gain unity of effect. He had to work on a small scale, at the same time, to prevent cracking. The Japanese woodcarver enjoyed an advantage over the Dahomey sculptor. He worked with a technique of his own, one borrowed from the Japanese carpentry described in the chapter on architecture (p. 98). He followed an "assembled blocks" procedure *—carving the whole figure in small-scaled separate blocks and uniting these with carpentry joints in order to complete the work. Proceeding like a whittler, he concentrated on each separate block in turn, shifting it about this way and that in his hands to cut it, to inspect the resulting effects, and to define the factual details ever more sharply.

Unkei, leading master of woodcarvers and head of a workshop of numerous assistants, brought realism in this technique to a final climax. In such masterpieces as their two giant warriors of A.D. 1203, still standing guard at the Main South Gate of Tōdaiji, Buddhist temple in Nara, Unkei and his collaborators managed to unite subject, style, and medium in a perfect fusion. They created two of the largest sculptures ever shaped in wood, each a full 26 feet in height, the one illustrated (5.13) attesting to the way in which both profited by the scale and the expressive force of the realistic style which the assembled blocks technique made possible.

Sculptors see only what they have the eyes to see, but they see sharply and inquiringly. They discriminate in what they see, concentrating on such forms as have meaning. New goals in the handling of space and the treatment of materials have been turning the eyes of sculptors recently toward realms hitherto either unexplored or else visited casually. Whenever they have found in a sculpture of the primitive Occident or the sensuously expressive Orient kinship with their own experience, they have been heartened by it to develop a corresponding boldness of statement. They have endeavored to bring their materials into the happiest possible wedding with their subjects, to do triple duty in expressing themselves, their subjects, and their mediums.

In stress upon character of natural material and expressive way of working it, the English master, Henry Moore, has played a leading role.† With a piece of stone on his stand, for example, Moore has concentrated on the stoniness of the material and developed out of this quality forms as strong in structure.

Consider the recumbent figure which Moore designed to serve as a memorial on the campus of Dartington Hall in South Devonshire, England (5.14). *Memorial to Christopher Martin* was carved out of Hornton stone, a native, fine-textured limestone, which the English sculptor converted into broadly rendered human forms echoing the sweep of neighboring downs and promontories. The womanliness of the landscape was the suggested counterpart to the earthiness of the figure, but the stone making this allusion remains pure stone throughout. It was worked by a process paralleling nature's in the shaping of pebbles in a river bed—by grinding more than by cutting, by rounding off edges and developing knobs of slight but seemingly great roundness against a flattened bulk for contrast. Stone has, as noted in our intro-

---

* For a summary of the techniques of early Japanese sculpture, see Wallace S. Baldinger, "An Early Japanese Buddha," *Allen Memorial Art Museum Bulletin* (Oberlin College), Spring, 1954, pp. 122–136.

† Herbert Read, *Henry Moore: Sculpture and Drawings* (London: Lund Humphries, 1946; 1st ed., 1944), and James J. Sweeney, *Henry Moore* (New York: Museum of Modern Art, 1946). See also the documentary film, *Henry Moore*, directed by John Reed (distributed by British Information Service, New York; black and white; 16-mm; English sound track; 26 mins.).

5.14. Henry Moore (1898–): *Memorial to Christopher Martin.* 1945–1946. Hornton stone. Length, 56". Grounds of Dartington Hall, South Devonshire, England.

5.15. Henry Moore: *Reclining Figure.* 1945–1946. Elm wood. Length, 75". Buchholz Gallery, New York. Courtesy of the artist.

duction to this chapter, natural compressions. The light falling on it is evenly distributed. Hence the gradualness of shape in Moore's carving, its lack of localized emphasis, its sense of impersonal breadth.

How different the case can be with wood carving is impressively demonstrated by a sculpture based on the same reclining-figure motive as the Martin memorial, done by Henry Moore at about the same time (5.15). Carved from elm, the piece reveals most vividly the properties of wood and its behavior under the mallets and gouges used to carve it. Like the African Negro sculptor, Moore recognized how much emphasis the uneven and subdued light falling on wood requires. He saw how wood inclines toward the upward-reaching forms of its growth, its fibrous consistency adapting it to cutting and splitting rather than to rubbing, its grain undulating around and through it in a single direction. He noted how hard and tough elmwood proved beneath his tools. He drew from every such feature the motives for his work, to give it the peculiarly expressive character which it has. Hence the sharp-edged and deeply shadowed hollows which invade the masses of his *Reclining Figure,* the continuous bulgings of its forms, their branchings from each other like tree growth, and their openings into space. Hence the light mottlings on the surface of his piece—signatures, so to speak, of his gouges and rasps. Hence, finally, the underlining of every long sweep of form by the play of the grain along it.

Carvers of Moore's generation have tended to deprecate modeling as trickery unworthy of true sculpture. As a reaction against romantic excesses such an attitude is understandable. We can see, on the other hand, what little justification disparagers of ceramic sculpture have, when we reconsider such terra-cotta masterpieces as the Chinese tomb statuette (5.5) or the colossal Etruscan image (Pl. II). Far from being an agency fit only for sketches or classroom exercises, clay modeling can be one of the most difficult and challenging of all sculptural mediums. The same holds true of sculptural metalworking for the artist who

treats metal as a modeling or structural, rather than a casting, medium. Here again, if he designs for the process, he develops qualities uniquely appropriate to the medium.

Combinations of materials, largely metals, have developed at mid-twentieth century into a new technique of metal construction. More tectonic than plastic in character, this additive medium consists in joining metal sheets, wires, and knobs together, usually by welding. It resembles architecture in this structural procedure, as it does in the customarily obvious hollows incorporated. We have noted the necessity for making life-size or colossal terra-cotta and bronze statues hollow (Pl. II and 5.6). But the "nothingness within" affects the external form of such sculptures only slightly if at all, whereas it plays a vital role in determining the composition of most metal constructions.

Among the younger constructivists Tom Hardy has developed animal sculpture into a specialty, interpreting each beast in forms uniquely appropriate to the techniques of metal joining. Hardy cultivated from early childhood on a farm in the Cascade Mountains of central Oregon a liking for both the barnyard stock and the wild creatures of the surrounding forests. He began to develop his art in ceramics, but he soon changed to metal construction because he felt metal better fitted to the semi-open planar compositions which he was striving to create. In following this new procedure, the sculptor felt, as he has himself declared, the influence of his home environment:

> From Eugene, Oregon, where I now live and work, it is possible within a couple of hours to reach the summits of the Cascade Range, the sagebrush deserts of the Oregon cattle country, or the Pacific Ocean. Within thirty minutes I can be at the farm—which is an isolated place, the quiet broken only by the sounds of birds and by my sheep and their bells. Being able to visit these interesting and pacifying places often leads, I think, to an attitude of calm intensity which I hope is reflected in my work.

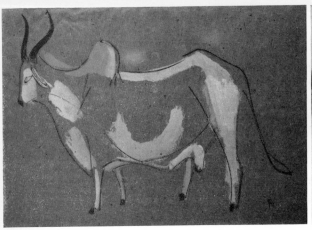

5.16. STUDIES FOR A SCULPTURAL CONSTRUCTION. a. Tom Hardy (1921–): Early literal study of zebu. 1955. Pen and ink and gouache on coarse cardboard. 15 x 22″. Collection of Alan Bennett, Eugene, Ore. B. L. Freemesser photograph. b. Tom Hardy: Later structural study of zebu. 1955. Brush and ink and gouache on paper. 15 x 22″. Collection of the artist. B. L. Freemesser photograph.

5.17. Tom Hardy: *Zebu*. 1955. Welded and forged steel. Height, 19″. Collection of Alan Bennett. Tom Burns, Jr., photograph.

Always in the Northwest the magnificent trees seem to establish man in a different scale than do the Midwest plains, or the skyscrapers of Eastern cities. There seems to be a parallel between the spatial relationships in the vertical and horizontal layering of trees, branches, underbrush, ferns and dry needles and the almost "post and beam" construction which I generally use in my sculptures.*

Hardy characterized each animal he knew, with increasing directness and intensity catching the essence of its anatomy, its movements, even its individuality. He came eventually to extend his range of subject to include the wild life of other climates and regions, finding in each subject new possibilities of organization in metal.

Take, for example, Hardy's rendering of the zebu, or Brahma bull, sacred ox of India but also a familiar animal on the Western cattle ranch. The artist began his re-creation of this animal with a series of drawings, thumb-nail sketches made direct from the animal, carried through progressive simplifications in the studio for translation into metal (5.16, 5.17). In the process of making these drawings he worked for balance of one form against another across space. He strove for emphasis on such contours and volumes as might convey the lumbering docile movement of the zebu and the features peculiar to its anatomy—the hump on its back, the dewlap beneath its throat. He worked out his forms to the point where he could decide the material to use—hot-rolled sheet steel—and the best way to cut it and join the pieces together. For greater certainty he cut out of heavy paper the pattern for each plane and transferred it to the steel.

When Hardy came to the actual rendering, however, he felt the necessities imposed by a change-over from paper to steel; he let the workings of the hard material dictate free modifications. In cutting the "core" piece and the subordinate sections, for example, he converted the sharp line of the drawings into the roughly beaded line made by the oxyacetylene torch. He forged the pieces into curves suggestive of the beast's configurations, and welded them together into shapes at once distinctive of the wrought steel and of the Brahma bull. He made certain pieces legs to support the whole sculpture, in place of a pedestal. Finally, for textural enrichment, he "built up" roughened passages for hair about the head and the tail (applying a heated steel rod to the semimolten surfaces), and incised the folds of the dewlap by laying the tongue of flame of the torch flat against the metal on either side.

Tom Hardy's *Zebu* became in this way one of those sculptural compromises to the creation of which metal construction contributes. It became neither absolute mass nor absolute space but a partial realization of both. Much as a modern building shows exterior and interior simultaneously (4.8a), Hardy's construction reveals both its outer surfaces and its inner structure.

SCULPTURAL USE OF THE NEW KINETIC ELEMENT

Metal constructions like Hardy's *Zebu* make refreshing departure from the sculptural conventions of closed mass and statically weighted form. We perceive these constructions by looking into them as well as by running our eyes and hands along their surfaces. We gain in the process of viewing an exhilarating sense of freedom. The sculpture remains fixed in one position and we remain fixed in another, but we feel at liberty to look anywhere, from without inward or from within outward. We feel that our vision is itself in motion.

The concept of vision in motion is new to art.† It obliges us to add to our basic list of

* "Metal Sculpture by Tom Hardy," *American Artist*, April, 1955, pp. 34–37, 74–75. Quotation from this article, p. 75.

† L. Moholy-Nagy, *Vision in Motion* (Chicago: Paul Theobald, 1947).

seven elements—point, line, plane, texture, color, mass, space—an eighth: the kinetic element, movement. The illusion of movement has always figured to some extent in visual works of art, and sometimes it predominates. But the simultaneous presentation of inner and outer space tends to fuse space with time and introduce a new element of movement beyond its illusion.

The idea of vision in motion began to affect sculpture as early as 1908, when Constantin Brancusi, Rodin's one-time follower who was then turning to Indian Buddhist and Hindu sculpture, began searching beneath surface illusions for the essence of reality in sculptures the direct carving of which was poised midway between the free forms of life and the geometric forms of the inanimate. Brancusi continued the rest of his life to develop sculptural equivalents to what he felt were the lowest common denominators of all organic forms: the sphere, the egg, the spiral. With such basic forms he endeavored to interpret not the living forms themselves but the functions by which their life was manifested.*

Let us consider an instance of Brancusi's art when he turned his attention to bird life. The forms of birds had been represented variously at the hands of other sculptors. But Brancusi made the form of the bird only his point of departure, going beyond the actual shape to convey nothing but a feeling for the bird's movements. He looked for sculptural equivalents to the sensation of a bird in darting flight and the sensation of a bird settling down for the night. He found equivalents in pure shapes, shapes rich in organic connotations but only distantly suggestive of the representational. Brancusi made the nucleus for his expression of each subject an elongated ovoid, but he developed around each ovoid a complex of contours and smoothly polished surfaces radically dissimilar from the other.

* Carola Giedion-Welcker, *Contemporary Sculpture* ("Documents of Modern Art," Vol. XII; New York: Wittenborn, 1955), pp. 112–129. Sculptures by Brancusi and Gabo, mentioned below, appear on pp. 116, 119, 121, and 161 of this book.

As the axis for *Bird in Space* (5.18a), Brancusi followed a rising curve of force. He developed the attenuated mass about it into a clean-surfaced and swiftly flowing shape, one which anticipated, in fact, that of the jet-propelled plane. As the axis for *Bird at Rest* (5.18b) the sculptor designed a sagging curve. He fashioned the bulging mass around it, though still tapering at either end, into a drooping form with subtly diminishing contours.

It was characteristic of the growing concern for medium that Brancusi should have sought for his pair of abstractions material and handling which seemed best fitted in each case to carry the subject. For *Bird in Space* he chose bronze, because it would adapt itself easily to the form required by the subject and would take a high polish contributing to the effect of speed. For *Bird at Rest* he chose marble, because its bulk would seem to weight the shape, and its granular texture and meandering grain would tend to retard the flow of the contours and increase the effect of quiet. In the second work, unfortunately, the influence of a theme led the sculptor to force his marble perilously beyond its capacity, carving the tapering ends to an extreme of thinness and elongation. An observer who understands the difficulty in doing this successfully will experience something of the same anxiety Brancusi must have felt lest the ends break off.

Actual Movement in Sculpture

So important did Brancusi consider the new concept of vision in motion that he contrived hidden mechanisms by which the pedestals for some of his sculptures could be made to rotate. He thus made an abstraction of a swan seem to float and abstractions of a fish and a seal to swim. The spectator stands still before such works, watching them reveal not only their full three-dimensionality of composition (having compositional appeal from all angles in depth, as well as in height and width) but also the four-dimensionality (fusion of space and time) which their actual movements effect.

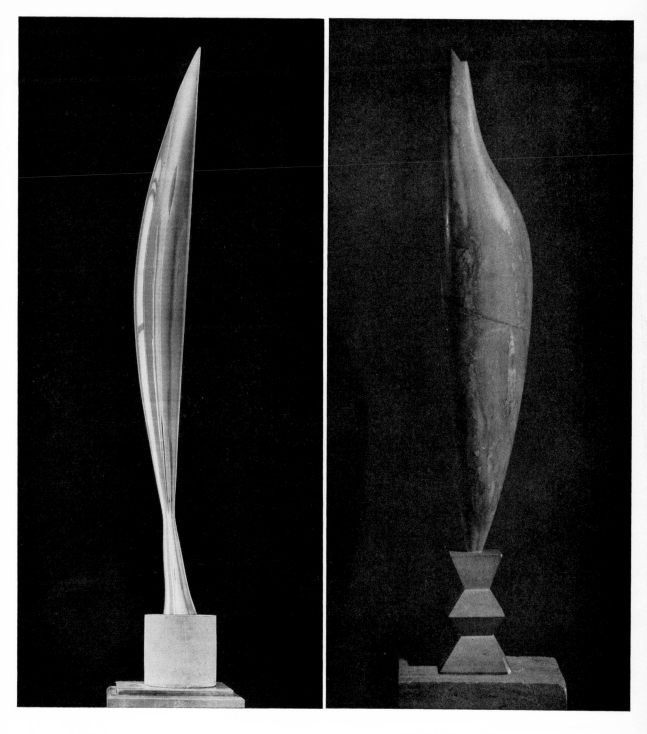

5.18. a. Constantin Brancusi (1876–1957): *Bird in Space*. 1919. Bronze. Height, 54″.
The Museum of Modern Art, New York. Soichi Sunami photograph. b. Constantin
Brancusi: *Bird at Rest*. 1920. Grained, pale yellow marble. Height, 54″. Collection of
Katherine S. Dreier. Courtesy of Miss Dreier and Yale University Art Gallery.

5.19. Alexander Calder (1898–   ): *Lobster Trap and Fish Tail.* 1939. Mobile, steel wire and sheet aluminum. Width, 15′. The Museum of Modern Art, New York, Gift of the Advisory Committee. Soichi Sunami photograph.

In Brancusi's creations the masses retain their original solidity, moving only with their pedestals and depending upon this for enhancement of their flowing effects. As long as a sculptor employs a conventional medium and retains the original compactness of his material as a single unit, he can bring the element of actual movement into his work solely by the expedient of a motor-driven base. In this respect the constructivist has the advantage. He cuts his material into pieces and reassembles them. In the act of rejoining his sections he can replace the usual welded joints with movable joints and flexible wire connections. He can support or suspend planes and points of metal by attaching them to lines of wire, developing systems of cantilevered construction and asymmetrical balance which merge the actual structure of the work with its compositional appearance. The constructivist opens up in this way a whole new realm of expression. He creates *mobiles*—sculptures in a continual state of becoming, in contradistinction to *stabiles*, fixed constructions which maintain only a state of being.

An American sculptor, Alexander Calder, originated these mobile variants of metal construction as early as the 1920's, and a third of a century later was still the leader in exploitation of the medium. Calder had few real precedents for his mobiles. American weather vanes and Swiss clockworks sometimes caught the germ of the idea. A work by Naum Gabo, *Kinetic Sculpture*, a steel spring that vibrates in space, dates from 1920, year in which the movement of constructivism began with it and kindred works in Moscow. Calder himself, son of a sculptor but trained as an engineer, invented mobiles out of his diversion of twisting wire and whittling wood into performers for a toy circus.*

---

* James J. Sweeney, *Alexander Calder* (New York: Museum of Modern Art, 1951; revised ed.; 1st pub., 1943). A 16-mm. documentary motion picture, *Works of Calder*, compares his mobiles with forms in nature (filmed by Herbert Matter, 1950; available from Museum of Modern Art, New York; color, sound; 20 mins.).

The artist succeeded in lifting his new medium to a level of true artistry in such mobiles as the *Lobster Trap and Fish Tail* (5.19), now hanging in the stairwell of The Museum of Modern Art in New York City. In this 15-foot-wide work Calder took the prosaic steel wire and sheet aluminum of industry and transformed them into a gossamerlike fantasy. Working like an industrial engineer with exacting laws of gravity, tension, and dynamics, Calder managed to introduce into his mobile a poetic wealth of allusion—to the litter on a sea-beach after a storm, perhaps, or to the seafarer's life and the phantoms of his legends.

Calder did not create his *Lobster Trap and Fish Tail* specifically for the stairwell of a museum. It fits, nevertheless, into the modern interior and holds its own, along with whatever works happen currently to be on view, in drawing the attention of visitors. As one stands on the stairway and watches the currents of the building's forced-air ventilation turn the mobile about, one tries to catch the relationship of each momentary effect to what preceded it and is about to follow it. One becomes intrigued not only by the moving forms of the construction itself but by the active play of shadows it casts on the walls.

Calder's mobile is most effective in those rare moments when museum attendance is light. When the stairway is crowded with visitors going from floor to floor, however, it interferes with circulation. People stop to observe its changing compositional effects, and the stairway grows congested.

The authorities of the Baltimore Museum of Art wanted a similar work for the stairwell of a new wing of their museum. They commissioned Naum Gabo, whom we have noted as one of the Russian founders of constructivism, to create it specially for the space in question. Some sculptors reject a commission like this on grounds that it enslaves them to the architecture, reduces them to mere selectors and arrangers. Not so Gabo. He had always insisted that in his kind of art, called constructivism by no accident, sculpture enters the domain of architecture and stands ready for the most intimate collaboration with it.* In this case he had to adapt his work to the architecture of a building already finished, where there was no chance to realize his ideal of a free give-and-take between sculptor and architect in their joint process of creation. But Gabo's chief concern coincided with the contemporary architect's—a concern with luminous space—and he felt no fettering as he approached his task.

Knowing of the congestion caused by Calder's mobile in the New York museum's stairwell, he proposed that his construction not hinder but actually encourage traffic flow. Instead of a mobile which tended to hold the spectator to one spot, therefore, Gabo projected a stabile that would prove so inviting of view from every angle above and below, as well as around, that the observer would in spite of himself keep on climbing or descending.

Challenged thus by the architectural setting, the sculptor evolved for suspension 15 feet into the space of the stairwell a construction as lightly airy in effect as Calder's and yet, unlike Calder's, as completely nonrepresentational as the architecture (5.20). Made of aluminum baked black, gold wire and steel wire, bronze mesh, and a transparent plastic, the sculpture thus integrates color with the material of the construction and material with space in the form of points, lines, and planes. Mass and texture are lacking, but deliberately lacking, as out of keeping with a construction aimed at capturing the poetry of space and light. Seen successively from various angles, the construction as it now hangs in the Baltimore Museum of Art seems to contract and expand with the rhythms of a breathing, moving thing (5.20, 5.21).

The Continued Importance of Mass

The character of constructivist sculpture as an art peculiar to the twentieth century does not argue, however, that it is destined to supplant other forms of sculpture. It widens our range

* Naum Gabo, "A New Construction for Baltimore," *Magazine of Art,* Vol. XLV, No. 2 (February, 1952), pp. 71–74.

of experience in art tremendously; it influences other sculpture, even architecture and industrial design, to their enrichment; but it remains only one important phase of twentieth-century sculpture. Whether stabile or mobile, whether representational or nonrepresentational, such sculpture rejects the element of mass. But bulk, even in a day of radar, jet planes, and space ships, remains essential to our existence. We are creatures of mass, inhabit an earth of mass, utilize for dwelling and tool much that has mass. And we still respond to sculptures which speak in terms of this element.

When its mass is joined with its normally representational role, sculpture is likely always to meet a need as vital to architecture as it met in ancient Greece or Gothic France. Whatever advances architecture may make in spatial expression, it still needs services which sculpture in traditional vein is alone able to render.

What the art of sculpture as a traditional art of mass can do for the interior of a public building was demonstrated by the statue used by Ludwig Miës van der Rohe in the German Government Pavilion at the 1929 Barcelona World's Fair (4.9). When an architect simplifies and refines his design as Miës did for this structure, and determines in the process exactly where and how sculpture is most needed to complete the composition, the resulting work becomes impressive. In this case, in fact, the very quality of the architect's design depended on his use of sculpture, for he made it the climax of the whole composition.

The architect installed in the exposition pavilion a bronze statue of a bather by his German sculptor-colleague, Georg Kolbe. He had it mounted above a reflecting pool in a garden open to the sky at the rear of the building, where it could strike a human note amid the impersonal forms of the architecture. More than this, he made it relieve, as only a work in mass can do, the uniformly flat planes of wall and glass, and effect between them the proper transition. So important did he make the sculpture in the ensemble that its removal would have returned the structure to a state of unfulfillment.

5.20. Naum Gabo (1890–   ): *Construction Suspended in Space,* view from third floor. 1950–1952. Aluminum baked black, transparent plastic, rolled gold wire, phosphor bronze mesh, stainless steel wire. Height, 15′. Baltimore Museum of Art, Saidie A. May Wing. Jerome H. Abrams photograph.

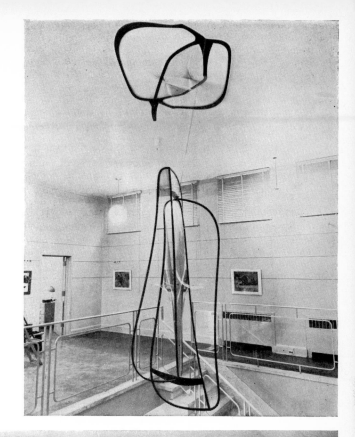

5.21. a. Naum Gabo: *Construction Suspended in Space,* view from third floor. Baltimore Museum of Art, Saidie A. May Wing. Jerome H. Abrams photograph. b. Naum Gabo: *Construction Suspended in Space,* view from stairway between second and third floors. Baltimore Museum of Art, Saidie A. May Wing. Jerome H. Abrams photograph.

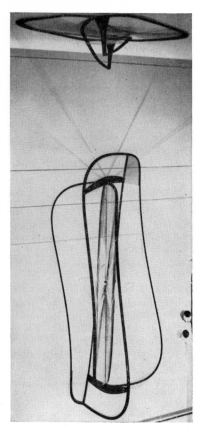

SUMMARY

Unlike the crafts and their extensions into industry, and unlike architecture, sculpture is a nonutilitarian art. It is an art of expression of personal experience, above all in volumes. Most often these volumes are of solid mass but sometimes, as recently, they include open space, defined and even set into motion by component lines and planes. Sculptures range from statues completely in the round, through various stages of high and low relief, to incision, a scratching of the surface closely akin to drawing.

Ordinarily, sculpture is a representational art. With few exceptions, even its more highly abstracted works bear traces of existent objects, and most sculptures remain identifiable in subject. For subject matter sculptures almost always draw on animate objects: birds, animals, human figures, especially human figures in the nude. They usually omit accidental or particular aspects of such objects in favor of their more typical and enduring qualities.

Sculptures are made of tangible and durable materials ranging from clay, wax, and metal through ivory and wood to stone. They are made in accord with one of two general classes of procedure: the additive, or plastic (modeling, casting, constructing), and the subtractive, or glyptic (carving, grinding, polishing). Out of these materials and processes artists in various ways draw inspiration to modify their representations of other objects. Works created by an additive process are characteristically extended in form, varied in contour, and modulated in surface. Works created by a subtractive process are characteristically contracted in form, simplified in contour, and generalized in surface.

The expressive realization of subject constitutes the sole function of much sculpture, and especially of studio sculpture (that branch of the art produced in the artist's studio simply to be looked at, touched, and handled). Beyond this function some sculpture is related by intent to works of other arts: architecture, landscape design, and city and regional planning. When sculpture performs functions of interrelationship, it complements other works in ways for which it alone is qualified, as an art of expression in volumes and representational forms.

RECOMMENDED READINGS

Read, Herbert. *The Art of Sculpture.* "Bollingen Series," XXXV: 3. New York: Pantheon Books, 1956.

The best book through which to secure an introduction to sculpture, this represents in published form the A. W. Mellon Lectures in the Fine Arts for 1954 at the National Gallery of Art in Washington, D. C. Except for some exaggerated emphasis on tactile (and "haptic") values of sculpture and some bias in judgment due to zeal to keep sculpture an independent art, the author offers a sound basis for appreciation. In his approach he reflects the strong influence of his sculptor-friend Henry Moore.

Clark, Kenneth. *The Nude: A Study in Ideal Form.* "Bollingen Series," XXXV: 2. New York: Pantheon Books, 1956.

This study was originally presented as the A. W. Mellon Lectures in the Fine Arts for 1953. It deals authoritatively with the chief subject matter of sculpture, tracing the changing uses of the nude in both sculptural and pictorial expression throughout the history of art. Abundantly illustrated and blessed by the author's wit and literary skill as well as critical insight and scholarship, it is a highly readable book.

Seymour, Charles, Jr. *Tradition and Experiment in Modern Sculpture.* Washington, D. C.: The American University Press, 1949.

Like Herbert Read's and Kenneth Clark's books, Seymour's book began in lecture form in Washington, D. C., this time at the American University on the occasion of a special exhibition at the University's Watkins Gallery. Prepared with college students in mind, the text is shorter and more easily readable than the other two cited. It was written with serious intent, and it still holds its own as an introduction to sculpture, deep in insight, illuminating in treatment, and refreshingly concrete in illustration.

Rich, Jack C. *The Materials and Methods of Sculpture*. New York: Oxford University Press, 1947.

Indispensable alike to the student majoring in sculpture and to the student of art appreciation, this reference work on mediums in some ways surpasses its nearest competitors: William Zorach, *Zorach Explains Sculpture* (New York: American Artists Group, 1947); and Jules Struppeck, *The Creation of Sculpture* (New York: Holt, 1952). It is moderate in size but encyclopedic in coverage, failing only to cover the field of metal construction (probably because this medium seemed too new in the United States at the time of writing).

Lynch, John. *Metal Sculpture: New Forms, New Techniques*. New York: Studio-Crowell, 1957.

Owing to its omission from all general technical manuals, the medium of metal construction is here singled out for a special reference. This book by Lynch, himself a constructivist sculptor, covers some of the historical background of the medium as well as partially surveying works by Lynch's contemporaries in the field. It is small in format but generously illustrated.

Slobodkin, Louis. *Sculpture: Principles and Practice*. Cleveland and New York: World Publishing, 1949.

A successful sculptor-teacher here goes beyond the usual technical manual to carry the pupil into the studio and direct him through a whole professional course in sculpture. Salty with the flavor of actual instruction, illustrated abundantly with detailed photographs and diagrams covering technical processes, and criticizing intelligently such works of the past as are illustrated, the book makes excellent preparation for visiting sculptors' studios and developing a "feel" for the tangible nature of their productions.

Ritchie, Andrew Carnduff. *Sculpture of the Twentieth Century*. New York: Museum of Modern Art, 1953.

There have been many books prepared in recent years to introduce the developments in Western sculpture since Rodin. Probably the best balanced in critical judgment and in range and quality of illustration are still three by Stanley Casson published by the Oxford University Press, *Some Modern Sculptors* (1928), *XXth Century Sculptors* (1930), and *Sculpture of Today* (1939). Ritchie's book brings such studies up to the middle of the twentieth century and makes a pregnantly suggestive analysis of the various movements in terms of relationship to the outside object. It includes a stimulating section devoted to passages by sculptors on their art, a convenient set of biographical notes compiled by Margaret Miller, and a selective bibliography drawn up by Bernard Karpel.

Giedion-Welcker, Carola. *Contemporary Sculpture: an Evolution in Volume and Space*. "Documents of Modern Art," XII. New York: George Wittenborn, 1955. Revised ed. of *Modern Plastic Art*. Zurich: Girsberger, 1937.

This is the most comprehensive reference for all Occidental sculpture of the twentieth century, particularly valuable because its author maintained close personal touch with the leading European sculptors of the time covered. Inquiry into late-nineteenth-century sculpture, especially that by painters who turned increasingly to sculpture as a means of solving problems of expression, makes a stimulating introduction to later developments. The book is richly illustrated and interlarded with specific comments on the works represented. The biographical notes by the author and the bibliography compiled by Bernard Karpel are more exhaustive than the corresponding features of Ritchie's book.

Damaz, Paul. *Art in European Architecture: Synthèse des Arts*. New York: Reinhold Publishing, 1956.

This is the most complete in coverage and the best illustrated (many color reproductions) among the works on architectural sculpture. It holds the same position for its subject as Giedion-Welcker's book holds for sculpture in general. The comparative study of garden design and mural painting and photography, made during the course of the survey of architectural sculpture, qualifies the book as the standard reference for those arts as well. Continuous quotation from both the spoken and the written words of the artists involved gives the whole study a ring of authenticity which is borne out by the author's text and documentation of each work illustrated.

6.1. Pirkle Jones (1914–   ): *Drops. c.* 1950. Photogram. 8½ x 6¾″. Collection of Ansel Adams, Yosemite, Calif. Ansel Adams photograph.

Photography and the Motion Picture

PHOTOGRAPHY IS THE ART of creating pictures by action of light on surfaces chemically prepared to respond to it. Its nature is suggested in the two Greek words from which its name is derived, *photos*, meaning "light," and *-graphia*, meaning "writing": a "writing" or "drawing" with light. The term "photography" is thought to have been invented by Sir John Herschel, English astronomer and physicist, in 1839. In order to make light produce pictures, two devices are essential, devices which together form the modern type of camera. One is the chemically treated surface, a light-sensitized plate, film, or paper. The other is the camera obscura (Latin for "dark chamber") in which this sheet of material is placed.

If we wish to see how light-sensitized paper functions, we must take a package of photographic printing paper into a darkroom, remove a sheet of it and lay on it a comb, leaf, feather, or other small object. We then throw a light on the paper for a second or two. Wherever the silver emulsion coating the paper is exposed, the light-sensitive silver salts begin reduction to metallic silver, while the unexposed emulsion lying under the object remains unaffected. We render the latent image visible by completing the reduction (bathing the paper in a "developer" solution of hydroquinone and other chemicals to complete the separation of the image-forming silver from its salts). The image is made permanent by immersing the paper in a "fixing bath" of "hypo" (hyposulphite solution), and the process completed by washing away with water the undeveloped salts. The direct action of light on sensitized paper has made a ghostlike register of the object, a fairylike picture which the first man to make one,

Fox Talbot, called a "photogenic drawing," a drawing rendered, as he put it, with "the pencil of nature." *

Talbot treated his photogenic drawings less as works of art than as illustrations of reality. When at the end of World War I such artists as Laszlo Moholy-Nagy revived the medium, they explored its possibilities for artistic abstraction as others were exploring in sculpture the possibilities of metal construction. Moholy-Nagy adopted for his abstractions the name *photograms*, which has now come into general use to refer to any photograph made without a camera.

The artist making a photogram must restrict himself to small, flat objects, but with them he has a surprisingly wide range of effects at his disposal. He can use opaque objects in conjunction with translucent ones, the latter yielding textural effects when light passes through them. He can manipulate the shadows cast by superimposed objects by modulating the lighting around them. He can lay over the paper a pane of glass on which forms have been painted, and on this glass place actual objects to diversify the shadows cast by both. He can press drops of water or oil or other liquid between two panes of glass and record by exposure to light their patterns on the paper (6.1).

With this same medium of the photogram artists have achieved images of widely varying character, from an extreme of literal representation of lace which fooled observers into

---

* Borrowed from the title of a book by William Henry Fox Talbot (1800–1877), a British scientist: *The Pencil of Nature* (London: Longmans, Brown, Green, and Longmans, 1844). This was the first book to be illustrated with actual photographic prints.

thinking it the actual fabric,* to an extreme of nonrepresentational abstraction which Moholy-Nagy used to open up a new realm of fantasy (6.10).

Unlike the photogram, which was invented little more than a century ago, the camera obscura has been known and used by artists for several hundred years. Like the photogram, on the other hand, it still lends itself to experiment. A camera obscura may be made by cutting one side of a light-tight cardboard box so that it can slide freely back and forth inside the box itself. A plate of ground glass is then inserted into this movable wall. A small aperture is cut through the opposite wall of the box and a lens installed across it. The aperture is then turned toward an object and the wall with ground glass moved forward and back until the image of the object comes to focus on the glass. Paper is laid over the glass and the image traced with a pencil. This is the procedure resorted to by artists in their more literal moments, from the days of Leonardo da Vinci down almost to the present.

The camera obscura can be converted into a simple box camera by bringing the ground glass into focus on some object, covering the aperture with a shutter, and replacing the ground glass with a photographic plate which has been carefully shielded from light until it is safely inside the camera. The shutter may be removed from the aperture momentarily, exposing the light-sensitized surface to the image focused on it through the lens. When the camera is taken to a darkroom and the exposed plate removed and bathed in a chemical solution, the latent image becomes visible in a negative form—light where the image itself is dark and dark where it is light (6.3b).

Since the plate is made of glass, all unexposed areas become transparent by this process of developing and fixing. Consequently, when a sheet of photographic paper is set under a negative in the darkroom, exposed to light projected through the negative, and developed and fixed in the same way, there is printed a positive image, that "drawing with light" which is the end product: the photograph itself (6.3a).

Whatever their refinements for creating or controlling light, adjusting aperture and timer, changing or focusing lenses, winding or developing film, all cameras have this basic structure. However elaborate the devices for measuring light, keeping track of time, controlling temperature and humidity, printing, cropping, and enlarging, all processes include at least a portion of the steps which we have described. If the photographer uses his camera properly and follows his procedure faithfully, he is bound to produce a technically commendable picture.

MAKING THE PHOTOGRAPH A WORK OF ART

The Experimental Approach

In order to create a photograph which qualifies as a work of art, however, the man behind the camera has to have more than technical dexterity. He has to have the makings of an artist with very special powers of patience, persistence, and calculated control. Consider B. L. Freemesser, for example, the photographer who converted a camera recording of a fountain pen into a work of art (1.9b). In this case the artist needed to enhance the features of an object so small as to escape notice in ordinary surroundings. He had an assistant hold the pen, therefore, a girl carefully chosen for fingers and fingernails as shapely as the pen itself. He focused not on the girl herself but on her hand as she held the pen. In order to give the pen major emphasis, the photographer used a progressive sharpening of focus from the

---

* Ill., *ibid.*, 1949 ed., p. 37. Talbot's description of observers' reactions, quoted, p. 203, and reprinted in full context, Talbot, "Some Account of the Art of Photogenic Drawing" (1839), Beaumont Newhall (ed.), *On Photography: A Source Book of Photo History in Facsimile* (Watkins Glen, N. Y.: Century House, 1956), p. 64.

blurred wrist through the hand and the fingers to a climax in the pen. In order to avoid the "ghost" images which blur the actual image in a carelessly made photograph, he reduced the glare of the chrome-plated top of the pen with a coating of grease specially prepared for the purpose.

Even then, for best effect Freemesser had to make a score of separate exposures, varying each exposure in lighting, in aperture-opening ("stop"), or in length of time. From the negative which he finally chose, he had to print a comparable number of positives, each similarly varied, until he exhausted every possibility and produced the best print. He found that this print surpassed his original conception. He had captured in it, for example, the best angle and distance of close-up for repeating rhythmically in the shapes of fingers and fingernails the shape of the pen, the best direction and intensity of lighting for accentuating the contours and plastic relief of the pen.

An outsider watching such a photographer at work is apt to deplore his apparent waste of time and film. If everything is set up to best advantage, the outsider asks, then why cannot the expert photographer go ahead, shoot his picture, and be done with it? The fact is that the photographer can seldom, if ever, achieve his objective with a single exposure. If he takes a chance on its being just right, stops shooting, and repairs with it to his darkroom to develop his negative and print his positive, more often than not he fails. By that time the subject may be lost or transformed beyond recall. He needs to assemble on the spot, therefore, a whole series of experimental exposures, a body of working material indispensable to his achievement. He proceeds to deal with these exposures much as a sculptor attacks a block of stone. He conceives in advance something of the form desired, but he sharpens his conception by following a subtractive procedure. Like a sculptor cutting surplus stone away, he studies his raw material carefully and proceeds to discard his negatives and positives ruthlessly until the ideal image emerges. Reducing the terms of his statement, he gains in force of expression.

Sensitivity and Perception

Photography has its own distinctive traits, and the man who recognizes and exploits them is certain to make of it an art uniquely itself. Gradations of light-intensity, or values, are its principal element of expression. The pattern of such values comes ready-made from nature. It may be simplified in number or heightened in contrast, but its structure remains rooted in an unstaged reality that is always fortuitous. It is this ready-made character of the pattern which accounts for the appeal of the photograph as a revelation of the unsuspected in daily life.*

Whatever the degree of its abstraction, this pattern is at heart representational. It may be fragmentary. It may leave much unsaid. But it draws us into active sharing with the experience depicted, arousing our desire to identify the objects represented. It exerts an esthetic appeal independent of its subject, but it exists less for art's sake than for life's. It invites us to peer more deeply into the things around us and grasp their significance.

Anything significant about the passing scene cannot be revealed merely by blind chance. It does not yield itself to the novice who simply points his camera and clicks his shutter at random. It responds, rather, to the artist-photographer who perceives its unique quality and calculates to evoke that quality by a delicate balance of representation against the form in which the photograph is couched. By striking this balance of representation and form, the photographer converts the transient into the monumental and enduring.

Artistic form has power even in photography. It documents, but still more it reveals and universalizes. It presents to the observer aspects of some other time, place, or personality as though they were his own. It fixes a pattern drawn from the subject and discoverable only by the photographer who comes to know the subject intimately.

* Rudolf Arnheim, "Accident and the Necessity of Art," *The Journal of Aesthetics and Art Criticism*, Vol. XVI, No. 1 (September, 1957), pp. 18–31.

The photographer is able to define this pattern in ways peculiar to his camera. He can condense the panorama which we see bit by bit, reducing our prospect to the limited compass of a print upon which we are able to gaze in its entirety (6.6). He can photograph a detail from an angle and at a scale to suggest the whole of which it forms a part (6.7). He can bring to light something so swift, remote, minute, or hidden that it is invisible to the naked eye—a bullet issuing from a gun, a galaxy of stars too far away to make their presence known to us on even the clearest night, an amoeba engulfing its prey in a drop of water—catching in such exposures of the unknown some suggestion of the cosmic.

Contrary to the claim sometimes made, that photography, a recording, cannot be converted into an art of creative expression,[1] the cameraman has as wide a range of expression open to him as has the modeler in clay. We have noted something of that range even when the photographer limits himself to the photogram or seeks merely to emphasize his subject by adjusting the angle of viewing and the focus of the lens. He does not need a thousand-dollar camera and a host of gadgets. All he needs is the artist's eye, hand, and brain. Possessed with the inventive imagination of a true artist, the photographer can produce a masterpiece with the cheapest box camera and the most makeshift darkroom and darkroom equipment. Only such a man can, in fact, put expensive equipment to proper use at proper moments. Only he deserves expensive equipment, since only for him is the range of effects unlimited.

The Problem of Reproducing Works of Art

Since a work of art is more important than anything written about it, we try in a book on art appreciation to bring the reader as close to the work as possible. Ideally, we should present each actual work exactly as it is. Since we cannot, we resort to illustration, counting on improved techniques of reproduction to do justice to the work.

In this respect we are better off than we would have been a hundred and fifty years ago. Then we would have had to depend on illustrations rendered and printed by hand—that is, on prints made in one of a variety of techniques. Although at times these illustrations were admirable works of art in themselves, the objects represented by them were necessarily transformed in the process of reproduction. However conscientious the craftsman in reproducing the image, his feelings and manner of using his tools always affected his work.

Now we depend not on hand-made representation to illustrate an object, but on photography. We photograph objects and reproduce the photographs by photomechanical processes. We assume that the resulting illustrations are trustworthy records because, as we say, the camera never lies. We even judge works of art from photographs alone, without ever seeing the original works.

The truth is that error creeps into a photograph when we least expect it. First of all, it reduces a third-dimensional object to a flattened image having height and width alone. It limits our point of view to that of the man who took the picture. It brings the background in around the object, forcing us to notice that background more than we would when facing the object itself. The photograph can, to be sure, reduce the forms of the background to a soft blur (1.8b), but it can as readily sharpen such forms indiscriminately, letting them impair by their "busyness" the clarity of the representation (2.3b).*

The photograph may serve as a visual record of the work of art, but used in this way it remains a product of science more than of art. It emerges out of the scientist's procedure of evidence-gathering and analyzing, recording and classifying, seemingly leaving little in the

[1] See Notes, p. 298.

* Clarence Kennedy, "Photographing Art," *Magazine of Art*, Vol. XXX, No. 4 (April, 1937), pp. 212–218, especially p. 212, middle of second column. See also Helmut Gernheim, *Focus on Architecture and Sculpture* (London: Fountain Press, 1949), and the foreword by Nikolaus Pevsner.

way of imaginative re-creation for the artist to do.

Any photograph of a work of art draws, nevertheless, on the powers of the cameraman as artist. The photographer seeking to record another man's creation has to enter sympathetically into its character. As he arranges the background and lighting of his subject, determines the position, height, and various controls of his camera, he is drawn into expressing personal reactions to the work being photographed. Sometimes, moreover, the photograph does itself qualify as a work of art: among the photographs chosen for illustration in this book, Will Hoagberg's table setting (3.11) would qualify, and so would G. E. Kidder Smith's Parthenon (4.2). Though made expressly to document other creations, each such photograph appeals to the senses, follows rhythmic orderings, manifests the photographer's experience with his subject. It possesses features essential to art—features calling for relationships of elements (point, line, plane, texture, and the like) developed according to the principles of design—balance, emphasis, rhythm, and proportion.

Consideration of a photograph of a work of art as itself a creation results in an ambiguity. Does the photographer strive to rival or to surpass the artistic quality of the work being photographed? Or does he so subordinate his artistry to the artistry of the subject that we forget his photograph and concentrate on the work represented? Ideally, we say that the latter alternative is the proper goal, because the subject of any representational work of art should be so fused with its form as to become inseparable, and again because a subject which inspires the artist's creation should come through so powerfully as to make the photograph an example of that art which conceals art. The more successful the photograph, on the other hand, the more distracting the photographer's creation as a thing in itself. Quality of appeal makes for loss in appreciation, leaving the photograph to compete with the work represented. Photographs of works of art belong, then, in a category by themselves. Though worthy of admiration when well-made, they remain distinct from photographs inspired by real life for subject, such photographs as constitute the main body of photography as art.

DEVICES FOR PHOTOGRAPHIC CONTROL

Lighting and Perspective

The photographer who has full command of his art can perform seeming miracles with lighting alone.* Let us suppose that he wants to abstract and emphasize the lines and planes of his subject. He adopts a front light, a light behind him that flattens the forms and eliminates deep space (6.16b). If he wants to bring out the textures and the masses, he resorts to a side light that stresses highlights and shadows (6.7) and a subordinate "fill-in" light that activates the reflected lights of his subject (6.9). If he wants to stress the atmosphere

and mood of his subject, he employs a back light that strikes his subject from behind (6.5). If he wants to accentuate the endless depths of space, the loneliness and monotony, felt to pervade a scene, he chooses a top light which illuminates everything near and far with equal intensity (6.6). If he wants to dramatize his subject, to enhance the weird and fantastic about it, he throws a footlight on to it, one that distorts shadows and introduces mystery into passages which are ordinarily commonplace and obvious (3.12).

The photographer utilizes such expedients of illumination not as mere formulas to be applied automatically but as means to be used sparingly as his sense of purpose dictates. Let a novice try any such device mechanically and

* Studies devoted exclusively to lighting are those by the motion-picture photographer, John Alton, *Painting with Light* (New York: Macmillan, 1950), and by the technician of the Eastman Kodak Company, Don D. Nibbelink, *The Complete Book of Lighting* (Forest Park, Ill.: Midland Publishers, 1950).

he is almost certain to end up with a photograph saying anything but what was intended, a chaos of confusing values and shapes. The expert knows, as the novice does not, the values of a photograph and their expressive potentialities, and he controls his means to get the particular value-effects required.

Since, as we have seen, the photographer represents on a two-dimensional surface objects and effects which actually exist in deep space, he has to work with illusions rather than with realities. Like a painter, he must work with perspective, that effect of relative distance and position of objects upon which the illusions depend.[2] He learns to control perspective, to draw from it a range of appearances extending from the "natural" to the "otherworldly."

For the "normal" view the photographer uses a standard lens. He sets the camera back from the subject and holds the instrument level. He stops the diaphragm down to a medium-size aperture and sets the shutter for an exposure time indicated by the exposure meter. He focuses on some point in the middle distance. Taking care not to jolt the camera, he snaps the shutter. He gets a documentary picture, deep in spatial illusion, sharp and clear in contour, one in which the objects themselves are allowed to tell the story (4.2).

For the panoramic view the photographer uses a telephoto lens. He chooses a distant and perhaps elevated vantage point. Since the telephoto lens tends to compress the effect of extension into depth, he seeks perhaps to offset that tendency by introducing a *repoussoir* (from the French *repousser,* meaning "to push back"), such as a tree or a human figure in the near foreground, which contrasts in its shadowed silhouette or flattened lighting with the values of the distance. He stops the diaphragm down to a small aperture, sets the time of exposure, focuses on "infinity," and shoots. He obtains a broadly expansive composition, serene, inviting, and occasionally, as in a mountain-valley view, excitingly spectacular (6.6).

[2] See Notes, page 298.

For the close-up the photographer uses a wide-angle lens. He gets as close to the detail chosen as his lens will permit and still yield sharpness of focus. He opens the diaphragm wide and shortens the exposure-time correspondingly to accord with the meter reading. He secures an intimately detailed picture in which objects or parts of objects appear either actual size or larger than life-size, with a sense of adventurous excitement in discovery as forms emerge with increasing sharpness from a background in blur (1.8a).

For a subject demanding emphasis on height the photographer tilts his camera upward from below to get an "angle shot" that makes for soaring proportions, dynamically inclined planes, and dramatic contrasts of dark mass against lighted sky (4.6). For the subject under foot which offers a rich array of pattern and texture, he tilts his camera downward to get a "bird's-eye" view which can be compellingly moving in its rhythmic sequences of line and plane and sense of expansiveness (6.8).

A black-and-white photograph allows no more direct transfer of color to its surface than it does transfer of three-dimensional space. For realization of the one as of the other, it depends on symbols and illusions which convey a feeling for these elements. Far from recording literally, it forces the photographer to abstract from nature whether he wants to or not.*

For contrasts in values of a photograph, for images to be separated or brought out clearly, the photographer has two principal means of control. One is his type of film; the other, his type of color filter. If for a given subject he uses orthochromatic film, film coated with an emulsion that is "blind" to red, he can make a red object register as black, thus heightening its contrast with a yellow object and differentiating both colors from a green background. If for a second subject the photographer uses panchromatic film, film coated

* Ralph M. Evans has written a profoundly technical exposition of color-control in photography: *An Introduction to Color* (New York: John Wiley & Sons, 1948).

with an emulsion that is more nearly equal in its sensitivity to all colors, he can record with convincingly clear definition a red and a blue against white, but he will fail to separate out the values of the first. If the subject is a distant one, with forms obscured by haze, he can use a hard film to keep the contrasts constant (4.17a). If the subject is cut up by extreme contrasts of light and dark, he can use a soft film to bring the values together and make the modulations register (6.7). If the photographer combines use of proper film with selection of color filter appropriate for a given purpose, he gains the power to control color-value contrasts much as other artists do. Color filters are mounted sheets of transparent glass or gelatine, each bearing a uniform coloring and functioning as a membrane between the lens of the camera and the forms of the subject. More than a hundred such filters are available for use in photography. Rarely if ever, however, does the artist use more than three or four, and these he uses simply to lighten (with the same color filter) or darken (with the complementary color filter) some given color in his subject, at the same time darkening or lightening the complementary in the subject.

Expression of Movement

We have noted in recent sculpture a tendency to embrace movement as an eighth compositional element, one giving the name *mobile* to the work exploiting it. Photography has put movement to work with comparable effectiveness, sometimes literally, sometimes only figuratively. If the artist finds in his subject such rhythmic flow of line and mass that its action is conveyed by these two elements alone, he takes an instantaneous exposure which catches them clearly as the sources of the effect (6.9). If the artist finds that motion can be conveyed automatically by the shape or position of the subject, he composes his photograph in such a fashion that its shape and position are emphasized. In a photograph of a ship's figurehead, for example, the oblique inclination at

the prow of the ship dictates placement toward the extreme upper right corner of the photograph and along its motion-expressing diagonal (6.2b).

Ordinarily, however, the photographer expresses movement by deliberately exploiting that blur of focus which amateurs are accustomed to regard as a defect. We see moving objects only indistinctly, and the photographer simply draws on natural experience in seeing when he decides in favor of blur. He makes a time exposure the length of which is determined by the speed of the movement, one so short as barely to miss stopping the action completely, because he knows that the slightest prolongation will result in a motion-registering blur (6.5). If he holds the camera still and catches the moving image in a time exposure, the background will be sharp but the subject blurred (2.5). If he follows the moving image with his camera while making his exposure, the subject will be sharp but the background blurred (2.4).

If the background is dark and the moving subject brought out with strong highlights, the photographer may resort to multiple exposure on the same negative. If the subject is moving slowly, he may either throw flood lights on to it or have it carry lights at its key extremities. If the subject is moving swiftly, he illuminates it in a series of rapid flashes with a stroboscopic lamp—an electronic device in which current at high voltage discharges through a gas-filled tube repeatable flashes lasting as little as 1/100,000 of a second. Whatever the device, the photographer may gain with his multiple exposure swirling lines of light or patterns of overlapping images extraordinarily strong in their emotional appeal (7.12).

Darkroom Control

Some artists insist that photography remain "pure." By "pure" they mean finding the right subject, focusing at the right angle, and determining through the finder or ground glass the most effectively composed view of the subject;

6.2. SELECTION OF DETAIL FOR ENLARGEMENT INTO COMPOSITION. a. B. L. Freemesser: *S. S. Balclutha at San Francisco Dock*. 1956. Photograph made with 4 x 5″ Graphic camera under daylight. Contact print, 4⁸⁄₁₀ x 3³⁄₁₀″. Courtesy of the artist. b. B. L. Freemesser: *Bow of S. S. Balclutha*, enlarged from cropped negative like that for Fig. 6.2a. 4⁸⁄₁₀ x 3⁸⁄₁₀″. Courtesy of the artist.

then making the exposure, developing the negative, and printing the positive by contact full size, without alteration. Artists have followed such restrictive procedure and produced photographs ranking among the greatest (6.7).

Other artists declare that every step taken before making the exposure is important, but that the best photograph is created by expressively controlled manipulation in the darkroom. Let us suppose that the artist has photographed a three-master ship with an excess of picturesque detail (6.2a). He then studies the positive print, searches for a passage which will stand enlargement and still convey the essence of the subject as a whole. In this case he hits upon the figurehead beneath the bowsprit of the ship—that sculptured mascot which the crew once cherished as their guardian and guide. He crops the negative, masks it out, that is, until only the figurehead and the form-contributing accessories immediately around it appear. He enlarges this detail, and in the process creates greater volume in the figure

and greater contrast with the sky— by "dodging" the figure (passing a piece of opaque cardboard rapidly back and forth between its image in the negative and the printing paper, while letting the rest of the lights in the negative register darker in the print). He creates in this way a photograph immensely more expressive than any the original exposure could offer (6.2b).

Again, let us suppose that the artist has photographed a detail of an architectural model of the Parthenon and from the negative developed a print strong in value-contrasts (6.3a). He may want to abstract from it to bring out the idea, perhaps for a book jacket or a brochure cover, that the original building has cast its spell over Western architecture for nearly twenty-five hundred years. He tries a reversal—that is, he makes a negative from the positive print, and prints a positive print from this second negative. Wherever shadow occurred in the original print, light now occurs, and vice versa—to convey a ghostlike effect

A

B

C

D

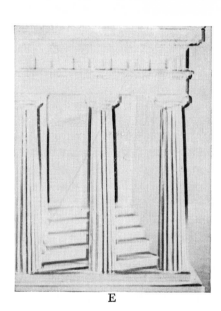

E

F

6.3. DARKROOM TECHNIQUES WITH THE SAME NEGATIVE.   a. B. L. Freemesser: *Detail of Student Model of Parthenon.* 1957. Photograph made with 4 x 5″ Graphic camera under photoflood illumination; positive print made by contact from original negative. 4⅞₁₀ x 3⅝₁₀″. Courtesy of the artist.   b. B. L. Freemesser: *Detail of Student Model of Parthenon,* complete reversal in development of positive print. Courtesy of the artist. c. B. L. Freemesser: *Detail of Student Model of Parthenon,* solarization during development of negative. Courtesy of the artist.   d. B. L. Freemesser: *Detail of Student Model of Parthenon,* print made from positive and negative films in conjunction. Courtesy of the artist.   e. B. L. Freemesser: *Detail of Student Model of Parthenon,* bas-relief print, underprinted.   f. B. L. Freemesser: *Detail of Student Model of Parthenon with Two Other Student Models,* multiple exposure in the camera. Courtesy of the artist.

suggestive of age-long continuation of the classic spirit (6.3b).

Or the photographer tries a solarization. He makes another negative from his original negative, and at a moment in the process of developing he exposes it for a few seconds to a white light before carrying the development on to completion. If the duration of the development before and after the second exposure and the duration of the exposure itself are all exactly right, the resulting blackness, which spreads from the thinnest areas toward those which are already black, yields a negative of fine white seams through which to make a positive print of sharply defined contours—one expressive of the ancient Greek ideal of steady, clear-eyed vision (6.3c).

The photographer tries a bas relief. He makes a positive print from his negative on to a lantern-slide glass of the same size as his negative. He places his original negative and his lantern-slide positive together, the emulsion of each facing that of the other. He moves the negative slightly out of register with the positive, and proceeds to make an enlarged positive print from the coupled positive and negative. He obtains through this procedure a bas-relief print curiously sculptural in effect, with the width of line that defines the contours determined by the degree to which the lantern-slide positive was set off register with the negative. With such a print he indicates something of the firmness of grasp of the tangible world upon which the ancient Greeks insisted (6.3d). If he underprints his positive from this staggered positive-negative combination he carries his abstraction of the subject so far that it seems almost an exercise in that geometry of which the ancient Greeks were enamored (6.3e).

The photographer tries, finally, a multiple exposure on the same negative—one exposure to a corner of the Greek Doric temple model already photographed for the other devices; one exposure to the end of another temple model with a single Ionic colonnade in front; and one exposure in between the two to a more primitive temple model set well back into the distance. Since everything in the room except the sharply illuminated temple model is kept in complete darkness, he secures an effect of disembodied, but classically framed-in and bounded, space—a photograph symbolizing the Greek search for universal and timeless form (6.3f).

On some other occasion the photographer may find it advisable to resort to reticulation —soaking a negative in water until its emulsion is softened and then causing the emulsion to swell and crackle in warm water. Unlike the uniform effect of a screen under which he sometimes develops his negative, he creates through the reticulation process a network which actually follows and emphasizes the essential forms of a photograph and obliterates its details. He creates an abstraction of textural overlay sometimes as imaginative in appeal as the freest sort of experimentation in sculptural construction.*

The photographer gains startlingly new effects from experimentation with these graphic techniques, but the test which proves him the artist is that rightness of feeling toward a given subject which turns him instinctively to the sole device by which he knows that he can heighten its qualities. Self-disciplined and clearly conscious of his aims, such a photographer practices an art of the darkroom as free as that of sculpture but in range of subject far wider.

* For a representative example, see Andreas Feininger, *Feininger on Photography* (Chicago and New York: Ziff-Davis, 1949), p. 406.

6.4. *Portrait of an Unknown Man.*
c. 1850. Daguerreotype. 4¼ x
3¼″. George Eastman House Collection, Rochester, N. Y. Courtesy
of Beaumont Newhall.

SUBJECT MATTER OF PHOTOGRAPHY

Shooting the Unposed Picture

From the earliest appearance of the camera-made picture in the eighteen-twenties down to the most recent refinements of color transparency and radiograph, the photographer has had at his disposal any possibility of effect we have been describing. If he took advantage of few possibilities at a given time, the limitation was not due to lack of ability but rather to a positive "will to form" shared with his fellows—a demand, sometimes called a state of mind, that a work of art assume a particular character. This "will to form" has imposed itself on photography ever since its invention, just as much as it has always imposed itself on painting or sculpture or any other art.

Through the middle decades of the nineteenth century, daguerreotype portrayal was the chief manifestation of the "will to form" prevailing. As one mid-century daguerreotype (6.4), now in the George Eastman House Collection, eloquently attests, mastery of medium could, when joined with artistry sensitive to the current state of mind, produce a masterpiece of individual characterization.

6.5. Alfred Stieglitz (1864–1946): *Winter on Fifth Avenue, New York.* February 22, 1893. Photograph: original negative made with 4 x 5″ Detective hand camera; original lantern slide, 9¾ x 6¼″. George Eastman House Collection, Rochester, N. Y. Courtesy of Beaumont Newhall.

Toward the end of the nineteenth century, in response to a new "will to form," pictorial photography came to replace the portrait daguerreotype with landscape, interior, and storytelling genre (or subject matter). This pictorial photography was facilitated by the newly invented hand camera and the new gelatinous film. With such equipment a man could roam at will in search of a picturable subject. When he found it, he could snap it immediately and keep the exposed film safe inside his camera until he got home to develop it in his darkroom.

People at first thought that the hand camera would work properly only when the subject was brilliantly lighted from in front, over the photographer's shoulders, producing pictures monotonously flat and cut up. The American photographer Alfred Stieglitz, however, refused to be bound by this convention.* He experimented, and succeeded in producing unprecedented pictures, true milestones of the art.

One of Stieglitz's most remarkable achievements with the hand camera is a photograph taken by him on February 22, 1893, in the midst of a blinding snowstorm (6.5). Conditions of lighting were the direct opposite of those declared prerequisite to good exposure. The photographer had been out in the storm for three hours, standing at a spot on Fifth Avenue where he sensed a possible picture. He was struck by the way in which the veil of snow at this point speedily shut from view the receding lines of street and building. He waited, shivering but patient, for the right gust of wind and flurry of snow to coincide with the proper relationship of passing carriages to the selected setting. He kept his aperture wide open, his shutter set for as little under a second's exposure as he figured would record the moving traffic without excessive blur.

* Account based on an article by Alfred Stieglitz, "The Hand Camera—Its Present Importance, "first published in the *American Annual of Photography* for 1897, pp. 19–26; reprinted in W. I. Lincoln Adams, ed., *Sunlight and Shadow* (New York: Baker & Taylor, 1897), pp. 69–78, and in Newhall, *On Photography, op. cit.*, pp. 133–140. Further based on information provided the author in a letter from Beaumont Newhall, November 20, 1957.

The moment came. The artist braced himself against the gale. He managed with benumbed fingers to snap the shutter without jarring the camera. He rushed back to the Camera Club to which he belonged, if not to warm himself, then at least to develop his negative and determine what he had. Fellow club members examined the negative as it emerged from the "hypo," only to scoff at its blurred images and urge him to discard it. They could not appreciate the blur essential to the effect because they were habituated to sharpness of focus as an unvarying standard of quality.

Stieglitz saw it otherwise. Following the practice of his day, the new convert to hand-camera usage made his positive print on another glass plate like that, 3¼ inches square, which supported his negative. In this way he created a lantern slide for projection at enlarged scale on a screen. He counted for his major effect on that "magic lantern" which had already, long before the invention of photography, given rise to the illustrated lecture using hand-rendered images on glass. Stieglitz did not, however, make his lantern slide a direct contact print from the whole negative. He estimated that particular complex of forms in the scene most likely to make the picture. He devoted utmost care to focus and exposure. But he treated the exposed negative, not as the finished composition in reverse, but merely as an intermediate study—source material from which to work creatively in the darkroom. He planned from the outset to mask out all less essential forms in the negative and to enlarge the remainder on to the positive as a heightened realization of the whole general subject.

When Alfred Stieglitz threw this photograph on a screen before his skeptical critics, he confounded them. The rhythmically graduated spots of dark made by the carriages in the picture overwhelmed his spectators by effectiveness of contrast to the pervading gray void. Stieglitz's photograph caught the mood of the storm. It made a telling commentary on a city's battle to keep moving in the snow— a commentary, in fact, on man's age-old struggle to survive.

6.6. Ansel Adams (1902–   ): *Yosemite Valley, Thunderstorm,* from *My Camera in Yosemite Valley* (Boston: Houghton Mifflin Company, 1949). Photograph on hard paper (Velour Black "T"), D.W. #2, developed in Beevy #6; made with a 10″ Kodak camera widefield Ektar lens, and a K-2 (light yellow) Wratten filter (for slightly clarifying the haze): Kodak Panatomic-X film in a Kodak D-23. 7⅝ x 9½″. Courtesy of the artist.

Consider again a California photographer's picture of Yosemite Valley in storm (6.6). Ansel Adams undertook in it a subject that overawed most cameramen. But Adams was no run-of-the-mill photographer. He belonged to a school of "straight photography" well qualified for such subjects. With Stieglitz in his later years,* this school was reacting against the excesses to which pictorial photography eventually went in trying to make a photograph

look like a painting. It was declaring itself for "pure" photography, for that kind of picture which we have already described as possible only with the camera.

Adams's straightforward approach to his Yosemite subject necessitated more than a quick focusing of lens and snapping of shutter. It required the most painstaking analysis and deliberative procedure. Adams reviewed the architecturelike structure of the Valley itself —its level floor, towering crags, quiet meadows, rearing pines. He found in this structure his cue for stationing his camera: bolt upright

* Dorothy Norman, "Alfred Stieglitz on Photography," *Magazine of Art,* Vol. XLIII, No. 8 (December, 1950), pp. 298 and 301.

and level, facing straight out, like the colossal rectilinear image spreading before it. He analyzed the spatial extensions of the Valley—its magnificent distances, majestically succeeding planes, and superhuman scale. He traced these spatial effects to the module that made them comprehensible to the eye—pine boughs sharply detailed nearby but obviously contributing to the shape of distant trees. He found a point in the nearer middle distance on which to sharpen his focus while stopping his diaphragm down (to extend the depth of field, or zone of relative sharpness) as far as the intensity of the light allowed. He noted the color effects peculiar to the Valley—blue top-lighting unmodified by those yellowish tinges apparent in the lower reaches of a sky above an expanse of prairie, quiet grays reflected into the shadows from the canyon walls. Adams let this coloring find its own large simplifications of gray on his film, using only a light-yellow filter to clarify the haze, lower the value of the sky, and enhance the luminosity.

The photographer knew that, even after resolving all problems imposed by the locale, he could heighten the true impressiveness of the panorama by catching the scene under some typical late-afternoon storm commensurate with the Valley's drama. Much waiting and trial "shooting" eventuated in that precious moment when cloud shadow and sunburst, silhouetted mass and illuminated detail, alternated in the interplay of space. Camera ready, Adams snapped the shutter. To heighten the effect, he developed the negative slightly more than normal, and from it printed a photograph rivaling Stieglitz's in its epic quality.*

The Camera-revealed Detail

For the rendering of a mountain valley in storm Adams used a view camera, one equipped, as the name implies, for just such panoramas: a camera with a spacious compartment, a "wide-angle" lens, and a large sheet of film known as cut film. With such a camera the photographer was able to secure at once the bigness of the containing forms of the Valley and the detailed life within it. He was able to make a negative so big that a contact print of equal sharpness could in turn be produced with no enlargement in the grain of the negative to soften the effect. Unlike his eyes, which he could focus in such a vista on only one spot at a time, Adams could make his camera grasp with equal clarity many spots at once. He could produce with his camera an assemblage of elements impossible to the naked eye, an array which assumes in the photograph new meanings of relationship.

A purist like Adams can command a surprising range of expression. He can create at one end of the scale a vast panorama of Yosemite. He can create at the other end a delimited detail. Alone essential to it, as to the panorama, is the artist's judgment. If he sees a detail imaginatively, if he abstracts it creatively, he can condense the essence of the whole and catch its flavor as he could not by photographing the whole itself. He can point up the structure of the mountain in the boulder on its slope, the ceaseless movement of the surf in a bit of froth and driftwood at its edge, the personality of human beings in the odds and ends of a living room from which the occupant seems just to have departed. In making such a close-up the photographer suggests the imminence of the mountain's looming up, the waves' dashing in, the dwellers' return.

Among the members of the "straight" photography school, none achieved a sense of the cosmic in the close-up more poignantly than Edward Weston, master whose precept and example inspired the whole group.† Fellow Californian of Adams, Weston came to know as intimately the diverse countryside and life of

---

* This account of Ansel Adams's procedure is based on a page of text accompanying the publishing of the photograph, Ansel Adams, *My Camera in Yosemite Valley* (Boston: Houghton Mifflin, 1949), Pl. I. It is further based on information provided by the photographer in letters dated February 23 and April 16, 1952.

† The clearest definition of the objectives of "straight" photography was written by Edward Weston in an article entitled "Photography—Not Pictorial," *Camera Craft* Vol. XXXVII (1930), pp. 313–320; reprinted, Newhall, *On Photography, op. cit.*, pp. 165–168.

6.7. Edward Weston (1886–1958): *Church, Hornitos*. 1940. Photograph. 7⅝ x 9½″.
Courtesy of the artist.

his state.[3] He came to know, for example, the ghost towns once booming under the Gold Rush; and he learned to single out their most powerful details.

Into a bit of the padlocked door to the sun-baked church at Hornitos he projected the essence of the abandoned community around it (6.7). The artist came upon this detail with an eye for its significance. He saw in it a registry of nature's triumph over the works of man. He noted how like the wrinkled face of age this warped and cracking entranceway was, how eloquent of disuse its padlocked barrier. Unlike the photographer-pictorialist, Weston made no effort to rearrange the forms. He simply studied them for their compositional and expressive

[3] See Notes, page 298.

possibilities. He chose the particular part to emphasize. He waited for the moment when the sun would throw a surface-revealing cross-light on it. He focused his camera on it: a portion of the door about the knob and bit of wall beyond it—a flat passage that would facilitate sharpness of image and heightening of texture. With motionless tripod and carefully adjusted stop and exposure, Weston clicked the shutter and fixed the image on his film.

Much of a "straight" photographer's job was now accomplished, but Edward Weston still had to exercise further artistry in the darkroom. In order to hold the grain of the wood without losing the transparency of its shadows, Weston had to maintain complete control over the transparencies and opacities of his negative as

The Photogenic Nude

For all of the revolutionizing innovations introduced into photography, from photograms to Kodachromes, probably nothing will ever replace the "straight" photograph made by the discriminating artist with the conventional view camera, printed in the same size by direct contact with the negative, and exhibited without retouching, frankly and unashamedly itself. Amid the myriad motives open to the "straight" photographer, moreover, probably none will ever replace the human figure.

Since photography shares with sculpture its prevailing character as a representational art, arguments in favor of the nude for subject hold for it as for sculpture. Photography cannot, to be sure, exploit the figure's actual masses. It cannot set the human form into organized depths of space. It can only, as we have already pointed out, create illusions of mass and space by recording relationships of values on a two-dimensional surface. In so doing, however, it achieves in the genre of the nude qualities of luminosity and textural appeal peculiar to human flesh, qualities of light-reflection, translucency, and value-modulation once sought only by painters. When we bring to our viewing of a creative photograph of the nude our delight in such qualities, we find in such a work an irresistible appeal. Nothing could be more appropriate to an art of light-recording, then, than that pre-eminently human subject, the human form. Photography draws with it on an inexhaustible source of sensuous attraction.

The "straight" photographer is not the only artist able to record the human figure artistically. Another artist can assume a more active role. He can control his lighting and direct his screening. He can dispose his model on the stand as purposefully as a sculptor. He can isolate the figure from its ordinary workaday environment. He can glorify it, monumentalize its masses as grandly as Maillol (5.11a and b).

Peter Gowland insisted on this more active role. He hired his model not, as Rodin had for sculpture, merely to move about oblivious to her posing. He had her adopt attitudes predetermined by his understanding of the character of her form, his feeling for the relationships of mass and movement in the given situation. He resorted to every studio device in order to heighten the figure's tactile, plastic, and luminous appeal in any position taken under his direction.

Sometimes conscious posing ended in forced and labored effects, as artificial as they were unconvincing. When Gowland succeeded, however, he created as momentous a work as the photograph reproduced (6.9). He posed the model in a seated position, had her turn with a corkscrew twist of torso and rest her weight on one arm while encircling her head with the other. The result was a pyramidal composition with the model's head at the apex and a decidedly sculptural disposition of the masses of her body. The photographer heightened the dynamic effectiveness of the pose by composing the figure in the ground glass before making the exposure. He cut the form in such fashion that the torso extended obliquely into the picture from a lower corner.

Gowland later made two prints from his negative, one a reversal of the other. The print in which the torso rose from the lower right corner proved decidedly superior to the other, because in it the torso seemed to move against the direction of the observer's viewing from the lower left corner, that which psychology has identified as the "spectator's corner," the position in which we feel ourselves to be as we look into a picture.* The resulting impact in viewing joined with a certain psychological reassurance that the spectator could examine the masses of the figure apart from any disquieting tendency to identify these masses with himself (which the torso in rising from the lower left corner actually seemed to prompt). The artist was able thus to determine the better print, not by theory nor formula but by actual experiment and judgment.

A conventional photographer might have argued that the pyramid described by the outer

* Mercedes Gaffron, "Right and Left in Pictures," *Art Quarterly*, Vol. XIII, No. 4 (Autumn, 1950), pp. 312–331.

contours of torso, arm, and head was so interesting that it called for solidity of effect. In the attempt to make it so, he would have adopted top-lighting or side-lighting to fill with cast shadow the open space between the right arm and the torso. Gowland had the imagination to see other possibilities. He provided back-lighting instead. He drew up behind the model a neutralizing background screen and threw his floodlights against it rather than against the figure.

The artist was able thus to envelop the figure in a luminous space. He was able to develop out of the space between the arm and the body a dominant form motive for the whole picture, a space the shape of which found echo in the positive forms. Against the contrasting brilliance of his background of reflecting screen, Gowland was able to give emphasis to the masses of the figure, brought out unexpectedly by the muted character of the values. He trained a soft reflected light to play over arms, breasts, and torso, thus intensifying the subject's appeal. The result is a genuine example of the ennobling power of art, depersonalizing and monumentalizing the figure to create a magnificent rhythmic composition.

Photography of the nude in the studio has advantages of controlled lighting and setting. The artist can do with the subject much as he pleases. Photography of the nude in the outdoors lacks these controls, to be sure, but it gains enormously in associative values when forms in the landscape find analogy in the figure. The appeal of Mother Earth is a very real one, we have seen, when it resides by association in the shapes of a pot (3.10) or a statue carved in stone (5.11b). It is no less real when a figure in a landscape is photographed imaginatively. It owes much of its power in such a picture to man's age-long worship of Earth as Goddess of Fertility, to man's everlasting urge to read into woman's forms the shapes of mountain, wave, and dune, and into nature's forms the shapes of torso, hips, and breasts. It profits by man's tendency to associate such forms with a goddesslike sublimity or with a promise of fruitfulness.

André de Dienes specialized in this genre of figure-in-landscape.* He saw the structure of forms in nature transfigured by their echo in the forms of the human body. He posed his models on a mountain crag, to repeat its fissures in their action of limbs and torso, to recline about its summit with the supple grace of a seal. He had his models lie in the surf as though they were fish gliding through it. He caught his models emerging dripping from the sea, arms upraised, head tilted backward, as though they were sea monsters momentarily disgorged.

The photographer drew heavily thus on associational values when he photographed the nude female figure lying face downward on a dune (2.5). He saw how footprints in the sand made points of accent along the lines of windswept ripples and bodily contours. He saw how much in keeping with this apparent movement were the lines of low-lying clouds. He saw how distant dunes seemed to rise and fall against the sky, their rhythms repeated in the middle-distant "hillocks" of the model's body.

FUSING SPACE WITH TIME IN PHOTOGRAPHY

De Dienes managed with his setting of dunes under high fog, no less than Gowland with his setting of back-lighted screen, to suggest in nude photography something of that universality which transcends space and time. Through the illusionary lights and darks peculiar to their art, these photographers achieved a spaciousness of effect characteristic of much recent building and open-volume sculpture.

Other photographers have in their own right gone as far as architects and sculptor-constructivists in presenting in the same composition

* André de Dienes, *The Nude* (New York: G. P. Putnam's Sons, 1956).

the inside and the outside of a thing. They have in such creations invited us to enter, so to speak, into the reality of existence, there to feel a pulsebeat of creation. In so doing they have achieved a version of that "interiority" through which, according to Henri Bergson,* the essence of existence can alone be perceived. It calls on the observer to enter imaginatively into a given object, to look around inside it and outward from it, to move along with it in self-identification.

The measure of the change effected in photography by Bergson's formulation of this idea can be taken in a before-and-after comparison of photograms. Let us consider again, as we did early in this chapter (pp. 163–164), Fox Talbot's direct registry of lace on silver-coated paper, so tangible in effect as to deceive the inventor's friends. Compare this primitive photogram with one by Pirkle Jones made a hundred and sixty-five years later (6.1). Jones used drops of water and oil squeezed out between two panes of glass. By controlled manipulations of drops and rays of light, the artist achieved a composition no less lacy of effect but also fantastically spatial in suggestion. He created a fairyland in which overlapping planes and netted lines are shot through with luminous depths. The spectator feels himself drawn by the photogram ever deeper into space until he is lost in it.

Laszlo Moholy-Nagy was one of those who led the way toward spatial emphasis in twentieth-century art. He experimented with sculptural stabiles and mobiles, with multiple-exposed, bird's-eye, worm's-eye, and other kinds of photographs, and above all with photograms.

Taking time out from his teaching at the Bauhaus in Weimar (where Marguerite Wildenhain taught pottery), Moholy-Nagy learned to carry the medium of the photogram far beyond a merely mechanical translation of ghosts of objects to silver-coated paper. He learned to manipulate materials and lighting in a variety of ways, using objects tilted at angles as well as laid flat, using mirrors, lenses, light filters, tissue paper, water, oil, and acid. Through or past such materials he learned to throw rays of light either directly or from a reflecting screen on to sensitized paper.†

For one of his photograms of 1923 (6.10), for example, the Hungarian artist-teacher laid a steel ring directly upon the photographic paper. A short distance above the paper he placed a piece of glass, and on the glass he laid another steel ring and semitranslucent celluloid, the latter at a point from which the light rays would seem to project it into the first ring so as to assure its serving as the principal center of interest. He propped the end of a paint brush and the edge of a piece of perforated steel lath on this glass plane so that they would lean obliquely away from it. He set a funnel-shaped shield around his lamp and from an angle threw the light across the whole ensemble on to the silver-coated support. Once he had fixed the paper thus exposed, his photogram was complete.

The means resorted to by Moholy-Nagy sound prosaic in the telling. But the photogram which he created is extraordinarily suggestive of cosmic depths. By play of lights and shadows in reverse on the silver surface, the artist developed a series of phantom shapes that recede from the sharply registered ring into darkness.

When Moholy-Nagy shifted his floodlight here and there in search of the proper effect, h became intrigued by the possibility of rec ing successive effects of lighting in a series of photograms.‡ Once he freed h by operating his mobiles with motor control his lighting sufficiently to c series, and with it to parallel the "photo-interview" or "photo-st holy-Nagy reached the point

* First formulated in his doctoral dissertation at the University of Paris, 1888: *Essai sur les données immédiates de la conscience;* Eng. trans. as *Time and Free Will.*

† L. Moholy-Nagy, "Light: pression," *Broom,* Vol. IV printed, Newhall, *On Ph* 152.
‡ An account of this by L. Moholy-Nagy (*New Vision; and A'* Modern Art," New

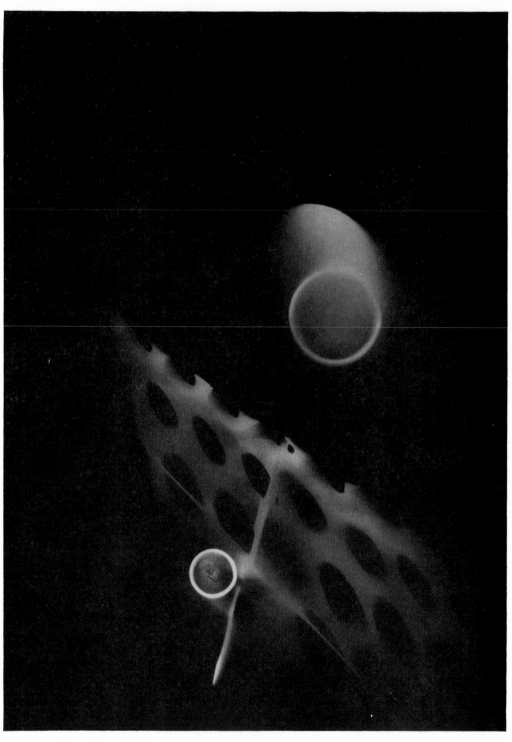

6.10. Laszlo Moholy-Nagy (1895–1946): *Photogram Using Steel Rings and Perforated Metal Lath. c.* 1923. 14⅝ x 10⅝″. Courtesy of Sybil Moholy-Nagy.

densing his series of photograms to a single sheet of photographic paper, he was approaching, in fact, the novel effect gained in photography proper by multiple exposure of the same negative to moving lights against a background of total darkness. Called a chronophotograph, such a creation made utter fantasy out of no more poetic a subject than the act of tying a necktie or swinging a tennis racquet (providing only that the model first attached a flashlight to his wrist). The chronophotograph of the movement seemed in its boldly linear pattern of white on black to project the subject into outer space.

When the stroboscopic lamp was invented in 1931, still more startling transformations were effected in the field of action-recording. This lamp could "freeze" on a time-exposed negative in the darkroom a bullet moving so fast as to be invisible to the eye. More impressive from the artistic point of view, however, the lamp could fix on the single negative a series of overlapping images of the moving object. Herbert Matter put the stroboscopic lamp to effective use, for example, when he created a series of photographs emphasizing through repetition of a woman's legs climbing stairs the wearisome nature of the effort (7.13b).

THE NATURE OF THE MOTION PICTURE

When multi-exposed "still" photography is extended to include projection of a filmic sequence of photographs (or drawings) of a moving subject on to a screen at a rate rapid enough to make the subject seem to move, then this branch of the art becomes motion picture photography, the art of the movies or cinema. It requires both the use of a camera specially equipped for making exposures at high speed on a roll of film and the development of the subsequent positive images on a corresponding roll. The illusion of movement when the positive film is projected depends on that phenomenon of persistence of vision in which our remembered images tend to merge with those which we anticipate.

Cinema is a composite art, having as much to do with time and sound as it has to do with sight. It covers a realm of such complexity and magnitude that we can give it only a meager introduction, dealing with but a few of its visual aspects and technical developments.

Cinema is an art, but few of us realize the fact or appreciate it as such. Only industrial design is a newer art, but behind many branches of industrial design we have found ancestors in the long-familiar crafts, and out of its branches have seen emerging familiar objects of use. We cannot bring to cinema even our experience with the stage, because the movies are entities distinctly different from play production. Without a cultivated basis for the appreciation of this unique form of expression, we bring no more than our own experience, hoping to find a comparable experience simulated in the illusions of the screen.

A problem of the motion picture has been its expansion into an industry dependent on mass consumption for its existence. Even the shoddiest of factory products reflect some sort of restraint deriving from utilitarian need. Movies have been free of such restraint. They have been produced merely to amuse by counterfeiting a life in which unpleasantries are glossed over and tensions relaxed. They have been created to please only the greatest number of admissions-paying patrons.

Popular support need not always spell mediocrity. We have seen widespread patronage evoking portrait photographs as characterful as were ever made in any other art (6.4). But the motion picture has been different. It has often suffered the artistic impoverishment of an industry designed to entertain and whet the appetite for ever more entertainment.

Whether or not we enjoy the movies, we are apt to have no clear idea of the way to judge a film. We do not know what to ask of it, what values to look for, what criteria to refer to in treating it critically.

Our lack of standards becomes particularly obvious in those films of our own making. The amateur home movie is apt to be the work of one member of a family recording the others. Father focuses and runs the camera. The rest of the family go through their acts. A commercial firm develops the film, but father, or some member of the family acquainted with the complications of threading the film, runs the projector.

The procedure is direct and simple, but the esthetic results are frequently painful, especially to an outsider trapped by social obligations into seeing the show. There is never enough film devoted to a sequence. The film jumps from one subject to the next with nerve-wracking suddenness. Something is always out of focus. One boring bit of incident succeeds another, leading nowhere, saying nothing, appealing only as reminiscence to the immediate family.

On a correspondingly modest scale it is possible for a professional artist to create single-handedly a film with boldly direct expression, rhythmic variations within a unified structure, and richly personal quality. Maya Deren comes to mind.* This film-maker of southern California has created a series of shorts which achieve remarkable effects of time and space in fusion, and always with the eerie suggestion that one is viewing the moving images through the eye and brain of the artist herself. In the making of such a film as *Ritual in Transfigured Time,* completed in 1946, Maya Deren called in to assist her a photographer, a choreographer, and two principal performers. But the work was chiefly hers. By cinematic means alone she made a dance out of the participation of nondancers, a "ritual" (or art form) in terms of the time created by the camera.

Even accomplished artists, however, have to depend on others to help them when they create a motion picture. They have to depend on whole teams of collaborators, teams sometimes numbering hundreds or thousands of individuals.

The idea for a film usually starts with a person whom the industry calls the sponsor. He develops his idea in consultation with the producer, shaping and reshaping it in terms of such practicalities as financing, staging, and appeal to audience. Sponsor and producer finally draw up a contract. They commission a scenario writer to prepare the script.

When the script finally satisfies the sponsor and the producer, the director takes over. Unlike the drama, where a playwright serves as creator while director and actors serve as interpreters, the director in cinema becomes the actual creator. He holds the responsibility for determining all phases of the film production and keeping them together. He modifies the script wherever needed; he directs the cameraman as the latter shoots the scenes; he edits the film and supervises the cutter as this specialist carries through the all-important process of montage: taking the single length of film as exposed by the cameraman, cutting it up into carefully selected sections, discarding some, and splicing others together to form new sequences.

The motion picture director is the master builder, as crucial to the film as is the architect to the skyscraper. His name belongs with the motion picture as the name of the architect belongs with the building or the name of the sculptor belongs with the statue. Except when a star like Charlie Chaplin serves also as the film's director, it is usually inappropriate to couple the name of the leading man or lady with the title of the work.

Techniques Peculiar to the Motion Picture†

A motion picture implies by its very name that element of motion which distinguishes it from every other art. We may think such a premise too obvious to mention; yet many movie-mak-

---

* Maya Deren, *An Anagram of Ideas on Art, Form and Film* ("Outcast" Series, 9; Yonkers, N. Y.: The Alicot Book Shop Press, 1946).

† The best reference for techniques is Raymond Spottiswoode, *Film and Its Techniques* (Berkeley and Los Angeles: University of California Press, 1953).

ers take no advantage of this trait, while a true artist-director realizes that the life of cinema is summed up in its action. He sees that without action he can produce only a film strip of "stills" but that with it he can catch those rhythms of life which draw a movie audience into moving with them.

The creator of a motion picture has four types of motion to work with, each capable of conveying its own effects if properly utilized: (1) motion within the frame; (2) panning motion; (3) motion of camera on moving support; and (4) accelerated or retarded motion.

Motion within the frame is the simplest, the most elementary, of the four devices. One has merely to set the camera up, focus the lens, and start the mechanism going. Whatever transpires in front of the camera will be recorded. Motion within the frame relies on movement of forms in front of the camera. If there is no movement of these forms, there is no motion within the frame. Let a man stand up. Let him make a gesture, take a step. He provides the movement, the film registers it in a succession of frames, and we focus our attention on him as he seems to move in the film projected.

Motion within the frame secures initial emphasis, but when used by itself it usually results in nothing but stilted, monotonous effects. A more expressive kind of motion is needed to vary the effect of such conventional shots. One possible variant is the motion gained by the panning technique. When a motion-picture photographer holds his tripod steady but turns his camera on it, he secures a panning shot. He gains the effect of one's remaining seated while turning one's head to look at another person entering the room and moving about. With such a shot he helps to draw the audience into the film. He makes the camera seem to operate in our behalf—glancing from side to side, peering downward, looking upward. By panning he is able to convey a sense of immediacy which a motion-within-the-frame shot is powerless to give, arousing our empathic response.

If we set a camera up in a classroom and focus it on the door through which students are entering, we are able to shoot a passage of motion within the frame. With such a sequence we can indicate the spot where action is about to take place, whetting the audience's interest and arousing its expectations.

A boy enters the room. He walks down an aisle and takes a certain seat. He would move completely out of range of the camera were it not for the panning technique. By panning we make the film follow him to his seat. By fluidity of movement we focus attention on this particular boy. We even begin to stir in the audience an emotional response. If instead of panning we catch the boy simply in a series of action-within-the-frame shots, we lose the smooth rhythm of his walk and create only a series of jerky transitions.

The cameraman rejects the idea that his camera needs to stay fixed on a stationary tripod. He makes frequent dolly shots. He establishes the camera, that is, on a movable carriage like the low-slung platform-on-wheels called a dolly, or else on a crane. By moving the carriage while the film is being exposed, he is able to explore a whole new realm of expressive effects.

Dolly shots allow a kind of watching beyond that which panning affords. They do not stop merely with our imagined turning of our heads to watch the boy entering the classroom and going to his seat. Dolly shots allow us, so to speak, to get up and walk over for a closer look at the boy. They give us a feeling that we are participating in his very feelings and behavior. Instead of letting us simply look on from the sidelines, as panning shots do, dolly shots project us into the midst of the action and its tensions.

As our boy is getting seated, the camera (which was not sitting on the floor after all, perhaps, but hanging from a crane) starts gliding over the heads of other students to bring us up to him. We hover over him as he settles himself, opens his notebook, and discovers a folded paper inside. We watch his face as it registers surprise and curiosity and then joy, as he discovers the paper to be a message from his girl friend. During the course of the sequence we go through all three types of action: within-the-frame, panning, and dolly. We experience an increasing emotional involvement which only the motion picture so created can invite.

The photographer may exploit the possibilities of still a fourth technique of motion. Through the magic of the camera he speeds up or slows down any movement drawn from nature. A plant, for example, taking weeks to struggle upward from the seed, put out its leaves, and burst into bloom, can be made on the screen to pass through its entire pattern of growth in as many minutes or seconds. The beat of a hummingbird's wings, too rapid for the naked eye to follow in nature, can be captured and reduced in tempo until the eye can easily trace every phase of its flight. A diver or golfer can be made to go through his motions so slowly on the screen that a novice can perceive them.

The picture by Maya Deren already mentioned, *Ritual in Transfigured Time*, showed a youth posing on a pedestal as though he were a statue. A maiden strolls by. The "statue" comes to life, leaps from the pedestal, and dashes off in pursuit. The maiden flees until the ocean engulfs her. But the movement of the pursuing youth on a separate strip of film is so slowed up for rephotographing before incorporation with the montage that the figure of the young man bounds floatingly into space like the phantom of a dream.

The techniques of montage and camerawork all point to the outstanding criterion by which to judge cinema as art: creative use of that eighth element, time. Lapse of time is essential to movement, and movement is the pulse of cinema as it is of life.

If we are to put our first criterion to work in judging motion pictures, we must learn to recognize along with montages a device which Americans call the "dissolve" and English call the "mix." A dissolve is the optical effect gained by the gradual disappearance of one shot from the screen while another is coming into vision.

By means of dissolves film-makers telescope and prolong time at will beyond the direct ac-celeration or retardation of film-movement or the practice of montage. Consider, for example, one conventional problem often encountered in film narration. Someone is performing an action that takes a long time to complete. How can the showing of the thing being done keep from being tedious and still get across to the audience the idea that much time is passing? In dissolves the artist finds his answer.

The heroine, let us say, devoted six months to a triumphal tour of the opera houses of Europe. A novelist might simply write that "Six months flew by while Jenny was sweeping all before her with her golden voice in every opera house from London to Vienna." But the movie-maker has to bear in mind that he is not writing a novel nor producing a play; he is creating his story with moving images on a screen. He resorts to dissolves. He gives us a close-up of the heroine's face as she sings. He shows her first in one costume and then in another and again in a third. He fades in on her image the Paris Opera House, La Scala in Milan, the Schauspielhaus in Dresden. Through these dissolves the film-maker declares that time is going by.

Distinguishing Qualities of the Motion Picture

Since cinematography is in reality an extension of photography, many considerations that go into the making of a good photograph enter likewise into the structure of a good motion picture. The photographer can show us, as Howard Dearstyne did (6.8), a bit of the commonplace of nature as seen from an unexpected point of view. The cinematographer can do exactly the same, using many kinds of angle shots. He plays with light and shadow like the still photographer, until he achieves the effect best calculated for emotional appeal. He works in similar fashion for repetitions and oppositions, of point or line, of plane or mass and space. He seeks for angles of lighting and depths of value-enrichment that bring out textures and suggestions of color.

Every principle of design that other artists use is called into service by the film-maker for eye-appeal. He does not guarantee that every shot be a "pretty" one, but he does seek to vitalize every scene with forms cultivated to grow easily out of his feelings for the subject, for the film, and for the techniques of shooting, cutting, and splicing which he employs.

The maker of a film strives for lifelikeness, knowing that the illusions on the two-dimensional screen will always give him the expressive freedom he needs, if he keeps their nature in mind and tries not to be mechanically literal. The criterion of verisimilitude demands being true, among other things, to what is being portrayed. It also demands that a film be consistent in its treatment. If the film is grimly realistic, then nothing in it should ever betray the fact that it is make-believe. If the movie is a fantasy, then nothing in it should ever be allowed to bring our minds and feelings back to earth.

We have talked about empathy in other connections. Appeal so strong as to arouse actual physical response in us is just as important a quality for the motion picture as it is for the sculpture or the building. Has the director handled all component parts of his film so effectively that we empathize as we sit and watch it? If empathy fails to take place in us, and if we have really tried to hold the door open for it, then, as far as we are concerned, the motion picture has failed to meet its objectives.

Empathy alone cannot make a movie good. Most Hollywood films are technically so slick that we find it easy, especially when in an uncritical mood, to empathize before them. At the same time, if there is no empathic appeal, the film is lacking. Many foreign films are made crudely by our standards; their settings are strange, their situations completely alien to our experience. In spite of such handicaps, some of them succeed supremely well in arousing our empathic responses. The German film of 1924, *The Last Laugh*, comes to mind, as does the French film of 1931, À *Nous la Liberté*, or the British film of 1944, *Henry V*. If, on the other hand, the situation is so handled as to seem silly, if anachronisms or obviously faked scenery obtrude, if the acting is forced and

hollow, the film prevents us from empathizing and proves itself wanting.

Back in the days of the silent film, lest the moving pictures be regarded as strained and awkward because of the unrelieved demands made on the eye, it was thought necessary always to have a pianist drumming out accompaniments. Now sound has become an integral part of the film-production itself, and not always a beneficial one. The silent film left the senses of the spectator less jaded. It carried an air of simplified abstraction which facilitated its appreciation as art. The incorporation of the sound-track increased the opportunities for creating illusions of reality but often to the detriment of the film's expressive powers. Too much sound is worse than none at all, especially if that sound runs counter to the quality of the story or interrupts the progress of the narrative.

The true artist of cinema can master sound as completely as he can sight, however, and nowhere does he bring this mastery more effectively to bear than in those films in which he intersperses periods of prolonged silence among sequences with sound. This mastery is evident in the French film, *Rififi*, for example. Its long bank-robbery sequence was shown in utter silence, with a resulting emotional impact that proved almost unbearable.

The motion-picture director has four different kinds of sound to exploit in connection with the visual organization of his film: imitative, cacophonous, musical, and human. By imitating at appropriate places in the progress of a picture sounds recognizable in nature, he can intensify the emotional effect tremendously. We may consider the sound of the cricket through the darkness of a marsh in which danger seems to lurk, water dripping into a barrel to break the silence of an abandoned farmhouse, the muffled moan of a foghorn as the ship inches forward, the long-drawn-out whistle of the train as it approaches the canyon where the bridge has been mined.

Cacophonous sound is just noise. It is the clatter of that unorganized racket which assails us in our daily round. Used discriminatingly by the director, it can contribute impressively to the mood of the setting for a given passage—people chatting in an adjacent room, a mob muttering below a window, the roar of machinery in a factory, the wail of a siren in the street. Even the mention of such sounds summons up images and evokes emotional states.

Music has always served as collaborator with the drama and the dance, and sometimes it has accompanied spoken poetry. In a good film, music functions properly only when it is unobtrusive. One is often not aware of its presence. Yet when used expressively with the moving picture it can heighten tremendously the effects of the imagery.

We have seen how much the composition of the film depends upon the quality of the montage. When the cutting and the splicing are done by a master, one scene succeeds another with maximum force of contrast, powerful rhythmic drive, positive sense of direction, and a feeling of epic inevitability in the unfolding of the narrative. Upon the judgment of the director depends the choice of filmic sequences and the way that they are joined. A film may be jerky and confused, with flash-backs within flash-backs, fade-outs and fade-ins, monotonous successions of long-shots, mid-shots, and close-ups—technical fireworks and chaos. Or a film may be coherent and clear of statement, enriched to a point of emotional effectiveness, growing easily and naturally out of its theme, its shooting, and its editing. The difference depends entirely upon the powers of the film-maker as artist.

GENRES OF MOTION PICTURE

The motion picture functions largely like photography in a realm of representational subject matter. Out of the objectives motivating the film the art evolves forms expressing them. Such forms vary greatly, but they can be boiled down into three essential types: film "reportage" (documentary), film "fiction" (narrative), and film "poetry" (fantasy).*

The Documentary

The first of these types corresponds to the "straight" photography of Edward Weston and his school. It is the documentary or eye-witness film in which things and activities are exactly recorded. Accuracy of observation outweighs anything else. Shots give the effect of having been taken more or less at random, even though they were not. Characters move about as though caught unawares, even though shot after much rehearsing. The atmosphere of the place pervades the various scenes. If cinema, like photography, is peculiarly an art of observation, then the documentary film is that genre in which the art realizes its essence.

Film reportage calls for backgrounds of real life. It calls for people moving around in their settings as though they belonged there. If actors must be hired to move among such people in order to get some point across to the ultimate viewers of the film, then these actors must look and behave exactly like the natives.

Film documentation is not what it would seem at first. It is not the automatic shooting of whatever comes before the camera. It calls on the director for the utmost artistry in planning, selecting, editing. His materials belong inextricably to the outside world. Rarely can he bring them into his studio and reshape them as a modeler does clay. Instead, he has to try to enter into them on the spot and share in their existence, at the same time remaining objective enough to recognize what is significant. He has to know instinctively the right techniques to use. He has to weld into an indissoluble whole the passages featuring characteristic details. In cutting, splicing, reshooting, and reorganizing, he has to develop cinematic

* Hans Richter's classification, in "Easel-Scroll-Film," *Magazine of Art,* Vol. XLV, No. 2 (February, 1952).

rhythms corresponding to the rhythms of the life being featured. Much is demanded—and the maker of the documentary does not always transform the film into the genuine work of art which fidelity to the recording of the subject would ideally require.

We have already said something about the problems of photographing other works of art. We have noted certain of the photographs of other works which are reproduced in this book to be works of art themselves. One subdivision of the documentary film is equivalent to this form of photography, that type of film made specifically for instructional purposes in studio courses and courses in the history and appreciation of art.[4] Notes for the preceding chapters have mentioned especially important examples of such films: (a) of the "how-to-do-it" type, *Handwrought Silver* and *How to Build an Igloo;* (b) of the factually descriptive type, *Rhythm Is Everywhere* and *Rodin;* (c) of the interpretative and critical type, *Looking at Sculpture;* (d) of the biographical type, *Maillol, Henry Moore,* and *The Photographer;* and (e) of the poetically evocative type, *Works of Calder.*

The documentary film-maker who undertakes to record and interpret another work of art is confronted with the same dilemma as the photographer engaged in a similar assignment. Is the work of art documented to be so revealed in its essence that its film-recording is forgotten? Or are the film-maker's personal reactions to that work of art to loom so large that the motion picture becomes expressive of them, to the distortion or even to the neglect of the work of art motivating the film?

Documentary films important to the study of one or another of the arts yet to be dealt with in this book will be referred to in connection with appropriate passages. When, however, the motion picture deals in documentary terms with materials other than works of art—the as-yet-unformed raw materials of the outside world—it demands the same critical attention that we have accorded "straight" photography and camera reporting. Microphotography, telephotography, and the whole new realm of photography of the unseen and seldom-seen find their most striking cinematic parallel at mid-century in the nature-filming directed and produced by Walt Disney (1901–   ):[5] *Seal Island* (1938), *Beaver Valley* (1951), *Nature's Half Acre* (1951), *The Living Desert* (1953), *The Vanishing Prairie* (1954), *African Lion* (1955), *Perri* (1957). Nothing could be more difficult to produce than these recordings of wild life, hidden from man, unstaged and unrehearsed. Disney and his associates try to enter intimately into the spirit of each scene and its protagonists, whether the film features the prairie dog being dive-bombed by the hawk, the praying mantis stalking its quarry, or two bull alligators fighting before a female. Disney and his cameramen try to make an expressive creation out of every sequence, seeking that camera technique which seems best able to catch the character of the scene. He and his directors edit, cut, splice untold miles of film recordings, condensing them into revealing passages and cultivating for each the proper cinematic rhythms. Under Disney's direction a film comes thus to be, telling to the utmost in transitions, contrasts, and sound-track accompaniments.

For fullest artistry in reporting, no subtype surpasses that to which the Scotch film-maker, John Grierson, gave the name of "documentary" and defined as the "creative treatment of actuality." * Himself an accomplished film-documentarian and leader of the documentary movement in England, Grierson was originally inspired by the American innovator Robert Flaherty (1884–1951).

Under Flaherty's initiating hand the documentary became a filmic means for exploration and interpretation of the life of a people. It became a work of art the forms of which evolved out of the effort to meet this epical objective, forms which still distinguish the genre from any other type of reportage. These forms are

[4] See Notes, page 298.

[5] See Notes, page 298.
* Forsyth Hardy, ed., *Grierson on Documentary* (London: Collins, 1946), p. 11. In a review of Flaherty's *Moana,* originally published in the *New York Sun,* February, 1926.

6.11. Robert J. Flaherty (1884–1951): A frame from *Nanook of the North:* "Battle with the walrus." 1920. Silent documentary film. Production by Revillon Frères; direction, scenario, and photography by Robert J. Flaherty. Photograph of frame, courtesy of Film Library, The Museum of Modern Art, New York.

evolved organically out of the character of human existence recorded and the medium chosen as best fitted to enhance it. They are built up into monumental proportions—sometimes only for the sake of impact in revelation, sometimes to reach a further goal of propaganda, persuasion, inducement of viewers to favor a cause or adopt a course of social action.

Flaherty completed his first documentary, *Nanook of the North,* in 1922, after twelve years of life among the Eskimos of the Hudson Bay region. Though commercially motivated (commissioned by Revillon Frères, furriers of Paris), the film had no special view to present beyond conveying realization of the harsh rigor of life in the Arctic wastes. It maintains icily clear contrasts of value deemed by Flaherty

appropriate both to the subject matter and to the orthochromatic film deliberately chosen for the recording (6.11). In contrast to *Nanook,* Flaherty's second essay, *Moana,* was filmed in Samoa in 1926. It assumes a pace in keeping with the mellow tropical existence which it documents. It takes on a consistent subtlety of value-modulations befitting not only the physical and spiritual warmth of this life but also the panchromatic film adopted for its shooting (6.12).*

* Paul Rotha, *The Film Till Now* (New York: Funk and Wagnalls, 1948; 1st ed., 1929), pp. 203–204, and *Documentary Film* (London: Faber and Faber, 1936), pp. 81–83. A biography was written by Richard Griffith, *The World of Robert Flaherty* (New York: Duell, Sloan, and Pearce, 1953).

6.12. Robert J. Flaherty: A frame from *Moana:* "Love-making sequence." 1926. Silent documentary film. Production by Famous Players—Lasky; direction, scenario, and photography by Robert J. Flaherty. Photograph of frame courtesy of Film Library, The Museum of Modern Art, New York.

The Narrative

What is the motion picture? What is it supposed to do? We have seen Robert Flaherty, John Grierson, and their followers answering in a particular fashion, and evolving in accord with their answer the documentary film. Others have answered the question by declaring that the ideal of film should be the visual presentation of a story. They have thought in terms of cinematic visualizations of literature.

In so doing they have established a connecting link between the motion picture and the novel. This connection could never result, however, in a literal filming of a play or a novel, a direct carry-over from the art of literature into the art of cinema. Adolph Zukor once thought

it could.* He ended by proving the incompatibility of the two arts. As an early producer and exhibitor of motion pictures, Zukor imported into the United States in 1912 a four-reel film featuring Sarah Bernhardt's stage production of *Queen Elizabeth.* He followed it with a series of motion pictures entitled "Famous Players in Famous Plays." Lack of spoken dialogue proved only one of the deficiencies of such films. There were innumerable others. A cast trained to project their gestures and expressions, in order to carry the action of a play from the stage to the audience, became grotesque caricatures before the close viewing of

* Richard Griffith and Arthur Mayer, *The Movies* (New York: Simon and Schuster, 1957), pp. 28–29, 50–55.

the camera. Brilliantly successful stage personalities were apt on the screen to seem only pompous and brittle; few were able to transform themselves into truly photogenic personalities and express anything significant. Traditional stage sets, effective when viewed from a distance, were revealed on the screen as the artificial backdrops that they were, ridicuously out of keeping with the figures of the cast.

Other troubles arose in the attempt to pictorialize on screen the forms of a written novel. Literary composition owes much to the wealth of imagery associated with words, phrases, figures of speech. We tarry over the passages of a great novelist, probing with our imaginations the depths of the author's meanings. We enjoy at the movies, moreover, an occasional carry-over from literature to screen in which certain expressions of the writer are transformed into visual metaphors, hyperboles, and the like, such expressions as "the striking of midnight," "the morning after," "the clack of hoof." * Let the full richness of the word-evoked imagery of the novel get packed into a film, however, and the result is stuffiness and confusion. Our eyes simply cannot keep up with the flashes of imagery which an author summons up as we read.

Fictional literature does occasionally lend itself, on the other hand, to cinematic rendering. We may take the novels of Charles Dickens as a case in point. So closely akin are they to good scenarios for film productions that one critic has described them as "proto-cinematic." † The great Russian film-maker, Sergei M. Eisenstein (1898–1948), testified eloquently to the debt which he owed, through David W. Griffith, the American director most profoundly inspiring his own art, to the fiction of this nineteenth-century author.‡

* Sergei M. Eisenstein in chapter entitled "Word and Image" (Joy Leyda, trans. and ed.), *The Film Sense* (New York: Harcourt, Brace, 1947; 1st ed., 1942), pp. 3–65.
† David Harrah, "Aesthetics of the Film: the Pudovkin-Arnheim-Eisenstein Theory," *Journal of Aesthetics and Art Criticism*, Vol. XIII, No. 2 (December, 1954), p. 165.
‡ Sergei Eisenstein (Joy Leyda, trans. and ed.), *Film Form* (New York: Harcourt, Brace, 1949), pp. 195–255.

Out of Dickens's novels Eisenstein drew motivation for developing the montage as a peculiarly cinematic way to tell a story. He employed montage as Dickens did his "breaks" in narrative: to clarify and contrast, to further progression of parallel scenes, to interlock separate episodes. Through montage he learned to relate a story purely in terms of motion picture.

Sergei Eisenstein started out in an atmosphere of complete freedom for experimentation characteristic of the early years of the Bolshevik regime. He sensed the need for some form of art which might enlist popular support for the revolutionary government of Russia. Eisenstein discovered how the cinema demands attention, guides observation, and compels the viewer to follow its direction and tempo of movement. He saw as a perversion of the art the current tendency to provide a mere escape into daydreams of wish-fulfillment. He saw such escapism as inconsistent with the harsh realities of the Russian revolution. Seeking every means of introducing reality into his own films, therefore, he went to unbelievably subtle lengths to convert that reality into the artistry of emotional appeal which would sway the masses.

With his five-reel picture, *Potemkin*,[6] Eisenstein perfected a cinematic language that was truly universal. He drew his subject from recent history: a story connected with that Revolution of 1905 which, abortive though it was, had paved the way for its triumphant successor of 1917. He re-created the mutiny of the sailors aboard the armored cruiser *Potemkin*. The people of Odessa, hearing the news, crowded the steps of their city's waterfront and cheered the sailors' heroism. Czarist troops charged the people from above and massacred them. But the sailors of the other ships in the Black Sea fleet responded to the greeting of "Brothers!" from the mutineers and allowed the *Potemkin* to escape.

In planning for the production of *Potemkin* Eisenstein saw the inappropriateness of actors.

[6] See Notes, page 298.

6.13. Sergei M. Eisenstein (1898–1942): A frame from *Potemkin:* "Odessa steps sequence." 1925. Silent narrative film. Production by Goskino; direction and scenario by Sergei M. Eisenstein, assisted by Gregori Alexandrov; photography by Edward Tisse. Photograph of frame courtesy of Film Library, The Museum of Modern Art, New York.

Motion-picture recountal in general tended properly to merge actors with the setting and to relegate to filmic sequences alone the burden of the story's telling. How much more, then, should a revolutionary narrative! In direct contradiction to Hollywood's star system, Eisenstein decided to abandon actors entirely. He resorted to what he called "typage."

In accord with such procedure the Russian director made the hero of his film not an individual but a people. He hired townsfolk of Odessa who had never acted before and probably never would again. He chose them for their typical and not for their individual qualities. He showed them what they should do and coached them through the successive inci-

dents of the story on the very spot where the historical event had occurred. In filming each type for its first appearance on the screen he had the image recorded as vividly as possible. He aimed so to fix the image in the spectator's memory that it would be recognized and responded to as a known element of expression every time that it reappeared. The film-maker then proceeded, as he put it, to "orchestrate" his typage.

Eisenstein made still more extensive use of the device of montage. For *Potemkin* he started with single sequences of frames on various strips of film. Each frame in a sequence corresponded to a still photograph like that here chosen for illustration (6.13), but the film-maker's basic unit was the entire sequence which included it. Such a sequence could present no more than a bit of action as yet uncomposed—a man running, a woman turning, or whatever.

When Eisenstein cut out a portion here and there for discarding and then rejoined the remainders, he was following a conventional process called horizontal montage. He was doing little more than speeding up the actions originally recorded. Only when he joined dissimilar sequences for the sake of effects of conflict was he really composing. He was practicing vertical montage, the essence of his art as he conceived it.

When, in the thirties, color began to invade movie production, problems of brightness-darkness range and related exposure-time came to plague cinema photographers as much as they were plaguing "still" photographers. Absorbed in such problems, cameramen set as their criteria of excellence nothing but the widest range of hues and the highest intensities. The resulting color films dazzled the theatergoer. They so blunted his sensibilities that he was no longer satisfied with the quiet harmonies of the black-and-white film. Such films played on all of the dramatic stops at once, making each color try to outshout the others.

It is interesting to note that credit for finally integrating color with film in a truly creative expression belongs to the Japanese. We have already noted how heavily Japanese artists drew on the tangible nature of materials and the contrasting emptiness of space—in shaping a tea-bowl, in building a house-and-garden, in joining hollowed blocks of wood to form a statue. We discover in such a twentieth-century film-production as Daiei Studios' *Gate of Hell*,[7] for example, a sensitivity to color which the Japanese have always cultivated. Instead of utilizing color photography to record natural hues unfeelingly, they drew on it to heighten the narrative's emotional appeal. They brought to cinema a traditional Japanese use of color tonality—that all-pervasive coloring of a given

composition which is capable of evoking a mood. With color tonality alone, of course, a Japanese director could have done nothing expressive. But when he combined color tonality with creative editing, he succeeded in eliciting an overwhelmingly emotional response.

Path-breaking films like *Gate of Hell* launched a new epoch for movies. Introducing color as a predominant element of expression on the screen, they influenced the biggest Hollywood producers to treat film-making more as art than entertainment. Metro-Goldwyn-Mayer undertook in one case to deal with the life of an artist for subject. M-G-M executives looked for a story with popular appeal and found it in a fictionalized biography of Vincent van Gogh written by Irving Stone in 1934. Under the title *Lust for Life*,* this best-seller had touched off a chain reaction of exhibitions, classroom study projects, magazine features, and illustrated lectures, until millions of Americans knew something about the late-nineteenth-century Dutch master and his art.

The Metro-Goldwyn-Mayer motion picture was extraordinary. For its creation the company went to infinite pains to make all settings authentic, going to film on the spot in Holland and France the places where van Gogh lived and worked. The motion picture characterized the painter and his associates with a sympathetic understanding of each personality. It presented the paintings of van Gogh in connection with the exact situation in which each work was created—paintings never faked but recorded from the originals in the collections of the world. The company sought, in short, to meet to the fullest extent the criterion of verisimilitude.

Vincente Minnelli, director, managed thus to build his motion picture on a solid factual foundation. Kirk Douglas, the actor cast as van Gogh, projected himself into the artist's personality, to relive van Gogh's life in all of its consuming zeal and repeated frustrations (6.14). Norman Corwin, scenario writer, drew imaginatively on both Stone's book and a col-

[7] See Notes, page 298.

* Irving Stone, *Lust for Life: The Novel of Vincent van Gogh* (New York: Longmans, Green, 1936).

6.14. Vincente Minnelli: A frame from *Lust for Life:* "Van Gogh painting the draw-bridge at Arles." 1956. Narrative film with sound and color. Production by Metro-Goldwyn-Mayer; direction by Vincente Minnelli; scenario by Norman Corwin; Cine-mascope photography. Photograph of frame courtesy of Metro-Goldwyn-Mayer.

lection of letters written by van Gogh to his older brother, Theo.* The director introduced into the sound track at appropriate points, therefore, not merely the assumed words which the actor represented the painter as uttering, but the painter's actual words.

Beyond all such achievements in verisimilitude, however, Minnelli succeeded in putting color to tellingly expressive use. He took van Gogh's paintings as the motivation for the color effects of the film and caught through

them the exact emotional state of each era in the painter's life. The years of groping uncertainty in Holland, chill and impoverished, were rendered in the dull browns and greenish blacks of the pictures of peasant life which van Gogh was then painting. The excitement of the discovery made by van Gogh in Paris, that light can brighten color and atmosphere can make it dance, was conveyed in variegated colorings of heightened intensity. His "following of the sun" to the South, attended by ever more frenzied researches into emotional equivalents of colors, was paralleled by ever brighter tonalities of orange-yellow and lemon-yellow, until the arrival of the final scene of the artist's suicide in the crow-ridden and wind-blown wheat field, when color gave way almost totally to black and white.

* Irving Stone, ed., *Dear Theo: the Autobiography of Vincent van Gogh* (Boston: Houghton Mifflin, 1937). Abridgement of J. van Gogh-Bonger, ed. and trans., *The Letters of Vincent van Gogh to His Brother, 1872–1886* (Boston: Houghton Mifflin, 1927), and *Further Letters of Vincent van Gogh to His Brother, 1886–1889* (Boston: Houghton Mifflin, 1929).

The Fantasy

We have seen the importance of verisimilitude as a test for filmic documentation or filmic narration. Yet the very conviction of reality achieved by the best of such films depends on the director's ability to abstract his elements and use them for emphasis. Consider Flaherty's varying treatment of values in *Nanook of the North* and *Moana,* or Eisenstein's exploitation of motion through montage in *Potemkin.* Wherever art is involved, even reality of effect calls for a departure from literal reality in technique.

In filmic fantasy, comedy occupies a place next door to filmic fiction, often overlapping it. Like narrative, one type of comedy adheres to reality in structure. It deals with real settings. It determines the actions of real people. It features their fleeting moments of good luck, their more prevalent moments of mishap and frustration. In adhering to the stuff of real life, this type of comedy reduces the number, and shortens the duration, of life's moments of happiness. It multiplies the moments of woe beyond all probability until we are thrown into laughter over them. We sympathize with the hero's efforts to maintain his dignity and climb continuously out of the holes into which adversity tosses him, but we laugh as we recognize that he is trying to do exactly what we should do in like situations. We laugh again as we see him solving his problems by supernatural means—just what we do when we indulge in daydreaming.

Comedy may be close to reality, but it offers us imaginative escape from that same reality. It presents as though they were real such situations and actions as could not possibly be. We roar with delight over the liberties which cinema can take with time and space; slowing motion down, speeding it up, or stopping it abruptly; exaggerating a figure's foreshortening, distorting a scene's perspective; setting side by side scenes which never could approach each other in actuality; reversing a sequence of film to send the action back again to its starting point.

It is thus that the prize-fighter can be made to proceed with ludicrous deliberation to flatten his opponent's nose. Police can be made to chase bandits in a haste hilarious to watch. Pickpocket and intended victim can be suddenly made rigid as the hand is spied creeping toward the purse—in a comic rendering of suspense. A roller skater's feet can be made to loom up grotesquely in a spill as the diminutive body behind them goes down. A bicyclist can be made to pedal a hundred miles in less than ten seconds. A vase smashed over the villain's head can be made to draw all of its pieces together again as though they were magnets, restoring itself to its original shape.

Much of the magic of motion-picture comedy is accounted for by technical devices which reduce the role of the actor and even replace him. Such devices alone can never, of course, make up the comedy. When treated merely for their novelty and out of context, they can scarcely evoke a smile. But when joined with the pantomime of a master comedian they can lift the film to a level of humor equal in quality to the heightened reality of the documentary or the epic grandeur of the narrative. It is this fusion of filmic techniques with comic acting which produces, in fact, the star comedian: a Fernandel of France, a Cantinflas of Mexico, or an Alec Guinness of England.*

As with documentary and fiction films, so with comedy pictures, however—nothing can be done without the direction of a truly creative artist. Thanks to the star system, actors tend to overshadow directors in comedy as much as in narrative film production. This is true even in that rare instance in which a great artist of comedy directs his own pictures. Charlie Chaplin was acclaimed by every theatergoer for a generation as the greatest star of comedy who ever lived. Hardly anyone recognized him as a director of fully comparable merit, and yet without his own directing Charlie Chaplin would probably never have got beyond the ranks of the Keystone Comedians with whom he began his cinema career in 1913.

* For a factual history see John Montgomery, *Comedy Films* (London: George Allen and Unwin, 1954).

6.15. Charles Chaplin (1889–   ): A frame from *The Gold Rush:* "Shoe-dinner sequence." 1925. Silent comedy film. Production, direction, and scenario by Charles Chaplin. Photograph of frame courtesy of Film Library, The Museum of Modern Art, New York.

Chaplin reached the full maturity of his powers only when he broke away from commercial producers and began directing, as well as acting in, his own comedies. Only then was he able, as in *The Gold Rush** of 1925, to create a rounded masterpiece. Chaplin based his scenario for *The Gold Rush* on a tragic expedition of prospectors to the Klondike. He satirized through it America's money-getting madness of the twenties. He developed the comedy merely as a string of anecdotes but he projected into them all the heartfelt suffering and disillusionment of both his boyhood and his current wealth and fame.

* Detailed description and illustration of "stills," Theodore Huff, *Charlie Chaplin* (New York: Henry Schuman, 1951), pp. 187–198, and pls. ff. p. 210.

How did the comedian-director manage to transform tragedy into comedy? He abstracted from his subject matter only the barest essentials. He isolated these. He treated them as visual metaphors; he distilled from them pungent local flavors which ordinary theatergoers could understand and relish. Then he gave to each a subtle twist of mockery which made it all the more uproariously funny because of the vivid reality of its background.

Look, for example, at the shoe-dinner scene from which we have selected our "still" (6.15). Thanksgiving Day has come. Charlie and his lumbering fellow prospector are cooped up in a tiny Arctic cabin. They have exhausted their larder and grown desperate in their hunger. For their Thanksgiving feast Charlie contributes one of his shoes. With all of the flourishes of an expert chef, he cooks his shoe, tries it with his fork for tenderness, carves the nail-studded sole from the uppers, and tries to get his companion to accept the sole. When his fellow feaster seizes the uppers instead, Charlie meekly attacks the rejected serving. He wraps the shoe-laces around his fork as though they were spaghetti. He picks up a bent nail and offers one end to his companion as though it were a wish-bone.

Chaplin recognized how much the enlarged projection of the film to the screen magnified every slightest hint of facial expression or gesture which he might give the picture. He made the most of it. He introduced for emphasis both close-ups and super-close-ups of portions of his face and other details. He resorted to camera-distortions to render selected details more meaningful. He cut his film into telescoped actions making sequences more telling. He developed montages into flawless continuities, timing each montage down to the last frame of film. Chaplin sought the simplest and the most directly filmic of means. He created movies organically.

Animated Film

Another genre of fantasy derives from the nature of the motion-picture camera as an analyst of time. No matter how rapidly it exposes its film to a moving image, it does so intermittently. It ends every fraction-of-a-second exposure by closing its shutter down, making a still photograph out of each frame. When the stills are run in sequence through a projector at approximately the speed at which they were snapped, they produce, as we have seen, the orthodox moving picture.

The motion-picture camera does not always, however, have to be run at rapid speed. It can be operated one frame at a time, with any interval in between, whether that interval be a minute, a day, or a year. When so operated, it is creating film for single-frame animation, that kind of cinematography in which the inanimate can, when projected at normal projector-

speed, be made to seem to move. Such single-frame animation makes the flower pop out of the ground and hastily unfold. It makes the chick grow within the shell until ready to peck its way out. It makes a line extend itself across a map or gradually disappear.

Single-frame animation makes possible, above all, that art of animated cartooning which was once restricted to the animated novelty booklet. A little paper-bound-album of drawings of the same figures in successive poses was held in one hand and the pages flipped rapidly by the other to give the illusion of little figures going through their antics. If these same drawings were photographed on motion-picture film, one frame to a drawing, and projected through the cinematic projector, they would be, in rudimentary form at least, an animated cartoon.

Walt Disney brought the animated film to a climax of popularity with feature-length productions like *Snow White and the Seven Dwarfs* of 1937.* He gained fame through such art, and justly so, considering how much experiment and heroic resolve had to lie back of it. The name of Disney has become synonymous with the name of his art, and the creatures of Disney's fancy have rivaled even Charlie Chaplin in their popular following. Mickey Mouse, Donald Duck, and Bambi are names known to all the world.

For all of his genius as a cinematic magician, however, Disney has sometimes slipped into error. Holding consistently to realistic representation in his nature documentaries, in filmic animation he mixed his categories. Against characters made up entirely out of fancy and kept appropriately flat and abstract, he set human figures either modeled literally or shot from life. Resulting contrasts became painfully awkward. Creatures of fantasy simply refused to cooperate happily with human beings. They

---

* Robert D. Feild, *The Art of Walt Disney* (London and Glasgow: Collins, 1947). Techniques comparable to Disney's are described by Roger Manvell, *The Animated Film*. A documentary film presents the early history of the animated cinema: *The Toy That Grew Up* (Roger Leenhardt, dir.; produced by Campas Films; black and white, sound; 17 mins.).

pulled apart every film in which they appeared together.

Filmic animation tends to liberate the moviemaker from conventional representation. It leads him eventually to the realm of "pure form" occupied by the sculptural constructions of a Gabo (5.20 to 5.21b). It divorces itself from all storytelling associations with the immediate world but offers excitingly new experiences. Before our eyes creatures as exotic as those of a submarine garden fade in and out, dart here and there, dance about in time to the sound track.

Absolute film, sister art to the popular animated comedy, is, paradoxically, the least known and understood. Intended by its champions as a "universal language," it remains the secret tongue of initiates. It does not really need to be so. If people approached it without preconceptions, they could learn to enjoy its formal relationships in time and space as fully as they enjoy corresponding relationships in a sculptural mobile.

Among the pioneers of "pure form" cinema, Norman McLaren has brought animation to a point of development comparable to Flaherty's in documentary and Eisenstein's in narrative film production.* Unlike Disney, McLaren had to learn to "say" the most with the least means. On the severely delimited budget of the National Film Board of Canada for which he worked, this artist from Scotland learned to eliminate entirely the intermediate use of the camera for recording cels—those celluloid squares on which artists draw images at conveniently large size, leaving to cameramen reduction to the size of the frames on 35-mm. film. McLaren found a way of working directly on each frame of the raw film itself, using apparatus which he invented for the purpose (6.16a).

Painting seven thousand frames in miniature on a strip of celluloid 1¼ inches wide, and painting them in succession to register the

* Alan Phillips, "The Inspired Doodles of Norman McLaren," *Macleans*, Vol. LXV, No. 24 (December 15, 1952), pp. 22–23, and 45–48; and Spottiswoode, *Film and Its Techniques, op. cit.*, pp. 24, 139–142, and 383–387.

essential action when run through the projector at the rate of twenty-four frames per second, was a severely disciplining task. McLaren learned in the process to which he had committed himself to strip every form down to its barest essentials. He learned to summarize in the fewest possible notations of line and color any character or movement which the subject demanded.

Take, for example, the four-minute short, *Fiddle-de-Dee*, which Norman McLaren made in 1947. As the sequence of frames illustrates (6.16b), the artist composed the movie in nonrepresentational terms alone. He eliminated even the simplified representations evolved in earlier films. He worked instead with the pure form of colored points, lines, and planes, synchronizing these motives with the song which he had a folk fiddler play for the sound-track recording, "Listen to the Mocking Bird."

McLaren actually interpreted in this way the melody and rhythm of a song. He rendered the film with the same directness of attack as he had earlier productions, using such inks, dyes, and transparent colors as would not dissolve and clutter the projector in the process of being shown. In addition to passages of frames conventionally rendered unit by unit, he introduced entirely new effects of continuous vertical action by painting long lines and bands of color across several frames at once. Sometimes, for spatial illusion, the artist rendered both sides of his film, and for expressive enrichment he diversified his textural effects. Certain areas he stippled or scratched. Others he covered with intermingled oil-based and water-based paints. Still others he treated while the colors were still wet, either dropping specks of dust into them to cause the washes to pull away and leave little holes, or else impressing them with fabric of various weaves.

The animator did not resort to such devices merely to display his cleverness. He seems in a showing of the film to have treated his medium with utter spontaneity and freedom. Yet he had to recognize for every passage the same necessities as those of a music or a dance composer at work, to develop his theme through a series

6.16. TECHNIQUES OF FILMIC AN-
IMATION.   a. Norman McLaren
(1914–   ): Animated UNESCO
film in progress. 1946. India ink
on raw film, with apparatus invented by the artist. Photograph
courtesy of National Film Board
of Canada.   b. Norman McLaren:
Fiddle-de-Dee in progress: continuous passages being rendered
across successive frames, in syn-
chronization with sound track (to
left). 1947. Animated 35-mm film
with sound and color. Production
by National Film Board of Canada. Photograph courtesy of National Film Board of Canada.

of repeats with variations that would seem inevitable to the structure of the whole. He succeeded in creating thus with *Fiddle-de-Dee* a masterpiece of pictorial dance. As the points, lines, bands, and textured areas gather and part, glide, leap, quiver, and skip on and off the stage, as though in ecstasy over the music, the film sweeps the viewer along with it at a headlong tempo which leaves him excited and breathless when it suddenly ends.

SUMMARY

Photography is the art of creating pictures by action of light on surfaces chemically prepared to respond to it. Cinema is an extension of the art of photography into the realm of movement. Consisting in the creation of images on successive frames of film to give the illusion of movement when projected on to a screen at a rapid rate, the motion picture depends for its effectiveness on a persistence of vision natural to the viewer.

Both photography and cinema exploit color as their major element—in their black-and-white versions, color-values alone, but in their color versions, hue, value, and intensity all at once. Film and camera operate merely to record, but the artist-photographer in the one case and the artist-director in the other manipulate one or all of the subelements of color for the sake of rhythmically expressive organization. Techniques of photography are shared with the motion picture, but they become much more complex and numerous in the latter.

Creative processes of treating and manipulating film produce two major types of photograph, the photogram and the photograph proper. They produce in like manner two types of movie, the camera-exposed film and the animated film. Creative processes of photography interact with subject matter in such selective fashion as to couple one particular medium with a definitely preferred genre. Daguerreotypy became associated thus with the portrait photograph, the hand camera and rolled film with the candid-camera shot, and the view camera and cut film with the nude photograph, the panoramic landscape, and the detailed close-up.

Cinematic genre divides into three major categories: documentary, narrative, and fantasy. The artistry of the camera operates in all three genres, as does the artistry of editing. The former includes such technical devices as the dissolve, the motion-within-the-frame shot, the panning shot, the dollying shot. The latter includes, above all, the technique of montage. Direct animation by hand on raw film tends to encourage the extension of what is normally a representational art into an art of pure form.

RECOMMENDED READINGS

Gernsheim, Helmut (Alison Gernsheim, collab.). *The History of Photography: From the Earliest Use of the Camera Obscura in the Eleventh Century Up to 1914.* New York: Oxford University Press, 1955.

Generous in size of page and abundantly illustrated, though seldom with fewer than three halftone reproductions to a plate, this book focuses on the development of photography in Great Britain, but gives secondary consideration to corresponding developments in France and the United States. It is fairly well written, but its encyclopedic coverage of the field makes it more valuable for factual reference than for continuous reading or for esthetic bases of judgment.

Newhall, Beaumont. *The History of Photography: From 1839 to the Present Day,* 3d ed. New York: The Museum of Modern Art, 1949.

Though much briefer than Gernsheim's book, this standard reference surpasses the English work in readability, factual condensation, and critical treatment of photography as an art. The author, Curator of George Eastman House in Rochester, is particularly successful in defining period styles and relating them to successive technical innovations.

Newhall, Beaumont (ed.). *On Photography: A Source Book of Photo History in Facsimile.* Watkins Glen, N. Y.: Century House, 1956.

This book of primary source material for an appreciation of the art of photography from various points of view plays the same key role in its field as Mumford's *Roots of Contemporary American Architecture* plays in the art of building (see p. 117). The background out of which each selected passage came is illustrated by facsimile reproduction of the format and type of the original document.

Adams, W. I. Lincoln (ed.). *Sunlight and Shadow: A Book for Photographers, Amateur and Professional.* New York: Baker & Taylor, 1897.

In a sense, this is likewise a source book. Adams drew for his reprints, however, on published studies of his own day. Himself a photographer and personal associate of the avant-garde photographers of the nineties, he preserves in this book much illuminating criticism which might otherwise have been lost. The current pictorialism of the time is now "dated." as is the stress on romantically sentimental subject matter. Many of the reproductions of photographs are scarcely larger than a postage stamp, but such features as a generous selection of photographs by Alfred Stieglitz help make the book valuable.

Feininger, Andreas. *Feininger on Photography.* Chicago and New York: Ziff-Davis, 1949.

Among the many technical manuals of photography, few manage to get beyond mere exposition, and fewer still undertake to lay down in the process a workable esthetics peculiar to the art. This manual succeeds beyond all others yet published in joining detailed technical information with principles of design in photographic practice. It was written out of the author's many years of professional experience as photographer for *Life* Magazine.

Feininger, Andreas. *Advanced Photography: Methods and Conclusions.* New York: Prentice-Hall, 1952.

Written as a sequel to *Feininger on Photography,* the *Life* photographer's second book offers even more helpful criteria for judging photo-

graphs as art. The author again restricts himself to black-and-white photography and even declares (p. 181) that color in nature is "of relatively minor importance" to the cameraman —which increasingly it is not. Within self-imposed limits, however, the author makes illuminating analyses of photographs well chosen to cover the expressive range of the art.

Steinert, Otto. *Subjektive Fotografie.* Bonn am Rhein, Germany: Brüder Auer, 1952.

Annuals like *U. S. Camera* (New York: Duell, Sloan & Pearce) provide good study material for sharpening critical judgment. Sometimes comparable with the annuals in coverage of subject and medium and often more discriminatory because of the quality of the photographs included in the art exhibitions occasioning them, catalogue-originating books such as this by Steinert make even more valuable reference.

Schmidt, Georg, *et al. The Film: Its Economic, Social and Artistic Problems.* Basel, Switzerland: Holbein, 1948.

The outcome of an exhibition first held in the Gewerbemuseum of Basel in 1943 in conjunction with a film festival, this book retains something of the format of a portion of the displays, though in content and choice of "stills" it is much revised. Among the co-authors, Werner Schmalenbach was responsible for treatment of the artistic problems of motion-picture production, and it is this part of the study which is most illuminating to the reader cultivating appreciation of the art.

Arnheim, Rudolf. *Film as Art.* Berkeley and Los Angeles: University of California Press, 1957.

Selected writings by a Gestalt psychologist who, perhaps more than any other author, laid the groundwork for an esthetics of cinema based upon organic principles of design, this book discusses the properties peculiar to the motion picture alone, and points out virtues of the black-and-white and the silent film deriving from their limitations. The book lacks the unity which a completely rewritten study would have afforded. It offers, at the same time, many brilliant flashes of insight. Available in an inexpensive paper-bound format.

Manvell, Roger. *Film.* "Pelican Books." Harmondsworth, England: Penguin Books, 1946. 1st ed., 1944.

One-time student of the documentary-film master, John Grierson, and an associate of the British Film Institute, Manvell in this and in his later "Pelican Book," *The Film and the Public* (1955), writes in an entertainingly British-colloquial manner but with sound critical judgment.

Livingston, Don. *Film and the Director*. New York: Macmillan, 1953.

This book was published in the same year as Raymond Spottiswoode's *Film and Its Techniques,* a work to which we have referred repeatedly in the preceding notes. Though focusing on the role of the director, it covers the same technical ground that Spottiswoode does—less thoroughly, to be sure, but in language more easily followed by the beginner, especially when read in conjunction with the admirably clear diagrams and photographic illustrations.

CHAPTER 7

Detail of Fig. 7.2a

Illustrating and Print Making

THE NATURE OF ILLUSTRATION

IN THE LAST CHAPTER we called attention to the power of the photograph to invite us imaginatively beyond its frame and the moment fixed by it. When we examine a photograph, we may identify ourselves with the things represented in it, speculating over circumstances which may have caused them to appear as they do and possibly making up stories about them when no narrative is at hand. Sometimes in this way, indeed, a photograph captivates us more than a movie does. The film gives us illusory action in real time; it spells things out for us. But the photograph leaves to our imagination the job of filling in; it launches us on a voyage of adventure, uncharted and fancy-free.

Publishers who intersperse pages of novels with photographs depicting episodes in the action are responsible for converting the independent art of the studio photographer into a collaborative art as interrelated with literature as architectural sculpture is with architecture. Photography becomes the art of illustrating, an art devoted (as its Latin root, *illustrare*, "to illumine or make clear," indicates) to clarifying a text with visual imagery. Photography figured in the making of illustrations for this book. Here it has been used merely to document works made for other purposes, however, and the kind of illustrations with which we are now concerned are genuine products of the art of illustration itself—pictures made for a specific text and designed to help a reader visualize the characters and the action of the story.

Some critics relegate illustrating to a level of minor art, disparaging it as a crutch to support a weak reader's imagination. They question its right even to be considered as an art at all. They hurl at an inferior picture their most damning epithet: "mere illustration." Consider, such critics say, what literature really is. Can the art of the written word not stand by itself? Are the words of a great novelist not vivid enough by themselves to evoke the proper images in the reader's mind?

From a literary point of view, argument against illustrations does carry weight. The average reader soon forgets the argument, however, when confronted with the direct sensuous appeal of pictures accompanying a text. They induce him to recall passages, reread passages, and extract new meanings.

Illustrating depends not only on the art of literature; it depends on a whole circle of arts called "the arts of the book." It is a collaborative art requiring for its appreciation grasp of the essentials of other arts which in one way or another influence its creations. We must learn (1) the qualities of the illustration as a picture by itself, a picture the form of which is determined by the paper or other support on which it is rendered and the medium in which it is executed; (2) the format (the size, shape, and other physical aspects) of the whole production as a work of layout-design and binding; (3) the physical nature of the text, whether calligraphic (in handwriting) or typographic (in print with movable types); and (4) the content of the story, its word-imagery, sentence-structure, stylistic flavor, development of plot.*

* The interrelated arts of the book are treated by Jan Poortenaar in *The Art of the Book and Its Illustration* (New York: Lippincott, 1935).

One major requirement for a good illustration is understatement. It must leave most of the visualizing of characters and action to the mind's eye alone and must never give the plot away. It must by its silences tease the prospective reader into filling in with text. Hand-rendered illustrations often meet this requirement better than photographic illustrations. They benefit by abbreviations, simplifications, abstractions, as natural to such renderings as complete documentations in light and shade and color are to photography.

Hand-rendered illustrations are products of the art of drawing. By drawing in this sense we mean that part of the art of painting by which some form is defined or "drawn out" into existence (1.4a and b). By coloring alone we mean that which would be left in a picture after all definition of form is removed: vague smudges of color like those left on a painter's palette (his mixing board or slab) after he has mixed his paints.* The moment that such smudges are variegated purposefully and given controlled variations of sharpness and softness of edge they are translated into drawings and set to work delineating and modeling.

Drawing is resorted to by the artist when he wants to jot down some detail or effect which impresses him as offering possibilities of later development into a picture: he calls this notation a *sketch* (1.5). Drawing is employed by him again when, reaching a general idea of his final composition, he seeks the assurance of greater factual knowledge in his final work, and makes a careful preliminary rendering of the part in question; he calls this exercise a *study*, whether for a painting or a sculpture (5.17a). Drawing is treated, finally, as an end in itself—as a framed picture to hang on a wall

(1.4b), as an album picture (1.4a), or as a story illustration (7.12).†

Be it sketch, study, or finished picture, a drawing tends to exploit the element of line as naturally as architecture the element of space and sculpture the element of mass. As we found in our introductory study of the elements of art, line in drawing offers a wide range of expression. It may rest firmly and unbrokenly on the paper, as two-dimensional a containment of form as the height and width of the sheet of paper on which it is made. It may expand and contract, advance into view and fade from sight, sharpen and blur, pursue a single definite track, and double and waver— to follow a rhythm which corresponds to the way in which the eye perceives a solid in deep space. It may break and jump about, contract itself to flecks suggestive of color notes and expand into crossings and crisscrossings suggestive of atmospheric shadows.

Advantages of Each Kind of Drawing

Linear drawing commends itself to illustrating because its natural flatness of effect corresponds to the flatness of the paper. It harmonizes with the strokes forming characters or letters in a passage of text (1.5 to 1.7). It sparkles like the calligraphy or typography against the white of the paper (7.12). It approaches the linear abstractions of the characters or letters themselves. It exerts a tactile appeal open even to a child's drawing (1.3a).

The American illustrator, Howard Pyle,‡ became a master of such line drawing. He condensed the individuality of the story's charac-

---

* This distinction between drawing and painting, together with emphasis on the role of drawing in painting, is made by Harold Speed, *The Practice and Science of Drawing* (Philadelphia: J. B. Lippincott, 1922), and Vernon Blake, *The Art and Craft of Drawing* (London: Oxford University Press, 1927). Charles de Tolnay makes a more thoroughgoing and historically comprehensive study in *History and Technique of Old-Master Drawings* (New York: H. Bittner, 1943).

† For examples of each type of drawing, see Joseph Pennell, *Pen Drawing and Pen Draughtsmen* (New York: Macmillan, 1920); Agnes Mongan, ed., *One Hundred Master Drawings* (Cambridge, Mass.: Harvard University Press, 1949); Monroe Wheeler, ed., *Modern Drawings* (New York: Museum of Modern Art, 1944); and the as-yet-untranslated standard reference: Joseph Meder, *Die Handzeichnung* (Vienna: Anton Schroll, 1923).

‡ Willard S. Morse and Gertrude Brinckle, eds., *Howard Pyle: A Record of His Illustrations and Writings* (Wilmington, Del.: Wilmington Society of the Fine Arts, 1921); and Ruth G. Patterson, "The Influence of Howard Pyle on American Illustration" (Unpublished Master's Thesis, Cleveland: Western Reserve University, 1954).

ters to its essentials, delineated them in the action of the story with an easy grace which complete knowledge of the subject and immersion in the tale made possible. We offer a choice example from *The Wonder Clock*, book of fairy tales written and illustrated by Pyle for each of the twenty-four hours of the day (7.11a).

Mass drawing, drawing which depends less on line than on modulations of value, is less favored by illustrators than line drawing, but mass drawing offers its own peculiar advantages. It enriches the imagery of a novel with a sense either of tangible substance through modeling in light and shade or of penetration into depths of light and shadow. Mass drawing evokes the mood sought by the author in the telling of the story. It suggests the atmosphere in which the action takes place (7.9), the state of weather, the movements of natural forces.

Color drawing, which uses black and white to suggest illumination, intensity, and hue, can make the most powerful impact of all. It may not harmonize with the text as well as a line drawing or a mass drawing will, but it makes up for its deficiency by the poignancy of its sensuous and emotional appeal. When color is employed expressively in an illustration, it can create mood-evoking tonalities as effective even as those of the American color film, *Lust for Life*.

The illustrator of a Japanese ballad of the thirteenth century knew what force of emphasis, for example, he could gain with bright accents of color introduced judiciously here and there into an otherwise completely black-and-white linear rendering (7.1 to 7.4a). N. C. Wyeth owed much as illustrator to his teacher, Howard Pyle, but Wyeth struck out in a new direction when he made color rather than line his specialty. Like a musician playing with the tones of an organ, Wyeth manipulated hues and intensities to heighten the themes drawn from the stories he illustrated. He charged adventure tales like *Treasure Island* * with an emotional appeal felt by even the most casual reader. Through his colored illustrations Wyeth invested blood-and-thunder scenes with a lusty veracity.

Format of Text as Determinant of Form

We referred to the format of a text as consisting of its height, width, and other physical characteristics. The term, in fact, embraces the whole general appearance of a literary production—the paper or other support used for the writing, the writing itself, and the binding. Prior to the fifteenth century in the Western world and to the tenth century in China, all texts were written or copied by hand, and for that reason we call them manuscripts (Latin: *manus*, "hand," and *scriptus*, "written"). As experts on handwriting know, the hand never repeats itself, so a manuscript always became a unique production. It was done joyously, but always from our point of view slowly and laboriously. Difficult to produce, it was precious. It prompted its patron, whether abbot or prince, to demand of its maker-collaborators nothing but the highest standards of craftsmanship and design.

Generally speaking, a manuscript is a collection of leaves of some material joined together and written on; in actual practice, however, it has assumed a variety of forms.† In ancient Mesopotamia, for instance, it took the form of slabs of clay into which cuneiform (wedge-shaped) characters were impressed with a stylus, a slender, pointed instrument, before being fired in a kiln. In ancient China it took the form of strips of wood or bamboo written on with pen or brush, then tied together with silken cords. In the Mediterranean world, until at least the fourth century A.D., the predominant material employed for manuscripts was papyrus—a reed having fibers which could be pounded into flat sheets, and giving its name to its successor, paper. Papyrus was brittle and vulnerable to dampness. It tended, therefore,

---

* N. C. Wyeth (1882–1945) illustrated Robert Louis Stevenson's *Treasure Island* in an edition published by Charles Scribner's Sons, 1911.

† David Diringer, *The Hand-produced Book* (New York: Philosophical Library, 1953) and *The Illuminated Book* (New York: Philosophical Library, 1958).

to be used in the form of the hand scroll, the *rotulus* of Latin-speaking peoples, corresponding to the *emakimono* of the Japanese.*

The rotulus consisted of sheets of papyrus or other material joined side by side, and sometimes mounted on a fabric backing, to form a strip 9 inches to 14 inches high and as much as 100 feet long. It was fastened, sometimes at one end, sometimes at both ends, to a roller made of wood, ivory, ebony, or metal. Often it was provided with a cord with which to keep the scroll rolled up when not in use. A little wooden box was usually made for protecting this hand scroll while in storage, its oblong but square-ended shape lending itself to filing. In use, the rotulus was unrolled horizontally from one end and rolled up at the other as one proceeded with its reading. Although it had to be rerolled laboriously back to its starting point before it could be read again, the rotulus, typically light and flexible, was easy to handle.

Ancient peoples seem always to have used tanned leather to some extent as a writing support. It was much heavier and more expensive than papyrus, however, and much less flexible. Rather than being employed for rotuli, therefore, it was reserved primarily for official documents. Even for this purpose, however, hairs and flesh in the leather interfered with the calligraphy.

Somewhere, perhaps at Pergamum in Asia Minor, the name of which gave the name "parchment" to the material, craftsmen devised a technique of treating the skins of sheep or lambs, goats or kids, cows or calves, so as to get rid of all hair and flesh and to produce a superior writing surface: enduring, even-textured and usable on both sides, white, and semitranslucent. Parchment, together with its refined calf-skin variant, vellum, lent itself to use in hand scrolls as leather did not, and to this day it enters into the creation of ritualistic scrolls for synagogues and the like.

The rotulus was, as we have noted, a nuisance for repeated reading. It confronted the reader with almost insurmountable obstacles when he wanted to make quick cross-references and comparisons among a number of scrolls. Anyone trying to use rotuli for such research was obliged to fall back on old-fashioned wooden tablets on which to make notes from the hand scrolls, stringing these tablets together with cords. He might in the interests of a less bulky set of notes fashion his book out of cut leaves of papyrus, bound along one edge to facilitate the turning of pages; if so, he could fold each sheet of papyrus over once, making a folio of four pages out of it and strengthening its attachment to the binding by sewing through the fold. But papyrus was too fragile to qualify for any further foldings or rough usage, and the cut-leaved, back-bound form of book had to wait for the tougher, more practical parchment to come into general favor in the fourth century A.D.

The manuscript with the format which the use of parchment helped to establish was known as the codex, precursor of the book as we know it today. This codex, named from the Latin word for "tree trunk," was a book of pages tied together along one side to facilitate leafing through, but with the gathering of these pages bound in turn to some protective backing.[1] If the covers were boards, they were usually encased in leather. Sometimes leather alone was used to make the covers. In either case the art of leather-tooling was pressed into service by the bookbinder—not only to cut and perforate and sew the leather but also to impress into the leather appropriate lettering and ornamental devices. Finally, the craft of the metal-worker was drawn on—to give the lettering accents of gold or silver, the corners of the covers protective bosses of brass. The result was a hand-bound volume of parchment or vellum, as convenient to consult as it was to hold, leaf through, and read.

In spite of its inconvenience, the rotulus worked well in encouraging an unbroken flow of story and pictorial accompaniment. The scribe would leave margins and gaps to be filled in by the illustrator, or the illustrator

* The chief authority is Kenji Toda, *Japanese Scroll Painting* (Chicago: University of Chicago Press, 1935).

[1] See Notes, page 298.

might do his work first, leaving spaces for the scribe to use. Whichever the case, when the organic ideal inspired the artist-collaborators, they let the format of the rotulus predetermine the character of text and illustrations.

Some rotuli carry illustrations isolated in their imagery and unrelated to their texts, but the best of the hand scrolls account through their pictures for much of the esthetic pleasure involved in unrolling and examining them. Such illustrations tie in with each other and the manuscripts bearing them in mutual complement. They provide that sense of continuity from episode to episode which parallels the progress of the story itself. Some rotuli even anticipated the cinema. Their mounts may have been static and neutral like movie screens, but their unrolling brought the element of motion into play in true cinematic fashion.

When manuscript-producers abandoned the rotulus in favor of the codex, they sacrificed much. They could no longer make their illustrations flow smoothly along. They had to submit to a different discipline. They had to accommodate their work to intermittencies of page and rectangularities of border.

The labor that went into the making of the codex, together with its relative rarity, made it a precious possession. Its creators often, therefore, made it look as costly as it really was. Illuminators filled every margin of its pages with ornament (7.6) and binders embellished its cover with precious metals and stones. Sometimes the craftsmen overdid their ornamentation and buried the text, forgetting the original reason for making any codex at all. But controlled ornament was in keeping with the character of the arts of the manuscript, and it lent itself well to emphasis on the organic sources of the form as a whole: function, material, and technical procedure.

Like the pages, the illustrations of the codex remained separate from each other. They gained their unity of effect only through consistency of style, characters, and accessories. Such illustrations said little in specific terms about the story's details. They aimed rather at

whetting a reader's desire to read the text—suggesting more, in accord with the principles of good illustration which we have already explained, than they actually defined, and often preceding those passages in the text to which they severally referred.

The printed book inherited much of the character of the codex, because it was the codex's direct descendant. The book kept the format of the codex. It held to the same margins, lines of text, distribution of illustrations, sometimes even repertory of ornamental initials and borders. It called for the same fashioning of pages out of larger sheets of paper—sheets folded together to make various numbers of pages.

Thanks to the peculiarities of mass publication, printed books came at the same time to assume qualities of their own.* Like other industrial products, every copy of a given publication had to emerge from the assembly line in a form identical with that of every other copy. If it bore any individual variations, it betrayed a fault in the machinery. Contrary to the decorative richness sought naturally by the craftsman, therefore, a simplicity of effect in the printed book seemed only proper to designers respecting the clean-cut precision of the printing process. It also seemed appropriate to the intended functions of a book in an industrial society—something for ready sale at the bookshop and easy reading at home.

What should a dust jacket do for a book if not catch the purchaser's eye, declare to him the character of the text, and make him feel the book a desirable acquisition? † When the jacket has been discarded, certainly the cover itself should continue to invite the book's

* György Kepeś and others, *Graphic Forms: The Arts as Related to the Book* (Cambridge, Mass.: Harvard University Press, 1949).
† For aspects of book design discussed in this paragraph, see the following: Charles Rosner, *The Growth of the Book-jacket* (Cambridge, Mass.: Harvard University Press, 1954); Joseph W. Rogers, "The Rise of American Edition Binding" in Hellmut Lehmann-Haupt, ed., *Bookbinding in America* (Portland, Maine: Southworth-Anthoensen Press, 1941); Rosamond B. Loring, *Decorated Book Papers* (Cambridge, Mass.: Harvard University Department of Printing and Graphic Arts, 1942).

reading, and withstand the wear of that reading, for many years. Certainly also this cover should bear lettering that reads easily and resists rubbing off. And the weight, size, thickness, and texture of the book should make it pleasurable to handle and hold open. What sort of end papers should join the inside of the cover to the cluster of pages enclosed? Such papers should at least be graced with a color, texture, or decoration, which accentuates their flatness while setting the mood for the text. What kind of paper should be used for the pages of the text? Whatever its other qualities, it needs at least to contrast with the blackness of the ink of the printing while sparing the eye fatigue occasioned by excessive glare. What type should be selected for the printing? [2] Surely it must correspond to the verbal content of the book, lend itself to organization into sentences and paragraphs which read clearly as wholes, and yet vary itself enough not to tire the reader's eye.

Do the illustrations contribute to the effectiveness of this reading? Do they follow some rhythmic pattern psychologically related to the progress of the chapter—from a minor detail recorded in a heading, perhaps, through marginal and half-page imagery to a full-page illustrational climax? Do they add to the book's imaginative appeal?

The present book might be subjected to a test of such questionings. It might be compared with other books of its kind more or less successfully meeting the criteria of quality in such arts of the book as page layout, binding and jacket design, and choice of illustrations. The closer it comes to meeting them, the more creative in the organic sense the book can be said to be.

Books are not always made to last forever, but they assume forms at least as enduring as the subject matter that prompted the printing. Books take months and even years to publish. They call accordingly for illustration as rich in expressive subtleties as is the text.

Periodicals are different. They specialize in the moment, whether or not that moment has anything of permanent value about it. They restrict themselves normally to current topics and events. Except when bound as books of reference in a library, they appear, in quality of paper, printing, and binding, as quickly disposed of as they are read. Newspapers and magazines aim only at such layout and illustration, therefore, as will catch the reader's eye and make the meanings of the accompanying text obvious at first glance. They admit only forms of such simplicity that they can be rendered speedily, reproduced inexpensively, and absorbed quickly.

The arts of the periodical have to operate under a far more rigid dictatorship of deadlines than do the arts of the book. They tolerate no mistake, admit nothing irrelevant or redundant. Hence the art of periodical-layout,* with its easily followed captions and headlines, its strong oppositions of blank space to black, its sharp, uncluttered definitions. Hence the art of commercial illustration: quick to deliver its message, fetching enough in theme to be remembered. Hence the art of the cartoon and comic strip, text-relieving, thought-provoking or heart-capturing, human, if not humorous, in appeal.

THE ART OF MAKING PRINTS

There has probably never been a time when cartooning was not practiced. It was certainly known in ancient Egypt.[3] The medieval Christian monk approached it at times when he illustrated his manuscripts (7.5). Hand-scroll painters cultivated it in twelfth-century Japan.[4] But the printed book was required to make cartooning really flourish, and the printed book could not even have come into existence without the use of paper. Parchment was too ex-

[2] See Notes, page 299.
[3] See Notes, page 299.

* Raymond A. Ballinger, *Layout* (New York: Reinhold Publishing Corporation, 1956).
[4] See Notes, page 299.

pensive and rigid a material. Papyrus was too brittle. Only paper could meet the need.

While lending itself to the advancement of printing, paper furthered the attendant rise of print making as an art. Print making is, as the Latin root of its name indicates (*premere*, "to press"), the art of duplicating pictures by pressing against a flat surface, usually of paper, a block or plate on which forms have been rendered and inked for transfer. Prints have been pressed on to or into a great variety of materials—from clay and butter to parchment and cloth—but never as satisfactorily as on to paper. When soaked in water, paper becomes limp and easily manipulable. It then responds to the pressure of the block or plate in a uniform adherence to the printing surface. It takes the ink from this surface with enough absorption to hold the coloring matter in place. And its gleaming whiteness offers contrast to the blackness of the ink.

In print making as in papermaking China pioneered [5]—first for seals impressed on documents; then for Buddhist-inspired prayers the multiplication of which by printing was thought to increase the chances of winning one's way to Paradise; and finally for illustration and text, whether for incorporation with a book or for separate production and sale as independent prints.

Considering the pictorial nature of Chinese writing (see p. 9 and 1.5a, b, and c) and the characteristic Buddhist scriptural stress on imagery, it was inevitable that Chinese printed books should be illustrated with prints rendered like the text itself—in blocks with the characters and the images in relief. But the cutting of the picture into a block was much easier than the cutting of the whole page, and the original "block books," printed one block to a page, were more apt than not to be illustrated—from their first appearance in China in the ninth century and in Europe in the fifteenth until printing with movable types led to their replacement a century or so later. In either case the impulse to enrich the text with illustrations printed correspondingly from blocks

[5] See Notes, page 299.

brought the newborn art of print making to early maturity.

Print Making by Relief

Block printing belongs to the first of four classes of print-making mediums: relief, intaglio, planography, and stencil. Relief came first in both Orient and Occident. In the Orient it prevails down to the present, but in the Occident it has been succeeded by each of the other classes of mediums, much in the order given, but with all four classes persisting in an active state today. Printing with the wood block has always been preferred to printing with any other material, because wood lends itself to cutting in relief, to impressing on to paper, and to uniform transferral of ink.

Relief includes a number of print-making techniques, ranging from the single block and the color block (with the block of wood cut the long way of the grain) to the wood engraving (with the block cut into the end of the grain), the linoleum block, and the commercial zinc cut. The single wood-block print has characteristically large and simple areas of black and white with a minimum of lines (7.8). The color wood block demands a series of blocks, one for each hue and one for each intensity or value of hue, resulting sometimes in a color print of considerable subtlety (7.7). The ink used for either type of wood block is soluble in water but thickened, with a starch like the rice paste used in the Orient, so that it will not run into the hollows of the block and blur the transfer of the forms standing out in relief.

When organically inspired, a print made with a relief medium will reflect the need for strengthening the areas to be printed by not cutting away too much.[6] It will assume big areas of black and white or areas of little variation in value or hue (7.8). Wherever lines occur, they will be sparing, firm, and sharp, or, if delicate, at least joined to stronger forms. A wood block does not lend itself to broken areas and cluttered lines; it succumbs quickly to overstatement. In doing so, it arouses our ap-

[6] See Notes, page 299.

prehension lest some detail of the relief break under pressure of the printing and ruin the block. It mars thus our pleasure in its viewing.

Print Making by Intaglio

Intaglio is engraving or cutting into, rather than cutting away to leave relief. It is the incising into a metal plate of grooves which hold the printer's ink after the surplus ink has been wiped off the plate, until dampened paper draws the ink out under the extreme pressure of a special press.

Dry point, simplest of intaglio mediums, consists in working directly on the metal plate (usually copper) with a triangular-pointed tool called the burin. The artist pushes forward into the metal with the burin, digging a groove and turning up a layer of metal like the sod along a plowed furrow. When he inks the plate so rendered and strikes (makes) a print from it, he obtains a picture the lines of which are shaded by the ink caught under the burr, the turned-up fold. When an artist removes the burrs in advance by scraping and polishing his plate, he converts the dry point into an engraving.* He then concentrates on the lines alone, letting them assume that sharpness of edge and rapidly moving effect given when they are dug out by the forward-pushing burin.

For softly tonal effects of line the artist may employ an intaglio medium called etching. He coats his plate, of copper, zinc, or iron, with a wax or varnish ground. He scratches his drawing through this ground with an etching needle, creating a rich array of lines and systems of line. He bathes the plate in nitric acid solution, letting the acid eat into the plate wherever it is exposed by the lines. He then stops out (covers) the lines to appear the lightest, and bathes the plate again. He stops out the next set of lines with more of the ground and bathes the plate once more, repeating this process until he has reached his heaviest set of lines, those subjected to all of the baths.

When the artist inks the plate so prepared, the bitten (acid-etched) lines hold the printer's ink until it is transferred to the paper in the etching press. He can introduce further tonal variations either by pulling the ink partly out of some of the lines in advance with a cloth or by wiping a portion of the plate in advance with a thin coating of ink.

A bitten-line etching has a characteristically rich diversity of tonal effects and spatial illusions. Owing to the fact that the metal exposed by the lines is eaten back raggedly under the ground to either side as well as straight down, an etching will take on a delicately wavering quality of line which the artist may actually accentuate in his rendering (7.9).

Softer variants of the etching are the soft-ground print and the aquatint, the latter of which consists of tonal areas rather than of lines; its true flavor derives, in fact, from the breadth and flatness of the value-areas and their proportional relations to each other, their contrasts of gleaming white to resonant dark. Color prints can be made in any one of these mediums, moreover, simply by preparing a separate block or plate for each color and impressing each in turn with the intended color on to the paper.

Print Making by Planography

Unlike intaglio with its many variations of medium, planography has only two: metal planography for commercial printing and lithography for both commercial printing and studio print making.† Since its invention toward the end of the eighteenth century lithography has enjoyed a tremendous vogue. In this medium the name "planography" indicates that the forms for transfer to the paper are on

---

* Stanley W. Hayter, *New Ways of Gravure* (New York: Pantheon Books, 1949). Hayter demonstrates and comments in a 16-mm. black and white A. F. Film produced in 1951 by Jess Faley, *A New Way of Gravure* (sound; 12 mins.).

† Bolton Brown, *Lithography for Artists* (Chicago: University of Chicago Press, 1929); and Grant Arnold, *Creative Lithography* (New York: Harper, 1941). Also, the 16-mm. silent black and white film prepared under auspices of the School of the Art Institute of Chicago, *Lithography* (International Film Bureau, 15 mins.)

the same plane with the block, while the name "lithography" (from the Greek *lithos,* meaning "stone"), indicates that the drawing for transfer is made on a block of stone. The block employed is made of a specially smooth limestone quarried in Bavaria in southern Germany, and the drawing is done with a crayon or an ink of grease mixed with carbon. The carbon permits the artist to see what he is doing, but once he has finished his rendering he washes the carbon off with benzine and "etches" (fixes) the remaining grease by applying to it a solution of nitric acid and gum arabic which keeps the grease from spreading beyond the areas originally covered by it.

The subsequent process depends on the fact that grease and water are mutually repellent. When the artist sponges the face of the stone with water, the areas untouched by the grease absorb the water, leaving the greasy areas dry. When he then rolls greasy printer's ink over the stone, the greased areas attract the grease in the ink, leaving the wet areas clear, but releasing the ink when paper is pressed tightly against the stone, by the scraping action of the lithographic press.

Soft crayon rubbed against hard stone assumes a visual effect peculiar to lithography. It registers at once the rigidity of the granular surface and the crumbly response of the crayon to the pressure exerted by the artist's hand. It can squash down into a velvety black or assume a luminous half tone. It can yield strong accents when applied crisply with a pointed end. It lends itself well to broad-stroked hatchings that suggest relief. It leads to boldly massive effects (7.10a).

Print Making by Stencil

A stencil medium calls for a sheet of metal, paper, or fabric perforated or otherwise treated to leave openings through which ink or paint is applied to paper to make the picture. It is not, strictly speaking, a print-making medium, but it is customarily grouped with such mediums and the pictures produced through it do qualify as duplicates.

The stencil medium most in use today is silk-screen print making, or serigraphy (Latin: *sericus,* "silk"). It is the newest of all print-making mediums, having been borrowed as recently as the nineteen-thirties from wallpaper manufacture. It depends for its practicability on the nature of woven silk—open enough in mesh to allow color to be forced through on to paper; fine enough to bring together into coherent areas the globules of color forced through it; strong enough to hold up under repeated squeezings-through of paint and stoppings-out of glue to make the stencil forms.*

The serigrapher starts with a sketch approximating the form of his ultimate print. He lays a screen of tightly stretched silk over this drawing. Since the drawing remains visible through the silk mesh, he is able to select areas suitable for the first application of color, tracing them out on the silk. He removes the drawing, paints the traced areas with a lithographic ink called tusche, and covers the entire screen, tusche and all, with glue. He removes the tusche and with it the glue lying over it, by dissolving the tusche in benzine. Since benzine will not dissolve glue by itself, however, he manages thus to keep the background of glue around these areas intact. He lays a sheet of paper under the silk screen and forces ("squeegees") the color on to it through the open mesh originally covered by the tusche. Using as many sheets as desired, ten or ten thousand (depending on the capacity of his drying racks), he squeegees the same color on to each sheet in turn.

The artist then washes the color out of his screen with benzine, and the glue out of it with water. He reinserts his drawing under the screen, traces off the areas for the second color, and repeats the stenciling for it. He does the same for a third color and a fourth, and so on, until the series of serigraphs is finished.

The most flexible of all print-making mediums, serigraphy permits the use of any color,

* Harry Sternberg, *Silk Screen Color Printing* (New York: McGraw-Hill, 1942); and Harry Shokler, *Artists' Manual for Silk Screen Print Making* (New York: American Artists Group, 1946).

from one end of the spectrum to the other, the use of any vehicle (agent by which to transport a pigment to a support), from opaque varnish to transparent water, and the development of any effect, from overlaying one color with another to stippling and spattering. It can be made to imitate almost any medium. If the artist working with it is inspired by the organic ideal, however, he will resist the temptation to try all possible effects. He will seek to draw from the medium some quality peculiar to it alone. He will recognize, perhaps, how dependent serigraphy is on the stencil, that pattern-making sheet through which color is applied basically in a series of flat areas. He will rest content, therefore, with applications of opaque coloring the texture of which is determined naturally by the silken mesh of the screen. He will respect each application of color through the screen as a distinct step in the process, and will make it register clearly (7.10b).

CASE STUDIES OF ILLUSTRATIONS

Now that we have surveyed the field of illustration and its sister arts of print making, we are ready to follow its artists in a few case studies. We shall see the artists in the process of developing their pictures, relating these pictures to the texts inspiring the pictures, and incorporating such qualities of their mediums as seemed appropriate.

A Feudal Hand Scroll

Our first study has to do with an unknown illustrator of thirteenth-century Japan and the way in which he dealt with the hand scroll and brought that particular format of manuscript to a climax of expressive realization. The Japanese illustrator was commissioned to create a series of emakimonos celebrating a civil war which had ended a little more than half a century before. Two rival clans had struggled for supremacy at the imperial court in Kyōto, and the man commissioning the series was undoubtedly Minamoto no Sanetomo, descendant of the head of the victorious clan.

The Minamoto clan had started the conflict in A.D. 1157 with a night attack on the Sanjō (Third Street) Palace of a retired emperor, the real power behind the throne, who favored the rival Taira clan. In order to kidnap the ruler and force him to shift his favor to their side, the Minamoto forces burned the palace and slaughtered its attendants. Although they succeeded in their initial venture, a Taira counterattack rendered their triumph fleeting. Eventually, however, the Minamoto recovered, overwhelmed and exterminated the Taira clan completely, and established a military dictatorship of Japan called the shogunate.

By the time the artist was commissioned to depict this war, the Minamoto exploits had become fit subject for the tales of ballad-singers and the texts of illustrated hand scrolls. He was following the vogue when he executed, presumably for his shogun patron, a score or more of spirited emakimonos. Of the three which have survived,[7] that in the Museum of Fine Arts in Boston is generally regarded as the best, and it is this particular masterpiece which is illustrated here (7.1 to 7.4). Under the series title of Heiji Monogatari (Tales of the Heiji), this emakimono carries the specific title, "The Burning of the Sanjō Palace."

The scroll begins at the customary right end, unrolling to the left as we examine it. Initial columns of text relate the story as an eyewitness might have told it.* They describe the situation at court, the arrival of the rebels at the Sanjō Palace at about two o'clock in the

[7] See Notes, page 299.
* English translation by Edwin O. Reischauer and Joseph K. Yanagiwa, *Translations from Early Japanese Literature* (Cambridge, Mass.: Harvard University Press, 1951), p. 451. Our account is based jointly on this translation and that by Kojiro Tomita, "The Burning of the Sanjō Palace (Heiji Monogatari): a Japanese Scroll Painting of the Thirteenth Century," *Bulletin of the Museum of Fine Arts*, Boston, October, 1924, pp. 50–55.

7.1. A JAPANESE HAND SCROLL.   a. *The Burning of the Sanjō Palace, A.D. 1157:* Introductory passage, "Crowd rushing toward palace"; emakimono from the *Heiji Monogatari (Tales of Battles of the Heiji Era). c.* 1250. Black ink and gouache on paper. 16¼ x 22′11″. Museum of Fine Arts, Boston.   b. *The Burning of the Sanjō Palace, A.D. 1157:* Intermediate passage, "Crowd meeting attacking force at palace wall." Museum of Fine Arts, Boston.

morning, the routing of the ex-emperor out of bed, the ironic exchange of words, the kidnaping, the firing of the palace, the massacre, and the spread of the news throughout the city, with the ensuing rush of townsfolk to the scene. Here the written account ends, to be briefly resumed at the end of the scroll, where a sequel mentions the burning of another residence the same night and concludes with the comment that the times became so troubled that everyone in Kyōto feared what the morrow might bring.

The painter of the Boston Scroll did his work first, illustrating the story as told in another text and leaving space at the beginning and the end for the calligrapher to fill in later with an abbreviated account. The Japanese collaborators created out of picture and text a coherent and moving unity. What gave them the advantage was the tradition, already centuries old in both China and Japan, that calligraphy is an art equal in importance to the arts of literature and painting and one to be practiced with a like freedom of expression. The Japanese collaborators enjoyed the further advantage of a written language that is pictorially symbolical, a language of variegated strokes written with the same water-color brush as that used in painting (see pp. 259–260).

The creators of the Heiji Scroll made much of their opportunity. In the rhythmic ebb and flow of the balladlike narrative, they found their cue for the structure of both the text and the picture. The calligrapher ended his main passage, before the space where the picture began, with a description of the spread of the news and the rush of the crowd to view the burning palace. The illustrator began his picture with the same incident, introducing it in the relative quiet of two running figures and a hurrying oxcart, but entering quickly on a wavelike massing of figures (7.1a). He drew this passage to an abrupt termination at the wall of the palace garden, where he turned the crowd forward and concluded its movement with the countermovement of a runaway cart (7.1b).

So powerfully did the painter develop a sense of movement through his scroll that it is almost impossible for us Western heirs of Beethoven to disassociate the work from a symphony.* The episode of the hurrying crowd is like the initial movement of a symphony, with its rapid drive through statement, restatement, and development of the major theme (the carriage motive) and the minor themes (men afoot and men on horseback). It is again like a symphony in its interspersed intervals and digressions, such as those along the lower edge of the picture, where groupings of carriages, of townsmen starting to run, and of monks eager to join the fray make repeated entries into the major wave of the movement above it.

That the artist was feeling his way through the painting much as a Western composer feels his way through a symphony, is borne out everywhere. Following the interlude made by the palace wall and the rearguard of rebels, looking cautiously over their shoulders at the onrushing throng, he carries us on into a majestically moving second movement (7.2a). He fits into this movement the scenes of major horror: the abduction of the ex-emperor, the burning of the palace (flame and smoke magnificently painted), and the massacre of the household. He closes the movement, just before the interlude of the rear wall of the palace, with the departing rebels in an incisive broken passage forecasting the third movement (7.2b). This third part, his most boisterous movement, he makes into a climax identical with that of the text: the convoy about the carriage which confines the ex-emperor (7.3a). Here he sets the horses into a merry canter, turns the bows and the long-handled knives upward, and makes the coloring of the armor vibrate. Speedily he swings into his final passage, concluding with a short and vigorous grouping made by the vanguard of the troops (7.3b).

* Analogies to symphonic composition in music were first suggested by Arthur Pope, "Design in Sequence of Time in the So-called Keion Scroll of the Boston Museum," *Art in America,* Vol. II, No. 2 (February, 1914), pp. 101–107.

7.2. a. *The Burning of the Sanjō Palace*, A.D. *1157:* Intermediate passage, "Giving troops orders, burning of palace, and slaughter of occupants." Museum of Fine Arts, Boston. b. *The Burning of the Sanjō Palace*, A.D. *1157:* Intermediate passage, "Departure of attacking force." Museum of Fine Arts, Boston.

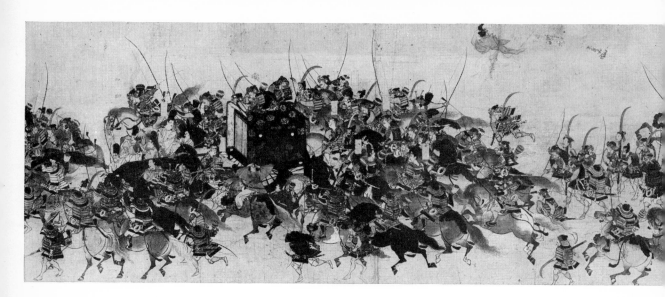

7.3. a. *The Burning of the Sanjō Palace*, A.D. *1157:* Intermediate passage, "Convoy of captive ex-emperor (Go-Shirakawa) and princess." Museum of Fine Arts, Boston. b. *The Burning of the Sanjō Palace*, A.D. *1157:* Concluding passage, "Vanguard of convoy suspecting ambush." Museum of Fine Arts, Boston.

7.4. *The Burning of the Sanjō Palace*, A.D. *1157:* Concluding passage, "Captain of vanguard reining frightened charger, while bodyguard prepares for ambush, detail." Museum of Fine Arts, Boston.

Just like the short commentary of text at the end, the Japanese master bases his concluding passage on a note of triumph that hints at an uneasiness rendering the captain and his bodyguard alerted by expectation of ambush (7.4). The archer sets an arrow to his bow, one soldier draws his sword, and the captain's charger leaps in fright. In this final rendering the artist makes the direct brushwork bespeak the essence of each object represented, delineating wiry muscles, watchful eyes, and warily treading figures. Overlaying the washes, he makes the substance of body color affect the weight and resistance of armor. Against paper elsewhere left untouched, he spots his darks in contrast. The Japanese painter creates thus for his picture a world of its own—shadowless and shadeless (although the attack took place at night) and featureless in landscape, concentrating on the telling of the story.

A Codex Psalter

The ideal of unity of text and illustration also inspired masterpieces in the field of the codex. One such was a book of psalms, called a psalter when produced separately from other books of the Bible. Dating from the ninth century and named after the library of the University of Utrecht in Holland at which it has been preserved for over two hundred years, the Utrecht Psalter accompanies its hundred and fifty psalms with illustrations extraordinary in their variety as in their number.*

The way in which this particular psalter was made typifies the practice of the medieval scriptorium, the studio in which the monastic scribes worked. Ebbo, Archbishop of Reims, needed a psalter for private devotions. He or-

* Reproduced in facsimile and described by E. De-Wald, *The Utrecht Psalter* (Princeton, N. J.: Princeton University Press, n.d.).

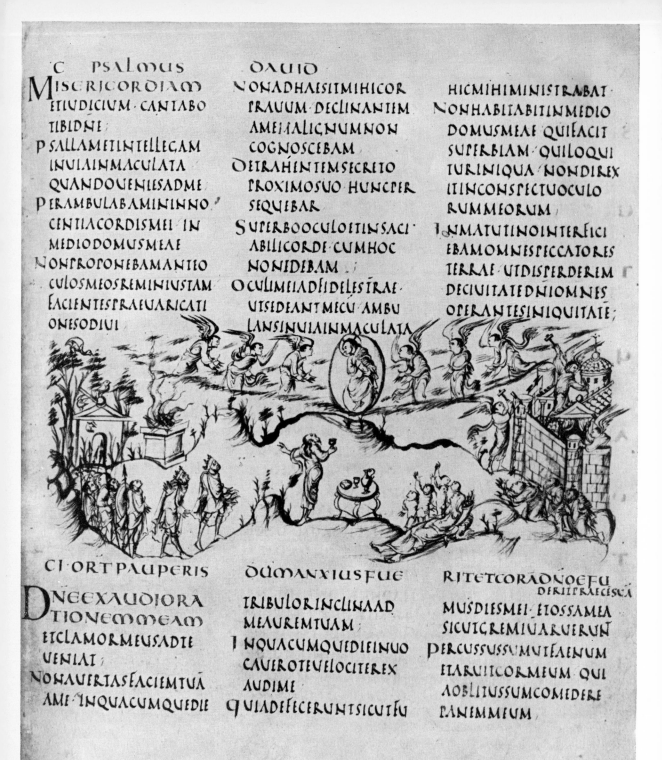

C PSALMUS DAUID
MISERICORDIAM
ETIUDICIUM · CANTABO
TIBIDNE;
PSALLAMETINTELLEGAM
INUIAINMACULATA
QUANDOUENIESADME
PERAMBULABAMININNO
CENTIACORDISMEI IN
MEDIODOMUSMEAE
NONPROPONEBAMANTEO
CULOSMEOSREMINIUSTAM
FACIENTESPRAEUARICATI
ONESODIUI

NONADHAESITMIHICOR
PRAUUM · DECLINANTEM
AMEMALIGNUMNON
COGNOSCEBAM
DETRAHENTEMSECRETO
PROXIMOSUO HUNCPER
SEQUEBAR
SUPERBOOCULOETINSACI
ABILICORDE · CUMHOC
NONEDEBAM
OCULIMEIADFIDELESTRAE ·
UISEDEANTMECU AMBU
LANSINUIAINMACULATA

HICMIHIMINISTRABAT
NONHABITABITINMEDIO
DOMUSMEAE QUIFACIT
SUPERBIAM · QUILOQUI
TURINIQUA NONDIREX
ITINCONSPECTUOCULO
RUMMEORUM
INMATUTINOINTERFICI
EBAMOMNESPECCATORES
TERRAE UTDISPERDEREM
DECIUITATEDNIOMNES
OPERANTESINIQUITATE;

CI ORTPAUPERIS
DNEEXAUDIORA
TIONEMMEAM
ETCLAMORMEUSADTE
UENIAT;
NONAUERTASFACIEMTUA
AME INQUACUMQUEDIE

DUMANXIUSFUE
TRIBULORINCLINAAD
MEAUREMTUAM;
INQUACUMQUEDIEINUO
CAUEROTEUELOCITEREX
AUDIME
QUIADEFECERUNTSICUTFU

RITETCORADNOEFU
DERIITPRAECISCA
MUSDIESMEI · ETOSSAMEA
SICUTCREMIUARUERUN
PERCUSSUSSUMUTFAENUM
ETARUITCORMEUM QUI
AOBLITUSSUMCOMEDERE
PANEMMEUM

7.5. A CAROLINGIAN CODEX. *A Prayer of the Afflicted,* illustration to Psalm 102; page from the Utrecht Psalter, executed in scriptorium of Monastery of Hautvilliers, Reims, under Archbishop Ebbo. A.D. 816–835. Stub quill pen and brown ink on vellum. 13 x 10″. Library, University of Utrecht, Utrecht, Netherlands.

dered it from the father superior of the local abbey, and the abbot in turn put his monks to work producing it. The psalter from which they were to copy was probably itself a copy of a copy of a copy, going back to some ultimate model five hundred years old.

Representative of the quality of the finished work is the page here reproduced (7.5), showing two psalms and the illustration to the second. Although the Roman numeral "CI," written below the space left by the scribe for the illustrator, refers to the number of the psalm in an earlier version, the King James version numbers this as Psalm 102. The details of the picture apply specifically to this psalm, but they represent centuries-old variations introduced by monks in order to break the tedium of their copying.

Since copying by rote inevitably betrays itself, we might expect to detect in the present miniature certain dull transcriptions. Instead, we find a vividness of expression everywhere maintained, and conclude that even where the illuminator borrowed a detail from the older psalter he transmuted it through his own experience. The artist, assigned to a routine job of copying, was a Christian devoting his life to the service of his Order and his Church; he was challenged to manifest his devotion by illustrating an inspired passage of Holy Writ. Such an illustrator could no more hold himself to duplicating another man's picture than he could deny his faith.

If we reread Psalm 102 with something of the freshness of the monk about to illustrate it, we experience something of the poet's power to inspire an illustrator to comparably great creation. We note the Psalmist's enriching figures of speech and wavelike progressions of verse, from prospect of the wretched on earth, crying for deliverance, to concentration of God in heaven, hearkening to their cry. We feel the force of the climax wherein David describes Jehovah's coming to build the city of Zion.

No mere copyist could take such a poem and, within the compass of the few square inches between its words and those of another Psalm, forge its imagery into equally inspired

depiction. The monk at Reims had to relive the psalm itself. He had to create afresh out of his own experience with the poem, with the page of vellum on his desk and the reed pen in his hand. Recognizing as the theme of the poem the give-and-take between David and the Lord, the artist made it the motive for his picture. Taking into account the rectangular shape of the page and its columns, he accentuated the rectangle of his picture.

In response to what we have already determined as the psychological effect conveyed by the path of eye-movement through a picture, the illuminator has induced us to identify ourselves with the heathen and the kings of earth, outcasts who are placed in the intimacy of "our side" of the picture (near the lower left corner) and there made to tremble at the name of God. On past the symbols of his and our wretchedness as enemies hunt for us (the "pelican of the wilderness" and the "sparrow alone upon the house top"), on past the altar of tribulation on which his and our bodies are consumed, the artist draws us to God in the arc of his heaven, attended by angels pressing to hear his words. Then in the psychologically distant right side of the picture he disposes the forms of the future—the ultimate building of the heavenly Jerusalem and the contrastingly anguished but hopeful generations to come, symbolized by an old woman lying at the point of death, with her offspring gathered behind her. The artist leads us finally back to his dominant motive: the figure of the Psalmist standing before his Maker.

Judicious placing of the pictorial allusions to the Psalm would still fall short of organic illustration were it not for the artist's having joined his visual metaphors to expressive rendering. He cut the reed of his pen into the same stub point as the pen of his scribe-collaborator, and wielded it with the same abstractions of line, converting the typically heavy down-strokes, thin upstrokes, and angular breaks of lettering into a pictorially dynamic language. This master of the pen-and-ink medium had to act decisively. He knew that ink on vellum would resist erasures and that he had no way of concealing a mistake. The monk at Reims gathered his powers into every passage, therefore, seeking to catch through varying quality and tempo of strokes the spirit of each thing represented: splintery and retarded for the figures of the awe-stricken kings; scalloped and swirling for the figures of the anxiously eager angels; clear and smoothly flowing for the figure of the Psalmist; and regular and firm for the figure of God. Far from copying, the creator of this picture lifted illustration to the level of great art.

An Album Miniature

It is not often that an artist can so command text and pictures as to make them inseparable. Sometimes, indeed, he does not even try. He sets for himself a goal of decoration only casually related to the text, if at all. He abstracts motives from either literature or reality and renders them so charmingly as to make the book into which they enter more precious as a physical possession than as a repository of poetic or informative writing. He delights the eye but stops short of compelling the reader that absorption in the text demanded by the illustrators of the Boston Scroll and the Utrecht Psalter. He may even treat his illustration as a detached miniature, a small-scaled, easily portable drawing or painting that accompanies no text but goes into a collector's album, ready to be enjoyed for itself along with other separate miniatures.

The illustrators of Safawid Persia and Mogul India in the sixteenth and early seventeenth centuries all worked in this direction. They were encouraged by their religion of Islam. Following the teachings of Mohammed, founder of their faith, they frowned on representational painting as idolatrous but held the written word in awe and set the calligrapher on a pedestal with the greatest of artists, as we have seen Chinese and Japanese doing. Naturally, therefore, the Moslems of Persia and India forsook the art of sculpture, which had always been the foremost art of India, and attached special importance instead to the arts

of the book.* They developed these arts along abstractly decorative lines—to create manuscripts for private enjoyment rather than for public display or religious devotion. They embellished these manuscripts to the utmost so as to make the works precious to the nobles ordering them. That they sometimes succeeded to a remarkable degree is evidenced by the practice of the great Shah Tahmasp II. So passionately devoted was this Persian ruler to his library of manuscripts that he packed it after him on camels whenever he made a journey.

Akbar as Patron of Illustrators

At his capital of Fatehpur Sikri, the Mogul emperor Akbar the Great (1556–1605) provided an Indian counterpart to the Shah. Near his palace in this city Akbar established a great workshop for manuscript production, together with apartments to house his army of bookmaking craftsmen. He assembled from Persia, India, and other countries over a hundred illustrators to collaborate in embellishing manuscripts or making illustrationlike miniatures.

Akbar demanded nothing less than the best from these artists. He held a weekly critique at which the painters were required to present their current works. He commented sharply on the quality of each work and awarded the artist making the miniature judged by him to be the best either a choice gift or a raise in the next month's pay. The emperor looked for sensuous charm of color and line, but he insisted that eye-appeal be undergirded by boldness of execution, perfection of detail, and a touch of that elusive vitality, that "life-movement of the spirit through the rhythm of things," which he himself described as a painter's "peculiar means of recognizing God." †

* Persian illustration is well represented by Laurence Binyon in *The Poems of Nizami* (London: Studio, 1928); and Mogul illustration by Maurice S. Dimand, "Mughal Painting Under Akbar the Great," *The Metropolitan Museum of Art Bulletin*, Vol. XII, No. 2 (October, 1953).
† Dimand, *op. cit.*, p. 48.

7.6. MINIATURE PAINTING. Kham Karan: *Prince Riding on an Elephant*. Probably 1595. Tempera. 8½ x 11⅝". Courtesy of the Metropolitan Museum of Art, New York, Rogers Fund, 1925.

The album miniature reproduced here (7.6) may have been just such a prizewinner at an Akbar review of 1595. Kham Karan, its artist, worked under two old Persian masters who ran the studio. He inclined like them toward the conservative Persian tradition of colorful embellishment. He drew on the usual Persian repertory of floral borders. He painted in the typically Persian medium of tempera which consisted of an emulsion of insect wax and gum arabic; he worked in the Persian manner, distributing patches of brilliant color much as though he were a jeweler studding a crown with precious stones; and he tended to adhere after the Persian fashion to two-dimensional areas.

Kham Karan painted his miniature at a time, however, when Jesuit missionaries were bringing to the Mogul court quantities of European altarpieces, illustrated books, and de-tached engravings. Under an emperor interested in painting as both a factual record and a feast for the eye, the miniaturist could not fail to be impressed by the refinement of detail and the portrait individualism displayed by these Occidental pictures. He adopted a subject certain thus to please the royal critic: a prince, maybe a son of Akbar himself, riding a fiery bull elephant which its keeper guides through a circuslike maneuver, while the bodyguard hangs on at the rear and waves his royal flychaser. The artist made concessions to Western realism when he individualized these three figures and the elephant. He may have made a further concession when he modeled the form of the elephant to suggest its bulk—although in so doing he was also reverting to the Hindu tradition of sculpturelike mass.

Kham Karan at the same time rendered the three figures in the frankly flat and gaily colorful manner of the Persian miniature—to make the elephant seem all the heavier by contrast. He isolated the group in a new manner typical of Akbar's day, setting it against a uniformly yellow background that increased the luminosity of the coloring and sharpened the contours.

Most tellingly of all, the Mogul illustrator composed in terms of the rectangular format of the picture. He tied the rear hoofs of the elephant to the lower edge of the border. He developed forms across space from this point in U-shapes and V-shapes the rhythmic repetition of which suggests the elephant's gait and its keeper's exaggerated leap.

Two Woodcuts

An isolated miniature like Kham Karan's portrayal in tempera satisfied artist and patron as long as it could be valued for its uniqueness and the prince's income remained sufficient for the artist's support. When, however, the patron-prince lost his power and wealth, as eventually he did in both East and West, by economic necessity he withdrew his support, and the artist had to count for livelihood on the patronage of passersby. Unless he chose to starve, the artist had to display eye-catching pictures with popular subjects. He had to offer such pictures at bargain prices, aiming at quantity production and quick turnover to make up for low returns.

With the decline of the aristocrat and the rise of the townsman in Orient as in Occident, print making for the masses came largely to supersede painting for a luxury market. It operated with the wood block, as we have seen, for the publishing of printed books.* It operated also in the production of detached and easily circulable prints. In both the book illustration and the separate picture it specialized in folk tales and the commonplace, and quickly passed from black and white to color for the

sake of sales appeal—with coloring first added by hand, then, in Japan at least, incorporated with the print making itself by the cutting and application of a separate block for each area of a different color.

By the end of the eighteenth century in Japan, middle-class patronage had brought forth a flourishing art of ukiyoye—"floating world picture." † It appealed to pleasure-loving townsfolk to whom the amusements of the aristocracy were barred. Instead of dealing with martial exploits like the Boston Scroll, it dealt with everyday life, the sensuous and sentimental delights of theater, lovers' rendezvous, and house of professional entertainment.

Following a tradition which we have already seen to be distinctive of the Orient—that literature, calligraphy, and painting must function to their mutual advantage as sister arts—a publisher (who often wrote popular songs as well) would initiate a print-making project and supervise the work. He would conceive of a series of pictures featuring the currently celebrated beauty queens, wrestlers, or actors. The publisher would commission a team of artist-craftsmen to make this series for him, a team consisting of designer, block-cutter, and printer.

The designer evolved the composition for each print in the series, carrying it out with brush and ink on a transparent sheet of paper. The block-cutter pasted this paper face down on a block of cherry wood, and proceeded to transfer the design, cutting through the paper and destroying the drawing in the process, but converting it into a wooden relief by gouging the surplus wood away.

From this block the printer struck a series of proofs on each of which the designer could paint in the areas of one particular color. The block-cutter transferred these color layouts to a series of blocks and cut the surplus wood away from each color area. The printer struck the designated color from each block in turn on to a sheet of soft mulberry-bark paper

* For the wood-block print as a form of illustration in Japan, see Louise Norton Brown, *Block Printing and Book Illustration in Japan* (New York: E. P. Dutton, 1924).

† James A. Michener has written a soundly critical and readable study, *The Floating World* (New York: Random House, 1954).

dampened for the purpose. He used colors thickened with rice paste for the printing. He applied them with a stiff-bristled brush, exerting pressure not with the Western type of press but with a bamboo-leaf pad, called a baren, which he rubbed and rocked across the back of the paper against the block.

Since the success of the enterprise depended on collaboration, each contributor had to adjust his own work to that of the others, designing for it and working effectively in it. It was inevitable, therefore, that their joint product should have become an organically expressive print, with a close adherence to the feel of both the medium and the subject.

Hiroshige's art * belongs to this collaborative kind of enterprise. Its production gained popularity among common folk in its own homeland; and it became so generally sought after and admired in the West at the end of the nineteenth century as to affect the course of Western art.

Utagawa Hiroshige was a print maker for forty-six years and during that time designed no less than 5,460 prints—more than all other print makers combined for two centuries. Born into a society restless under Tokugawa dictatorship, Hiroshige grew up with a wanderlust that he shared with his generation. He left diaries of his travels, and from the fragments which have survived we learn how zestfully he approached new scenery, appreciating it with the same hearty sensuousness with which he appreciated good lodging, food, and drink. Born into a family of hereditary firemen, Hiroshige himself served as fireman until the art of print making, which he learned between fires, so drew him that he turned his job over to a relative and devoted himself to the life of an ukiyoye designer. He brought to his print making of landscape a large fund of personal experience. He saw with new eyes the changes

of the seasons and the states of the weather, the subtleties of lighting by night as by day; with true genius he translated such effects to his prints. Hiroshige sought to stimulate sales by making sets of prints in preference to individual ones. Drawing on the Oriental predilection for classifying natural views, he found in ancient Chinese poetry the idea of developing sets around eight standard views of nature at its loveliest: (1) Evening Snow, (2) Full Moon in Autumn Twilight, (3) Evening Rain, (4) Temple Bells at Evening, (5) Boats Returning to Harbor, (6) Geese Flying Home, (7) Sunset, and (8) Clearing Skies at Evening after Storm. Applying these views with variations to certain specific localities, Hiroshige managed to create some of his most celebrated series: *Eight Views of Lake Biwa,* for example, or *Eight Views in the Neighborhood of Edo.*

The last-named set was commissioned by a poet desiring gift sets for his friends. This poet wrote a poem of four lines for each subject, a poem which Hiroshige had his block-cutter introduce into its proper composition. When the gift prints had all been distributed, the artist gained the poet's consent to issue a second edition (in each print of which only the first line of the accompanying poem appeared).

In the print from the later edition selected for illustration (7.7), the first line of the poem not only gives the title to the composition; it incorporates itself with the lines of the key block. "Asukayama bosetsu" it reads, meaning simply "Asukayama evening snow"; and with the same terse directness of statement Hiroshige rendered the scene, counting on overtones of familiar suggestion to make the print appeal to the average Japanese. Asukayama was a hill famed for the cherry trees which grew on its slopes, a hill to which crowds repaired every spring to celebrate the blossoming. They sat on benches in front of the teahouses at the foot of the hill, sipping their tea and eating their lunches as they absorbed the glory of the scene.

Instead of obvious illustration of the blossom-viewing festival, Hiroshige chose something more subtle to represent the scene under

* The best references on Hiroshige are Sei-ichiro Takahashi (Charles S. Terry, Eng. adapt.) *Ando Hiroshige* ("Kodansha Library of Japanese Art," No. 3; Rutland, Vt.: Charles E. Tuttle, 1956); Yone Noguchi, *Hiroshige* (2 vols.; London: Kegan Paul, French, Trubner, 1940); and Edward F. Strange, *The Colour-prints of Hiroshige* (New York: Frederick A. Stokes, n.d.).

7.7. Utagawa Hiroshige (1797–1848): *Evening Snowfall at Asukayama, near Edo,* sixth print in the series, "Eight Views of the Neighborhood of Edo." *c.* 1838. Woodblock print in black, white, and blue. *c.* 9 x *c.* 14". Courtesy of the Metropolitan Museum of Art, New York, Rogers Fund, 1936.

a winter's snowfall. He created poetic analogies which every Japanese would grasp: snowflakes like falling petals, snowdrifts like banks of blossoms. He created poetic contrasts no less easily understood: cold air, heavy snow, and a few lone wayfarers seeking shelter, as opposed to mild air of spring, harvest of fallen blossoms, and multitudes of viewers. He played in this way with a mood of gentle melancholy, a symbolism of fleeting life and the hush of death.

Hiroshige was fond of snow scenes, and he knew how to interpret them simply. Here, for instance, he reduced his coloring to the point at which only two blocks would be required beyond the key block: one block for the blue in gentle modulations, the other block for the masses of snow, masses which he had his printer blend softly here and there into the bluish tones of shadow and partly hidden earth.

The artist drew the few huddled figures of the landscape close to the spectator's corner, as though inviting us to shiver with them in the cold. He squeezed the houses and road against the left edge of the picture and made the mass of the hill there pinch them narrowly. He managed thus to convey a feeling of nature's resistance to the petty ways of man. Then, in contrast to the drooping figures and over-burdened horse, he rendered the trees in spirited upward thrusts against their pads of snow—as though they enjoyed in these same white cushionings a foretaste of the blossoms which they would later sport.

The Japanese color print has influenced Western art profoundly, has even evoked a corresponding school of the color wood block. It has never supplanted, especially in Germany, however, a traditional art of wood-block print making in black and white. This German art

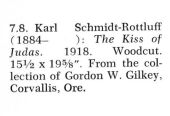

7.8. Karl Schmidt-Rottluff (1884–): *The Kiss of Judas.* 1918. Woodcut. 15½ x 19⅝". From the collection of Gordon W. Gilkey, Corvallis, Ore.

was traditionally linear in emphasis, but it underwent in the early twentieth century a sweeping transformation. It became a new type of print making with large-scaled areas of black into which "white lines" were engraved and about which heavy bands of shading were cut in relief. It achieved through such a technique at times a force of expression rarely equaled by other mediums.

Consider, for example, a wood block cut in 1918 by Karl Schmidt-Rottluff, *Kiss of Judas* (7.8).* Created by the German master at the critical moment of collapse before the Allied armies, it bore special meaning to the artist and his public. Amid their disillusionments, with the Kaiser fleeing and his officers surrendering, the print offered solace of reference to a corresponding betrayal in the life of Christ —His betrayal by the kiss of Judas.

Sensing the timeliness of the theme, Schmidt-Rottluff gave it intense treatment, developing forms to which the wood block seems itself to have responded with a certain in-

evitable air. The artist found his cue for the lighting of his picture in the play of highlights and shadows cast by the torches of the mob. Unlike many who had illustrated the scene before him, he avoided the distractions of the garden and the crowd. He focused on the heads of the two protagonists, magnifying them until they dominated the block. He concentrated on the eyes of these two heads, counting on them to convey the psychological tensions of the story. Judas's eye in profile he rendered half closed, covert in expression, the eyes of Jesus staring in mingled rebuke and sorrow. By placing Judas's head toward the familiar left corner, he suggested our sharing in the traitor's guilt; by placing Jesus's head at the termination of the path of eye-movement through the picture he made the impact of divine judgment fall on us as on Judas.

How effectively forces seem to have converged to produce the forms of this woodcut! In the schematized and flattened planes of the print, in its interpenetrating solids and voids, we detect the workings of gouges on the block, the total participation of the artist's imagination in the story illustrated. Though not commissioned for a book, Karl Schmidt-Rottluff's *Kiss of Judas* constitutes illustration at its best.

* For Karl Schmidt-Rottluff, see Joan Knobloch, "Berlin's Post-Naturalist-Revival," *Studio,* Vol. CXXXVIII (December, 1949), pp. 166–171, and the color reproduction accompanying the review, "Outburst of Art," *Life,* Vol. XXXVI (May 10, 1954), pp. 43–46.

7.9. Rembrandt van Rijn (1606–1669): *The Raising of Lazarus.* 1642. Etching. 5¾ x 4½″. Courtesy of the British Museum, London.

A Biblical Etching

As Schmidt-Rottluff exploited the possibilities of the wood block, so Rembrandt mastered the techniques of etching.* He learned to make the etched line tell the story, creating through its intricate development an illusory depth of space in which the story's action could take place. He perfected gestures of hand and body,

expressions of face, and touches of environment best calculated to enliven the story. Although Rembrandt never published his prints as book illustrations but offered them for sale solely as individual pictures, he effectively retained the character of his etchings as illustrations to literature, above all as illustrations to the Bible, which he knew by heart and drew on repeatedly for making prints.

Let us consider, for example, *The Raising of Lazarus* (7.9), an etching created by Rembrandt at the height of his career. The print derives its subject from Chapter 11 of the Gospel according to St. John, where one of

* Facsimiles of Rembrandt's etchings are published in Jaro Springer, ed., *Complete Etchings of Rembrandt* (3 vols.; New York: E. Weyhe, n.d.). A good critical study is that by Jakob Rosenberg, *Rembrandt* (2 vols.; Cambridge, Mass.: Harvard University Press, 1948), Vol. I, pp. 99–145, 204–210.

Jesus's miracles is described. The etching dwells, with a tenderness equaling the text's, upon the climax of the story. Jesus on his return to Bethany heard that his devoted friend, Lazarus, had died. Sharing in the grief of Lazarus's sisters but resolved to restore the man to life, the Master accompanied the sisters to the tomb. There he called on Lazarus to come forth from the tomb. The dead man came forth, bound hand and foot with graveclothes but speedily at Jesus's command released from their confinement.

Apart from fidelity to the story, the etching employs purely pictorial means to convey the story's appeal. The print presents the space before the cave as something removed from the everyday environment shown in the background. Through its disposal of the crowd to the lower left, where we imagine ourselves stationed, it invites us to share in beholding the miracle. Part way back to the right, it confronts us with Jesus, standing, so to speak, as a connecting link between the present life and the life beyond, while it represents Lazarus as rising from the tomb at the very spot psychologically most remote from us in the spacing of the picture. The etching profits thus by the artist's calculations to make the spaces in the reversal of the print give the true effect.

The etching further profits by the artist's response to the feel of the needle cutting through the ground on the surface of his plate. Its exhilaratingly free effect reflects the ease with which the lines were scratched and the rapidity with which the acid baths deepened and spread the lines. The very facility of the rendering with the needle might have lured the artist into overworking his picture, but Rembrandt held himself to an economy of means. Against the anticipated whiteness of the paper he made his lines move searchingly around the objects and fade into depth, but always with that rhythmic waver characteristic of an etching at its best—a deliberately expressive waver which accentuates the irregular bite of the mordant and weds the form to this graphic recount of an extraordinary miracle.

A Lithographic Cartoon

Even as Rembrandt utilized the subtle effects natural to etching to vivify a Bible story, the French print maker Honoré Daumier exploited the lugubrious darks of lithography to register his protests against injustice. This mid-nineteenth-century master found in the new medium of planography his happiest outlet for political expression. He perfected it as a source for the forms of his most characteristic creations. When he discovered its artistic possibilities, lithography had already evoked a whole new profession of printer-lithographers, men trained to reproduce commercially drawings handed them. By his choice of medium Daumier surrendered himself to the growing specialization that was divorcing craftsman from designer, but he assured himself employment at the same time as an illustrator for actual publications.

Thanks to his relations with a publisher of an illustrated journal devoted to political satire, Daumier came to specialize in cartooning. Cartooning had been practiced for many centuries, but Daumier in his work for the periodical *La Caricature* evolved out of it a novel form of journalism. Since the weekly championed new Republican ideals of liberty, equality, and fraternity against the attacks of King Louis Philippe, Daumier was asked to supplement his employer's editorials with cartoons calculated to heighten the indignation they evoked. These cartoons Daumier made so tellingly simple and direct that he attracted the unfavorable attention of the government itself. For a cartoon of 1832, indeed, one caricaturing the king as a monster swallowing the bribes of his ministers and disgorging commissions in return, Daumier was sentenced to six months in jail.

Undaunted by his punishment, Daumier resumed his cartooning attacks with even greater bitterness after his release. On April 15, 1834, military police of Paris, excited by rioting against the king, mistook for rioters certain passersby seeking shelter in the janitor's lodgings of an apartment building at 12 *rue Transnonain*, and slaughtered them all, including

7.10. LITHOGRAPH AND SERIGRAPH. a. Honoré Daumier (1808–1879): *No. 12 Rue Transnonain, April 15, 1834.* 1834. Lithograph. 11⅛ x 17³⁄₁₆″. Courtesy of the British Museum, London. b. Robert Gwathmey (1903–   ): *Share Croppers.* 1936. Serigraph in 7 opaque colors, printed with 10 tusche stencils. 14½ x 12″. Courtesy of the artist.

the janitor and his children. Daumier's cartoon memorializing this atrocity the editor of *La Caricature* published not only in his weekly but also as a separate print for sale to the indignant citizenry. People lined up before the windows of shops where the print was being sold, merely to get a glimpse. The police stopped the sale, of course, and soon afterward, with enactment of necessary legislation, put an end to the publication.

But his *No. 12 rue Transnonain, April 15, 1834* remains one of the best of Daumier's cartoons, a poignant expression of the artist's sympathy with his subject and his feeling for stone and crayon (7.10a). Beside the bed and the overturned chair, still in the nightshirt in which he was surprised, the janitor lies dead. Beneath him lies a baby, while into the shadows on either side the other victims extend. The expressive simplifications by which humorous effects are gained in caricature have been employed here for just the opposite effect: one of starkest tragedy. The foreshortened figure of the janitor has been made the type of outraged humanity, and everything around him has been expanded into monumental masses of epic proportion.

The rendering of the print accords with its theme. As pure lithography the middle tones of the composition scintillate, its modelings project in clearly crosshatched strokes, its darks recede in resonant, smooth accents. But through all such passages, unyielding as the grimness of the reality portrayed, the grain of the stone persists.[8]

A Contemporary Serigraph

When in the early nineteen-forties Robert Gwathmey turned to the art of silk-screen printing, he came to pioneer in serigraphy as Daumier a century earlier had pioneered in lithography. Gwathmey had just returned from a year as sharecropper on a tobacco farm. Though born and reared in Virginia, he had not previously appreciated the lot of this impoverished segment in Southern society. Stirred

[8] See Notes, page 299.

by what he saw, he created, like Daumier, a print making of protest, but through the silk screen medium rather than the stone.

One of Gwathmey's resulting serigraphs is *Share Cropper* (7.10b). In the master drawing for it the artist sought forms peculiar both to the silk-screen process and to his conception of the sharecropper as a type. He began by representing a man and his wife hoeing in a field, a study which he progressively simplified in subsequent versions until at length he felt ready to undertake his print.*

When he turned to the stenciling itself, he responded to the medium with a still closer approach to his original aim. Through his initial stencils he filled the largest areas: the mass of earth and the unbroken expanse of sky. He found in them the true motive for his picture, since against the monotony of these background areas the figures stood out in silhouette, white, flat, and shadowless, in their tottering attitudes the epitome of a precarious existence. He was careful to preserve this dominating motive, adding with the eight stencils that followed only the sparsest of incidents: a band of dark green to cover the overlapping of earth and sky; notes of Negroid flesh, blue overalls, yellow hose; finishing touches with a broken line prompted both by the unsteady action of the figures and by the mesh of the screen itself. Gwathmey in his simplifications gave his print the superficial effect of a poster, but through the social significance which he packed into it he carried his serigraph beyond any work fashioned merely for the moment.

The full impact of the Gwathmey print depends upon the color which our reproduction can only suggest. Only by chromatic contrasts, in fact, can the bleakness of the sharecropper's prospect and the pain of his struggle be felt. If the print had been conceived in black and white, the lack of color would have called for a compensating stress on line or value or texture, and a different picture would have resulted.

* The simplifying process is described for a comparable print by Gwathmey in his article, "Serigraphy," *American Artist*, Vol. IX, No. 10 (December, 1945), pp. 8–11. See also Elizabeth McCausland, "Robert Gwathmey," *Magazine of Art*, Vol. XXXIX, No. 4 (April, 1946), pp. 148–152.

ILLUSTRATING FOR MASS PUBLICATION

The quality of a photomechanical reproduction, like the quality of a print, one replica among many, does not need to be affected by its rarity. If well-designed for the process and clearly printed, it is bound to be good, whether belonging to an edition of ten or ten thousand. Only deterioration of printing surface under wear and tear of process can work to the detriment of the print or reproduction, and competent craftsmen know when to destroy the block or plate so that no further prints can be struck from it. Since a zinc plate "tires" easily, editions of etchings have to be severely limited in number. Since a wood block is sturdy, editions of woodcuts can run up to a hundred or more. And since a lithographic stone for a time actually improves with use, editions of lithographs can sometimes number thousands.

Even in regard to size of edition, therefore, every medium of print making or reproduction has its frame of reference. We refer to this when we criticize the picture and even insist, if we are purists, that its bounds be not transgressed. We ask that a woodcut stand out as pure relief, an etching as pure intaglio, a lithograph as pure planography, a serigraph as pure stencil.

The Organic Ideal in Book Design

We have explained how an illustration can evolve out of the nature of the story, of the book containing the story, and of the medium employed in its rendering. It is also influenced by the photomechanical process followed in making the reproduction for a published illustration. Such an illustration can be made as expressive as a manuscript illumination or a print.

The illustrations of Howard Pyle are a case in point. When we take into account the book of fiction into which they went, its special nature and format, any hint of mere embellishment or emotional exaggeration falls away, leaving bedrock integrity of form.

Under organic inspiration an illustrator might write his text as well as draw for it. Occasionally a versatile artist has distinguished himself in this double capacity. Howard Pyle was one such author-illustrator. He entered sympathetically into the publishing processes involved and designed exclusively for them. He conceived of text and pictures as one, even as the Japanese their house and garden, neither complete without the other.

For a volume of fairy tales, for example, the American author-illustrator achieved this level of super-unity in both text and pictures. In this volume Pyle gave to each hour of day and night, as implied by his title of *The Wonder Clock*, a story of his own invention.* He prefaced each story with a page announcing the hour for it, and he accompanied his announcement with an appropriate nursery rhyme, composed by his wife and hand-lettered and decorated by himself. He then carried his own text and drawings on into the story, paralleling the rhythmic ebb and flow of the narrative with alternations in size of picture: head-piece and initial letter, and full-page and half-page illustrations in sequence.

What the artist advised his students to do,† he did himself in his own writing and designing. He identified himself with his story, projecting lusty vitality into both text and illustrations. He subjected himself to the discipline of the composition of the whole. He gave to the narrative a properly quaint Old English flavor and to the illustrating its correspondingly reminiscent treatment of a romantic past in which anything could happen. Again in keeping with the typography, legible but Gothic in derivation, he perfected a pen line at once functionally reproducible (completely black) against white areas of paper kept scrupulously

* Howard Pyle, *The Wonder Clock; or, Four and Twenty Marvelous Tales, Being One for Each Hour of the Day* (New York: Harper & Brothers, 1887 and 1915).
† Henry C. Pitz, "Howard Pyle: Father of American Illustration," *American Artist*, Vol. XV, No. 10 (December, 1951), pp. 44–47, 81–83.

The three share the money amongst them.

7.11. Pen and Ink Illus-
tration. a. Howard Pyle
(1853–1911): *The Three
Share the Money amongst
Them;* illustration to "Story
for Five O'Clock: The Simpleton and His Little Black
Hen," *The Wonder Clock*
(New York: Harper &
Brothers, 1887). Page, 7³⁄₁₀ x
5²⁄₅"; original reproduction,
3¹⁄₁₀ x 4". Courtesy of Anne
Poole Pyle and Harper &
Brothers. b. Fritz Kredel
(1900–   ): *They Fought
with the Fury of the Lions
. . .;* preliminary study.
1944. Pen and ink on paper.
3 x 4". Courtesy of the artist.

clean and functionally expressive of subject.

So flavorful is each tale in *The Wonder Clock*, so much a part of it the accompanying set of illustrations, that one is at a loss to choose from context any single picture to represent the whole. Selected thus at random, the illustration here reproduced (7.11a) comes from the Five O'Clock Afternoon tale, "The Simpleton and His Little Black Hen." It tells about the dunce called Caspar; how in his very stupidity he outwitted his two clever, grasping brothers and their fellow-rascal friend.

When Howard Pyle came to illustrate the story of Caspar, he faced a subtle task which he had created for himself in his writing, the task of making Caspar look characteristically witless and his companions contrastingly shrewd and practical but ridiculous in their frantic zeal to turn everything to their own account. How well the artist succeeded at his task is shown in the half-page cut here illustrated. Pyle depicted Caspar sprawling on the grass at the roadside, dumfounded by his companions' behavior as they struggle to wrest from each other the treasure which he himself had found hidden in a tree.

The artist made his rendering bespeak the psychological states involved. He drew Caspar's figure in thin and wavery lines as though themselves affected by the simpleton's uncertainties in a practical world. He characterized the other three figures with lines heavily shaded and blunt, moving boldly but nonetheless limitedly. Pyle further accentuated these contrasts in character by grouping the three rogues together with a tree gnarled and twisted like themselves, in such fashion that they seem all the heavier and more earthy— lifting Caspar against a background field of grass as though he were on the short end of a seesaw.

The illustrator designed his picture for the very spot where it eventually appeared—the upper half of the right-hand page. Since the reader looks habitually upward from the bottom edge of the page and rightward from the spectator's corner, he sees an actual scene in this position much as Pyle conceived his illustration. Pyle gave the landscape background a low horizon line and the figures a foreshortening to accord with this point of view.

The designer further recognized our habits of looking from left to right and from a position below the lower margin of the pages when he placed the illustration on the right-hand page rather than on the left. He could have chosen the incident for illustration from a passage farther on in the text; as previously remarked, such would have been an orthodox procedure. Instead, he chose an incident already passed—with an idea that browsing in a book of fairy tales means looking at pictures first and only later reading snatches of the text. Through the appeal of the illustration he aimed so to arouse the browser's curiosity that the prospective reader would turn back to the passage referred to, either for a first reading or for a more careful rereading. Even in placing his picture with reference to his text, therefore, Howard Pyle encouraged that leisurely, reminiscent, and fancy-free approach that he wanted the reader to make to the whole production.

In regard to the relationship between text and illustration, let us consider, for another example, the illustrative work of Fritz Kredel, a contemporary German-American artist. His pictures are so much a part of the book for which they were designed as to seem fragments if separately considered. Unlike Pyle, he did not write the texts himself. But when commissioned by the Peter Pauper Press to illustrate its projected new edition of Voltaire's *Candide*,* Kredel entered wholeheartedly into the undertaking. He collaborated with editor, typographer, and binder to create an entity which would not just revive the original edition but which would effect a synthesis of the eighteenth-century novel with the modern visual forms inspired by it.

The artist began like Pyle by steeping himself in the work to be illustrated. He projected himself into all the lore of Voltaire: the au-

---

* J. F. M. A. de Voltaire, *Candide, or: The Optimist* (Mount Vernon, N. Y.: Peter Pauper Press, 1944; 1st ed. in French, 1759).

fore our arrival in Morocco! But let that pass; these things are so common that they are not worth mentioning.

Morocco was swimming in blood when we arrived. The fifty sons of the Emperor Muley Ismael had each a faction; and this produced fifty civil wars, of blacks against blacks, browns against browns, mulattoes against mulattoes. There was continual carnage throughout the whole extent of the empire.

Scarcely had we landed when the blacks of a party hostile to that of my pirate arrived with the purpose of depriving him of his booty. After the diamonds

7.12. Fritz Kredel: *They Fought with the Fury of the Lions, Tigers and Serpents of the Country to Determine Who Should Have Us;* illustration incorporated with page of text in Baskerville type, J. F. M. A. de Voltaire, *Candide* (Mt. Vernon, N. Y., Peter Pauper Press, 1944). Page, 9¾ x 6¼". Courtesy of Peter Pauper Press.

thor's life and times; the circumstances leading to the writing of *Candide;* the flavor of its expression in the original French and the need for illustration to help retain its vitality when couched in the less vivacious forms of English.

How completely Fritz Kredel made his illustrations a part of the book only the whole volume of the Peter Pauper edition of *Candide* can disclose. But a representative page can give some idea, a page like that on which one of the illustrations occurs to accompany the Old Woman's Story, Chapter XI, page 47 (7.12). The Old Woman is telling how as a beautiful girl of fifteen she and her mother, the Princess of Palestrina, were on a sea voyage captured by pirates and taken as slaves to be sold in Morocco. Upon their arrival, a hostile party of Moors wrested the women away from the pirates and then fell to fighting among themselves for individual possession. The daughter was saved miraculously, but she witnessed her mother, each leg and arm grasped by a Moor, hacked to pieces as the Moors fought each other to death.

Kredel chose for illustration of this passage in the story the incident of the fight over the mother; he planned it to appear toward the bottom of the page preceding the recountal. He aimed in this way to increase the reader's zest to continue with the text. In keeping with such intent, he merely suggested the scene, subordinating his illustration to the author's novel but seeking by his manner of rendering to catch the spirit of the tale. He managed to parallel the dashing momentum of the narrative with a lightly swirling line and a flickering play of darks. He found in the eighteenth-century paintings of Voltaire's contemporaries his precedent for this effect, but instead of trying to revive an eighteenth-century style he developed a new rendering of his own—one akin to it in spirit but with the scribblelike curves of a modern manner.

The illustrator developed this seemingly casual rendering through a series of preliminary versions, the first relatively stiff and factual (7.11b), those which followed progressively freer and more forceful.* With a view to the illustration to be printed ultimately from the photoengraving, Kredel made his final drawing twice as large as the reproduction to be, thus facilitating a gain in sharpness through the reduction later made by the camera, but maintaining nonetheless consistently a firmness of line throughout. Whatever rendering would have seemed to the outsider so slight and sketchily incomplete in this drawing as to debar it from exhibition as a finished work in itself, the illustrator allowed of no concern. He had alone in mind the illustration to one particular passage in one particular book. This he created, and its vitality when viewed in its context is the measure of his success.

Cartoons and Comic Strips for Newspapers

Voltaire's *Candide* was nearly two hundred years old when Kredel undertook its illustration. By comical exaggeration like that devoted to portraying the ferocity of Moors, the artist managed nonetheless to recapture the spirit of the satire of another day. Kredel's very exaggeration of rendering brought his drawing, moreover, to the threshold of the sister arts of caricaturing and cartooning.

There was a time when a cartoon (from the Latin *charta*, "paper") meant a drawing made full-scale on paper to serve as model for a painting (see pp. 252 *ff.*). It came by extension to include a drawing made for reproduction in a periodical—a picture featuring, usually with a touch of humor, some event or person in the news. It came in the form of this extended meaning to be used either in place of an editorial or as an accompaniment.†

Cartoonists have always recognized the crucial importance of that principle of emphasis to which we have repeatedly referred. They develop essentials in the tersest and simplest language of vision. Seeking the most economi-

* A process confirmed by the artist in a personal letter to the author, March 20, 1952. See also Norman Kent, "Fritz Kredel: Master Xylographer," *American Artist,* Vol. X, No. 5 (May, 1946), pp. 19–22, 38.
† A study of cartooning from the journalist's point of view: Dick Spencer III, *Editorial Cartooning* (Ames, Iowa: Iowa State College Press, 1949).

cal of statements, they adopt any device facilitating speedy identification and understanding. They invent and repeat such allegorical symbols, for example, as the Democratic donkey and Republican elephant.[9]

Cartoonists have usually resorted to caricature to heighten the impact of their drawings. As illustrated by line drawings for our first chapter (1.3b, and 1.4a), a caricature is an exaggerated portrayal of the characteristics peculiar to a human individual or type. It originates in an emotional situation, but becomes good only when based on physical characteristics already present to a certain extent in the given subject. Only then can it evoke an emotional response akin to that inspiring it in the first place, and draw on a common fund of observation and experience making it speak a universal language. When founded in reality, it can at the hands of a master cartoonist become a powerful instrument.

Cartoons are usually expected to arouse laughter. They do not need to amuse, however. Like George Grosz's drawing of survivors on a battlefield (1.4a), cartoons can be deadly serious. They can rouse people either to impassioned defense of a cause or violent attack on it. They can even spurn all caricature whatsoever, dwelling on starkly realistic representation so compellingly that a government under the cartoonist's attack is moved in self-defense to suppress the newspaper publishing his cartoons (7.10a). Cartoons have actually written history, shaped its course of events.*

One extension of the art of cartooning came around the turn of the present century to embrace the comic strip. Like the development of the fictional film out of primitive cinema, the comic strip emerged out of cartooning as a type of narrative. Like the hand scroll, it tells its story through a series of scenes in which the characters and their settings recur. It tells its tale in a succession of boxes strung out across the page.

In its brief career, the comic strip has become distinguished as the most popular type of art ever invented, more popular even than the motion picture. It has entered the fabric of our culture, won daily followers by the millions, influenced styles of dress, introduced new words and phrases into the language, and outdone the classroom in advancing education. The "funnies" have indeed played a key role in contemporary life.

Among the multitudes of strips which we now encounter, how can we tell a good comic strip from a bad one? We can apply standards operating in all of the arts, look for adherence to principles of design (see Chapter 2). We can watch for expressive employment of elements, especially elements of line and area (see Chapter 1). We can judge the composition in each box and consider its relationships to the composition of the strip as a whole. But we need further to note features peculiar to this branch of the illustrative art.† We need to distinguish first of all between the two components of a comic strip: the *visual*, consisting of delineations and groupings of figures and settings, and the *literary*, consisting of the story-line or plot, of captions lettered in each box or sayings lettered in the balloons emerging from the mouths of the characters.

Whether in terms of sheer fantasy, like *Krazy Kat* (7.13a), or in terms of everyday reality, like *Gasoline Alley*, a comic strip usually tells its story with the aid of a literary accompaniment. It may, like *King Aroo*, divert attention from its impoverished drawing by heightening the suspense of its verbal narration. It may, like Mik's *Ferd'nand*, dispense with text entirely and count on pictures alone. *Ferd'nand* has to be studied for its meanings, to be sure; sometimes the meanings elude the search, but the picture-puzzle appeal is effective and the drawing more than adequate for the purpose. Under the test of pictorial emphasis, *Ferd'nand* passes but *King Aroo* fails. Under the same test Gustavo Arriola's *Gordo*,

[9] See Notes, page 299.
* See, for example, Allan Nevins and Frank Weitenkampf, *A Century of Political Cartoons: Caricature in the United States from 1800 to 1900* (New York: Charles Scribner's Sons, 1944).

† Criticism along lines here laid down is in Coulton Waugh, *The Comics* (New York: Macmillan, 1947).

7.13. FUSED SPACE-TIME IN COMIC STRIP AND PHOTOGRAPHIC AD. a. George Herriman (1881?–1944): *Krazy Kat:* "Scratching Mother Earth's Back." Comic strip in pen and ink as it appeared in *The Oregon Daily Journal* (Portland, Ore.), April 15, 1930. Courtesy of International Feature Service, Inc. b. Herbert Matter (1907–): *4-Story Groceries?;* stroboscopic multiple-exposure photograph. 1942. 12⅝ x 10⅜". Courtesy of Container Corporation of America.

approaches an ideal relationship between drawing and caption.

A good cartoonist dresses his plot in appropriate clothing. He determines every line, area, and tone to meet the story's needs. He makes each element play its part with utmost economy. He spots every dark with reference to the lights. He avoids third-dimensional illusion and makes all flat areas conform to the simplified physical character of the boxes in the strip. He renders the given character in each box with the proper expression. He cultivates a personal style and holds to it consistently: he makes this style as readily identifiable as the appearance of a friend.

When subjected to the test of such special criteria, comic strips fare variously. *Gasoline Alley* claims effective spotting and competent delineation, for example, but it exerts its appeal through the story more than through the drawing. *Dick Tracy* has a tight, well-defined style of its own, but every form is reduced to a hard wooden outline curtailing its expressiveness. *Terry and the Pirates* borrows movie techniques of long-shots, close-ups, angle shots, and the like; it introduced characters drawn from posed models and details carefully studied from life; it once composed well but later came to suffer from confusion of spotting. *Joe Palooka* stands out for beautiful arrangements of black, white, and gray, of spotting in the darks; its faces are expressively animated, its figures move easily, and its pictures carry the bulk of the story.

An outstanding example of masterful fusion of story and visualization occurs in George Herriman's *Krazy Kat*.[10] This comic ceased in 1944 when its creator died, but it lives on in the files of old newspapers, because of a timelessness of appeal born of its very timeliness. Thanks to unexpected twists of narration and lunatic fantasies traceable to subconscious motivation, Herriman's *Krazy Kat* has staying qualities in all 10,000 of its separate issues.

When in 1913 Herriman christened his new-born strip *Krazy Kat*, Freudian psychology along with concepts of time and space that

[10] See Notes, page 299.

were revolutionizing every sphere of design, was invading the arts. Out of a dream world tapped by the subconscious the cartoonist was evolving entirely new creatures, beings which shared certain traits with men and animals but which lived nowhere but in their master's fancy and the strip itself.

Krazy Kat went through many adventures, some lasting many weeks. But the theme underlying every issue of the strip was the Kat's inextinguishable affection for Ignatz Mice. Married to an attractive female mouse, Ignatz was a confirmed realist who loathed the dreamy, philosophical Kat and who at every slightest pretext "creased the Kat's bean with a brick." By a feat of subconscious race-memory Krazy Kat resurrected out of ancient Egypt the idea that being hit by a brick meant that the heaver of the brick really loved his victim and was trying in this way to show his love. Always, as the impact of the brick on the back of her head sent Krazy Kat flying through space, under her illusion she passed out blissfully.

In every issue of his comic strip Herriman proved his powers as a writer. He developed a whole new language peculiar to the creatures of his strip, a sort of "hog-Elizabethan" exemplified in our reproduction (7.13a). He couched the spelling of this jargon on sounds which might have been uttered by someone with his mouth full of potatoes. He took liberties with figures of speech, with double and triple meanings, achieving uproarious comedy and at times even irony.

The American master exhibited still greater genius with his drawing and design.* He reduced his delineations to essentials; he transformed them into shorthand. Conforming to the rhythm of his recountal and its climax he variegated the boxes of a given strip in size and proportion.

* The best critique of *Krazy Kat*, Gilbert Seldes, *The Seven Lively Arts* (New York: Harper & Brothers, 1924), pp. 231–245. See also William Murrell, *A History of American Graphic Humor* (1865–1938) (New York: Macmillan, 1938), pp. 160, 162, and Coulton Waugh, *The Comics* (New York: Macmillan, 1947), pp. 57–62.

Such achievements are impressive enough. But the amazing feature is the continual change of time and place around a single line of talk. Sometimes the characters converse in fixed positions. Sometimes they merely hold their minds to the topic while going through a whole variety-show of situations and attitudes. Always, whatever the parts they play, they act them out in front of a landscape shifting cinemalike from box to box. In the comic illustrated (7.13a) the landscape is typical—a properly fantastic mesa borrowed from Arizona. It is a magic land in which rock, tree, cloud, and sun go through antics of their own.

The idea upon which this strip is built seems as madly eccentric as the drawing. It has to do with the association of cat's claws with fingernails needing a "menna cure," with plowshares ground on gravelly soil. Lunatic though the strip may be, it still speaks to us. It reaches us in some inexplicable fashion, tapping that body of experience which ordinarily lies buried in the subconscious.

Advertising Photography

Question has been raised whether commercial illustration has any right to be considered as an art. Admittedly, any industrial product like those studied in our third chapter makes its own best advertisement. And the attractiveness of the package containing it will have more to do with overcoming sales resistance than a score of cleverly designed ads in magazines and newspapers. Beyond the forms of both product and container, however, there is still need to acquaint a prospective buyer with the nature of the product before he goes to the store; and the art of advertising exists to meet that need.

Not all advertising can qualify as art, to be sure, much less organic art. An advertisement can evoke such a mist of sentimental associations as to blind one to the defects of the product being offered. If it is to qualify as an organically designed "spread," it has to be truthful. It has to register on a casual flipper of pages as readily as its magnified counterpart of the billboard registers on the motorist driving by. It has to intrigue him into stopping before it long enough to absorb its message and buy as recommended.

Organically effective commercial design * depends, like any other form of design, on a correct analysis of the factors involved in the situation. What is essential to the product, to its name and slogan, to the text describing it? How can such essentials be abstracted and symbolized? How can they be related to each other in order of importance? What style of lettering best suggests the nature of the product? How can the lettering be spaced and grouped for maximum clarity in reading and intelligibility of communication? How can the drawing, painting, or photograph reproduced with the lettering best intensify and develop the theme? When intelligent solutions have been found and the resulting forms integrated with each other, the resulting advertisement is bound to function properly and qualify as a work of art (7.13b).

Since we began our chapter with a look at photographic illustration, let us close it with the same art. Herbert Matter had done much experimental work with industrial design and typography as well as with the photogram and photograph and he had exploited such devices as time-exposure under stroboscopic lighting. Then Container Corporation of America approached him to enlist his photography and typography for commercial illustration.

The artist was to stress the importance of good packaging for sparing a housewife footwork as she shopped. Without efficiently designed containers, groceries would be so bulky as to require multistoried buildings for display and sale. Stair-climbing would make an ordeal out of every shopping expedition.

---

* Trace the progress of the art in such publications as *International Poster Annual*, W. H. Allner, ed., in English, French, and German (St. Gall, Switzerland: Zollikofer); and *Graphis Annual*, Walter Herdeg and Charles Rosner, eds., in English, French, and German (Zurich: Amstutz and Herdeg).

Matter developed this idea in terms of a simple repeat (7.13b).* He resorted to the stroboscope and the photomontage. With stroboscopic flashing he recorded on a frame of film under prolonged exposure successive images of a woman's legs in the act of climbing stairs. He made a series of strips by duplicating this photograph, and these he mounted obliquely across the upper part of the advertisement much as a stairway might appear to those below, groaning at the thought of climbing it.

In lighter value, Matter lettered parallel to one of the photographic strips the theme-fixing caption, "4-Story Groceries?" He sought by so doing to arouse in the reader not only an empathic weariness but a curiosity to learn how the alternative of a one-story grocery store is made possible. As a hint of answer to the question, the designer laid in at the bottom of the advertisement symbolically horizontal lines of lettering which point to packaging as the secret and to the name of the corporation as the source of the solution.

Matter's advertisement was carefully planned so as not to spell things out. It was calculated to exert the appeal of a puzzle, leaving the spectator to find the point. Too obvious an unfolding would have defeated the purpose. It would have been like depicting the climax of a story before it could be read in the text. It would have aroused sales resistance as inevitably as does the door-to-door agent, sticking his foot in while he extols the virtues of his merchandise. There is an appeal in the less obvious, the art that conceals art, and it is this appeal that Herbert Matter puts to use.

* Reproduced in black and white, Daniel Catton Rich, et al., *Modern Art in Advertising: Designs for Container Corporation of America* (Chicago: Paul Theobald, 1946), No. 66. See also Raymond A. Ballinger, *Layout* (New York: Reinhold, 1956), pp. 77, 135, and 223; and Eugene M. Ettenberg, "Herbert Matter: Designer and Photographer," *American Artist*, Vol. XX, No. 3 (March, 1956), pp. 36–41.

SUMMARY

Illustrating is the art of making pictures to illuminate or clarify a story. It is a collaborative art in which its practitioner joins with author, scribe or typesetter, papermaker, leatherworker, binder, to produce a book.

Illustrating is based on the art of drawing, the defining or drawing out into existence, on a flat surface, a representation of objects or phenomena existent apart from the picture itself. Drawing is employed to make sketches, studies, and finished pictures. In the third category, as ends in themselves, drawings function as the art of illustrating, but this art nonetheless depends on a text for its motives and its reason for existence.

Illustrating as an art of the book once functioned solely for the production of manuscripts. It was inescapably influenced by the format of the text, usually either a hand scroll (rotulus) or a book proper (codex). Sometimes color would be used, to increase the interest of the manuscript or the detached miniature.

The urge to duplicate books and illustrations, for increased revenue or other practical purpose, gave rise to the art of print making— the art of impressing the picture, usually on successive sheets of paper, from a block, plate, or screen. Print making developed through four classes of mediums: relief, intaglio, planography, and stencil. Although masterpieces in black and white have been produced by one medium or another in each of these four classes, desire for greater range of expression and added sales appeal led to a flourishing art of print making in color, and especially to that of the ukiyoye school in Japan.

Print making led in turn to printing, the multiplication of texts and illustrations by the industrialized printing press. And illustrating for the periodical divided up still further into arts for popular consumption: caricature, political cartooning, and comic-strip cartooning on the one hand, and commercial illustrating, packaging, and typographical layout on the other.

RECOMMENDED READINGS

Diringer, David. *The Hand-produced Book*. New York: Philosophical Library, 1953.

In highly condensed form this book brings its reader up to date on practically everything known about the hand-produced book up to the invention of printing and offers illuminating data found nowhere else within a single book.

Toda, Kenji. *Japanese Scroll Painting*. Chicago: University of Chicago Press, 1935.

Although Toda's study lacks the comprehensiveness of Diringer's, it is indispensable for reference on the Japanese version of the rotulus. It explains the format of the hand scroll in detail, traces the history of this form of manuscript in Japan, presents the important factual data about each of a large number of surviving works, and illustrates significant portions of these with some care in quality.

Watrous, James. *The Craft of Old-Master Drawings*. Madison, Wis.: The University of Wisconsin Press, 1957.

The usual book on drawing either concentrates on the practical aspects of drawing or its history in the narrow sense. This book embraces both in an extremely illuminating way, matching illustrations with text, and accompanying reproductions of carefully selected examples with photographs and diagrams of actual materials and tools and microphotographs of characteristic strokes.

Noma, Seiroku, ed. (Edward Strong, trans.). *Artistry in Ink*. New York: Crown Publishers, 1957.

This is the Oriental counterpart to the study made by Watrous. It goes farther than Watrous in presenting not only the materials and techniques of brush drawing in China and Japan, but also the philosophy and history behind it. It is profusely illustrated with offset lithographic reproductions of almost perfect clarity.

Simon, Howard. *500 Years of Art and Illustration: From Albrecht Dürer to Rockwell Kent*. Cleveland and New York: The World Publishing Company, 1942.

Simon has produced a magnificent picture book, generous in size of page, fascinating in choice of example, and uniformly high in quality of reproduction. The text consists largely of biographical summaries of the illustrators represented, informative but disappointing in its critical analysis.

Cory, J. Campbell. *The Cartoonist's Art*. Chicago: The Tumbo Company, 1912.

Cory was a highly successful cartoonist himself and he wrote as a master to a hopeful apprentice, providing a practical manual on various aspects of his art. Other cartoonists have done as much. But none ever managed to get as close to the drawing itself, showing how and why it was made, and what is good and bad about it. Cory's critical comments are all the more illuminating in view of the fact that he illustrated his book with his own cartoons.

Waugh, Coulton. *The Comics*. New York: Macmillan, 1947.

Waugh wrote about the comic strip with the same fresh gusto that Cory brought to the cartoon, even though thirty-five years lay between their respective literary efforts. More comprehensive in his coverage, Waugh interspersed his text with a wit that sometimes becomes slapstick.

Weitenkampf, Frank. *The Illustrated Book*. Cambridge, Mass.: Harvard University Press, 1938.

Since the history of the mediums of print making is closely bound up with the history of the printed book, this study by Weitenkampf makes a proper fusion of the two. The result is, to be sure, an unfortunate omission of those print makers who did not work as illustrators: Rembrandt in etching and Goya in aquatint. But the treatment and choice of mediums in the light of prevailing styles and states of mind more than makes up for the omissions.

Hayter, S. W. *New Ways of Gravure*. New York: Pantheon Books, 1949.

Few professional artists write with such clarity, insight, and historical perspective as Hayter does about his chosen art. He deals with all forms of intaglio print making, including new mediums and new ways of handling old mediums. The book is well illustrated.

Poortenaar, Jan. *The Technique of Prints and Art Reproduction Processes*. London: John Lane, 1933.

Few writers on print making bother to compare its mediums with corresponding mediums of photomechanical reproduction or attempt to trace relationships of each set of mediums to the forms of the pictures made with them. Hence the value of this book by an artist with professional experience in both the studio and the publishing house.

Kepeś, György, and others. *Graphic Forms: The Arts as Related to the Book*. Cambridge, Mass.: Harvard University Press, 1949.

This book was the outcome of a symposium on the arts of the book, a forum sponsored jointly by the Harvard University Press and The Bookbuilders of Boston. As the publication bears witness, this symposium succeeded in integrating publishing with design procedure. Though lacking in the unity which any one of the fifteen participants might have achieved by writing the study himself, the book offers many passages brilliant in their insight.

8.1. Murals in the chapel of the Tomb of Nakht, Thebes. *c.* 1450 B.C. Secco. Rear wall, 83 x 63″; chamber, 102″ long. Courtesy of the Metropolitan Museum of Art, New York.

Painting

PAINTING IS, like sculpture, an art of representing objects and natural phenomena, but unlike sculpture, it represents them on a flat surface with pigment or other coloring material. Again like sculpture, painting abstracts forms from reality, modifying them in accord with the artist's feelings about them, about his materials, and about his methods of procedure.

TYPES OF PAINTING

Painting used as illustration is utilitarian, owing its utility to its representational character.

A second utilitarian branch of painting serves the compositional needs of architecture. Since it has to do with picturemaking on walls (and ceilings and floors, by extension), it is called mural painting, *murus* being the Latin for "wall." When functioning as it should, mural painting enters like architectural sculpture into the visual effects of a building. By its powers of representation, denied to architecture, it calls attention to a building's functions. By drawing on remembered associations, it evokes a mood in keeping with the building's character, whether the building be a tomb (8.1), a church (8.3), an auditorium (8.16), or other type of structure. By employing effects of action or repose, lightness or gravity, and the like, mural painting, like architectural sculpture but less tangibly, completes or corrects a building's composition.

In keeping with the building's impersonal character, mural painting assumes the more generalized types of form. In response to forces felt to be at work in architecture (pressures, tensions, thrusts, and counterthrusts), it develops characteristically epical effects, with grandly sweeping contours and broadly rendered masses. In reaction to the substance of structural materials, it either flattens forms until they seem to hug the wall (8.1 and 8.4), or else models in light and shade until two-dimensional forms seem as solid as walls and piers (8.6). Mural painting may quiet the hubbub of a reception hall (8.6), inspire lofty sentiment in a place of public assemblage (8.16b), animate the abode of the dead (8.1).

The expanse of wall bearing the mural predetermines the way in which the observer has to view it. If he would see it whole, he has to stand at a distance; if he would see a part at close hand, he cannot see the other parts simultaneously. Recognizing these necessities, the painter develops boldly contrasting forms which spurn all detail. He avoids too dominant a center of interest, too softened or blurred a series of surrounding forms. He anticipates successive viewings of parts at close hand by giving them such character as rewards their study. He provides each part with a "follow-through" in motive and organization to draw the viewer to the next.

Critics who deplore a mural's limitations are conditioned by a studio painter's point of view, for the studio painter practices an art having qualities opposite to those of mural painting, qualities of mobility and intimate appeal. Easel painting is an art of picturemaking on a stand or tripod (from the German *esel*, meaning, humorously enough, the burden-bearing ass).

Unlike an illustration or a mural, an easel painting exists for its own sake. The artist making it may give little thought to pleasing anyone but himself. Accepting only restrictions of medium, and sometimes not even them, the easel painter may be as arbitrary as he likes. The illustrator may be less limited than the bookbinder, the muralist less so than the architect, but the easel painter is the least hedged in of all. No considerations of size, expense, client tastes and needs, site, or climate restrain the easel painter. He goes his own way.

Easel painting is as intensely personal an art from the spectator's point of view as it is from the artist's. We stand, more or less, on common ground when we judge a building; the height of a doorway or the width of a passageway must fall within practical limits. We stand on common ground when we criticize a mural; some of us may object to its distortions but its success or failure in meeting the building's compositional needs is usually not a matter for debate. The case is different when we try to evaluate an easel painting. When we weigh its pros and cons, we have no functional criteria to refer to and few rules. We depend on our reactions.

One sure test of a painting's worth is the test of living with it. It must be looked at and into often and intently. It must be seen under different lights and moods, in different settings and varieties of experience. If the painting has something to say, it will go on saying more and more to the man who views it. Paradoxically speaking, the painting may as time passes reveal out of its immediate timeliness of expression a certain timelessness of appeal —a treasury of enduring qualities the consideration of which once led a picture-book compiler to entitle his work *Art Without Epoch.**

* Ludwig Goldscheider, *Art Without Epoch: Works of Distant Times Which Still Appeal to Modern Taste* (New York: Oxford University Press, 1937).

When an easel painting measures up to its potentialities, it can be distinguished from a mural as easily as a studio sculpture can be distinguished from a piece of architectural sculpture. For all of its variables, it offers qualities which it shares with all other organically inspired paintings of the studio.

For example, the portability of an easel painting, easily hung and easily taken down, encourages its maker to exploit fleeting effects and simulate movements (8.5). Unlike the sculptural mobile or the motion picture, on the other hand, the easel painting has to remain stationary for viewing. In its fixed position it throws the burden of suggesting movement on the patterns of its composition.

The easel painting may be limited in size, but it is boundlessly receptive to the artist's arm, wrist, and hand. Its maker concerns himself less with monumental themes, therefore, than with subtleties of coloring and manipulations of paint (Plate IV), illusions of deep space and hints of extension beyond the picture's boundaries into a changing world (8.10). The easel painter tends to design his work for simultaneous vision from a single vantage point. He seizes on a single dominant note or on two or three notes of accent, and plays the other passages of his picture around them in strictly subordinate roles (8.2).

Purpose determines form. Purpose likewise determines medium. The peculiar natures of a material and a process make them appropriate to realizing the painting's intent. And the study of the relative appropriateness of mediums to the job at hand has led during the course of history to a grouping of mediums into two general classes: [1]

A. Mediums of mural painting
  1. Secco　　4. Stained glass
  2. Fresco　　5. Ethyl silicate
  3. Mosaic
B. Mediums of easel painting
  1. Encaustic　4. Water color
  2. Tempera　　5. Gouache
  3. Oil

[1] See Notes, p. 300.

Such a classification is not absolute. Artists have painted successful murals in oil; they have tried repeatedly to fashion easel pictures out of fresco or mosaic.[2] But the trouble with a mural in an easel-painting medium is the way in which the illusions of deep space which are natural to the medium contradict the actual spaces of the building. Or it is the "busyness" of too much subtle detailing for a room in which the actual movements of people would compete. The mural is apt to look strained and unhappy over a servitude for which it was not intended. And the trouble with an easel painting in a mural medium is just the reverse. It does not have enough illusion of space. It assumes a monotonous, barren effect discouraging the close viewing which its modest scale invites.

Like the sculptor, the painter is essentially a representational artist, but he is less restricted in his choice of subject. He can concentrate on the human figure, nude (8.5), or draped (8.6), or seen every way at once (8.12). Much more readily than the sculptor, the painter can group a multitude of figures together (8.6). If he specializes in the figure, he adopts a figure genre (class of subject): nude, draped figure, portrait, figure-in-interior, figure-in-landscape, and so on.

Or the painter can ignore the human figure entirely. He can roam at will over the landscape, exploiting themes drawn from the life of natural creatures (8.15), the structure of trees, rocks, and houses (8.9), the changing states of weather (8.10). He can focus his attention on ordinary household objects or bric-a-brac of unusual textural or chromatic quality, and evolve out of groupings of such material a painting known as a still life (8.18). He can carry the shapes of objects, their relationships with each other and the atmosphere, the play of sunlight and shadow over them, beyond the limits of ordinary representation to any degree of expressive distortion and abstraction, and even to total nonrepresentation (8.14).

[2] See Notes, p. 300.

Fallacious Criteria

Review of painting's genres reminds us of the genres of photography which we have already studied. These genres do partly correspond, in fact, because both arts are essentially representational. Until photography was invented, of course, they were the exclusive monopoly of painting. And many people thought that the primary objective of painting in any one of them was an eye-tricking (trompe-l'oeil) illusion of the real thing.[3]

This idea of painting as imitation is ancient. It was current, for example, in the Roman world when Pliny the Elder, first encyclopedist of history, referred to it as the criterion for judging masterpieces of Greek painters five hundred years before him:

> The story runs that Parrhasios and Zeuxis entered into competition, Zeuxis exhibiting a picture of some grapes, so true to nature that the birds flew up to the wall of the stage. Parrhasios then displayed a picture of a linen curtain, realistic to such a degree that Zeuxis, elated by the verdict of the birds, cried out that now at last his rival must draw the curtain and show his picture. On discovering his mistake he surrendered the prize to Parrhasios, admitting candidly that he had deceived the birds, while Parrhasios had deluded himself, a painter.*

Zeuxis and Parrhasios may indeed have painted in this illusionary way. None of their paintings have survived, however, and the trompe-l'oeil effect referred to was likely familiar only to Pliny's culture and certain later cultures like that of an America which brought forth the still life illustrated (8.18). At any rate, the Roman writer was betraying his limitations as critic when he related such a tale without comment. However far the illusionism of Zeuxis may have gone, the Greek master could never have achieved the fame that he did if he had offered illusionary deception alone. Any tendency in that direction would

[3] See Notes, page 300.
* Eng. trans., K. Jex-Blake, *The Elder Pliny's Chapters on the History of Art, op. cit.*, pp. 109 and 111.

have been offset by his expressiveness of design.

The idea of art as imitation was betrayed most interestingly during the nineteenth century when photography came to invade one genre after another formerly regarded as the province of painting. Portraiture, figure painting, landscape painting, and still life fell one by one to the advances of the camera man, and some thought it only a matter of time until photography would supplant painting entirely. Artists tried desperately to compete with the camera man on his own ground, copying photographs or trying to make their paintings look like photographs.

Photography is now seen to do much better what painting could once do alone. When a master-photographer can create a portrait as personable as that which we have reproduced, a nude study as moving as Gowland's, a landscape as sublime as Stieglitz's or Adams's, a detail as sensuous as Weston's or Dearstyne's, even a fantasy as captivating as Jones's or Moholy-Nagy's, then we may be forgiven for asking in all seriousness: What is left for the painter to do? The truth of the matter is that any approach to painting as an imitation of nature is a blind alley. We owe exposure of this fallacy to photography's coming of age as an art, since, as we have seen, not even a camera master ever created a work of art by holding a mirror up to nature, and not even a camera-inspired master like Degas ever offered a portrait that has endured merely as "a photographic likeness" (8.8). There has always been something more, and it is this "something more" which really counts in art.

In the art of painting, this "something more" is the handiwork, the manipulation of colors and shapes, by which the artist expresses his feelings about the subject represented. Subject matter starts the painting, but is soon transformed into something beyond itself.

A painting is a world in itself, self-contained and different from our own. It is not meant to be a corroboration of our sense-experience, but rather an expansion of it, a liberation from it, a sudden disclosure of new feelings and new ideas about it. It achieves its beauty not merely by representing a beautiful girl or other object of beauty. It achieves its beauty by revealing new aspects of familiar objects. While maintaining the identity of the object inspiring it, a painting presents the object as though it had never before existed. It is a discovery or a revelation, not an imitation.

The fallacious concept of painting as imitation is matched by a second fallacy, as persistent and pernicious. This fallacy declares that any painting to be good must look slickly rendered, must display a dazzling technique. It must appear "finished" and "hard to do." Whether or not it says anything, it must make a graceful flourish.

Technique is a means. Unless it has solid fare to chew on, it becomes empty and futile. Solid fare can make a good painting by itself, even though its execution is at fault. Albert Pinkham Ryder was anxious to realize images in his painting which were perceived only dimly in his mind's eye. In quest of realization he painted and repainted on the same picture sometimes for years, whether or not the coloring underneath had dried and regardless of the composition of his colors. As time passes, consequently, Ryder's pictures blacken and crack. In spite of such defects in his works, however, critics agree that Ryder was one of the greatest painters in American history.

John Singer Sargent, Ryder's contemporary, was, on the contrary, a master technician. He could turn out a portrait so speedily that his sitters had no time to get weary. He dashed his coloring on and pushed it around, bringing forth as though by magic a pleasing likeness. He flattered, glossed over warts and moles, bathed his sitters in glittering light. But he had nothing more to say; the inflated reputation which he won scarcely survived his death.

Although painting is not just a matter of technical display, it is inescapably involved in technical matters. In spite of Ryder's example, it can ignore craftsmanship to such a glaring extent that even the noblest of subjects fails to be communicated. No painting can be effective without a tangible physical presence; and, if we would learn to appreciate the artist's work, we have to find out what his medium really feels and smells and looks like. More with painting, perhaps, than with any other art, we need to supplement our studies in this book with actual visits to museums and studios, actual viewings at first hand, and, when possible, actual experiments in techniques.

MURAL PAINTING

Within the field of each type of painting distinctions exist between one medium and another. Each medium has its own peculiar ways of behaving, assumes its own effects. When respected for its unique qualities, it leads to a form of picture unlike any other.

Secco

There is secco, for example. Named for the Italian word meaning "dry," the medium consists of painting on walls of dried plaster. The pigments (granulated coloring materials) are mixed with slaked limewater for vehicle (agent by which the pigment is transported to the support). The pigments are further mixed with a binder (substance serving to hold both the color together and the pigments to the wall), commonly casein, the fresh white curd of skim milk.

The artist wets the dried plaster ground thoroughly with a limewash. If he wants a blended effect, he paints into the limewashed area while it is still wet. If he wants either a crisp-edged or a glazed effect, with one color overlying another semitransparently, he waits until the limewashed area has dried. Otherwise, he works as he pleases, over the entire surface at once or exclusively bit by bit.

The resulting mural is open to a variety of effects, but it is usually distinguished by its opaque, flat coloring, its airy effects if wet-painted, its sharp contourings if dry-painted (8.1). The coloring becomes a separate skin attached to the plaster—and it looks its separateness. If moisture works through the wall from the rear or if the air in front changes abruptly in temperature and humidity, the painting demonstrates its separateness disastrously; it flakes and peels off.

Fresco

Artists find for painting on plaster that the medium of fresco is more exacting, but also more inspiring and durable. Named likewise by an Italian word, meaning "fresh," fresco consists of painting on freshly applied plaster before it has had a chance to dry and set. The pigment is mixed with limewater, as in secco. Unlike secco, on the other hand, the medium requires no binder. In the process of drying, the lime in the plaster absorbs carbonic acid gas from the air to form a glass coating that incorporates the colors with the wall, giving the mural a characteristically beautiful sheen and making the painting completely insoluble in water.

More than the secco painter, the frescoist has to respect the properties of his medium. He knows that colors must be applied only while the plaster is wet; otherwise he cannot interrelate them properly in values and secure them firmly to the wall. He knows that the wall can be worked on only piece by piece, with fresh plaster applied each morning over an area just large enough to receive that day's coverage of color, with new areas painted in day by day in a gradual progress toward completion of the whole. He knows that plaster which has dried even so much as to "pull" the brush can take no further rendering, no correcting nor retouching, but that alterations or additions require the given area of plaster to be chipped away and replaced with a fresh layer, ready to start all over.

Disciplined by knowledge of the medium, the artist makes extensive preparations. He predetermines in sketches the effect of the whole, in studies the character of each detail, in drawings from the model the action of each figure, and finally in a cartoon the salient features and their relationships to the architecture, giving the linear structure of the work at full scale.

Satisfied that his preliminary essays are as good as he can make them, the muralist and his assistants set to work preparing the support. Lest the plaster dry too fast, before applying it to the wall they soak the underlying stone or brick masonry. Lest the plaster crack and break away from the wall later on, they apply it in at least four distinct layers: a rough-cast coat against the masonry itself, an equalizing coat with which to level off the wall, a scratch coat on which to ascertain the area for the labor of each day, and an intonaco coat on which to do the final painting. The painter transfers his cartoon to the scratch coat—either by tracing it (pressing the tip of the brush handle into the plaster along the lines through the paper), or by pouncing it (shaking powdered charcoal through holes made in the paper by running a "roulette wheel," a wheel with spikes extending from it, along the outlines). He uses the outlines so transferred as a guide for scheduling each day's progress, laying the intonaco coat within the outer contours only far enough for coverage before having to quit for the night.

The artist aware of the medium's unique qualities finds in fresco's piecemeal procedure a prompting to stress contour, to model form, to set dark areas boldly against light areas or light against dark (8.6). He finds in his preliminary studies a means to simplify coloring and sharpen the definition of images rather than merely to fix "molds" by which to translate the studies to the wall. His success depends almost entirely, in fact, on the clarity of definition of everything about his picture before he even begins to paint on the plaster.

Joints between successive days' applications of plaster are almost certain to show by variations in value due to unevennesses in mixture of color and in drying—unless they are made to coincide with the contours of objects represented. Hence again the good muralist's emphasis on contour, refining it, shading into it,

opposing background values to it, as though it were the steel skeleton of the whole organic structure, which indeed, in a way, it is. The colors of fresco dry lighter in value than they seem when applied. Hence the strength of statement in the good muralist's rendering—overstatement like that to which the actor resorts in order to make his lines carry to his audience.

Mosaic

The medium of mosaic consists in the making of pictures by inserting tesserae into a bed of cement or other ground capable of holding them in place when thoroughly set. As its meaning in Latin signifies, a tessera is a square piece or cube of solid material. It can be made of almost any substance: colored pebbles, glazed or unglazed potsherds, marble, enameled or gilded glass.

The mosaicist is more dependent on a cartoon than even the frescoist. He is obliged not only to follow the design worked out in line and color in his cartoon, but also to lay out on his support beneath the mortar-bed-to-be an exact copy of his cartoon. If it is a large mosaic, he must draw this copy only section by section, because it is as necessary as on a large fresco to complete each day's section by itself before going on to the next.

The artist who works according to the direct method develops his composition exactly as it appears in his cartoon; that is, without reversing it. He sets each tessera directly by hand into the mortar bed. He has to know exactly what he is doing. Once he has gotten under way, he can do no experimenting, make no mistakes.

The inherent beauty of a good mosaic lies in its utter simplicity and flatness, its jewel-like radiance of color, its sense of wall-like stability (8.3 and 8.4). The element of line counts for much, because the width of the tesserae makes the mosaic broad and heavy. The element of area counts for much, because the tesserae go naturally into rows, discouraging subtleties of modeling in light and dark and following the already flattened area of the mortar underneath. The two subelements of color, hue and intensity, play important roles, since the color is incorporated in the body of each tessera where it can never fade nor react to its detriment with any color under, over, or beside it.

As can perhaps be detected in the Byzantine mosaic detail illustrated (8.4), the handwork results in irregularities of surface. One tessera sticks out a little, another recedes; the face of one turns obliquely this way, another that way. These irregularities set up a play of glinting lights and fluttering shadows which account for much of the vitality of effect peculiar to such mosaic. When the spectator moves along the course of the mural, he sees the play of light shift, create continually changing aspects. His eyes are quickened by this play, drawn into active participation with the movements of the forms.

A sensitive mosaicist can develop the richest of textures. The same hue and intensity in a marble tessera will offer a textural quality clearly different from that of a glass tessera. Tesserae an eighth of an inch across will give an area a markedly different feel from one covered with tesserae an inch across. Then, again, tesserae that follow each other in straight rows describe a different surface from tesserae set in zigzag or herringbone fashion or around the arcs of circles. In our opening chapter we noted the importance attached to the element of texture in much contemporary art. The mosaic medium is peculiarly well fitted to meet this demand for textural expression, and it is perhaps that qualification, as much as any, which accounts for the increasing number of murals now being executed in it.

Stained Glass

One very striking variant of the glass tesserae used in mosaic is stained glass. Unlike enameled glass, which is opaque, stained glass has the pigment incorporated in its body, to make the glass translucent. All translucency is lost, of course, if stained glass tesserae are embedded like any other tesserae directly in the mortar. But if the pieces of stained glass have a leaf of gold or silver, or, best of all, of aluminum, set behind them in the mortar, the metal or metal alloy will reflect the light back again through the glass, rendering its coloring extraordinarily brilliant.

Better still than into mosaic, the artist can introduce stained glass into a window opening. Not only by so doing can he integrate his mural more fully with the actual structure of a building; he can also achieve a brilliance of coloring unmatchable with any other medium. Reflected daylight or direct sunlight will come through from outside, transforming the mural into a glory of illuminated color. It will give an effect approximating that of the color slides projected onto a frosted-glass screen from behind.

European artists of the age of the Gothic cathedrals brought the art of stained glass to a peak of development, above all in the windows of Chartres Cathedral (4.5). So tremendously moving did stained-glass windows become, in fact, that they actually determined the course of development of the architecture itself—toward ever more daring skeletal construction for increased expanse of window. Craftsmen later debased the art, to be sure, by trying to make it imitate fresco and other mediums, but in such collaborative enterprises as the Church of the Sacred Heart at Audincourt, France, artists have again found virtue in its unique qualities.[4]

In the twelfth and thirteenth centuries the master artisan and his apprentices brought all materials and equipment to the building while it was still under construction. They began by drawing carefully to scale a miniature study of each window. They enlarged the study into a full-size cartoon and worked out carefully on the cartoon every detail of shape and color of glass, and of lead framework, called leading, to hold the pieces in. They made the lines indicating this leading as thick as the actual framing would be, sometimes an inch or more in width. In order to determine the actual size of each piece of glass, they made another

4 See Notes, page 300.

drawing from the cartoon, substituting thin lines for the thick ones. This final drawing they laid out flat on the cathedral floor where they could cut each piece of glass to match exactly the area designated for it.

Once the drawing was entirely covered to the master's satisfaction, the craftsmen turned to the waxing-up stage: on sheets of clear glass, tilted at an angle to let the light shine through, they transferred each piece of stained glass to its proper spot in the composition, securing it by applying drops of melted wax to the corners. Thus waxed up, the design could be studied approximately as it would finally appear, and pieces either altered in the oven or completely replaced. It could even be painted on, piece by piece, with the proper pigment.

When everything was ready finally to go into the window itself, the master and his assistants returned to the line drawing lying flat on the floor. They replaced each piece of glass on it and shaped the leading around it in accord with the heavy black outlines of the cartoon. They attached the leading in turn to a grid of iron rods called the armature, so that, when the section was ready, it could be lifted safely and installed in the window opening. The armature served to hold the glass firm against a wind; it found anchorage in turn in a network of stone masonry called the tracery. Tracery spanned the opening and echoed in its skeletal effect the system of piers, rib-vaults, and flying buttresses in the rest of the building (see p. 90).

Throughout this process the artist-craftsman enjoyed a surprising latitude not only in format but in color. He continues to enjoy it today, but imposes for the sake of artistic effectiveness the same self-restraint as did the medieval workers in stained glass. He simplifies, abstracts, depersonalizes. He may lend a touch of character to a face, of roundness to a figure, but in general he insists that everything remain flat within its heavy outlining in lead— an outlining which we have already seen in our study of drawing flattens as it detaches.

Far from treating the heavy leading as a defect to be disguised, the artist actually welcomes it. Since he recognizes its structural necessity, he insists that it prevail over any possible demands for literal representation. He treats it as a truly functional line. Learning by observing at the site, he realizes that a weak line looks all the weaker when daylight encroaches on it from behind. He finds in the thick line, therefore, his cue for abstracting his figures. He segments them earthwormlike, squares off their contours, and breaks across them abruptly. He respects the principle of emphasis, sacrificing illusions of mass and depth in favor of line, area, color-hue, and color-intensity.

Ethyl Silicate

We have been thinking of stained glass, as of other mural mediums thus far, as intended only for indoor murals. To be viewed from inside may indeed be the primary intent of a mural, but it is not the only intent. In a stained-glass window, tracery and leading are always visible from the exterior of the cathedral. On the shadow side of the building, with sunlight coming through from the opposite side, or at night, with lights burning inside, such a window also registers in its full brilliance of coloring to a viewer out of doors. Mosaic is entirely weatherworthy and fitted for outdoor murals, as the architect-muralist, Juan O'Gorman, impressively demonstrated in the Library on the campus of the University of Mexico, almost covered with mosaic from ground to roof.*

Secco is totally unsuitable for an outdoor mural and fresco is not much better, because of the way in which rain attacks plaster. But the artist who would render forms akin to those of fresco on the outside of a building can now paint them directly on concrete. This structural material has always proved too porous to hold the color of any ordinary medium. But the newly developed medium of ethyl silicate adheres permanently to a concrete wall in the face of the severest conditions of weather and also harmonizes perfectly with the porous sup-

* Reproduced in color from photo by Eliot Elisofon, *Life*, December 3, 1956.

port by presenting in itself a porous consistency.

Much like the waterglass (sodium silicate) in which our great-grandparents used to store eggs to keep them fresh, ethyl silicate holds the pigment in uniform suspension, but, unlike waterglass, it does not react with the colors to their detriment. The vehicle giving the medium its name is a compound of alcohol and silica. Neutral in itself, it carries the pigment within its transparent body, first in a solution of alcohol and water, and then, on being brushed out, in the form of a tenacious gel. This gel when dry becomes converted to pure silica, to preserve the color in all its natural brilliance against atmospheric acid, soap, or variation of heat, cold, or dampness.

Like any conventional medium, ethyl silicate has properties capable of serving as an organic source of expression (8.16c and d). The even consistency and quick initial set of the medium permit any area to be painted over a second time within a few minutes of the original application, thus giving the painter a chance to attack his whole composition simul-

taneously. The rapid evaporation of the alcohol and the absorbency of the concrete impel the artist, on the other hand, to develop flat coats of color in preference to smoothly blended passages. They influence him to resort only to hatchings and cross hatchings of brushwork for any possible modeling, to keep his coloring thin and to hold his overpainting to a minimum lest the pigment peel off.

The texture of the concrete and the markings left on its surface by the wooden planks, originally used in the molds for the pouring, appeal to the painter as an asset, to be retained and incorporated wherever possible as an adjunct to the painting. The colors best adhering to concrete he discovers to be those grayed with black and lime white; he makes areas of gray predominate, therefore, reserving for color accents either acidproof colors or actual pieces of metal embedded in the concrete. He feels the hardness of the concrete under his brush, its uniformity of texture, its solid structural strength, and he works accordingly, to evolve big-scaled structural axes of line and unbroken areas of tone.

EASEL PAINTING

In the art of easel painting mediums tend to vary less than they do in mural painting, to resemble each other in certain important respects. For one thing, they all employ a support uniformly flat and opaque, whether made of wood, cloth, or paper. For another thing, they depend on brushes, or rods wielded like brushes, as their major tools. Finally, they utilize a vehicle for their coloring which at time of application is liquid or semiliquid.

Art is, to be sure, so much a matter of synthesis that function can scarcely ever be set off in actual practice from material and technique. Characteristics born of one consideration merge at the artist's hands with characteristics born of the two other considerations, and he is not long in discovering qualities of his medium which come close to coinciding with realization of his subject. Generally speak-

ing, the easel painter's mediums encourage him to elaborate detail, to variegate coloring, and to play more or less freely with lighting, contouring, and atmospheric environment.

Encaustic

The story of Zeuxis and Parrhasios which Pliny related not only reflects a popular idea that painting should imitate nature. It also bears witness to the fact that ancient Greek artists painted easel paintings as well as murals, and that the medium in which they did their portable pictures must have been well suited to creating illusions. The medium in which the Greek masters rendered their competition-pieces was in all likelihood encaustic. No classic Greek examples of this medium have survived, it is true. But Greeks and Romans living in Egypt during the early centuries of the Christian era practiced it with a high degree of sophistication.

The medium is fittingly named, for the Greek word *enkaustikos* not only reflects the nationality of the first people to perfect it but also describes the "burning in" of the process. Workers in encaustic painted directly on the surface of a wooden panel, using beeswax for vehicle and heating the wax to mix the pigment with it. They applied the coloring to the panel either with a brush or with a metal tool called the cauterium—pointed at one end for accenting, spoon-shaped at the other end for spreading. Once the pigment was applied, they heated the cauterium and went back over the surface with it, modeling the wax, fusing layers together, and "burning" the pigment more deeply into the wax for safekeeping. Then, for final smoothing and fixing, they ran over the surface once more with the metal grid of a burning charcoal brazier.

A contemporary artist like Karl Zerbe,* alert to the medium's possibilities, may achieve organically expressive forms comparable to those of an ancient Egypto-Roman portrait (8.2). He develops a rich impasto (from the Italian word for "paste," referring to thick application of paint) appealing to touch as well as to sight. In portraiture or figure painting, for example, he makes the slight ridges of wax left by the cauterium an equivalent to the downy, porous texture of flesh. He accentuates such a rendering of skin by contrast, perhaps, with smooth, thin passages of background or drapery representation.

Every application of melted wax cools and sets quickly, permitting the artist to superimpose other layers at will. If sensitive to such behavior, he takes care not to mix his colors unduly in any single application, but to introduce a glaze on another color underneath. He creates in this way an optical gray, one vibrant with light as compared with the usual dull gray obtained by mixing pigments for a single application. Thanks again to the quick set of the wax, he can resort as readily to scumbling as to glazing—brushing one color so lightly over the one beneath that only the ridges of the impasto catch the new color. He finds in this procedure a most effective means of textural as well as of chromatic variation, one which he often uses for the rendering of hair, beards, unshaven chins, and the like.

A master of encaustic makes a straightforward attack on his painting, confident that no partially dried color underneath will cause his overlays to crack, confident that the body of the wax will hold the pigment in suspension exactly as he applies it. He cultivates that quietly luminous glow of color to which the medium lends itself. He brings his impasto to bear on the colors underneath, playing one against the other to their mutual enrichment.

Tempera

Tempera (from the Latin word meaning "to temper," or "to regulate") consists of painting with glue for vehicle and binder. The glue may be animal (milk, cheese) or vegetable (cherry tree, gum arabic), but when not otherwise designated, it is assumed to be egg. Tempera paint is applied to a wooden-panel support. Unlike encaustic, which goes directly on to the wood, tempera requires an intermediate protective layer, or ground, of gesso.

A painter in tempera may work with the whole egg or with the yolk alone, because the yolk contains an oil which dries into a tough film almost impossible to wash off.

Even if the artist dilutes his egg with water to make the mixture flow a bit, his coloring dries almost instantaneously on its gesso ground. It changes in hue as it dries. It remains so transparent and resistant to removal that it cannot be hidden or corrected. It rules out all modulations of a wash, all attempts at trial-and-error experiment. Tempera is so difficult to work with that it resembles fresco in its exacting steps of procedure. Again like fresco, it withholds its final effect until the work is completed.

* A work by Zerbe, illustrated in color, is in Frances Pratt and Becca Fizel, *Encaustic Materials and Methods* (New York: Lear, 1949), opp. p. 48.

The artist planning to work in tempera has to make any number of preliminary sketches and studies. He has to map out and think through every minute passage of shading in each successive layer. He has to complete a cartoon as painstakingly exact as that for fresco but in even finer line; he has to transfer this accurately to the gesso surface.

A tempera painter starts out by indicating in a shorthand of light washes where his major lights and darks are to go. He makes these in monochrome, to form a sort of underpainting. Over these washes he develops his painting gradually. Knowing that only tempera color with body in it will register properly on the eye, he does little diluting with water and no consequent brushing-in of large areas of color. Working with such a quick-drying medium, he draws only lines with his brush, thin, sharp lines, hatched, crosshatched, and overlaid, which must do duty for every bit of modeling and every detail.

The artist can indicate the lighter values and highlights with body-color of white, to be sure, but every time he does so he contradicts that ground of gesso, wonderfully smooth and gleaming in its whiteness, with which he starts. He recognizes in it his only true source of light, since it reflects light back through the transparent pigment. He endeavors, therefore, to retain the gesso in all of its original freshness by keeping his shading transparent or translucent, and seldom if ever opaque. In shaded overlays, therefore, he achieves even more successfully than the encaustic painter those vigorous optic grays which we have already described as natural to wax.

A good tempera painting is an organic product of a severely delimited procedure. It owes to its exacting techniques and its creator's willingness to accept its disciplines the qualities which distinguish it. A good tempera painting stands out for its clarity of form, its inner luminosity, its sheet-ice smoothness of impasto (Plate III, 8.5). It distinguishes itself for its sharpness of line and bright transparency of color. It seems actually to cherish the tangible features of the object represented.

Oil

The fullest possibilities of easel painting are realized in the medium of oil. For record of preferred use and high achievement, oil is to easel painting what fresco is to mural painting. So closely coupled are they that oil is often treated as synonymous with easel, and fresco with mural, painting.

Pigment ground into cold-pressed linseed oil that has been properly aged and filtered yields an even-colored and pastelike substance called an oil paint. Diluted with a little turpentine, it is fluid enough to use easily until the turpentine evaporates. Beeswax may be added to increase its buttery consistency, stabilize its pigment in suspension, and reduce its glossiness.

Like encaustic or tempera, oil painting can be done on a wooden support. It can also be done on a host of other materials—plywood, cardboard, composition board, glass, brick, stone, plaster, metal. Ordinarily, however, because of its resilience under pressure of the brush, artists prefer to paint their oils on tightly woven linen canvas. Whatever the support, it can hardly ever be painted on directly; it is usually either too smooth or too absorbent. If too smooth, it fails to lodge the paint. If too absorbent, it soaks up the oil and gives the paint an unpleasantly "mat," dead look. More than other mediums, oil requires a tooth, a roughened surface, on which to paint. Otherwise, there is nothing to "pull" the paint off the brush and hold it in place for the picture.

Let us say that the artist is preparing canvas for an oil painting. He stretches it over a demountable wooden frame of stretchers of a given size. Unless the canvas has already been sized and primed, he applies successive layers of size, usually a rabbit-skin glue, and over them a final priming coat or series of coats of whiting, usually white lead ground in stand oil.

The painter is now ready to set his palette. He is ready, that is, to lay his colors out on a mixing slab. Here the artist's sense of direction is put to the test. What colors shall he use? The range of possibilities confronting him is enormous—earth colors, artificially prepared mineral colors, animal colors, aniline colors. Among the reds alone, for example, the array is bewildering—from Pompeiian red, Persian red, English red, to cadmium red, alizarin crimson, burnt sienna.

He may prefer a limited palette. He may set out no more than a flake white, an ivory black, and a burnt sienna. If he knows his medium well, he can get an astonishing variety of color effects with these three paints alone, a tone of white or black actually seeming blue or green, for instance, when set next to a certain tone of burnt sienna.

A painter may prefer a highly varied palette. Instead of three or four colors, he may choose fifteen or twenty or more. He chooses each of them in a given situation for a certain quality which no other color could catch. He may spread all these hues on his canvas and still create a composition remarkable for its unity.

The key to the artist's success is his eye for color relationships and his coordinated brain and hand. In an art as flexible as that of painting in oil, rigorous discipline is needed. A set palette helps to maintain such discipline. But no palette ever automatically produced a masterpiece. Only a good painter can produce a good painting.

The craft of the oil painter is subject to great diversity, but within its over-all limits two basically different methods can be detected. One is the direct method, sometimes called *alla prima* after the Italian expression meaning "at the first." The other is the indirect method, the underpainting-overpainting method which involves a predetermined stage-by-stage procedure.

Direct painting can mean either "painting directly on the prepared canvas" or "painting directly from the objects being represented." In accord with the first practice, the artist can attack the white-primed canvas "head on," introducing with stiff hog-bristle or sable brushes a stroke here, a touch there, trying to finish the picture in a single day. In accord with the second practice, he may set up his easel in front of a subject, indoors or out, and try to transcribe whatever he sees and thinks im-portant—before the subject has moved or changed in atmosphere and lighting. Usually the two practices combine, as they did at the hands of the plein-air (open-air) painters of the nineteenth century. Rarely, they are transformed into the most carefully thought-through and felt-out operation, one requiring months of daily struggle at the same spot to pierce to the essentials behind the fugitive aspects of the subject—the case pre-eminently with Cézanne (8.9a).

By indirect painting we mean a procedure akin to that of the mural. It includes exhaustive preliminary sketches and studies and the careful transfer of the cartoon to the ground. It requires underpainting in thin monochrome to indicate the masses and the modelings of form. It calls for successive glazings here and there to localize the coloring, to accentuate the shading and yield a play of light. It involves painting the lights thickly, often with scumblings for accent and textural variation, but painting the darks thinly, usually with transparent colors, for suggesting depth and recession. It means leaving the underpainting as much as possible for the half-tones. It demands prolonged drying of any given passage before adding fresh color to it, or else painting wet-in-wet for a single day's work only—with no work in between, lest the paint crack and slide around in drying.

Each type of handling results in a distinctly different form of picture. For direct painting, let us consider the Cézanne (8.9a) already cited as an example. It has a single skin of paint, but this skin is continually opening here and there to reveal flecks of the white or toned ground and traces of the original drawing underneath, characteristically done with the same brush as the painting. It has a vivacious sparkle about it, eloquent at once of the painter's momentary experience and of spontaneous brushwork.

For indirect painting, let us consider a detail of a portrait by Rembrandt here reproduced in color (Plate IV). It bears, not just one skin of paint, but several successive layers. Through the upper layers, wherever they are semitransparent, the coloring underneath shows subtly, mingling with that on top to set up a play of rich optic grays. The painting assumes an impasto of rich variation, thick to thin, rough to smooth, mellow and yet spirited to a degree of controlled expressiveness seldom reached in a directly rendered work. It supplants the sparkle of the direct painting with a deep-toned resonance possible only with prolonged reflection and carefully considered brushwork. It has richness, rather than variety of color— a richness dependent on a muting of most of the colors by graying against a contrastingly bright accent, such as that of yellow ochre, which becomes positively golden in its context. Thanks to the amount of seeing, thinking, feeling that went into its execution, the picture offers depths under depths of meaning seldom found in the directly painted work.

Whichever the method generally followed by an oil painter, he varies it freely from one picture to the next in actual studio practice. He may start out indirectly with elaborate underpainting and much glazing, and finish up with an *alla prima* attack. He may start out directly, drawing freely with his brush and disposing his painted passages openly and freely, and then scrape everything out with his palette knife until only its ghost is left, proceeding to paint over it in layer after layer of glazings, palette-knife plasterings of body color, and scumblings.

Water Color and Gouache

We mentioned in the preceding chapter certain mediums of illustration which function equally well in easel painting: tempera, water color, and gouache. We have already considered tempera as a medium of easel painting. Let us now look at the other two mediums in the present light. Water color and gouache are sister mediums, for they both employ water as a diluent, not, in spite of the name, the medium. Actually, gum arabic is the medium of water color, while Chinese white, a zinc oxide paste, is the medium of gouache. Both gum arabic and Chinese white are readily soluble in water.

The two mediums have been employed with a variety of supports—ivory, porcelain, parchment, vellum, silk, but above all, in both Orient and Occident, paper. For water color, Western artists have usually preferred a hand-made linen rag paper with a medium or coarse grain to hold the pigment readily and a glue sizing to reduce its absorbency. Chinese and Japanese artists have preferred a mulberry-bark paper almost as absorbent as blotting paper; they have learned to calculate exactly how far a stroke will spread and have often painted detail first and run washes over it afterward, the strokes for the detail having soaked in deeply enough not to be disturbed. For gouache, artists have found the demands for the paper much less exacting, a toned paper offering the same advantages in painting in lighter colors as a toned ground offers in oil, and the brown wrapping paper used in grocery stores often proving ideal.

The sable brushes useful for blending oil colors work equally well for either water color or gouache. Camel's-hair brushes are those most commonly used, although such brushes are misnamed; they are usually made of squirrel's hair. The hog's-bristle brushes used for oils give occasional effects in water color or gouache impossible with any other brush.

Water colors are composed of more or less transparent pigments which the gum medium binds to the paper and covers with a thin protective film (so easily dissolved by exposure to moisture that water-color paintings have to be framed under glass for additional safeguard). Gouache colors may be composed of exactly the same pigments and ground into exactly the same gum medium, in which case they depend on the further mixture with Chinese white to render them opaque—as the nature of the art demands. More properly, however, gouache colors are made opaque at the outset by having added to them some such white filling material as chalk—to form colors commercially produced today under the name of poster colors.

A water-color wash corresponds to an oil glaze. It is a liquid coating of color over a white or a lightly tinted ground. It depends for its value on the degree of its transparency; the less pigment diluted with water at time of application, the more the ground shows through to lighten the effect of the wash. The Occidental water-colorist normally works from a loose, lightly sketched-in pencil drawing, through a series of light but increasingly dark washes, to the final dark accents, made with the point of a brush, and sometimes with the point of a pencil.

Much more than in oil painting, the nature of the support and the behavior of the medium at the moment of application determine the form of the finished work. Correct procedure and decisiveness in following it are as rigorously demanded as they are in fresco. Water-color painting counts for much of its appeal on its sparkling freshness and openness, its immediacy of statement, its sense of the informal, accidental.

Right or wrong, the wash has to go down without delay once it has started. Other colors can be fused with the color of the wash while it is still wet. Or the wash can be gradually darkened or lightened while being floated on to the paper. While it is drying, however, it has to be left absolutely alone. In the drying process, the color concentrates more along the edge of the wash than in its center, giving added luminosity to the area by its suggestion of reflected light, and at the same time adding crispness of accent to its shape. Other washes can be laid over the initial wash when it is dry, providing they are darker and drier than the original application; but there is a strict limit to their number and to the pressure with which they are rendered; otherwise, the underlying pigment gets dislodged and mixed up with the pigment on top, to destroy the uniformity of tone and to muddy the color.

The water-color painter has open to him a variety of techniques, each with its own particular qualities. If he has something to say and knows exactly the technique which will help him say it best, he is likelier to produce a picture that communicates effectively. The water-colorist can follow the dry method, painting

"wet-on-dry" to get maximum sparkle in his lights, brilliance of color in his washes, sharpest accents in his contours. He can follow the wet method, painting "wet-in-wet" to get mysteriously blurred effects, with light mounting out of fog to a sunburst of climax, with vague suggestiveness of shape and softly saturated contours.

The painter can follow the drybrush method, stroking most of the water out of his brush on to blotting paper each time he loads it with color, then rendering a given form in his picture with a slow, dragging stroke for a dark and a light, quick stroke for a half tone, leaving after each stroke, depending on how lightly he made it, little dots of color on the tooth of the paper. He may in actual practice follow one or another of these methods exclusively, or he may, because the subject seems to demand it, combine two or more of them in a single work (8.10).

Pastel is a hybrid medium halfway between charcoal in drawing and gouache in painting. It employs the same pigment and filler as gouache, but it is made up in the form of a crumbly crayon using the least possible amount of binder (gum tragacanth). Pastel colors are drawn and rubbed broadly on to paper, a fine-grained sandpaper often being preferred for the support because of the tooth in which to lodge the powder. The looseness of the medium lends itself easily to paintinglike effects which are actually tricky and pretty without being designed. This very freedom makes pastel, paradoxically, the most difficult of all mediums to handle successfully, and few artists have ever done anything significant with it.

It takes the restraining and disciplining power of the Chinese white body to convert the pastel chalk into the truly workable medium of gouache. When out on the palette for use in the form of a paste, gouache color looks and acts like oil. On the paper support, however, it dries out flat, mat, and chalky, to reveal its true nature. Like water color, it dries out also to a lighter value than it has when wet; as in oil, on the other hand, it covers most, if not all, of the support with its many opaque layers. When utilized for its essential nature, gouache gives rise to a painting like that of Morris Graves here illustrated (8.15)—dense and weighty, yet blonde in tone and crisply tactile in appeal.

A good gouache gives expressive vent to its opacities. Still, it needs a "window," so to speak, lest its tightly closed-in layers seem too dense. Graves provided this "window" in the untouched outer areas of his support. The artist can further open his gouache to light and air by resorting to the water used as his diluent. The more water he uses, the more he converts a layer of gouache into a transparent wash. Because of the chalk in both the pigment and the vehicle, he never quite reaches the transparency of a water-color wash. But he can let enough of the white paper show through to provide a refreshing counterfoil to the thick layers of paint in the rest of the composition.

Chinese and Japanese artists often use gouache in this free transparent-translucent-opaque fashion. They do not employ gouache always as a mere adjunct to ink-painting (monochromatic water color), as did the artist of the Japanese hand scroll (7.1 to 7.4), to give body to details. They also work in the other direction, depending chiefly upon opaque color to carry the painting through, but rendering the flatter or more distant forms in transparent washes. Recognizing how difficult it is in successive layers of gouache to represent a rounded surface like that of a bird's breast or a flower's petal, they strive to model the entire form in a single stroke, with three or even four colors introduced onto separate parts of the brush at the same time, where the strokes will register properly for the form by a turn of the wrist as the arm moves.

PAINTING STYLES AND SUBJECT MATTER

Every medium of painting, mural or easel, plays a leading role in shaping style. Its fellow star in the process is the man who uses the medium, and style is a synthesis of his nature with the nature of his medium. In discussing automobile design, we noted (p. 43) how little an individual style emerges but how distinctly a cultural style and a period style stand out. In the art of painting an individual style draws more attention than either of the others. It even induces authorities to invent names for artists whose individual styles are clearly evident in a number of paintings but whose actual names have never been discovered: such names, for example, as Berlin Master or Master of the Narbonne Altarpiece. Often the works of artists following a certain master or living in a certain town develop a familylike resemblance in style that justifies their being studied under such captions as School of Rubens or School of Antwerp, School of Giotto or School of Florence. Painting is so flexible and responsive an art that its variations of style according to personality, time, and place seem more important than those of other arts.

Painting for Religion

We found (pp. 132–133) a deep-felt need impelling the practice of architecture and allied arts in ancient Egypt. It occasioned the creation of such masterpieces of portrait sculpture as the bust of Queen Nefertiti. Out of a longing for assurance that the soul would indeed live on forever, the sculptor creating this work looked to every possible means to monumentalize and animate his protrait. In his search he did not hesitate, therefore, to unite with his limestone carving the most vivid possible painting, perhaps even calling into his studio a collaborating painter.

Need to prepare for eternity was a source of livelihood for artists in ancient Egypt, for painters as well as sculptors, and especially for mural painters. Muralists were called in to decorate mansion walls with flowers and grape

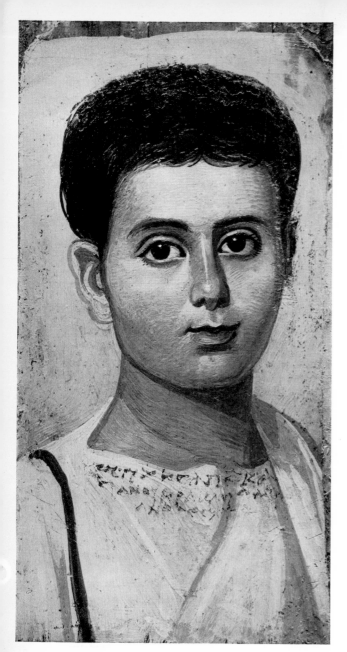

8.2. Mummy portrait of a boy, from the Fayum Valley, Egypt. 2nd century A.D. Encaustic on wood panel. 15 x 7½". Courtesy of the Metropolitan Museum of Art, New York, Edward S. Harkness Gift, 1918.

arbors as retreats from the desert. They were called in to decorate tomb walls in corresponding fashion, since life in the hereafter needed to be provided with all the good things of the present life, and since it was popularly believed that only the possessive magic of a good mural could properly do the job.

The ceiling of the tomb chamber had to be painted to look like the straw mats hung in the ordinary house for the sake of greater coolness (8.1). The top of the wall had to be painted to look like a clerestory window. The wall itself had to be covered with tier after tier of paintings representing daily existence in its multiple rounds—from tilling to harvesting, butchering to serving food.

On the walls of the Tomb of Nakht (8.1), a scribe who lived fourteen hundred years before Christ prepared for his own immortality by having a muralist guarantee in advance that his soul would be provided with all of life's necessities. He had the painter perpetuate his piety and friendly relations with his gods by portraying him and his wife making religious offerings (on the south wall to our left). He had the painter further guarantee the good luck of his future life by portraying bearers kneeling to either side of the "false" (imitation) West Door, there to welcome him back from vacation jaunts to the Land of the Dead in the West.

We are struck by the lengths to which Nakht's muralist felt obliged to go in isolating and defining every figure. He avoided wherever possible the confusion of overlapping forms. He stuck to the safe, sure flatness of the wall. With his secco medium on the mud-plastered masonry he banished shades and shadows, highlights and reflected lights. He reduced his figures to brightly colored silhouettes tied down tightly to the ground line of each zone. He avoided the complications of foreshortening in the figure, resorting in place of it to "fractional representation": the depicting of fragments most easily visualized and their joining without concern for their departure from reality—profile of head with full-face eye, profile of arms with full-face shoulders, and so on down to profile of feet.

We have seen what an important matter the soul's identification of its own body was in ancient Egypt and how it led to vivid portrait sculpture. Such portraits entered the tomb as substitute homes for the soul in case the body were destroyed, even became incorporated with the lid of the coffin itself.

When under Roman imperial rule the illusionistic realism of Greek and Roman encaustic painting became known in Egypt, people recognized its superiority for individualized portrayal. They abandoned tomb sculpture in favor of tomb painting in encaustic, portraiture on gessoed planks which could be painted from life and then placed over the coffin at death.

One surviving example of this new Egypto-Roman funerary portraiture is a picture of a boy (8.2) now hanging in the Metropolitan Museum of Art in New York. Probably it was commissioned by the boy's parents with the idea that as long as the boy lived it could hang on the wall at home, reminding everybody who saw it what the man once looked like in his youthful freshness. When he died, maybe half a century after the panel's painting, it was laid away in the tomb.

Vivid likeness, objective of the commission, was exactly what the artist caught. In portraying the boy this artist made good use of his encaustic medium. He used the impasto natural to encaustic to convey not only the look of the boy's flesh but also its feel. For emphasis by contrast he flattened the garment's coloring and the background area. He welcomed the tonality of the wax as a means of suggesting the atmosphere of the studio.

The portraitist followed a disciplined procedure. He sought to make the head look solid. He restricted his palette severely, therefore, employing only burnt sienna for the half-tones of the flesh, lead white shaded with blue for the garment, and dark green for the background. If he had widened his palette to include every note of color about the actual sitter, he would have achieved variety only at the expense of that physical presence of the youth which the parent-patrons were demanding.

The painter underscored the forms of his portrayal by giving them heavy outlines. Such outlines always operate to flatten forms, contradicting the illusion of relief which the modeling of the face was calculated to achieve. We might call this inconsistency a flaw in the composition, but we are obliged to admit as we do so that the Egypto-Roman artist has handled it successfully. He has created tensions between the outlining and the modeling and with these tensions given the portrait its own peculiar appeal. He has paid tribute with his outline to the Egyptian tradition of two-dimensional painting, and Egyptianized the illusionistic kind of painting imported from Rome.

The dark and cool retreat to which the dead repaired when they returned from the Land of the West to their tombs was not thought of by the living as a place of barren waste from which all life had departed. It was thought of as the very opposite of the scorched desert waste which Egyptians knew only too well as a place of annihilation. In the dark the living could not see either the paintings on the walls or the mummy portrait over the face of the deceased. But the soul of the departed could, by a magic, enjoy the multitude of details of real life with which the artist had surrounded him. The very darkness made this animation of painting effective by contrast.

In sunbaked Sicily, across the Mediterranean to the northwest of Egypt, Christians a thousand years after the painting of the encaustic portrait were looking for a correspondingly shadowy retreat into which to escape from the light and heat outside. They were seeking such a retreat not for burial, however, but for worship.

When Norman builders set to work about A.D. 1132 to erect a chapel for King Roger II at Palermo, they found in their environment inducement, beyond the other-worldly traditions of the Eastern Orthodox (Byzantine) Church to which they belonged, to make it dark and cool (8.3). They built its walls so massively, pierced them so sparingly, that one might easily imagine the Divine was lurking in the shadows.

Lest undifferentiated darkness fail to arouse the worshiper's devotion, they joined diverse structural elements into a fantastically rich ensemble: ancient Roman columns with Corinthian capitals, a Byzantine dome on shelflike devices called squinches, an Islamic ceiling of stalactite decorations suggesting the fantasies of caverns.

8.3. Murals in the nave of the Palatine Chapel, Palermo, Sicily. A.D. 1143. Mosaic executed by direct method. Photograph courtesy of De Magistris, successor to V. Bellotti y Fratelli, Milan.

8.4. *Saints of the Eastern Church: Gregory, Basil, John Chrysostom*, detail of Palatine Chapel murals. Photograph courtesy of De Magistris, successor to V. Bellotti y Fratelli, Milan.

All of this would have proved merely diverting, however, if the designer-builders had not enlisted painters to cover their walls with murals. There was no question over the medium to employ; only mosaic could pick up the little light admitted and make images visible. The painters so ordered their tesserae as to convert the chapel walls into a vision of heavenly hosts.

Let us look, for example, at one sequence of Fathers of the Church on a side wall (8.4). The figures are flat. They stand separate from each other in formal array. They hold themselves rigidly upright like the weight-bearing wall of which they form the face. They comport themselves as though gravely conscious of their dual role as structure-stressing ornaments and champions of Christ. They press tightly against the wall between the windows. Yet such is the light-reflecting power of the gold tesserae in the background that they are made to seem real saints silhouetted against the radiant depths of Paradise.

Painting for Humanism

Byzantium, though the source of the tradition and even perhaps of the artists for Palermo's mosaics, is a paradox of history. This capital of an empire nurtured for a thousand years that art of disembodied representation which we have been examining. Yet it treasured through the same millennium Greek texts bearing the germ of an ideal which had once inspired (4.2 and 5.7) and would again inspire (5.9) a totally different art. Byzantine Christians conceived of man in forms divested of all substance. But these texts championed the concept of man as a physically perfect whole, after whom the Greeks had patterned their gods and determined their systems of measurement and proportion.

When Constantinople fell to the Turks in 1453, Byzantine scholars fled to Italy, bearing these same Greek manuscripts with them. Largely because of their books, it would seem, the refugees met an especially cordial reception at the court of the Medici in Florence, a banker-family whose enlightened patronage was making the city the leading art center of the age. The Medici and their circle subjected the Greek texts to minute study and evolved out of that study a modified revival of the ancient philosophy of Neoplatonism.

According to Neoplatonism, man was once incorporated with God and God was Ideal Beauty. Through some disastrous accident, he became separated from God and condemned to lead a miserably incomplete existence. Man longed to become reunited with God and his longing constituted the instinct of love. Since anything beautiful on this earth was an emanation from God, man could with proper religious sanction love it as a way to unity with God. He could appropriately love a beautiful woman, or a painting of one. Naturally thus, Neoplatonism resurrected something of the cult of the goddess whom the Greeks had called Aphrodite and the Romans Venus. It encouraged adoration of any lady whose charms might seem to attest to her being invested by ideal beauty—or the spirit of Venus.

The Venus legend often inspired Renaissance pageantry, one of the most remarkable of such occasions being a tournament given by Lorenzo de' Medici in 1475. At this affair Lorenzo staged a series of tableaux which featured the birth of the Goddess and her annual springtime return to the realm of mankind. According to one legend, Venus was born of the foam of the sea (*Aphrodite* means "foam-born" in Greek). She floated in off the sea on a scallop shell, wringing brine from her hair while zephyrs blew her along and nymphs waited on shore to receive her. Some versions of the account have it that she landed at Paphos on the island of Cyprus; others that she disembarked at Cythera on the island of that name; still others, that she first went ashore at Porto Venere on the Bay of La Spezia in northwestern Italy.

The Birth of Venus would have been a perfect subject for such a tableau. Stage sets could be painted to simulate waves and shore. A concealed carriage could carry the shell across the stage. Persons could be readily engaged to act the roles of zephyrs and nymphs. But who

8.5. Sandro Botticelli (1444–1510): *The Birth of Venus. c.* 1485. Tempera on canvas. 5′3¼″ x 8′11″. Uffizi Gallery, Florence. Alinari photograph.

could be found worthy of and willing to take the role of Venus?

There happened to be at the Medici court a certain lady celebrated for both her beauty and her charm of personality. Simonetta was her name. Born in Porto Venere itself, she was the perfect answer to the Neoplatonists' ideal of female beauty. They made her Beauty Queen for the pageant; this we know. That she further served as the Venus of this tableau is a strong possibility.

One year after the tournament Simonetta suddenly died, leaving memory of her role at the pageant to haunt the minds of all who had seen her. The poet Poliziano wrote a poem describing the presumed tableaux in detail.* And Sandro Botticelli, favorite painter of the Medici court, created some ten years later the third and best of his series of pictures commemorat-

ing in allegorical form the features of the pageant.

Botticelli seems to have had no thought of being literal. He was intent on achieving an interpretation worthy of the subject itself. The goddess had to seem light enough to float convincingly shoreward before the breezes. In order to make her so, the artist found tempera a perfect medium. He found in it his cue for linear emphasis—and over line he was already master. He subordinated all modeling to it, therefore, making his tempera hatchings so delicate as to appear to caress the contours instead of hiding them.

If the Venus figure was to be lightly airy, so must the picture as a whole. Botticelli found his cue for this quality, too, in the tempera medium. Keeping his coloring limpid and transparent, he achieved to a remarkable degree that sense of inner luminosity which the reflected light of the gesso was ready to offer. He abolished almost all cast shadow and rendered the little shadow remaining so indefinite as to seem likewise bathed in radiance. As our

* Agnolo Poliziano (1454–1494), "La Giostra di Giuliano de' Medici," pub. in part in both It. and Eng. trans., W. Parr Greswell, *Memoirs of Angelus Politianus,* etc. (London: Cadell and Davies, 1805), pp. 4–13.

8.6. Raphael Sanzio (1483–1520): *The School of Athens*, Room of the Signature, Vatican, Rome. 1509–1511. Fresco. Alinari photograph.

color reproduction of the head of Venus indicates (Plate III),* he converted his coloring largely to tints subordinate to the lines, and in such fuller-bodied accents as the red robe extended by the nymph, and the blue garments of the zephyrs, took care never to lose a contour (8.5). He made plastic gold, formerly reserved by convention for haloes over the heads of saints in tempera altarpieces, serve as highlights of the golden hair of Venus and a glowing frame for her features.

Against a background of ornamental details rendered in linear shorthand (for waves, shell, flowers, leaves, and the like), Botticelli then devoted his fullest powers to perfecting a dancelike rhythm of line about the foreground figures. With a detached but tactile-appealing line,† he caused the zephyrs to sweep in from

the left in bulging lines, the nymph to rush in from the right in fluttering lines, and Venus to sway upward and rightward at the center in smoothly gliding lines. Botticelli created in this way the most expressive of all climaxes— a gently moving form against activated flanking forms for contrast. His tempera painting is limited in what it says, but limited by design to say what it has to say all the more strongly.

Neoplatonism not only succeeded in reviving the cult of Venus in such a tempera as this Botticelli. It also succeeded in revolutionizing the Christian Church at Rome. In the name of union between ancient Greek philosophy and traditional Christian theology, it inspired the Church to resist the tide of criticism that was to culminate in open revolt under Martin Luther in 1519. Against this tide the Vatican sought to protect itself by annexing the prestige of ancient Greece and Rome, and in the realm of art to propagandize the union in a grandly classic manner. It called in to cover the walls of the Papal palace the ablest frescoists of all

---

* Reproduced in color, double-page fold-out, Lionello Venturi, *Botticelli* (Phaidon Press Series; New York: Oxford University Press, 1937), Pl. 34.
† Stressed by Bernard Berenson, *The Italian Painters of the Renaissance* (New York: Phaidon Press, 1952; 1st pub., 1894–1907), pp. 67–69.

Italy, among them one destined to bring the Renaissance classic ideal to culmination: Raffaello di Sanzio, better known by his Anglicized name, Raphael.

For the ruling Pope, Julius II, Raphael began in 1509 frescoes calculated to reaffirm the Church's claim that the Pope was appointed by God to head Church and State. He planned his painting specifically for walls of four reception rooms on the second floor of the Vatican. Although the overburdened artist died in 1520 before completing the murals, leaving them for assistants to finish, he did execute by his own hand paintings in the first room befitting its use as Stanza della Segnattura—room in which the Pope affixed his signature ("segnattura") to official documents.

In one of the frescoes in this first room Raphael attested to the thesis that Christian theology was the legitimate heir to ancient Greek philosophy (8.6). He represented as gathered at the entrance of what was probably meant to be the new St. Peter's, only then under erection, all leading philosophers of the Occident.* He represented them as rapt in solemn argument around Plato and Aristotle at the center; within their august company he actually portrayed himself, crowded modestly against the frame at the extreme right, documenting himself in this way as the fresco's creator.

The painting fits easily into its wall, a skillfully painted arch serving to enclose it and unite it to the actual architecture of the room. It utilizes a door cut awkwardly through the wall at the lower left as though the door were a desired feature of the composition, to accentuate the illusion of the painted space behind it. The painting seems to open the wall out into a deep recession but it so groups the figures and overlaps the planes of the architecture represented as to refer repeatedly to the flat plane of the wall on which the work was painted. Everything about the picture is under

* Each figure in *The School of Athens* is identified in a diagram accompanying a reproduction of the painting, Sewall, *History of Western Art, op. cit.*, pp. 674, 675.

control, bounded and definite, symmetrically disposed in relation to everything else. Far from a stereotype of academic formula, the mural seems to pulsate with life. It derives its vitality from the telling counterpoise of heads, limbs, whole figures, and groups of figures, and the bell-like swinging movements which such units maintain. It derives its vitality from the buoyant space seeming to fill the vaults of the building depicted. It derives its vitality, finally, from the recognition that only fresco frankly treated could embody the classic ideal that Raphael sought.

Portraiture

Efforts made by Pope Julius II and his successors to hold Christendom together were destined to fall short of their objective. When Raphael died in 1520, the Protestant Reformation had already started. Before the century was out, much of northern Europe had disclaimed allegiance to the authority of the Vatican, and the Netherlands (Lowlands) had broken in two, the southern provinces, remaining with the Church, to form Belgium, the northern provinces, declaring their independence, to form Holland.

There was more to this cleavage, of course, than rivalries of church and state and scruples over ritual. The cleavage had to do with emergence of a new outlook on life, one which encouraged an individual to go his own way, study the Scriptures for himself, and work out his own destiny. Individualism supplanted centralized authority. An ideal of personal character development replaced the classic ideal of physical beauty. A search for the godlike in man took over from the old concept of God as glorified man.

As always, because art is expression of deeply felt experience in sensuous and rhythmically organized form, painting had to change with the change in way of life and thought To an individual trying to discover things for himself, the whole idea of submission to authority, even Greco-Roman classic authority in art, came to seem intolerable. The disciplines of tempera and fresco painting failed to jibe with the new frame of mind. Only such freedom in self-expression as oil made possible could really satisfy.

It was not by accident, therefore, that oil painting came to predominate in the Lowlands of Jan van Eyck, the medium's pioneer. With oil as with no other medium, these northern artists could pursue light, penetrate shadow, get down under the surface of things, and reveal their inner life. With oil they could catch the moods of weather in a landscape, the hustle of the market in a cityscape, the camaraderie of the inn or bonhomie of the home in an interior. They could catch especially in a portrait the impress made on character by the struggles of existence, the graces left on the countenance by all the joys, sorrows, and agonies involved in the act of living. These were things that mattered most to Dutch burghers, things that they looked for most in the pictures they hung on their walls at home.

We have already seen how one Dutch master, Rembrandt, came to identify himself, and to draw us into the same identification, with an intimately personal Bible subject—in his etching called *The Raising of Lazarus* (7.9). Counterpart in oil to this intensive reliving of a subject is such a painting by Rembrandt as his *Man with a Magnifying Glass* (8.7). The work is a portrait, and it is with it that we mean to tarry, because Rembrandt thought of himself as primarily a portrait painter and left no less than four hundred portraits (self-portraits, single portraits, and group portraits), at least two-thirds of his lifework in painting.

The man who posed for the portrait is unknown. He was probably a wealthy Jewish friend of Rembrandt's in Amsterdam, city in which the artist lived and worked. The patron commissioned of his painter-friend at the same time a companion portrait of his wife, now hanging under title of *Lady with a Pink*, with his own portrait in the Metropolitan Museum of Art in New York City. The sitter had already commissioned a double portrait of himself and his wife, one probably intended to commemorate their marriage since it bears

8.7. Rembrandt van Rijn (1606–1669): *Man with a Magnifying Glass*. 1665–1669. Oil on canvas. 36 x 29¼". Courtesy of The Metropolitan Museum of Art, New York, Bequest of Benjamin Altman, 1913.

the title of *The Jewish Bride*. This picture is now in the Rijksmuseum, Amsterdam.

For want of the sitter's name, the portrait reproduced here has been given a peculiarly apt title, for Amsterdam in the seventeenth century led the world in the manufacture, trade, and utilization of glassware—and the lens held in the sitter's hand calls attention to the fact. It also points to the painter's interest in glassware, something which he frequently introduced into his pictures and made an important part of his daily life. Rembrandt used mirrors, not just to shave with but to study his own features from, painting from his mirrors some sixty portraits of himself! He did this not out of vanity—there is nothing flattering about the surviving self-portraits—but out of an urge to pierce beneath his features to his inner self and try to understand it.

By the time, toward the end of his life, that Rembrandt came to paint the *Man with a*

Magnifying Glass, the artist had suffered much and found a bond of sympathy with other men. He had learned just what to seize about a man's features as best revealing character. The richer the subject's personality, the greater the challenge and the higher the painter rose to meet it.

Rembrandt had also learned to master the techniques of oil so that they were no longer a problem to him. With pigments on palette and with brushes and palette knife in hand, he could absorb himself in the portrayal at hand. He could peer into his sitter's features, search for the soul beneath them, and register, unconsciously as in writing, exactly what he found.

The detail of the *Man with a Magnifying Glass* here reproduced in color (Plate IV) indicates how Rembrandt fused his portrayal and his handling. Starting out with a warm gray underpainting as though it were a fathomless abyss, he sought to feel in it the same presence of the spirit which the Byzantine mosaicists had suggested by setting their tesserae onto walls in actual spatial darkness. Gradually, with thin but darker accents and transparent glazings and thick lights, he evolved a more and more solidly defined head—until the form most vividly suggested the soul beneath but still did not conceal it, when he stopped abruptly.

Rembrandt exploited in the process the widest possible range of effects open to oil. He manipulated the paint with tactile variations, now floating it on like a wash, now brushing it in with subtle changes of value and plastic turnings of stroke, now plastering it on with palette knife, molding it with his thumb, incising it with his brush-handle. He varied his edgings rhythmically—sharpening, blurring, merging with background—to give the picture a loose and freely open form. He reserved the major portions of his canvas for quietly modulated grays, and against them struck his boldest accents about the face as it came into the light, in notes of scarlet and vermilion, heavy-bodied Naples yellow and white lead. Through such a technique Rembrandt achieved a magic of coloring, unified in its red-yellow tonality and plastic in its impasto.

Rembrandt followed the "light-into-dark" method of painting which he mastered probably more fully than any other painter. So varied, however, is the art of painting and so responsive to every subtle shade of feeling, that it would be wrong to set such a portrait on some "unapproachable" pedestal. The ways of painting are infinite and their forms no less.

A portrait (8.8) by the French painter, Edgar Degas (1834–1917) is a case in point. According to a method diametrically opposite to "dark-into-light," it was painted *alla prima* on a white-primed canvas. If Degas had been asked why he worked in this way, he would probably have had no answer; he disliked talking about his art almost as much as he disliked people. One of his fellow "luminists," as they sometimes called themselves, however, might have volunteered the explanation that white canvas was necessary because, as a fusion of all colors, it left a faithful registry of any hue, value, or intensity set against it. And a faithful registry of such an attribute of color was necessary if one were painting from nature (as one should, if one desired to parallel the scientist of the day in making an analytical study of reality).

The only proper subject of a painting was, he would declare, the light, and no other subject mattered much except insofar as it brought out accurately the fugitive nature of light. To do so required just as subtle a weighing of hues, values, and intensities against each other as Degas managed brilliantly in the portrait. Instead of *Head of a Young Woman*, the apologist for Degas might have concluded, the painting ought to be called *Study in Light*.

In 1867, when the young lady posed for her portrait, photography was turning the Paris art world topsy-turvy. Lured by it, one-time patrons of the portrait painters were lining up to await their turn before the "salons" of popular portrait photographers. They were willing, when their turns came at last, to have their heads clamped into an iron frame to keep them from moving during the prolonged exposures required by daguerreotypy. They were willing to suffer such discomfiture in the hope that they might have the joy of taking home after its development at least one daguerreotype of first quality in sharpness of focus and lifelike effect.

Degas looked with envious eyes at the photographers of his day. He was one of the artists convinced that the new art might one day take the place of the old. In the meantime he was resolved to make the most of what photography had to teach him about visual appearances. Involuntarily he introduced dabs of coppery coloring into this portrait to suggest that there was a copper plate like that of the daguerreotype underneath.

Otherwise, as though anticipating the days of the snapshot and the action photograph, days which were yet to come, he introduced over his whole painting of the girl's head a soft blur of contour, a delicate shimmer as though the subject were in motion.

In his attempt thus to suggest movement, Degas in his own way was seeking the effects of the fleeting moment featured in the Japanese color prints which he was collecting and studying. As in these prints, which, as we have noted, their makers called "floating world pictures," the French artist was seeking to convey effects of the passing scene, casually caught and informally presented.

In spite of his desire to suggest the accidental, Degas was too much the artist to miss the lessons offered by such master prints as Hiroshige's *Evening Snowfall at Asukayama, Near Edo.* He learned from such prints to create effects of movement in keeping with the fleeting nature of his subjects—through rhythmically ordered lines. He developed such a system of lines for the contours of the girl's features, veiled under their blur, but nonetheless present to enliven the portrayal.

Degas further learned from Japanese prints to value the shapes of the negative background areas as much as the shapes of the positive areas out in front. He designed them tellingly to repeat each other with variations from side to side in the picture. Whatever the protestations of fellow luminists that they were looking only for the accidental in theme and treat-

8.8. Edgar Degas (1834–1917): *Head of a Young Woman.* 1867. Oil on canvas. 10⅝ x 8⅝". Courtesy of the Louvre, Paris.

ment, he evolved through such devices in design a pleasing picture of a pleasing subject. Like the Rembrandt, the Degas was painted to hang on a wall at home, but it was different in its nature as a portrait because its objectives were different.

Landscape

This casualness of approach to portraiture applied more fittingly to landscape painted outdoors before the actual scene itself. It developed into a more or less formless rendering of momentary effects in broken color. Coming to be known as impressionism, it divorced its devotees increasingly from traditions of composition, craftsmanship, and considered subject matter. It tended to reduce its followers to mere eyes, its works to confettilike dabs.

Within fifteen years of its first appearance about 1870, impressionism was revealing even

8.9. The Natural Landscape and Its Painting. a. Paul Cézanne (1839–1906): *Village of Gardanne*. 1885–1886. Oil on canvas. 36¼ x 28¾". Courtesy of the Brooklyn Museum, Brooklyn, N. Y. b. John Rewald: Photograph of the village of Gardanne, made at the spot where Cézanne originally set his easel. Courtesy of John Rewald.

to some of its champions how much of a blind alley it really was. Some, like Paul Cézanne, who had learned his coloring from impressionist friends, became convinced that color need not be the destroyer of form but the stuff out of which pictorial structure could be created afresh. Cézanne, too, painted landscape, but he painted it in a radically dissimilar way.

Consider, for example, the *Village of Gardanne* (8.9a) which Cézanne painted in 1885 and 1886 at the height of his reaction against impressionism. His theme was a village which he had known from childhood, near his home in Provence in southern France. The church on the hill, the emplacement of one-time mills above it, every house and tree below it meant something to him as a native of the locale. When he came to paint this subject he was growing impatient with the literal recording of landscape under sunlight, whether handled in the impressionists' or any earlier manner. He was still looking to nature for the motives of his paintings, but he yearned to set on canvas only those aspects of the visual world which seemed "solid and enduring, like the art of museums."

Now it is true that this region of southern France is adapted to abstractions. The sun shining through cloudless air seems to simplify the planes of the barren, rocky landscape, to vivify their contours. The people and their dwellings seem as timeless as the weather; they seem never to change nor to want to change.

One might think that Cézanne could have gained a corresponding effect of permanence simply by transcribing Gardanne in a pre-impressionistic, realistic manner which photography had encouraged in the art of Degas two decades earlier. The painter did station himself on a hill overlooking the town. He did follow that *alla prima* method of painting which we have described Degas as following in his portrait of 1867. If he had rendered the scene literally, however, he might have made it look much like the photograph which the painter's biographer took many years later, not as a work of camera art but merely as a record

(8.9b).* He would have conveyed the general look of the place, but he would have missed the *feel* of the town. He would have missed the drop into the valley, the rise from housetop to housetop up the opposite hillside, and, above all, the apparent growth of one element from another.

The forms taking shape on Cézanne's canvas were not the forms recorded thus casually by the camera. They were the forms sifted out from nature, transposed, distorted, and simplified, even as the artist felt was necessary to capture their structural essence. Encouraged, no doubt, by the vertical format of the canvas upon which he worked, Cézanne retained of the foreground mass of trees only shapes leading upward. He increased the distance between the housetops, merged the churchyard wall with the walls of the church itself, and elongated the proportions of the building. He exaggerated the narrowness and steepness of the hilltop but rounded off its contour in a final passage of return to the forms below it.

By developing these abstractions, Cézanne followed a technique of almost infinite deliberateness. Against the white canvas, at some spot lending interest to the proportions of the intervals around it, he struck in a single note —a stretch of roof, perhaps, or the branch of a tree. Responding then to the spaces affected, the artist recognized the need for another note, located exactly where it would seem to balance the first. That the tension between these two forms might be resolved and one of them allowed to dominate, he sensed the need for a third note. The new passage seemed naturally to evoke a fourth, the fourth a fifth, and so on, until ultimately the picture could be regarded by the artist as complete. Much trial and error was involved in the process, much scraping and doing over, but the beauty of the process lay at every step in the retention of invigorating intervals of white, and these spaces func-

* Similar comparisons, John Rewald (Margaret H. Liebman, trans.), *Paul Cézanne* (New York: Simon and Schuster, 1948); and documentary film: *La Provence de Cézanne* (Franco-American Film Bureau, distrib.; black and white, sound, French; 20 mins.).

tioned in conjunction with the positive forms no matter at what stage of completeness the painting happened to be.

Although the artist may never have considered the *Village of Gardanne* complete, we find it, for all of its areas of exposed canvas and loosely sketched-in notations, perhaps in part because of them, a peculiarly satisfying work. The oil may still seem to be evolving, but its apparent lack of finish is deceiving. We have only to examine the work to discover how carefully its careless-looking elements have been put together. Not a form nor a stroke but has been calculated for its effect upon the whole.

The forms of the landscape painting do more than represent objects; they serve in the same way as posts serve to compose a building. They have structural power. The secret of their power lies not so much, however, in their architectural analogies; it lies rather in the extraordinary value Cézanne was able by disassociation to attach to the elements which we have already noted as going to make a painting: line, area, texture, mass, space, and color. The filled-in areas maintain their own rhythmic relationships, but the lines keep time with them in a syncopated manner, invading an area or departing from it, sharpening an edge or doubling it. Some areas bear in graduated values expressively toward an edge; others unfold in hatched or scalloped or smoothly merging strokes. Each passage describes a texture; it further contributes its own brief run of movement. The very intervals, as in the Japanese prints, shaped from voids by the positive areas around them, become participants in a symphonic ensemble.

Chief among the elements composing this Cézanne is its color. The artist discovered that by bringing color to its richest realization he could make a painting assume its fullest form. He developed the composition of the *Village of Gardanne* primarily by an ordering of its hues and intensities. Mixing warm colors with warm, and cool colors with cool, he increased the brilliance of the passages to be emphasized and gave them luminosity. Mixing warm

colors with cool, on the other hand, he produced a series of more or less muted grays which he used to subordinate certain areas to others. He set complementaries against each other to their mutual enhancement, and related hues in plastic modulations. In the complex of rhythmically protruding and receding passages thus created, Cézanne replaced the conventional modeling in the light and dark values of a single color by the expressive use of oil colors in their full range of hue and intensity.

The French master realized, on the other hand, that he could not in the same picture maintain color at its maximum brilliance and represent objects at their maximum roundness. Such features are mutually incompatible. He reduced the apparent roundness of surfaces, therefore, by bounding them with lines, blue lines that tend both to flatten as they define and to increase the vibrancy of the adjoining colors.

Prior to Cézanne's creation of such a picture as this, pictures were customarily painted to be looked at from without. Objects were represented each from a single point of view, however much that point of view might shift up or down from one object to the next. Beginning with such works as the landscape by Cézanne, pictures tended more and more to reflect a totally new attitude towards space. The remarkable openness of Cézanne's rendering, the frankness with which it betrays the canvas and the initial notations between the brushstrokes, may seem crude to the unaccustomed eye. Such qualities are the inevitable result of the artist's endeavor to place himself and the observer in the very midst of the landscape, not just out in front of it. They are the consequence of his endeavor to move along, and to make us move along, with the forms ascending the hill. Cézanne wanted us to feel the invisible energy which seemed to be animating everything in view, not just to look at the countryside superficially.

Cézanne's landscape represents in this way the newer kind of painting. It marks that revolutionary break with the past which requires

8.10. John Marin (1870–1953): *Barn in the Berkshires*. 1925. Water color on rough paper. 14⅛ x 18⅛". Courtesy of the Brooklyn Museum, Brooklyn, N. Y.

of us as observers a correspondingly radical adjustment. In viewing works of the past we have been obliged to remain more or less detached, viewing them through a sequence of moments. Whether two-dimensional or three-dimensional, space was always treated as something separate from the objects represented, at times, as in the Rembrandt, intermingling with the objects but still remaining separate. In viewing works done since Cézanne's day, on the other hand, we are asked to enter into the very heart of the work and become a part of it all, looking from the inside out. We are called upon to respond to the objects represented as though they were shot through with energy and space.

The increasing openness of form necessitated by this concept of "interiority" * drove

Cézanne more and more toward water color. He died before he could concentrate exclusively on water color, however, leaving to a younger generation development in the more fluid medium. John Marin (1870–1953) was an American painter distinguished for producing water colors comparable for carrying power with works in the weightier medium by Cézanne.

Marin had from the beginning of his career in the first decade of this century shown a predilection for water color. He had come progressively to master it as a means of hinting at the formative forces behind external appearances. On one sketching trip in the Berkshire Hills of New York, he found especially intriguing the land-and-sky effect following a shower. Through the electrically charged at-

* First formulated by Henri Bergson (1859–1941) in doctoral dissertation at Sorbonne, Paris, published,

1889: *Essai sur les Données Immédiates de la Conscience.*

mosphere he watched the forms of nature busily rearranging themselves after the downpour, the water-soaked fields reflecting the drama in the sky. Under a rift in the clouds he perceived how for brief moments of suspense the landscape offered elements so well attuned as to invite a series of notations on their form and color.

Equipped with his jottings, Marin returned to his studio, there to settle himself at a sheet of coarse-grained paper and to create on it an abstraction of his experience (8.10). The artist started with the lighter tones of his painting. Progressing methodically towards the darker tones, though sometimes stroking in a major accent for reference, he reserved till last the deepest notes of emphasis. Some of the later forms he rendered in a drybrush technique; by the stippling so gained he made a spirited variation in shading and texture. Throughout the course of the painting he preserved the original white of the paper; he not only used it for the highlights but heightened by its contrast the sparkle of the colors and the sharpness of their boundaries.

The resulting painting captured one of nature's fleeting moments but it was not for that reason hastily rendered. Meant for pictorial analysis, it became a carefully thought-through study. Although it now seems to us electrified into action, each apparently hasty stroke was made to follow its predecessor only after minutes, or even hours, of deliberation.

Like the process creating it, Marin's water color became a concentrated thing. It dwelt less upon the landscape itself than upon the movements occurring within it—the massing of clouds, the driving of rain by wind, the sag of sodden earth, the upthrust of barn and silos. In almost explosive openness of form it operated as much through its intervals as through its positive passages, intervals set off against each other to compose, within a margin left to recall the original support, the structure of the picture and the realization of its subject. Toward the utmost forcibleness of expression, it received the gesture and radiance of every wash of blue-gray water, yellow ochre soil, or blue-green turf, every stroke of ultramarine shadow or Indian-red wall.

Fusing Space and Time

Cézanne's and Marin's landscapes were pioneering works, but the trails which they blazed went only part way in the new direction. The paintings which we are now about to introduce have gone the whole way. The measure of their strangeness, like that of the Calders and the Gabos of sculpture, is a measure of that transformation wrought upon our habits of seeing and feeling by automobile, airplane, radio, television, and still more startling contrivances for conquering space and time. Once we have learned to see such pictures as intended, we can share with their creators artistic reactions to an experience into which, willy-nilly, we are all being plunged.

The earliest of such paintings stemmed directly from Cézanne's. They developed naturally out of the desire to realize the "interiority" of experience in a painting. If, as in Cézanne, the planes of an object had been emphasized, loosened so much that the support showed through, it eventually became necessary to think about what the planes looked like from other angles—above, below, behind, inside—to speculate over the means whereby to represent in a single picture all aspects of the object.

Examination of the actual object would require space and time. Thanks to the freedom of painting, on the other hand, space and time could be telescoped together. Renderings of separate planes could all be assembled on the flat surface of the canvas and made to present thus simultaneously aspects viewed originally only in succession. For simplification and emphasis, planes could be squared off, contours accented by outlining or shading. Illusions of mass and deep space could be abolished and planes which overlapped sometimes, to be sure, could be made to seem never to recede behind the picture plane.

Thus was created a cubist painting, exemplified by that shown here (8.11) by Georges

Braque (1881–   ), a French founder of cubism. Not at all a representation of cubes, as the name cubist erroneously implies, this picture is two-dimensional. It gives an occasional hint, through the texture, color, or shape of a plane, of the identity of the objects with which the abstraction started, but it has gone so far in the process that it can no longer lean on representation as a substitute for weak composition. It stands alone on its own structural legs, every area of plane and background carefully spaced, every shape sensitively proportioned.

In the process of trying to arrive at a satisfactory ordering of planes, as Braque did in this painting, the artist might facilitate his job by cutting pieces of paper to correspond to intended planes, and by pushing them around on the canvas until they seemed just right. If movable pieces of paper worked so well, he might ask, why not make them the final forms and render them as such? Why not use planes of other materials, chosen for their natural textures and colors, and eliminate most of the work of actually painting them?

It was through some such process of free experimentation and adaptation that a new medium came into existence. Called collage, after the French verb *coller*, meaning "to paste," the name of this medium indicated at least the adhesive, if not the vehicle, used in the process. And collage played a prominent role in the course of cubist painting until it came to an end about 1925.

Collages were usually small, but Braque took the medium seriously enough to create colossal works with it. One such canvas (8.11) can even be accepted today as of major importance. The artist used the back of an oil on canvas for the purpose; perhaps he thought that if he failed he would not be wasting canvas; thus ridding himself of inhibitions, he was able to work more freely.

Braque undertook to create a still life based on the various odds and ends lying in his studio—easel, canvas, palette, side-table, guitar, and the like. He strove to match the planes of these objects with cardboard trimmings

8.11. Georges Braque (1881–   ): *Collage*. 1918. Miscellaneous fragments pasted on canvas, additional painting in oil. 52 x 29½". Philadelphia Museum of Art, Philadelphia, Walter C. Arensberg Collection. Sam Little photograph, courtesy of Walter C. Arensberg.

and crumpled papers salvaged from the waste basket, fragments of wall-paper advertisements and of newspaper cut at random, and pieces of sandpaper and wood veneer. Keeping these pieces chiefly rectangular in shape, he assembled them and pasted them down to overlap each other and incline in strong axial movements inward from the frame. He maintained an active relationship between these fragments and the surrounding areas of canvas, and seized eagerly every chance to enhance the effect with newsprint, photographic reproductions, and the like for the sake of textural variations.

The artist did not stop in this case with a simple collage. The canvas seemed to call for the addition of oil paint, and Braque met this demand with passages of deep-toned, mellow grays. He invaded some areas of pasted-on paper with these painted passages, knitting the composition together while obliterating no portion. He even managed with additions in oil to create around the collage proper a spatial illusion that seemed to project it forward. Within the space of this illusion he introduced, as though he saw them in a half-waking state, fragmentary glimpses of the studio and its trappings—to complete a composition surprisingly full and mellow in appeal, considering the casual way in which it began.

We have remarked at the hint in Braque's collage that he was creating in a semiconscious state. In the process of improvising, fancy did, as a matter of fact, become a fertile source for another kind of painting. It led to creation of a technique for probing the hidden recesses of the mind. Called "automatic writing" or "psychic automatism," this process started with aimless scrawls, often made blindfolded. When the artist came to examine these lines with a mind vaguely abstracted, he found that they combined into all sorts of monstrous shapes. With a little development of line here and there and a little filling-in of color, he professed to complete his painting.

No great change was necessary to transform doodling into the subconsciously expressive techniques by which Freudian psychology was thought to apply to art. Clinical in aim, to evoke fantasies from levels of personality below the conscious, the painter was supposed to employ such techniques much as a psychoanalyst's patient is encouraged to employ the techniques of free association and stream of consciousness. The resulting art of surrealism ("above realism") came to embody in its forms the carefree spirit which followed the First World War. Although it survived that era, flourished through the Great Depression and the Second World War and the war's aftermath, it never lost its original casualness of approach nor its alertness to the picture-worthy aspects of accident.

As the 1927 *Seated Woman* (8.12) by Pablo Picasso (1881–   ) bears witness, surrealistic painting constituted much more than a technical innovation. It gave rise to a complex of shapes directly opposed to those of cubistic art: elaborately double-curved instead of angular, continuously interpenetrating instead of overlapping. In viewing such a picture as this, one gets the eerie sensation of looking through the figure and walls of the room, as well as at their surfaces. There is no foreground nor background, no mass nor void, no planes turned toward light nor planes turned toward shadow. All is one intricately interwoven complex—a complex in which the near and the far, the positive and the negative, seem by double-imagery always to be taking each other's places. The time-honored laws of composition still hold. But the forms themselves in their sensitive adjustment to contemporary forces could have been conceived in no other time than one of aerial flight, radio-listening and X-ray seeing.

Picasso seems to have felt that a composition of such complexity required machinelike smoothness for balance. He eliminated all variegated impasto, therefore, to make his picture coldly impersonal and withdrawn. He was able to hint in this way at the character of the dreamworld in which the forms originated. He was able to suggest that a rift in the fog of rationality was affording a glimpse of that great ocean of being which has no tangible bounds.

Joan Miró (1893–   ) in *Figures in the Night* (8.13) produced a different version of surrealist painting. Spanish, like Picasso, and as perversely faithful to subconscious meanderings, this younger artist put his canvas support and his oil medium to more expressive use. Salvaging from the trash can a tiny frag-

8.12. Pablo Picasso (1881–
    ): *Seated Woman*. 1926–
1927. Oil on canvas. 51½ x
38½″. The Museum of Modern Art, New York.

8.13. Joan Miró (1893–
    ): *Figures in the Night*.
1940. Oil on canvas mounted on composition board. 6⅝ x
8″. The Miller Company Collection of Abstract Art, Meriden, Conn. Courtesy of the Miller Company and Fred Heidel.

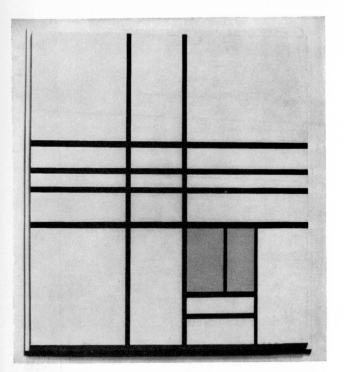

8.14. Piet Mondrian (1872–1944): *Abstraction.* 1936. Oil on canvas. 33¼ x 30½". Philadelphia Museum of Art, Philadelphia, Walter C. Arensberg Collection. Sam Little photograph, courtesy of Walter C. Arensberg.

ment of canvas, he emphasized its irregularity of shape by mounting it on a black-surfaced mat, emphasized its character as refuse by smudging it with paint.

The first thing that strikes us, when confronted by the fantasy, is a pair of irregular black blots (are they human beings, insects, amoebas, or all three at once?). Next come scrawlings in between, apparently aimless but actually tying the two major blots together. These silhouettes and lines alone, as proved by our black-and-white reproduction, would still make the painting function. But it is the coloring of the original work which gives *Figures in the Night* its particular charm. This coloring underlies the silhouetted shapes as intensified open space—floating like cloud in the infinite depths of the sky. As scrubbings of violet, viridian, crimson, and yellow, it emits its own inner glow.

Representation vs. Nonrepresentation

Cubists and surrealists went far in abstraction, but they always managed somehow to keep one foot in the realm of representation. They depended for much of the appeal of their art, in fact, on associations made by the observer with creatures existing apart from their works. Another style flourishing in twentieth-century painting denies all representational significance whatsoever. It is appropriately called purism, but it is also known as nonobjectivism, neoplasticism, and Suprematism.

Chief advocate of purism in painting was Piet Mondrian (1872–1944). Native to the same Lowlands that produced Rembrandt and van Gogh, Mondrian reacted to his countryside in totally different fashion. He found the cue for his painting, not in overcast skies and scurrying patches of light and shadow, but in the dikes, canals, and drainage ditches which everywhere sliced the land into rectangles. Mondrian made straight lines and rectangles the constants of his paintings and freed them from all service to representation.

In quest of what he called "pure reality" the Dutch purist created such completely nonrepresentational oils as the *Abstraction* of 1936 (8.14). He followed in its painting a procedure that was indeed a model of self-discipline. Stripping himself, as he put it, of all the trappings of outside shapes, he left nothing to befog the pictorial structure and seduce the observer into poetic associations.

Relieved thus of all conventional impedimenta, ready to start afresh, Mondrian faced his canvas. Like many another before him, the artist felt the hypnotic spell of that bare white rectangle. Unlike others, obliged at times to break this spell by messing colors across it aimlessly, Mondrian gloried in the immaculate purity of the support. He made his subject, in fact, this very plane of canvas. He felt the apparent upward drive made by its vertical against its horizontal edges, and the corresponding rise which the slightly longer vertical axis seemed to occasion. He sensed the tension of the apparent oppositions of one side to another, resolved by the tautly stretched skin of canvas.

Mondrian found thus in the shape of his support ample motive for his picture, and out of nothing but rectangles he developed it. He constructed these rectangles with strips of black tape, stuck on and moved about until the complex pleased him. When everything seemed to be "working" just right, Mondrian replaced the tape with black bands, painstakingly laid in against a straight-edge ruler. He reduced the elements of expression to a minimum, eliminating all simulated masses, illusory spatial columns, textures of impasto or brushwork. The sole elements which the Dutch master allowed himself were line (in a sort of network across the picture), hue (in a pair of red oblongs), and area (in the untouched spaces of canvas between the bands).

Mondrian worked strictly in accord with his objectives. By suppressing any hint of his medium, he made his oil affirm the canvas alone. By freeing his forms of all representational associations, he created a pictorial equivalent to pure music. He claimed to go even farther— beyond music into some utopian society of the future. He declared that he was projecting into his paintings "a dynamic equilibrium of relationships" like that of the ultimately perfect world. Once humanity had evolved into this ideal state, he went on with a certain suicidal ruthlessness to explain, then painters would cease to exist because men would have no further need of pictures!

Despite Mondrian, we continue to need painting around us, and we trust that our Utopia may be a long time in coming if its advent would require us to forego even the limited visual satisfactions of one of his oils.

Representational imagery is still central to the art of easel painting, and the range of expressive emphasis open to the painter who does not accept puristic dogma is indeed unlimited. Let us look, for example, at a gouache (8.15) by Morris Graves, created within four years of the Mondrian abstraction. Everything that the Mondrian was, it is not, and vice versa. It suggests; it does not define. It is indetermi-

8.15. Morris Graves (1910–   ): *Woodpeckers*. 1940. Gouache on brown wrapping paper. 32¼ x 22¼″. Seattle Art Museum, Seattle, Eugene Fuller Memorial Collection.

nate in its illusions of depth. It abjures the straight line in favor of the acute point, the boundary in favor of the infinite extension. It is intensively representational, offering identifiable fragments of form to serve as starting points for revery. It cultivates spontaneity of statement, but hides its meanings under vaguely suggestive shapes. This romantic painting by Graves is properly done in gouache, ideal for the purpose in its fragile-edged strokes, chalky tones, rippling luminosities, and subtle grayings of color.

It is indebted, moreover, to the influence of the Pacific Northwest in which the painter was born and reared and inspired to develop his art. The landscape of the extreme northwest corner of the United States is cut by mountains into many miniature valleys, each with its own vegetation and wild life and pattern of change. So small is the miniature subregion in which Graves made his home and established his studio that, by standing on a bordering butte, one can readily look across from one range to another, and down its length, too, for a considerable part. The valley floor is lush with grass, but grasslands give way to scrub oak on the lower slopes, and oak in turn to dense fir forest on the higher slopes. Added to the varied textures of this vegetation is a constant play of rain, fog, mist, and softened sunlight, forming a complex of mysteriously veiled forms well disposed to cultivate that richly imaginative art which we have already seen in the sculpture of Tom Hardy (5.17).

Graves identified himself with this heavily forested region, immersing himself in its typically quiet abundance. Within the forest depths he would encounter an unexpected glimpse of wild life. From out of the stillness, for instance, he would be startled by a sudden staccato of drummings nearby. Investigating, he would discover a whole community of woodpeckers hunting their meal on a fir trunk.

In keeping with the accidental nature of the theme, Graves chose for his support nothing more pretentious than brown wrapping paper. He stretched a piece of it loosely over his drawing board, and on the paper introduced a ragged, blue-black blot of color. Over the blot he laid some vague meanderings of gray, to affect the shaggy texture of the bark. Then, with a sudden change in pace and abrupt heightening of emphasis, corresponding to the surprise of his discovery, he struck in patches of black, red, and white. With them he did not actually define or model the forms of the birds. More important, he captured their personality, the essence of their existence. He caught the exact effect of their protective coloration. He grasped the direct equivalent to their movements: their intermittent hoppings up and down the trunk, their trip-hammerlike borings into it.

Lest we be tempted to leave off at this point, observing the forms as nothing more than red-headed woodpeckers working on a tree trunk, Morris Graves purposely kept the structure of his picture slight. He wanted us to pass quickly from it to the symbolism of the subject. He wanted us to regard the birds on the aging trunk as a miniature counterpart to existence, to think of the periphery of brown paper as standing for the void out of which comes creation, and the irregular fragment of bark as standing for the decay out of which life springs afresh. He wanted us to sense in the rhythmic movements of the birds the heartbeat of nature. The painter thought as a poet, and as a poet created images for their symbolical significance.

Symbolism: Painting a National Epic

Easel paintings may be created freely in the studio for the sake of self-expression alone, even though they become subject to architectural conditions when put to use in a home. But mural paintings, rendered typically on a large scale and fixed immovably on a wall, are, as already described, much more closely interrelated with the building. The interrelationships are most impressively demonstrated for the twentieth century in the work of Mexico's muralist, José Clemente Orozco (1883–1949). During the course of his career this artist undertook projects on a scale surpassing even that of Raphael or Michelangelo. He did not always succeed in integrating his painting with the architecture. But one mural completed by Orozco toward the end of his life stands as a landmark of integration, not merely with a room or building but with a whole complex of buildings, with a campus, and even, in a sense, with a whole capital city and nation around it.

This was the painting Orozco completed shortly before his death for the stage wall of an open-air theater in Mexico City's National School for Teachers. The architect, Mario Pani (1911–   ), had designed both the new campus and the new buildings for this normal school, and construction was under way when he commissioned the painter to create a fitting climax to the ensemble. As shown by an air view of the campus at completion (8.16a), Pani designed the buildings on the plan of a triangle bisected by a central axis. He aimed with this formally geometric plan to lend to the buildings of the campus an atmosphere of dignity comparable with the task which the institution would face in training teachers. The architect left the apex of this triangle open to view from Mexico City's main artery of approach. He carried the view of passersby from that point across a series of reflecting pools to the central tower of administration, a tower flanked with laboratories and workshops and backed with a library and lecture-hall unit. He bounded the axis at its base, finally, with a wedge-shaped building six stories high, its wings serving not only for classrooms but for balconies looking down over an open-air theater in the middle. At the apex of this segment, against an unbroken expanse of curving concrete wall as high as the building, he set the speaker's platform and stage.

The arrangement of the buildings of the normal school seemed to lead inevitably to the open-air theater. There, at times of public assembly, everyone connected with the institution would congregate. They would sit facing the stage and the gigantic wall behind it (8.16b). This wall was a logical culmination to the campus, and as such it had to have an interest equaling its importance as the heart of the institution. To break the great plane into panels or coffers or otherwise to decorate it architecturally would seem makeshift. As architect, the best that Pani himself could do was to insert at the base of the wall, as a memorial to the buildings of the former campus now being replaced, the frame of the gateway of one. This single motive of a revival style of architecture was sadly out of keeping with the building Pani designed; it was also totally inadequate to give the wall the interest needed. Only a great mural could fill the role required, and the architect turned for it to Orozco.

The task confronting Orozco was a formidable one. The wall was one of the largest any painter had ever been asked to cover. A painting applied to it would have to meet the convergence on it of all of the buildings, and its theme would have to be as noble as the task to which the school was dedicated. An obvious subject might be the history of Mexican education, or a typical country teacher's life. It could consist of incidents in successive zones, to offer the student seated before it a lesson more vivid than his textbooks could offer. Many such murals had been painted, but the painter saw serious objection to a mural of this sort. Tiers of anecdotal scenes would set up irritating competition with groupings of actors in a play below it, or with gatherings of speakers at a meeting. Worse still, zones in the painting might compete in scale and play of light and shade with the actual architecture of the balconies.

Orozco's choice of subject and method of presenting it were as telling a solution to the problem as they were unprecedented. The artist chose the theme of Mexican life itself. Orozco gave form to this subject by developing a complex of allegorical shapes richer in content and structural significance than a literal representation could have been.

If we choose to look at the painting (8.16d) for its subject matter, we enter the painting quietly from its lower left-hand corner—that "spectator's corner" which we have noted in many other pictures. Through a subdued passage standing for the native past, we rise with increasing momentum over forms describing the legs of a man mounting the steps of a pyramid, his trunk lost in a cloud of smoke, his head left to be imagined against the sky above the painting. This symbol of aspiration of the Mexican people gives way to revolutionary struggle symbolized by blue spirals, orange flames, and a sweeping red column of smoke. Beams float serenely above the chaos, bearing inward toward the right as though to prophesy that the forces impelling revolt will ultimately be resolved.

The apparent movement of these beams leads to a central motive dominating the entire composition. It is the serpent held in the ea-

A

8.16. An Outdoor Mural as the Climax of a Campus. a. Mario Pani (1911–   ): National School for Teachers, Mexico City, air view of entire complex. 1945–1948. Compañia Mexicana Aerofoto photograph, courtesy of the architect. b. Mario Pani and José Clemente Orozco (1883–1949) collaborating painter: Open Air Theater, National School for Teachers Mexico City: *National Allegory*. Mural in progress, November, 1947, to April, 1948. Ethyl silicate on concrete. Mural, 59 x 72′. Guillermo Zamora photograph, courtesy of the architect. c. *National Allegory*, detail at lower right corner. Manuel Álvarez Bravo photograph, courtesy of the artist. d. *National Allegory*, completed mural. Manuel Álvarez Bravo photograph, courtesy of the artist.

B

C

D

gle's beak, emblem of the Mexican nation. As the painter himself indicated, this emblem at the same time represents Life and Death, the Soil of Mexico. We are drawn down the straight-lined back of the bird into a field of ordered architectural forms which contrast sharply with the drama enacted on the other side of the picture, and into which is thrust the fist of a man, polishing a stone in token of human power. We finally come to the conclusion of the painting in a maze of motives associated with the study, the laboratory, and the factory—forms suggesting that it is on learning, science, and industry that the future of Mexico must rest.

Now let us look at the mural as a whole. It welcomes the sweeping curves of the concave wall, it seems to suck the doorway into it, lifting this relic of weak revivalism into the surging motives of revolutionary change. We feel the counterpull of return in the strongly accentuated verticals at the center. We note the echoing by these central motives of the tower beyond, and the opening of the composition at the top, to give play to forms that seem to continue beyond the painting into the spaces around the tower. We observe how the staccato repeat of piers and parapets forming the balconies is made to trip lightly into the painting; the colors themselves pick up and intensify the earth reds of the bricks, the bluish reflections of the concrete, and the variegated grays of the stones. The shadowed forms gather toward the left side and bottom, as though they were the bass to mounting passages of a symphony in progress.

The choice of medium proved the most difficult problem, because conditions were exacting. The mural would have to adhere to a porous concrete surface. It would have to withstand every kind of outdoor weather. It would have to carry to great distances and still relate well to the architecture. Only ethyl sili-cate could meet these demands, and Orozco became the first artist to use this medium on a major scale. He made the properties of ethyl silicate contribute directly to the forms of the painting. Starting with the concrete wall itself, he retained its texture and even accentuated the marks of the boards used in the forms for its pouring (8.16c). For a network of lines on which to develop his areas, he built the concrete up here and there into bands of actual relief. He painted his colors in flat areas and reduced all modeling to a minimum. He made areas of grayed coloring predominate, but gained powerful accent by inserting into the concrete actual strips of metal—brass, aluminum, galvanized iron—which glitter like gold, silver, and precious stones against the quiet areas surrounding them.

In the state of flux characterizing Orozco's mural there is a certain conditional element, a sense of suspense, upon which much of the picture's significance depends. Double images give a key to it. The eagle of social order is also the building. Its plumage is machinery. Its perch is scaffolding, factory construction, ancient Indian gods. The serpent of social change is the helpless prey of the eagle; in death it also seems, by virtue of its metal incrustations, to emanate life. The sword is a shaft of light, a tower, a symbol of creation. The climbing man is rock, space, time.

Within this mural, as one critic close to the painter remarked, possibilities of life or death confront the Mexican people. In an extraordinary integration of painting with architecture, Orozco's mural points to the role of art in future society greater even than that which his art and the architect's could together fill. This is the art of planning and shaping man's environment—the art of developing whole regions and cities set in them. In order properly to introduce this super-art, another book would be needed.

LIVING WITH PICTURES

A mural painting in a public building belongs to a people. It conveys its proper epical message to crowds. For life at home, however, only the easel painting can truly satisfy and only then when it is effectively presented. An easel painting is made to be lived with continually and not just looked at in passing. Once made, it needs to be bought by an observer, taken home, and hung where it can be enjoyed, for only then, under repeated daily observation, can its full significance be grasped.

Owing to its modest size and variegated detail, an easel painting exerts an intimate appeal. It functions best under the relatively close viewing afforded by the room at home. Even more than a piece of sculpture, it serves to humanize the interior, giving a room warmth of personality and making it livable. Unlike sculpture, which occupies deep space and picks up for emphasis the volumes of mass encompassed by the building, a painting in the home occupies an area on the wall, to alleviate the wall's bareness and give it interest.

All this the easel painting does, providing it is not distorted by poor presentation. It creates within itself by its nature a miniature world apart. The illusions of depth inherent in its forms have to be kept distinct from the actual depths of the room. The concentrations of form, color, and action within its limits have to be set off by themselves. Hence its need for a frame.

The conventional frame employed for an oil or a tempera is a wood molding of generous width, the straight-edged grooves and ridges of which provide a foil for the action of the picture and a transition to the straight lines of the architecture. It is true that fashions in frames change almost as radically as fashions in women's dress, and for that reason paintings are usually photographed, as they have been for illustrations in this book, without any frames. Whatever the vogue for treatment of the molding, waxed or varnished, gilded, painted, carved, or elaborately overlaid with stucco in relief, the principle still holds, that a frame must be an adjunct to the picture, enhancing its appeal but never competing with it for attention. Let us for demonstration compare alternative framings of a particular given picture, applied to identical reproductions of a given work in order to make the comparison valid (8.17a and b).[5] Let us first consider the picture itself. It is a double portrait of two lovers of fifteenth-century Swabia, a mountainous district of Bavaria in southwestern Germany. The Swabian artist who rendered it in tempera felt enough at home with his medium to bring out its qualities. He kept the surface of the picture as smooth and hard as the gesso underneath. He made his coloring sharply local and lively in its transparent optic grays. He defined his forms precisely in fine-lined hatchings. He pushed his figures out against the picture plane, and treated his Black Forest setting as though it were a backdrop.

Now let us look at the frames. The first employs a pattern drawn from the ornamental border of a page of manuscript of the day. It conventionalizes foliage like that appearing in the picture's background. It carries a gilded surface reminiscent of the gold leaf commonly used in tempera altarpieces if not in this particular portrait. The other frame foregoes these ornamental allusions. It, too, bears gilding, but the gleam of the gold is softened by the irregular rubbing of grayed colors over the surface. The molding consists of uniformly straight lines in a series of rhythmically disposed groupings, but these are stopped short of the picture itself to allow insertion of a lighter-toned strip for distinguishing more clearly between the third-dimensional substance of the frame and the two-dimensional surface of the tempera.

After weighing the pros and cons carefully, we finally decide in favor of the second frame. Its simple rectilinearity makes the few re-

[5] See Notes, p. 300.

A

B

8.17. FRAMING: RIGHT AND WRONG. a. *Two Lovers*, New York Graphic Society color reproduction of a painting in Cleveland Museum of Art, Holden Collection. Original, late 15th century; tempera on canvas. In 19th-century frame by The House of Heydenryk. Courtesy of Henry Heydenryk, Jr. B. L. Freemesser photograph. b. *Two Lovers*, color reproduction in suitable frame by The House of Heydenryk. Courtesy of Henry Heydenryk, Jr. B. L. Freemesser photograph.

strained curves of the portrait effective by contrast. Its ample width gives the picture a feeling of spaciousness from side to side. Its subdued coloring, with the gold merely peeping through here and there, holds it strictly subordinate to the tempera in its brilliance. The delicately wrought groovings of the molding comport perfectly with the sharp contourings and hatchings of the picture. The other frame is stingy in its narrowness, shrill in its gilding, offensively slovenly in its deep-grooved ornamentation.

Now let us consider, for a second comparison, alternative framings of reproductions of a still life in oil by the celebrated late-nineteenth-century American painter, William Michael Harnett (8.18a and b). The work depicts a grouping of kitchen objects on a marble table. Everything is painted with absolute honesty of craftsmanship, modeled to give the utmost illusion of relief, and rendered texturally to convey its actual feel. The coloring is dark but the fresh greens of one of the clusters of grapes key up the rest of the colors refreshingly.

The first frame used to enclose this picture is severely square and plain. Its straight-lined moldings enhance the stabilizing effect of the table top in the picture. Its softly gleaming silver coating keeps itself strictly subordinate to such highlights in the painting as those of the pewter and the copper vessels. Like the painting itself a work of the nineteenth century, this frame employs a mat-finished walnut inner liner to disassociate the canvas from the silvered portions of the frame.

The second frame is by contrast a gloriously frilly importation from Italy made about the same time as the still life was painted (1891). It cost more than the first to make, and its

8.18. FRAMING: RIGHT AND
WRONG. a. William Mi-
chael Harnett (1848–1892):
Just Dessert, color reproduc-
tion by Triton Publications,
New York, of a painting in
Art Institute of Chicago, The
Friends of American Art Col-
lection. Original, 1891; oil
on canvas; 22½ x 26½".
In suitable frame by The
House of Heydenryk. Cour-
tesy of Henry Heydenryk, Jr.
B. L. Freemesser photograph.
b. *Just Dessert,* color repro-
duction in 19th-century Ital-
ian frame by The House of
Heydenryk. Courtesy of
Henry Heydenryk, Jr. B. L.
Freemesser photograph.

age makes it more expensive still. Only an expert woodcarver could have cut the leaf and shell motives making the ornament of the frame; they stand out so thinly and in such high relief that they compete for our admiration with the painter's *trompe-l'oeil* treatment of the leaves in the painting. We usually get only what we pay for in this life. The second frame is much the more expensive of the two. Should we choose it in preference to the first?

In much the same way as mural painting is needed as an art of collaboration with architecture, the art of framing is needed by the art of easel painting. There is also an art of *hanging* pictures, and failure to practice it judiciously can ruin the effect of even the best. Here the Japanese have a distinct advantage over us in the way that they design their interiors. We have already described the tokonoma as a niche actually built into the wall for the specific purpose of displaying works of art in an orderly fashion. In using the tokonoma as the center of interest for the whole room, chances of error in the hanging of a picture are definitely minimized. And knowledge of the exact spot where the picture will be displayed helps the painter and the professional mounter of his painting to design organically.

Unlike the Japanese house, the American dwelling usually offers nothing but undifferentiated walls on which to hang paintings. Paintings are framed rigidly; they cannot be unrolled or rolled at will and stored in cupboards when not in use. They leave light-marks or dirt-marks on the walls after they have hung for the length of time usual in American homes—another deterrent to making changes. But there is a right way to hang an easel painting on the wall at home, and only by hanging it correctly can it truly grace our existence. It is hung properly with its center of interest at a level with the eye of a person of average height, for that is the height at which it can be seen without accidental distortion (1.12b). It is placed squarely on the wall in relation to the furniture below it, and the space around it is kept free of disturbance. It is suspended from hooks driven into the wall, and the wire across the hooks is carefully concealed as alien to the effect; or, if the wall is such that hooks cannot be driven into it, it is hung from a wire or a pair of wires attached to the "picture molding" at the top of the wall, and the wire is made to hang at right angles to the top of the frame.

The custom of hanging a picture from the picture molding with a single hook and an inverted V-shape extension of wire detracts from any picture for which it is used. The converging lines of the wire make an irresistible distraction and source of irritation to the eye when nothing at the point of intersection rewards their being followed.

Pictures that are too numerous and too small in scale for the space around them prove still more irritating. By grouping them, with generous space allowed to either side of the grouping, and by lining them up at top or bottom or through their centers, the irritation can be reduced. But the best practice of all is to reduce the number of pictures in a room to three at the most, and to see that the pictures themselves are of generous size.

SUMMARY

Painting is an art of representing objects or phenomena existent apart from the picture itself. It depends for its representation upon the manipulation of pigments on a flat surface, but it treats this representation more or less abstractly, to accord with the artist's feelings.

Painting is divided into three functional branches: illustrating, mural painting, and easel painting. Like illustrating, treated in the preceding chapter, mural painting is a utilitarian branch; it covers walls of buildings with pictures and aims to complete the effect of the architectural composition. Easel painting parallels studio sculpture in being an art of free expression independent of use outside of itself. Effective realization of subject matter drawn from experience makes up its proper function and gives it its reason for existence.

The only sure test of a painting's worth is the test of time. In the process of testing it, however, qualities of expression are seen to derive, as in any other art, from the artist's deeply felt reactions to function, material, and techniques. As based on subject matter, painting divides into genres: figure, portrait, landscape, still life, and the like. As based on medium (material and technique combined), it divides into other classes: for mural painting, into secco, fresco, mosaic, stained glass, and ethyl silicate; for easel painting, into encaustic, tempera, oil, water color, gouache, and collage. Each medium predisposes the artist in favor of certain definitively expressive forms in his work, in favor of a selective emphasis, an expressive distortion, which will help him guard against either the imitative or the technical fallacy.

Every medium joins with the man who uses it in an interaction producing what we know as style. In painting, individual style looms up as of more importance than it does in other arts, although cultural style and period style also make themselves conspicuous. Among our case studies, for example, in ancient Egyptian mural painting, cultural style predominated as a sort of fixed period style called archaic. In more recent easel painting, both the individual style and the period style stand out—the style of Degas and the style of Luminism of the eighteen-sixties, the style of Cézanne and the style of reaction against impressionism (one called postimpressionism) in the eighteen-eighties, the style of Braque and the style of cubism in the early years of the present century, the style of Picasso and the style of surrealism in the late twenties. Orozco's mural in the National Normal School of Mexico City would seem to represent thus, not only a style of Orozco but the styles of cubism and surrealism in a state of fusion for socially expressive purposes, to form a synthesizing style which might be called postsurrealism. Orozco's mural at the same time points ahead to an art of regional and city planning.

The ultimate effectiveness of a mural painting depends on its complementary relationship to the architecture into which it enters. The ultimate effectiveness of an easel painting depends, in like token, on its framing and its hanging.

RECOMMENDED READINGS

John Canaday. *Metropolitan Seminars in Art.* 12 Portfolios. New York: The Metropolitan Museum of Art, 1958–59.

> As a painter himself, former Director of Education at the Philadelphia Museum of Art, and art editor of the *New York Times,* the author profits by much personal experience. He places himself in the position of the untutored layman and writes in simple terms. He makes an illuminating interpretation of each of the twelve paintings represented in each portfolio (both by a color reproduction and by details in black and white accompanying the text). The color reproductions, of highest quality, are offered in loose-leaf form in an envelope at the front of each portfolio. The series was originally issued to subscribers one per month, distributed by the Book-of-the-Month Club, Inc.

Norman Colquhoun. *Paint Your Own Pictures.* "Penguin Handbooks," 22; Baltimore, Md.: Penguin Books, 1953.

> Though unillustrated and written, as the title implies, solely for the prospective "Sunday painter," this little paper-bound volume makes a particularly helpful study of various mediums. The author has explained with great clarity of definition the qualities of each medium employed by the easel painter.

Bartlett H. Hayes, Jr. *The Naked Truth and Personal Vision.* Andover, Mass.: Addison Gallery of American Art, Phillips Academy, 1955.

A study published as the outcome of a 1952 exhibition prepared by the author-instructor and his students at the Phillips Academy, this book explores the different ways of thinking and seeing which have governed the artist both in painting and in other arts. It provides a good introduction to styles.

Mary Chalmers Rathbun and Bartlett H. Hayes, Jr. *Layman's Guide to Modern Art: Painting for a Scientific Age.* New York: Oxford University Press, 1949.

Likewise a publication growing out of an exhibition, this time held in the Addison Gallery of American Art, Andover, Massachusetts, in 1947, this book, written and rewritten in response to reactions of visitors at the exhibition, is couched in simple terms. Though intended to acquaint the beginner with the expressive necessities and meanings behind the more difficult styles of twentieth-century painting, it an-alyzes and illustrates, often in color, the elements and the principles of art.

Robert J. Goldwater and Marco Treves, eds. *Artists on Art,* New York: Pantheon Books, 1945.

Painters sometimes fall short in trying verbally to describe their objectives and their reasons for doing this and that. Their statements need to be read and considered only with reference to the actual works, and then they can sometimes become not only challenging but revealing. The editors of this volume have performed an extraordinarily discriminating task of sifting the literature, from medieval times to the present, and evaluating the passages quoted.

Ralph Mayer. *The Artist's Handbook of Materials and Techniques.* New York: Viking Press, 1941.

Most technical handbooks are dry for any but the professional craftsman. This handbook is not. It covers arts other than painting, but it does not neglect any phase of painting nor certain other subjects, like perspective, ordinarily overlooked. It is much the best manual of its kind for repeated consultation.

Notes

CHAPTER 1

1, page 3. Two film strips produced and distributed by Charles A. Bennett Company, 237 North Monroe Street, Peoria, Illinois, develop the theme, "Art Is Everywhere": *Art in Nature* and *Art Has Many Uses*. Two books reproducing photographs exceptionally high in quality and illuminating in regard to the sources of art forms in nature should be consulted by the serious student at the beginning of such study; Andreas Feininger, *The Anatomy of Nature* (New York: Crown, 1956), and Wolf Strache, *Forms and Patterns in Nature* (New York: Pantheon Books, 1956).

2, page 9. Calligraphy, the art of writing, was introduced into Japan by way of Korea from China in the fifth century A.D. and developed there, as in China and Korea, into an art rated even higher than poetry or painting. In this art, line was carried to lengths of subtlety in expression only suggested by the following passage of a Chinese master of the second century A.D., which co-authors Lucy Driscoll and Kenji Toda translate in *Chinese Calligraphy* (Chicago: University of Chicago Press, 1935), p. 13:

> In its forms writing should have images like sitting, walking, flying, moving, going, coming; lying down, rising; sorrowful, joyous; like worms eating leaves, like sharp swords and spears, strong bow and hard arrow; like water and fire, mist and cloud, sun and moon, all freely shown—*this* can be called calligraphy.

The book by Driscoll and Toda makes an excellent introduction to the subject, but a more thoroughgoing study, which also relates calligraphy to the expressive use of line in drawing and painting and to its source of inspiration in nature, is that by Chiang Yee, *Chinese Calligraphy: An Introduction to Its Aesthetic and Technique* (London: Methuen, 1938). The abstractions of line impelled by calligraphy and carried over into the conventions of pictorial representation are introduced by Henry P. Bowie, *On the Laws of Japanese Painting* (New York: Dover Publications, 1951; 1st ed., San Francisco: Paul Elder, 1911).

3, page 10. Studies of lettering and typography as arts practiced in the Occident exploit a field less rich in expressive use of line than do studies of Oriental calligraphy. Probably the most useful books on the subject are those by Frederic W. Goudy, *The Alphabet and Elements of Lettering* (revised and enlarged ed., Berkeley, Calif.: University of California Press, 1942; 1st ed., New York: Mitchell Kennerley, 1918), and by Alexander Nesbitt, *Lettering as Design* (New York: Prentice-Hall, 1950).

4, page 15. In this oversimplified account of the element of color we start with the Prang system and go on to a modified version of the Munsell system. A color system is a diagrammatic frame of reference designed to provide standard identifications for colors in all of their attributes. The *Maxwell system,* useful especially in the theater, applies to colors in light, as represented by an isosceles triangle with the primary colors, red, green, and blue-violet, at its angles. The three major systems applying to colors in pigment (those with which we are concerned in the present study) are the Prang, the Munsell, and the Ostwald.

The *Prang system,* based on a two-dimensional concept, is represented by the "color wheel" described in the text. See the Prang Company's *The Graphic Drawing Books,* Vols. I–VIII (New York: 1914).

Unlike the Prang system, the *Munsell system* recognizes the deep-spatial character of color. It conceives of the three attributes of color as the equivalents of dimensions going to form the structure of a *color solid* or sphere. See A. H. Munsell, *A Color Notation* (Baltimore: Munsell Color Company, 1941; 1st ed., *c.* 1913), and the *Munsell Book of Color* (Baltimore: 1929).

The *Ostwald system* is a variant of the Munsell system, the diagram for it being a rhomboid rather than a sphere. See Wilhelm Ostwald (S. Scott Taylor, trans.), *Color Science* (3 vols.; London: Winsor and Newton, 1931–1935) and Egbert Jacobson, *Basic Color: An Interpretation of the Ostwald Color System* (Chicago: Paul Theobald, 1948).

5, page 23. The Hindu concept of existence, and the technique by which one grows in the spiritual power of *prana* and climbs through the successive levels of the material to ultimate absorption in the Absolute, are described with relative simplicity in a small volume by Swami Vivekananda, *Raja-Yoga: or Conquering the Internal Nature* (New York: Ramakrishna-Vivekananda Center of New York, 1946).

CHAPTER 2

1, page 27. The idea that "form follows function" in nature originated in researches of the French biologist, Jean-Baptiste Lamarck (1744–1829). That "form follows function" in art seems first to have been advanced by an American sculptor, Horatio Greenough (1805–1852). See the Recommended Readings for the present chapter, reference edited by Small. Louis Sullivan (1856–1924), Chicago architect, advocated the same idea so eloquently in his writings, so convincingly in his practice, that a whole generation of American architects came to subscribe to it. See especially Sullivan's *The Autobiography of an Idea* (New York: Press of the American Institute of Architects, 1924; 1st ed., 1922).

Sullivan's one-time apprentice, Frank Lloyd Wright, quarreled with his master's dictum and substituted one of his own: "Form and function are one." Wright wrote even more voluminously and vigorously in support of his own principle. See especially Frederick Gutheim, ed., *Frank Lloyd Wright on Architecture: Selected Writings 1894–1940* (New York: Duell, Sloan and Pearce, 1941).

The idea that "form actually determines function," making the artist the initiator rather than the follower, was first advanced by the American architect, Matthew Nowicki (1910–1950). See his article, "Origins and Trends in Modern Architecture," *Magazine of Art,* November, 1951, pp. 273–279. See also Richard J. Neutra, *Survival Through Design* (New York: Oxford University Press, 1954), pp. 107–118.

2, page 29. Emphatic reactions have occurred as long, probably, as man has lived on this earth. It is remarkable, therefore, that the theory of empathy was not expressed in the Western world until the nineteenth century, when Robert Fischer wrote his *Drei Schriften zum Ästhetischen Formproblem,* first published, 1872–1890, but republished in Halle, 1927. Most aptly, Fischer called the response *einfühlung,* a word invented to mean literally "feeling into." For a critical study of this theory, read Wilhelm Worringer (Michael Bullock, trans.) *Abstraction and Empathy* (New York: International Universities Press, 1953; 1st ed. in German, 1908).

3, page 35. *Rhythm Is Everywhere* is a film which follows a small boy on his way to school, finding wherever he turns some irresistible rhythm in the life about him. Accompanied by sound, the film makes an effective tie-up between obvious auditory rhythms and those which are visual. It is a CIF (Classroom Instructional Film) 16-mm. ten-minute reel produced by Teaching Films, Inc., and distributed by Carl F. Thahnke Productions, Des Moines, Iowa.

CHAPTER 3

1, page 42. The status of the art of industrial design as here described extends into history no earlier than the year 1930. As recently as 1936 an exhaustive investigator could report that 90 percent of the industrial products of Great Britain, first nation to undergo the Industrial Revolution, were lacking completely in any esthetic merit. See Nikolaus Pevsner, *An Enquiry Into Industrial Art in England* (Cambridge, England: University Press, 1937), p. 12.

2, page 42. An idea of the complicated detail of such data can be gained by looking through a book by Wesley E. Woodson, *Human Engineering Guide for Equipment Designers* (Berkeley, Calif.: University of California Press, 1954). A much more readable account, illustrated with drawings as informative as they are entertaining, is that by Francis de N. Schroeder, *Anatomy for Interior Designers and How to Talk to a Client* (New York: Whitney Publications, 1948).

3, page 42. This three-fold relationship of artist, observer, and personified art work originates in conceptions of the nature of art held by Gestalt psychologists. See K. Koffka, "Problems in the Psychology of Art," *Art: A Bryn Mawr Symposium* (Bryn Mawr, Pa.: Bryn Mawr College, 1940), pp. 180–272.

4, page 44. Early variations in the form of the automobile can be studied comparatively in Joseph Floyd Clymer's book, *Treasury of Early American Automobiles, 1877–1925* (New York: McGraw-Hill, 1950). The study can be brought more nearly up to date in Philip Van Doren Stern's *A Pictorial History of the Automobile as Seen in Motor Magazine 1903–1953* (New York: Viking, 1953), and in Allan Nevins's *Ford: The Times, the Man, the Company* (New York: Scribner, 1954). For an industrial designer's own account of his work for the automobile, see Raymond Loewy, *Never Leave Well Enough Alone* (New York: Simon and Schuster, 1951).

5, page 56. Japanese raku ware was named after a family of potters originating it in the sixteenth century and continuing to specialize in it down to the present day. Bernard Leach describes it out of intimate personal experience with Japanese masters, *A Potter's Book* (London: Faber and Faber, 1948; 1st ed., 1940). One of the best accounts of clays and of methods of preparing them was written by Leach in this book, pp. 43–62. Chapter I is worth reading as a whole for its inquiry into qualitative standards for all ceramic wares.

6, page 69. The Stocksdale salad set was created by woodturning as an art of practical utility. Woodturning as an art for art's sake is dealt with by Barbara Morgan, photographer, and Edgar Kaufmann, Jr., author, in *Prestini's Art in Wood* (New York: Pocahontas Press and Pantheon Books, 1950).

7, page 72. A competition and exhibition conducted by The Museum of Modern Art of New York motivated Eames to embark on this project in collaboration with Eero Saarinen. Eliot F. Noyes wrote the catalogue, *Organic Design in Home Furnishings* (New York: Museum of Modern Art, 1941). This merely provided a start, however; the ensuing complications took Eames years to straighten out. See Wallance, *Shaping America's Products, op. cit.,* pp. 108–113.

CHAPTER 4

1, page 78. The term "interval" for space has been borrowed from the art of music. The concept of space as essential to a "figure-and-ground" relationship is emphasized in Gestalt psychology. Read Rudolph Arnheim's thoroughgoing investigation of the element in *Art and Visual Perception* (Berkeley, Calif.: University of California Press, 1954), pp. 177–244. The importance of volumes of open space to a work of architecture, newly emphasized in the Western world, is traditionally recognized in Chinese architecture. Read Amos Ih Tiao Chang, *The Existence of Intangible Content in Architectonic Form Based upon the Practicality of Laotzu's Philosophy* (Princeton, N. J.: Princeton University Press, 1956).

2, page 78. Ideal procedure in choosing the site involves intimate collaboration of architect with landscape designer. The landscape designer is perhaps more aware of this need than is the architect. See, for example, three works written from the landscape architect's point of view: Christopher Tunnard, *Gardens in the Modern Landscape* (New York: Charles Scribner's Sons, 1948; 1st ed., 1938); Ralph Rodney Root, *Contourscaping* (Chicago: Ralph Fletcher Seymour, 1941); Garrett Eckbo, *Landscape for Living* (New York: Duell, Sloan and Pearce, 1950).

3, page 79. Architects have invented instruments for determining the angle of incidence of the sun's rays. One is the heliodon, invented by G. Beal in the nineteen-thirties. In its use, the model of a building is set in the middle of a circular platform. A steel arc is adjusted over the platform to correspond to the degree of latitude of the site in question. A telescoped steel arm coming out of this arc is then extended to the proper point for the day of the year. A floodlight is attached to the end of the arm and a motor turns the arc with the light corresponding to the sun through the course of a day's passage from sunrise to sunset. The stopping of the motor at any time during this course indicates on a dial the exact hour and minute of that interruption, showing exactly where the sunlight and the shadow would fall. A careful diagrammatic analysis, based on heliotropic studies and their optimum relationship to densities of population, is contained in Ludwig K. Hilberseimer's *The New City* (Chicago: Paul Theobald, 1944), pp. 76–86, and a summary of this analysis is published in the revised edition, *The Nature of Cities* (Chicago: Paul Theobald, 1955), pp. 203–207.

4, page 79. Materials have played such an important role in the art of Frank Lloyd Wright that the architect's biographer, Henry-Russell Hitchcock, Jr., was prompted to give his book the title *In the Nature of Materials* (New York: Duell, Sloan and Pearce, 1942).

5, page 80. A motion picture produced in color and sound by the National Film Board of Canada, *How to Build an Igloo*, documents the process as it occurs typically in the Arctic wastes. Within an hour and a half (11 mins. for film-showing) two Eskimos erect their dwelling. The commentator explains the choice of snow, the spiral method of setting the blocks, and the means of lighting and ventilating.

6, page 96. Bruno Taut, another architect of German origin contemporary with Miës van der Rohe, visited Japan in the middle nineteen-thirties for the express purpose of living in traditional-style houses exactly like the Japanese, determining thus at first hand the reasons for every structural detail. His findings were published in German in several books, two of which have been translated into English: Estille Balk and H. Vere Redman, *Houses and Peoples of Japan* (Tokyo: Sanseidō, 1937), and Glenn F. Baker and H. E. Pringsheim, *Fundamentals of Japanese Architecture* (Tokyo: Kokusai Bunka Shinkokai, 1936). In spite of factual errors, confused organization, and faulty translation, both books remain standard references.

7, page 98. Frank Lloyd Wright had the opportunity while still serving as an apprentice to Louis Sullivan to obtain first-hand knowledge of Japanese architecture and methods of building. Representing Sullivan on frequent trips to Jackson Park, Chicago, where the pavilions for the World's Columbian Exposition were in process of erection in 1892 and 1893, Wright watched a crew of Japanese carpenter-builders construct a replica of a historically famous temple building, the Hō-ō-dō (Phoenix Hall), built at Uji, south of Kyoto, in 1053. This replica served as the Japanese Government Pavilion at the fair. On this subject, consult the article by Grant Carpenter Manson, "Frank Lloyd Wright and the Fair of '93," *The Art Quarterly*, Vol. XVI, No. 2 (Summer, 1953), pp. 114–123.

8, page 110. For early evidences of the discovery of the Japanese house-and-garden, read not only various passages by Frank Lloyd Wright, such as that in *An Autobiography* (New York: Duell, Sloan and Pearce, 1943), pp. 194–201, but also Edward S. Morse, *Japanese Homes and Their Surroundings* (New York: Harper & Brothers, 1885), and Ralph Adams Cram, *Impressions of Japanese Architecture* (New York: Japan Society, and Boston: Marshall Jones, 1930; 1st pub., 1905).

9, page 110. Much of the information on both the Tanaka House and garden and the Harada House interior, as well as the original photographs for them, was kindly provided by Dr. Jirō Harada, staff member of the National Museum in Tokyo. He has written introductions to both the Japanese house and the Japanese garden. See his *The Lesson of Japanese Architecture* (Boston: Charles T. Branford, 1954; 1st ed., London: Studio, 1936); *Japanese Gardens* (London: Studio, 1956; revised ed. of *The Gardens of Japan*, 1928); and *A Glimpse of Japanese Ideals* (Tokyo: Kokusai Bunka Shinkokai, 1936).

10, page 113. The Baldinger garden is analyzed and illustrated with the same diagrams as used by the author, and with a number of additional views, in Carroll Calkins, editor, and Tom Burns, Jr., photographer, "We Take a Garden Plan Apart . . . and Study the Pieces," *Sunset*, November, 1953, pp. 50–51. "Before and After" views are illustrated in Garrett Eckbo, *The Art of Home Landscaping* (New York: F. W. Dodge, 1956), p. 55. Other details as well as a sketch plan are reproduced in this same book, pp. 72–74, and p. 151, Fig. 3.

CHAPTER 5

1, page 120. In one peculiar form of relief assumed in ancient Egypt, no protrusion was allowed to extend forward beyond the original surface, and that surface was retained around the whole work as a sort of frame. Known by the French term, relief *en creux* ("in the hollow"), it is illustrated in Jack C. Rich, *The Materials and Methods of Sculpture* (New York: Oxford University Press, 1947), Pl. III.

2, page 122. An imaginary reconstruction of the Parthenon's interior, showing the image of Athena in place, is exhibited by the British Museum and illustrated in Herbert Read, *The Art of Sculpture* (New York: Pantheon Books, 1956), Pl. VII.

3, page 123. Augustus Saint-Gaudens was one noteworthy exception in American sculpture. He rendered sculptural monuments of historically important figures, each attired in the dress of his day. Compare such sculptures, illustrated in C. Lewis Hind, *Augustus Saint-Gaudens* (New York: John Lane, 1908): *Admiral Farragut* (unveiled, 1881), *General Sherman* (1903), and so on.

4, page 123. This eclecticism, practiced in both ancient Roman sculpture and in European sculpture of the nineteenth century, is bitterly attacked by R. H. Wilenski, *The Meaning of Modern Sculpture* (London: Faber and Faber, 1932), pp. 49–69. It is dealt with from the literary point of view by Stephen A. Larrabee, *English Bards and Grecian Marbles* (New York: Columbia University Press, 1943). Pliny the Elder (23?–79 A.D.) in his 37-volume *Natural History* repeated the mistaken notion already current in his day, when he described the Greek master, Zeuxis, as painting an ideal female figure from the respective "best parts" of the bodies of the five fairest maidens of Agrigentum, selected after having inspected all of the city's maidens naked. See the translation by K. Jex-Blake, *The Elder Pliny's Chapters on the History of Art* (London and New York: Macmillan, 1896), p. 109 (Ch. XXXV of the *Historia Naturalis*, 64–65).

5, page 125. A *netsuke* is a counter-weight attached to the draw-cord of a small receptacle, called an *inro*, which the Japanese carried tucked into the sash of his kimono. Both *netsuke* and *inro* have prompted a highly variegated sculpture in miniature.

6, page 131. Charles F. Ramus, in "Siva Nataraja" (*The Denver Art Museum Spring Quarterly*, 1949, p. 1), declared it to be of bronze. Coomaraswamy, *Catalogue of the Indian Collections, op. cit.*, Part II, pp. 12 and 38, explains it to be incorrect to call such sculptures "bronzes," stating that the majority are of copper and the rest of brass.

7, page 134. The absolute fidelity of the carver to the law of frontality is evidenced in a front view of the head, ill. in Ranke, *The Art of Ancient Egypt, op. cit.*, Pl. CXXX. Compare our color plate with that in Ranke, opp. Pl. CXXX.

8, page 144. Rodin's approach to sculpture is explained in his own words in a published interview: Paul Gsell (Mrs. Romily Fedden, trans.), *Art, by Rodin* (Boston: Small, Maynard, 1912). His sculptures are presented in a documentary 16-mm. film directed by René Lucot, *Rodin* (distributed by Franco-American Audio-Visual Distribution Center, New York; black and white; English sound-track; 29 mins.).

9, page 145. The way in which Banyuls, fishing port near the Spanish border and home of Maillol in his later years, helped determine the serenity of the master's art is presented poetically by Jean Lods in a documentary 16-mm. film made in 1945 shortly before the sculptor's death: *Maillol* (Franco-American Audio-Visual Distribution Center; black and white, English sound track but French passage by the sculptor himself; 20 mins.).

CHAPTER 6

1, page 166. The early British master of photography, Peter Henry Emerson (1856–1936), wrote in this vein out of personal disillusionment with an art which failed to meet painting-derived standards. See his pamphlet of 1891 in the Royal Photographic Society archives, London: *The Death of Naturalistic Photography*; Newhall, *On Photography*, pp. 125–132.

2, page 168. A historical sketch of the various devices invented to study and transcribe illusions of perspective, all of them in one way or another anticipations of the camera, was written by Heinrich Schwarz, "Art and Photography: Forerunners and Influences," *Magazine of Art*, Vol. XLII, No. 7 (November, 1949), pp. 252–257.

3, page 178. Edward Weston's photographic discovery of California is presented in a report of a year's work made possible by a Guggenheim Award: Edward Weston and Charis Wilson Weston, *California and the West* (New York: Duell, Sloan and Pearce, 1940). See also Edward Weston, *My Camera on Point Lobos* (Boston: Houghton, Mifflin, 1950). Many of the photographs included in these two publications are shown in process of being taken in a documentary motion picture on Edward Weston, *The Photographer* (Willard Van Dyke, director; produced by United World Films, Inc.; black and white, sound; 26 mins.).

4, page 191. For documentary films on art, see George Amberg, "Art, Films, and 'Art Films,'" *Magazine of Art*, Vol. XLV, No. 3 (March, 1952), pp. 124–133. Excellent catalogues with accompanying critical reviews are published by UNESCO (United Nations Educational, Scientific and Cultural Organization, 19, Avenue Kleber, Paris): *Films on Art: A Specialized Study* (1950), *Films on Art: Panorama 1953*, and others.

5, page 191. Story books for children are based by Walt Disney and his associates on these nature documentaries, and published by Simon and Schuster of New York: *Vanishing Prairie* (1955), *Living Desert* (1956), *Beaver Valley* (1956), and others.

6, page 194. Exact replica of *Potemkin* in original state, available for rental in 16-mm. size, Film Library, Museum of Modern Art, New York.

7, page 196. *Gate of Hell, Jigokumon* in Japanese, was based on a play by Kan Kikuchi, *Kesa's Husband*. The film was directed by Teinosuke Kinugasa and produced in 1954 by Daiei Studios of Tokyo. Available in 16-mm. size through Cinema Guild, Mount Vernon, N. Y.; 89 mins.

CHAPTER 7

1, page 210. Written as a technical manual for bookbinders and librarians, but useful as a source of information for others: Douglas Cockerell, *Bookbinding and the Care of Books* (W. R. Lethaby, ed., "The Artistic Crafts Series of Technical Handbooks"; London: Isaac Pitman and Sons, 1927; 1st ed., 1901). See also the 16-mm. Encyclopaedia Britannica film, *Making Books* (black and white; 12 mins.; accompanied by a teacher's guide).

2, page 212. The art of calligraphy was dealt with briefly in our discussion of line in the first chapter. Its industrial-art descendant, typography, can be studied in a variety of publications. See especially David Diringer, *The Alphabet; A Key to the History of Mankind* (New York: Philosophical Library, 1948); Clayton Whitehill, *The Moods of Type* (New York: Barnes and Noble, 1947); and Charles Rosner, *Printer's Progress: A Survey of the Craft of Printing, 1851–1951* (Cambridge, Mass.: Harvard University Press, 1951). Also, two Encyclopaedia Britannica films, 16-mm.: *Writing through the Ages* (10 mins.) and *Printing through the Ages* (10 mins.), both accompanied by teacher's guides, and a Bailey 16-mm. film, *Here's How We Print* (10 mins.), all three in black and white.

3, page 212. Ancient Egyptian caricature, on flashes of limestone called *ostraka*, is dealt with briefly by Mary Hamilton Swindler, *Ancient Painting* (New Haven, Conn.: Yale University Press, 1929), p. 36.

4, page 212. Cartooning then reached a climax of expressiveness equal to the best in modern America. See Toda, *Japanese Scroll Painting*, *op. cit.*, and a 16-mm. color film documenting and interpreting an emakimono: *Conspiracy in Kyoto* (produced by Indiana University; 18 mins.).

5, page 213. Thomas Francis Carter (L. Carrington Goodrich, ed.), *The Invention of Printing in China and Its Spread Westward* (New York: Ronald Press, 1955; 1st ed., 1925), pp. 3–10, 211–213. Introduced from China into Japan not later than the seventh century A.D., papermaking developed to lengths of great complication and subtlety. Actual examples of its wide range of character in Japan are presented by Thomas Keith Tindale and Harriett Ramsey Tindale, *The Handmade Papers of Japan* (Rutland, Vt.: Charles E. Tuttle, 1952). A 16-mm. black and white film features at its

beginning the traditional craft as practiced today in Japan: *Moku Hanga* ("Woodblock Print"), distributed by the Government of Japan Information Services and the Japan Society of New York. The art of papermaking had evolved to a state of extraordinary refinement long before Westerners had ever heard of it. Arabs first learned the secret of papermaking from Chinese prisoners captured at the battle of Samarkand in A.D. 751, but no European shared in the secret until Spaniards extracted it from Arab prisoners during the twelfth century.

6, page 213. A very conservative approach to the medium is made by J. J. Lankes, *A Woodcut Manual* (New York: Henry Holt, 1932). See also the 16-mm. silent black and white film of 1937 directed by Elias Katz, *Lynd Ward at Work* (15 mins.)

7, page 216. See Toda, *op. cit.*, pp. 88–90. One of the scrolls is preserved today in the Iwasaki Collection near Tokyo and the other in the Matsudaira Collection, now housed in the National Museum in Tokyo.

8, page 233. That this is not the only organic way to express the medium, even at the hands of a master like Daumier, is emphasi 1 by William M. Ivins, Jr., in *Prints and Books: Informal Papers* (Cambridge, Mass.: Harvard University Press, 1926), pp. 265–293. See also Michael Sadleir, *Daumier: The Man and the Artist* (London: Halton and Smith, 1924), and Jacques Lassaigne (Eveline Byam Shaw, trans.), *Daumier* (Paris: Hyperion Press, 1938).

9, page 239. The donkey and the elephant as symbols of political parties originated with Thomas Nast (1804–1902), America's first great cartoonist. See Albert Bigelow Paine, *Th. Nast: His Period and His Pictures* (New York: Harper & Brothers, 1904).

10, page 241. Krazy Kat first appeared in 1911 as a minor actor in the cast of Herriman's strip, *The Family Upstairs*, but quickly achieved independent status in the New York *Evening Journal*. Under the title *Krazy Kat* the strip spread after 1913 to other newspapers, especially to those of the Hearst chain.

CHAPTER 8

1, page 248. Books describing the methods given here and the various types and styles of painting discussed and illustrated are easily available. Also of interest are the following films: *The World of Mosaic* (Ernest Rose, University of California at Los Angeles, prod. and distrib.; Richard Widmark, narr.; 1956; color, sound; 28 mins.); *Making a Stained Glass Window* (University of California of Berkeley, distrib.; 1943; color, sound; 22 mins.); a series on water color produced and distributed by Encyclopaedia Britannica Films; *Adolf Dehn's Technique in Water Color* (Harmon Foundation, prod. and distrib.; 1945; color, silent; 30 mins.); a film on gouache, *Out of a Chinese Painting Brush* (Wango Wêng, dir.; Harmon Foundation and China Institute of America, prod.; 1943; color, sound; 11 mins.).

Among individual artists named in the text, the following have had noteworthy books, periodical articles, or films devoted to their work: Albert Pinkham Ryder, John Singer Sargent, Raphael, Rembrandt, Edgar Degas, Paul Cézanne, John Marin, Pablo Picasso, Joan Miró, Piet Mondrian, Morris Graves, José Clemente Orozco, and William Harnett.

2, page 249. The Maria de' Medici series (1621–1625) by Peter Paul Rubens (1577–1640), originally in the Luxembourg Palace, now in the Louvre, Paris, is one example of a mural in oil. A reproduction appears in Adolf Rosenberg, *P. P. Rubens: Des Meisters Gemälde* ("Klassiker der Kunst," Vol. V; Berlin: Deutsche Verlags-Anstalt, n. d.), pp. 243–263. A report on experimentation with mosaic for an easel painting is Leonard Kimbrell, *A Series of Paintings, Lithographs and Mosaics* (Unpublished manuscript, Eugene, Ore.: University of Oregon Library, 1954), pp. 21–23.

3, page 249. The problem of the extent to which the representation can remain literal and still qualify as creative has plagued artists and critics for at least two thousand years. See Etienne Gilson, *Painting and Reality* (A. W. Mellon Lectures in the Fine Arts, 1955, National Gallery of Art, Washington, D. C.; "Bollingen Series," Vol. XXXV. 4; New York: Pantheon Books, 1957); and John Canaday, *What Is a Painting?* ("Metropolitan Seminars in Art," Portfolio I; New York: The Metropolitan Museum of Art, 1958).

4, page 253. Stained glass designed by Fernand Léger as glass block masonry for Church of the Sacred Heart, Audincourt, France, is illustrated in Anton Hentze and Theodor Filthaut (Cecily Hastings, trans.), *Contemporary Church Art* (New York: Sheed and Ward, 1956), pp. 21 ff.

5, page 287. This pair of framings and that which follows were originally displayed in an exhibition assembled by Henry Heydenryk, Jr., head of the House of H. Heydenryk, Jr., a New York firm specializing in framing. The exhibition was circulated from 1956 to 1958 by the Western Association of Art Museums. The color reproduction of this double portrait, by an unknown artist of the Swabian school, late fifteenth century, was made by the New York Graphic Society.

Index

(Italicized numbers refer to pages on which illustrations occur.)

Date Due

OCT 2 6 '62		
NOV 9 '62		
JAN 4 '63		
MAR 9 '63		
JUL 2 3 1963		
AUG 3 0 1963		
JAN 1 7 1964		
JAN 2 2 1964		
JUL 2 1964		
OCT 9 1967		
JAN 2 0 1968		
MAY 5 1970		
APR 2 8 1982		
5/3		

Library Bureau Cat. No. 1137